EXTRAJUDICIAL COMMUNICATION

This is the first book to comprehensively address the phenomenon of extrajudicial communication.

With contributions from leading legal scholars, it offers a detailed examination of what judges say outside of the courtroom, when, why, and to what end. The book explores extrajudicial communication through both varying perspectives on its use, and the forms that it takes, including judicial speeches, interviews, life writing and more. It does so with a principal focus on the UK judiciary, but also with reflections on its practice in other common law jurisdictions and at international courts and tribunals. The text unpicks the relationship between these communications, constitutional principles and the modern understanding of the judicial role.

A fascinating and truly novel work on how judges communicate outside the courtroom and why it matters.

Hart Studies on Judging and the Courts: Volume 4

HART STUDIES ON JUDGING AND THE COURTS

Series Editors
Erin F Delaney, James Lee & Andrew Lynch

The primary focus of this series is on appellate courts in the common law world, but we welcome submissions beyond this, including those offering a comparative angle, such as from civilian jurisdictions, or jurisdictions in developing nations. The series supports innovative work by emerging and established scholars in the field.

Volume 1: Values in the Supreme Court: Decisions, Division and Diversity
Rachel J Cahill O'Callaghan

Volume 2: Foreign Judges in the Pacific
Anna Dziedzic

Volume 3: Judicial Individuality on the UK Supreme Court
Lewis Graham

Volume 4: Extrajudicial Communication: Perspectives and Practice
Edited by Hélène Tyrrell and Conall Mallory

Extrajudicial Communication

Perspectives and Practice

Edited by
Hélène Tyrrell
and
Conall Mallory

•HART•
OXFORD • LONDON • NEW YORK • NEW DELHI • SYDNEY

HART PUBLISHING
Bloomsbury Publishing Plc
Kemp House, Chawley Park, Cumnor Hill, Oxford, OX2 9PH, UK
1385 Broadway, New York, NY 10018, USA
Bloomsbury Publishing Ireland Limited, 29 Earlsfort Terrace, Dublin 2, D02 AY28, Ireland

HART PUBLISHING, the Hart/Stag logo, BLOOMSBURY and the Diana logo are
trademarks of Bloomsbury Publishing Plc
First published in Great Britain 2026

1

A catalogue record for this book is available from the British Library.

A catalogue record for this book is available from the Library of Congress.

Library of Congress Control Number: 2026935506

ISBN: HB: 978-1-5099-8183-0
ePDF: 978-1-5099-8185-4
ePub: 978-1-5099-8184-7

Typeset by Lumina Datamatics Ltd

For our girls: Rosalind and Nina; Niamh and Áine.

Foreword

FEW WOULD NOW question that judges occupy a central position in any democratic system. In the United Kingdom and similar societies, until recently the convention was that judges should only speak through their judgments. In this way it was thought that their reputation for wisdom and impartiality was unassailable. As the contributions in this excellent book clearly demonstrate, this convention no longer holds sway and has been seriously attenuated. In recent times, senior judges have shown a growing appetite to travel outside their judgments and speak and write on a range of topics. These are usually connected in some way with substantive law or questions of policy relating to the justice system. But some more adventurous souls are starting to show an appetite for painting on a broader canvas. This departure from the safe haven of their judgments has been accompanied by a growing public interest in the identity of senior judges and their views about important matters of general concern. Some of these matters concern issues of general policy, politics and morality.

The chapters in this timely book have been written mainly by academics, but also in one interesting case by a former Judicial Assistant to the Supreme Court of the United Kingdom. They have been thoroughly researched, as is evident from the plethora of footnotes. The extrajudicial communications by serving and retired judges that are considered in the book include what they say in Parliament, and what they write in lectures, speeches, textbooks on legal topics, memoirs and their personal diaries.

The chapters express a rich range of views. For example, some defend the traditional reticence of judges and refusal to travel outside their judgments. Letting judgments speak for themselves is the safe course to adopt. Anything else is fraught with danger, especially where the issue is controversial and gives rise to strong emotions and vehement disagreements. Others say that the trend towards more openness on the part of judges is to be commended. Their position is that transparency is an essential element of judicial accountability and that this is particularly important when so many court decisions have a political flavour. The public has a right to know something about the authors of important decisions which can affect us all. After all, judges exercise enormous and largely unchallenged power. The most striking exposition of this view appears in Chapter two: 'Speaking Out: The More the Better' by Allan C Hutchinson. He says that law and adjudication are *'thoroughly political'* and that democracy is better served by an acceptance of this fact. The corollary of this is that judges should put their values on the table. It is unreal to suppose that the values that they hold do not affect their decision-making. I suggest that there are many who will disagree with this challenging thesis. But it is powerfully expressed and should stimulate much debate.

There is much else to savour in the book on a considerable range of topics. For students of the United States, there is an interesting chapter by Christopher Schmidt entitled 'The United States Supreme Court and the perils of Extrajudicial Speech'. This contains a description of what, to UK eyes, is the extraordinary behaviour of some US Supreme Court Justices and what is seen by some as the transformation for the Court from an institution of law to one of politics. Hélène Tyrrell discusses the issue of retired judges and what they should or should not be able to do. This is a thoughtful contribution to a subject which seems to be gaining momentum as an important topic.

I will confine myself to mentioning one more contributor by name. She is Jacqui Kinghan. She was a Judicial Assistant in the UK Supreme Court. She saw the workings of the Court and the Justices at very close quarters and was involved in some of their work. It is of particular value and interest to have her perspective on the issue of the extrajudicial discourse of the Justices in the wider public domain. To invite her to contribute to the book was an inspired idea.

It would be invidious to single out more of the individual contributions. Suffice it to say that this is an important book. I have no doubt that it will be of interest to anyone who reflects on the part played by senior judges in the United Kingdom constitutional system, and beyond.

Lord John Dyson
(Justice of the Supreme Court 2010–12
and Master of the Rolls 2012–2016)

Preface

THIS BOOK EXPLORES the perspectives and practice of extrajudicial communication. It draws on the way in which judges communicate with an array of discrete and general audiences outside the legal process, and the importance of this engagement. The stimulus for the work was our recognition that many senior judges in the United Kingdom – and elsewhere – were communicating with such frequency and regularity that it was becoming an integral part of their role. Senior judges were not only applying and occasionally developing the law from behind the bench, but also making distinct contributions beyond the bench. Our interest in this phenomenon was greatly assisted by the support of the Society of Legal Scholars who funded a one-day seminar on the topic, titled 'Beyond the Bench: a seminar about extrajudicial engagement' at Newcastle University in September 2022. Our thanks go to Helen Hampson for her expert assistance in organising this workshop.

Following this event, we conducted a series of interviews with serving and retired judges from the United Kingdom's highest courts. The rich discussions we had with these judges greatly informed our understanding of the area and we are indebted to them for their time. These interviews formed the basis of our article, 'The Extrajudicial Voice', published in *Legal Studies* in 2024. Of the judges interviewed, we are particularly grateful to Lord Dyson for his support and encouragement on the project, as well as his willingness to write the foreword to this collection.

As editors, we are most grateful to the contributors for agreeing to be part of this collection and for both the quality of their chapters and their patience during the process. At Hart Publishing we are indebted to the support and professionalism of the production team. Particular thanks go to Sasha Jawed, Verity Stuart, Sinead Moloney and Jo Choulerton. We also offer our thanks to our respective institutions of Newcastle University and Queen's University Belfast for the institutional support they have provided over the course of the last three years.

Finally, our thanks go to our families for their patience, forbearance and support on this project, as on everything else.

Hélène Tyrrell and Conall Mallory
November 2025

Contents

PART II
PRACTICE

List of Contributors

TT Arvind is Professor of Law at the University of York, UK.

Rachel Cahill-O'Callaghan is Professor of Law at Cardiff University, UK.

Anurag Deb is a PhD researcher at Queen's University Belfast, UK.

Brice Dickson is Emeritus Professor of International and Comparative Law at Queen's University Belfast, UK.

Lewis Graham is a Lecturer in UK Human Rights Law at the University of Manchester, UK.

Alexander Horne is a Barrister (Lincoln's Inn), Counsel at Hackett & Dabbs LLP and Visiting Professor at Durham University, UK.

Allan C Hutchinson is Distinguished Research Professor at Osgoode Hall Law School, Toronto, Canada.

Jacqueline Kinghan is a Professor of Law and Social Change at the University of Glasgow, UK.

Dean Knight is a Professor of Law at Te Herenga Waka–Victoria University of Wellington and Co-Director of the New Zealand Centre for Public Law.

James Lee is Professor of English Law at The Dickson Poon School of Law, King's College London, UK.

Conall Mallory is a Senior Lecturer in Law at Queen's University Belfast, UK.

Gar Yein Ng is a Senior Lecturer in Law at the University of Buckingham, UK.

Alan Paterson OBE, FRSE, FRCP Edin, FRSA, FAcSS is Professor of law at Strathclyde University Law School and Director of the Centre for Professional Legal Studies, UK.

Erika Rackley is a Professor of Law at the University of Birmingham, UK.

Christopher W Schmidt is a Professor of Law at Chicago-Kent College of Law and Co-Director of the Institute on the Supreme Court of the United States (ISCOTUS), USA.

Hélène Tyrrell is a Senior Lecturer in Law at Newcastle University, UK.

Introduction

HÉLÈNE TYRRELL AND CONALL MALLORY

THE JUDICIARY OCCUPY a fundamental position in democracies across the world. They administer the rule of law, safeguard the rights of individuals, and resolve complex disputes. As the interpreters of the law, they mould, shape and sometimes even create it. They are experts in this work. The role of a senior judge also extends beyond the courtroom, involving frequent communication with a range of audiences beyond the judicial bench. This 'extrajudicial communication' takes many forms: television appearances, radio and print-media interviews, speeches, and written contributions to both academic and popular publications. But to what end? What purposes are served by judicial communication beyond the delivery of legal judgments, and what is the broader significance of extrajudicial communication within public discourse? How have these communications evolved over time and how might they continue to change in future, in response to changing societal and institutional contexts? What does extrajudicial communication tell us about the nature of the modern judicial role? This book explores these questions through a detailed analysis of perspectives on extrajudicial communication and its practice.

In this text we have adopted a broad and permissive approach to the understanding of extrajudicial communication. The collection has aimed to include any instance when a judge communicates with an audience beyond the courtroom and legal process. This excludes the nucleus of the judicial function – we are not concerned with what judges say when they are engaging with litigants and their counsel, writing legal opinions and administering court proceedings.[1] Instead, our interest is in what judges say outside of the judicial process. Unconstrained by the text of statutes, case-facts and precedent, judges can, in theory, speak freely on a diverse range of issues and to wider audiences. In some instances, this can afford the public a glimpse of who the judge is – their journey, personality, values,[2] and humanity.[3] The 'extra' in 'extrajudicial' not only denotes something extra to the judicial role, but also implies the potential for judges to offer an additional perspective, which may in turn provide us with additional insight into the persona of the judge on the bench.

[1] A similar approach is taken by Garoupa and Ginsburg in their assessment of 'nonjudicial functions', N Garoupa and T Ginsburg, 'Judicial Roles in Nonjudicial Functions' (2013) 12 *Washington University Global Studies Law Review* 755, 758.

[2] R Cahill-O'Callaghan, *Values in the Supreme Court: Decisions, Division and Diversity* (Oxford, Hart Publishing, 2020), 127.

[3] D Pannick, *Judges* (Oxford, Oxford University Press, 1987) 176.

The communication evaluated in this collection largely relates to high-profile judges on apex and senior courts, although many of the examples, lessons and arguments may apply to judges in lower courts. This is not to denigrate the power and the influence of a local judge on his or her community, or the significance of their public discourse. Rather it is to recognise that the higher the office, the greater interest and amplification in judicial communication. There is also a focus in this text on the extrajudicial communication practices of senior judges from courts in the United Kingdom and in other common law jurisdictions, although many of the authors in this collection are writing about cross-jurisdictional issues and using examples from outside the United Kingdom. We hope the arguments advanced and lessons learned can be shared across other jurisdictions and international courts. Finally, as a point of nomenclature, in this introduction and in our own chapters we have adopted the use of the term extrajudicial over extra-curial, and the unhyphenated 'extrajudicial' as opposed to the hyphenated 'extra-judicial'.[4] There is considerable divergence on the use of these terms in the scholarship and in judicial practice and, as a result, we have invited authors to the collection to allow individual preference to determine the form used. If pushed to explain our rationale for the unabridged *extrajudicial*, we would say that the hyphen adds an artificial distance when, in our view, the content and constraints of what judges say outside of the courtroom are inextricably linked to the judicial role. The reality is simply that we do not have a strong view one way or the other.

I. BACKGROUND AND CONTEXT

Extrajudicial communication is now a common feature of the legal literature and commentary but, in a number of jurisdictions, the cultural predisposition was, for a long time, towards a cautiousness in speaking out. For judges in the UK, restraint was shaped by the much-famed Kilmuir Rules of December 1955, which prohibited judicial office holders from participating in radio and television engagements. As Lord Chancellor, Lord Kilmuir's motivation was to insulate judges from 'the controversies of the day':[5]

> [S]o long as a Judge keeps silent his reputation for wisdom and impartiality remains unassailable: but every utterance which he makes in public, except in the course of the actual performance of his judicial duties, must necessarily bring him within the focus of criticism.[6]

This position was not grounded in law. The Kilmuir 'rules' assumed customary status, relying on an expectation that judges would follow the guidance of the Lord Chancellor.[7] Whatever the motivation for compliance, these rules shaped extrajudicial communication for the ensuing decades. In his 1987 book on *Judges*, David Pannick wrote:

> English judges rarely give press interviews or appear on television. Only occasionally do they write about the job they perform. They do not allow cameras into their courts.

[4] Our decision in doing so is consistent with the *Oxford English Dictionary*.
[5] Letter from Lord Kilmuir to Sir Ian Jacob KBE of 12 December 1955, reprinted in AW Bradley, 'Judges and the Media – the Kilmuir Rules' [1986] *Public Law* 383.
[6] ibid 384–85.
[7] G Rubin, 'Judicial Free Speech versus Judicial Neutrality in Mid-Twentieth Century England: The Last Hurrah for the Ancien Regime?' (2009) 27(2) *Law and History Review* 373, 382–83.

> They discourage sociological studies of their activities, such as sentencing. Like members of the Magic Circle who face expulsion if they explain how the trick is done, judges are eager to protect the mysteries of their craft. They do not respond to public criticism (on those rare occasions when they are subjected to it). Political scientists respect this desire for privacy by ignoring the judiciary when debating the nature of government.[8]

The Kilmuir Rules were abandoned by Lord Mackay in 1987.[9] Judges would no longer require the Lord Chancellor's consent before making comments to the media and would make their own determinations about when it was appropriate to speak in public. The contemporaneous expansion in the scope of judicial review, administrative law and human rights might also have stimulated a greater public engagement on the part of judges, flowing from a sense of judicial responsibility with respect to justifying contentious outcomes.[10] Simultaneously, the demise of the convention against political criticism of judges opened the space for extrajudicial speech in defence of the system and their role within it.[11] In the United Kingdom, a further turning point may have been the removal of the most senior judges from the House of Lords under the Constitutional Reform Act 2005, which removed the principal avenue by which the nation's most senior judges could engage in public life. As Lord Neuberger put it, the remaining avenues of extrajudicial engagement were inevitably 'likely to be more travelled'.[12]

Other common law jurisdictions are also now generally permissive of extrajudicial communication, although the journey to this point has varied.[13] In the United States, for example, there is a long history of engagement by members of the judiciary with the public, as well as periods of what has been characterised as 'judicial silence'.[14] As the culture of engagement from senior judges is tied directly to the constitutional position of the judge and their ascension to office, judges in America have increasingly started to speak about constitutional issues in public and to respond directly to criticism.[15] In Australia, the Kilmuir Rules were never formally adopted as part of the judicial custom but did frame the debate on extrajudicial communication for a number of decades.[16] Lindsay and Tomkins, for example, note a change in extrajudicial communication by Chief Justices in the last 50 years, involving more diverse media and a numerical increase in the instances of extrajudicial output.[17] New Zealand judges took a similarly

[8] Pannick (above n 3) 10.

[9] Lord Mackay would latterly reflect that he remained 'entirely convinced that it was completely right to get rid of the Kilmuir rules'. House of Lords, Lords Select Committee on the Constitution: Examination of Witnesses Lord Mackay (24 January 2007).

[10] eg Lord Dyson, 'What is Wrong with Human Rights' (Hertfordshire University, 3 November 2011) supremecourt.uk/uploads/speech_111103_85c8e61696.pdf.

[11] L Blom-Cooper, 'The Judiciary in an Era of Law Reform' (1966) 37 *Political Quarterly* 378.

[12] Lord Neuberger, 'Where Angels Fear to Tread' (Holdsworth Club 2012 Presidential Address, London, 2 March 2012) www.judiciary.uk/wp-content/uploads/JCO/Documents/Speeches/mr-speech-holdsworth-lecture-2012.pdf, para 34.

[13] See generally HP Lee, *Judiciaries in Comparative Perspective* (Cambridge, Cambridge University Press, 2011).

[14] B MacKenzie, 'Extrajudicial Speech: Judicial Ethics in the New Media Age' (2012) 2(2) *Reynolds Courts and Media Law Journal* 193.

[15] CG Geyh, 'The Criticism and Speech of Judges in the United States' in Lee (above n 13) 257.

[16] JM Williams, 'Judges' Freedom of Speech: Australia' in Lee (above n 13) 158.

[17] K Lindsay and D Tomkins, '*Hail to the Chief!* The Roles and Leadership of Australian Chief Justices as Evidenced in Extra-Curial Activity 1964–2017' (2017) 40(2) *UNSW* Law Journal 717.

restrained approach in the decades following Lord Kilmuir's pronouncement. As in Australia, the Kilmuir Rules were not officially adopted, but conformance flowed from a sense of 'judicial neutrality'.[18] The South African judiciary traditionally followed a similar approach of 'aloofness from political controversy',[19] until the development of a constitutional democracy with judicial review and a firm role for civil liberties made space for a 'flourishing of expression'.[20] Similarly in Canada, Roach identifies the adoption of the Canadian Charter of Rights and Freedoms as the turning-point in judicial communication: judges now make interventions on matters 'that would have been unacceptable in the pre-Charter era'.[21] Across several jurisdictions therefore, there has been a turning of the tide from an era of judicial reticence and constraint, towards one of judicial engagement. Indeed, some senior judges have stated a concern that judges now speak so regularly that 'their voices will have less weight when they speak out on matters of real significance'.[22] This book maps out how this new age has manifested, along with its potential benefits and perils.

II. FORMS OF EXTRAJUDICIAL COMMUNICATION

Extrajudicial communication comes in many shapes and forms. One of the contributors to this collection, Christopher Schmidt, has provided a useful framework for categorising different types of extrajudicial communication, in the context of US Supreme Court Justices. Schmidt breaks the outputs down into five different categories,[23] which we can broadly apply to communication by judges across multiple jurisdictions.

First, there are the *personal* outputs, whether in the form of autobiographies, books, notes or interviews, in which judges reflect on their own lives and careers. The defining feature of this type of output is that the contribution is by and about the judge themself. A common frame is the journey of the individual judge to the bench, and an obvious format is the judicial biography and autobiography. The popularity of these genres fluctuates across generations and different jurisdictions,[24] but reveals a steady interest in the lives and work of those on the bench.[25]

[18] G Hammond, 'Judges and Free Speech in New Zealand' in Lee (above n 13) 195.

[19] I Currie, 'The judiciary and freedom of speech in South Africa' in Lee (above n 13) 217.

[20] ibid 227.

[21] K Roach, 'Judges and Freed Speech in Canada' in Lee (above n 13) 175.

[22] M McMurdo, 'Should Judges Speak Out or Shut Up?' (Speech at Queensland Business Institute, Brisbane, 16 October 2001) archive.sclqld.org.au/judgepub/mcmurdo161001.pdf, 16. See also: Lord Neuberger (above n 12) para 53.

[23] C Schmidt, 'Beyond the Opinion: Supreme Court Justices and Extrajudicial Speech' (2013) 88(2) *Chicago-Kent Law Review* 487, 497. See Chapter 3 of this volume: C Schmidt, 'The United States Supreme Court and the Perils of Extrajudicial Speech'.

[24] The absence of judicial biography is lamented in Australian legal circles. See T Josev, 'Judicial Biography in Australia: Current Obstacles and Opportunities' (2017) 40(2) *University of New South Wales Law Journal* 842.

[25] D Sugerman, 'From Legal Biography to Legal Life Writing: Broadening Conceptions of Legal History and Socio-legal Scholarship' (2015) 42(1) *Journal of Law and Society* 9; P Scott, 'Judicial Biography in the National Security Constitution: Lord Diplock and a "Rather Silly Little Secret Racket"' (2024) 87(3) *Modern Law Review* 604; G Edward White, 'The Renaissance of Judicial Biography' (1995) 23 *Reviews in American History* 716.

There is also a practice of celebrating the legal lives of influential judges with Festschrifts, essay series and special issues of journals, many of which often include a contribution from their subject or former colleagues.[26] Op-eds and interviews present further opportunities. The rise and diversification in media platforms have extended the outlet for this style of extrajudicial voice to social media and podcasts, with potentially wider reach and where a judge's own voice may add personality to their prose.[27]

A second form of output is the *interpersonal*, where judges discuss other judges and the collegiate or professional behaviour of the bench.[28] This category differs across jurisdictions and judicial cultures. In the United States, Supreme Court Justices have frequently spoken of their relationships on the bench.[29] Indeed, much has been made of the friendship between the great judicial opposites of Ruth Bader Ginsburg and Antonin Scalia.[30] In the United Kingdom, it is generally seen as a convention that judges *do not* speak about the qualities of their colleagues, their experience, and in particular, their performance on the bench. And yet there are notable exceptions to this practice. One example considered in a number of chapters in this book is the publication of Lord Hope's personal diaries, which drew considerable criticism from the bench and beyond.[31] Lord Hope's comments on the judicial appointment process in particular drew ire from commentators. In Australia, federal and family court Justice Joshua Wilson was forced to apologise to colleagues and withdraw from an international conference when his draft speech – which contained accusations that the appointment process promoted diversity and progressive politics over merit – was circulated in advance.[32]

Third, judges engage in *educational* commentary, acting as 'civics teachers' of the workings of the courts and the constitutional system.[33] Unsurprisingly, judges are regularly invited to share their expertise at domestic, regional and international conferences, on a range of issues. Many speak at universities, societies and institutions, but their audience is not limited to the legal specialist or student. Judges, and courts, are increasingly engaging in outreach activities with the wider public, appearing on

[26] See for example: W Day and S Worthington, *Challenging Private Law, Lord Sumption on the Supreme Court* (Oxford, Hart Publishing, 2020) which includes an introduction from Lord Sumption, and B Dickson and C McCormick, *The Judicial Mind: A Festschrift for Lord Kerr of Tonaghmore* (Oxford, Hart Publishing, 2021) includes a foreword from Lord Reed and a chapter from Lady Hale.

[27] See for instance: The University of Law Podcast, 'The Judges: Power, Politics and the People' www.youtube.com/playlist?list=PLIr_gf3NNn2jvMHVS4oFnGTigu8mroujy; 'Baroness Hale of Richmond, Desert Island Discs' (*BBC Radio 4*, 19 September 2021) www.bbc.co.uk/sounds/play/m000zt7b.

[28] Schmidt (above n 23) 497.

[29] S Breyer, 'The Supreme Court I Served On Was Made Up of Friends', *New York Times* (New York, 3 April 2024) www.nytimes.com/2024/04/03/opinion/stephen-breyer-friendship-court.html.

[30] R Wolf, 'Opera, travel, food, law: The unlikely friendship of Ruth Bader Ginsburg and Antonin Scalia', *USA Today* (20 September 2020) eu.usatoday.com/story/news/politics/2020/09/20/supreme-friends-ruth-bader-ginsburg-and-antonin-scalia/5844533002.

[31] *Lord Hope's Diaries* volumes I–V (Edinburgh, Avizandumm, 2018–19); in this volume, see especially Chapter 14: Lewis Graham, 'Learning from *Lord Hope's Diaries*' and Chapter 15: James Lee, 'Judging Memoirs: Life Writing as Extra-Judicial Communication'.

[32] N Bucci, 'Australian judge apologises after claiming that colleagues are appointed regardless of merit', *The Guardian* (London, 26 May 2023) www.theguardian.com/law/2023/may/26/judge-apologises-after-claiming-that-colleagues-are-appointed-regardless-of-merit.

[33] Schmidt (above n 23) 500.

podcasts or documentaries, opening their courts for visits and tours, and meeting with school children. The general aim behind much of this is sustaining public confidence.[34] As Margaret McMurdo has said, public confidence in the judicial system can be fostered 'by ensuring the community understands the role of the judiciary as an essential arm of democratic government and the role of judges in administering justice according to law'.[35] Confidence on these fronts breeds legitimacy and authority. These qualities are vital for courts, not least in the instances where they render judgments which are divisive or unpopular. At these times, as Ginsburg notes, 'courts need allies'.[36] There is no better ally for the court and domestic judge than the public. And an informed public – invested in the importance of judicial independence – is much more effective an ally than an apathetic one.[37]

Connected to this, a fourth category of output is *jurisprudential*. This is where the judge takes up questions and interpretations of the law principally for academic and practitioner audiences. The audience might also include judicial colleagues. These types of communication tend to have a deeper analytical focus and may go beyond education in the sense that they can also represent attempts to influence legal practice. Consider, for example, the public conversations between Antonin Scalia and Stephen Breyer about the relevance of foreign case law in US constitutional cases or on the interpretation of the US Constitution.[38] Other examples include where judges write or speak specifically on the art of judging.[39]

A fifth category is *institutional* in nature: judges may speak out for, or in defence of, the judicial institution and its decisions. Senior judges in many jurisdictions have a responsibility to engage with the other branches of state. Thus, judges may attend legislative committees and hearings, issuing responses to questions and providing updates on key issues. There may be an expectation that they attend scheduled ceremonial events. Institutional responsibility may also lead judges (particularly in leadership positions) to respond to criticism of the judiciary.[40] There is also a detectible sense that judges have a responsibility to speak out, proactively, on political and constitutional developments which fall within their sphere of influence. Changes to legal aid, court fees and delays in hearings have all provoked judicial comment from serving and retired judges. Nonetheless, there are limits to the form and manner in which judges can effectively deal with politicians. As Joshua Rozenberg has noted, 'their authority extends no further than the courtroom. In any public spat between politicians and the judiciary, politicians will always win'.[41]

[34] Conall Mallory and Hélène Tyrrell, 'The Extrajudicial Voice' (2024) 44(1) *Legal Studies* 1, 10–15.

[35] McMurdo (above n 22) 6.

[36] T Ginsburg, 'Demographic Backsliding and the Rule of Law' (2018) 44 *Ohio Northern University Law Review* 351, 368.

[37] S Shetreet and S Turenne, *Judges on Trial* (Cambridge, Cambridge University Press, 2014) 357.

[38] N Dorsen, 'The Relevance of Foreign Legal materials in U.S. Constitutional Cases: A Conversation between U.S. Supreme Court Justices' (2005) 3(3) *International Journal of Constitutional Law* 519.

[39] See eg: T Bingham, *The Business of Judging: Selected Essays and Speeches* (Oxford, Oxford University Press, 2000); A Barak, *The Judge in a Democracy* (Princeton NJ, Princeton University Press, 2006).

[40] Schmidt (above n 23) 501.

[41] Joshua Rozenberg, 'Judges need help to counter the dark arts', *Law Society Gazette* (5 September 2025) 12.

We would make one addition to Schmidt's categories: *entertainment*. When judges move beyond the bench to communicate, they are often doing so at the invitation of another: a university, institution, society or interviewer. Judges are popular speakers in a range of venues, and have long been in high demand for lectures. Indeed, some influential lecture series have been dominated by the extrajudicial voice,[42] both within the United Kingdom and further afield. Many of their engagements may be framed through an educational lens, but it would be remiss not to recognise that their invitations can also take on an 'after dinner' quality.

III. THE PRINCIPLES AND PITFALLS OF EXTRAJUDICIAL COMMUNICATION

Whatever form extrajudicial communication takes, the chapters in this collection build a picture of expectations and principles which reveal that judges are held to explicit and implicit standards that are not applied to others. Extrajudicial communication sits at a conceptual crossroads – an intersection of principles where potential and perils converge to shape and define the judicial role.

To the one side of this junction are the reasons underpinning a judicial right to speak. Most prominently, when judges communicate extrajudicially they are manifesting the principle of judicial independence. Legal systems that refrain from imposing rigid rules on what judges say and how they say it help to safeguard this independence from undue influence. This principle was central to Lord Mackay's decision to abandon the Kilmuir Rules in 1987. Allowing judges to speak extrajudicially also affirms their individual rights to freedom of expression and,[43] if it contributes to the public understanding of law and legal process, extrajudicial speech has the potential to advance judicial transparency and promote the judicial office. Engagement or response to commentary and criticism can also constitute participation in a form of judicial accountability. This freedom of expression, however, is subject to some qualification given their judicial office: the right is balanced by the need to maintain 'the authority and impartiality of the judiciary'.[44] It becomes clear that judges carry 'special duties and responsibilities',[45] which, among other things, require them to 'preserve the dignity of the judicial office and the impartiality and independence of the judiciary'.[46]

Such qualifications carve out the other side of this conceptual junction: the reasons underpinning restraint on extrajudicial communication. These echo Lord Kilmuir's concerns that extrajudicial comment has the potential to risk the reputation of judges as neutral arbiters. Avoiding that risk may necessitate 'some degree of seclusion,

[42] Shetreet and Turenne (above n 37) 360.

[43] See eg Article 10 European Convention on Human Rights 1950 and *Perna v Italy* (Application no 48898/99) (2004) 39 EHRR 563; Article 19 International Covenant on Civil and Political Rights 1966 and Article 19 Universal Declaration on Human Rights.

[44] Article 10(2) European Convention on Human Rights.

[45] Article 19(3) International Covenant on Civil and Political Rights.

[46] *Bangalore Principles of Judicial Conduct*, adopted 1 June 2002 [4.6] www.unodc.org/pdf/crime/corruption/judicial_group/Bangalore_principles.pdf.

abstention from social and political struggles, restriction on the freedom of expression and the freedom to respond';[47] judges should 'retreat into monastic isolation in order to preserve the sanctity of the judicial office'.[48] More subtle reservations relate to the scope and style of extrajudicial communication. Ewing's concern about the rules on judicial free speech was that they may not be framed with 'sufficient humility about the propriety of the judicial role',[49] while Bartie and Gava have argued that extrajudicial writing on legal issues requires 'scrutiny, not unthinking acquiescence'.[50]

Thus, the very same principles which promote freedoms in relation to extrajudicial communication are those that attract the constraints, steering judges away from public statements which have the potential to erode perceptions of judicial independence and thereby also damage public confidence in the justice system. These constraints are reflected both in prevailing judicial conduct rules and guides on judicial ethics, as well as in informal or implicit shared conceptions amongst the judiciary.[51] Those constraints are unpacked by the contributors to this book, while charting this potential and peril of extrajudicial communication across several different practices and jurisdictions.

IV. OVERVIEW OF THE BOOK

The structure of this book differentiates between perspectives on extrajudicial communication and its practice. The chapters in the first Part focus on the history, significance, potential and perils of extrajudicial communication, alongside its legal and social impact.

TT Arvind begins the collection with a brief history of controversial extrajudicial communication, told through six historical judges with events occurring in the seventeenth, eighteenth and twentieth centuries. His account, in Chapter one, portrays the judges as falling into three camps: *lobbyists*, strategically seeking to achieve through political means what could not be achieved judicially; *evangelists*, encouraging a wide audience to adopt a particular view of the law; and *problem-solvers*, using their experience to identify tensions and pragmatically working to find solutions. He concludes with observations on the historical demarcations of extrajudicial communication – the legal and the political – and the lessons that can be learned from the historical judicial navigation of this terrain.

Allan Hutchinson's Chapter two explores the foundational question: whether judges should or should not speak out. He makes the case for challenging commonly accepted constraints around extrajudicial discourse. In particular, seeing law and its adjudicative function as unavoidably political and partial enterprises, he disagrees that judges should resile from revealing political views. He argues that judges'

[47] Barak (above n 39) 110.

[48] WG Ross, 'Extrajudicial Speech: Charting the Boundaries of Propriety' (1989) 1 *Georgetown Journal of Legal Ethics* 589, 589–90.

[49] K Ewing 'Judges and free speech in the United Kingdom' in Lee (above n 13) 356.

[50] S Bartie and J Gava, 'Some Problems with Extrajudicial Writing' (2012) 34 *Sydney Law Review* 637, 656.

[51] Mallory and Tyrrell (above n 34).

political views affect both the creation and application of the law, and that the nature and thrust of those political views therefore become a matter for public disclosure and public scrutiny. Judges should speak out more, not less.

Christopher Schmidt takes the opposing view, examining the perils of extrajudicial discourse. Through the lens of the United States Supreme Court, in Chapter three, he identifies three primary beneficiaries of extrajudicial speech: the public, the judiciary, and the judge. He weighs these against the dominant risk of extrajudicial communication – that what a judge says or writes off the bench will undermine public confidence in the judiciary. A significant factor in altering the balance has been the changing judicial attitudes in relation to extrajudicial speech. As extrajudicial speech becomes more commonplace, he argues, the distinctive value of extrajudicial speech diminishes. Extrajudicial speech has become a powerful way to further the individual interests of the justices but, on whether it advances the institutional interests of the Court, he is less convinced.

In Chapter four, Brice Dickson explores the extrajudicial role of judges as agents of change, focusing on three species of that role: their work as writers of textbooks for practitioners, as writers of courses of lectures, and as chairs of official commissions and inquiries. He suggests that judges have occasional opportunities to change the law through their extrajudicial work and that those opportunities may even be more obvious. Outside of the courts, judges are not trammelled in their thinking by the pressures exerted by having to establish facts and consider the specific arguments put by the parties. These opportunities license judges to be freer in their thinking and more imaginative in their problem-solving. He argues that, even if it is difficult to point to many specific legal changes which have been an obvious consequence of extrajudicial work, speaking extrajudicially can and has been influential in 'moving the dial' of the law's development.

Conall Mallory, in Chapter five, considers the nature of extrajudicial discourse on the part of international judges. He positions the international judge as experiencing an inherent 'legitimacy deficit' when compared to their domestic counterparts and therefore argues that a core motivating factor behind extrajudicial communication of the international judge is the opportunity to respond to this deficit. It follows that the audience for extrajudicial comments on the part of international judges is a series of key constituencies upon whose approval their existence is dependent. Using the practice of the President of the European Court of Human Rights as a case study, he outlines how leadership judges at that Court effectively use rhetorical appeals of *logos, ethos* and *pathos* in their communications with key constituencies. In doing so, they adopt and deploy a judicial voice that would not sit naturally within the courtroom.

In Chapter six, Erika Rackley considers the potential for extrajudicial discourse as a changemaker. She considers the role judges have played, as individuals and through their institutional leadership roles, in shaping and inhibiting judicial diversity debates in England and Wales. Her argument is that extrajudicial discourse about diversity in the judiciary is characterised by an over-reliance on personal testimony and a reluctance (with notable exceptions) to address 'uncomfortable truths', or to confront received clichés and real dilemmas. But it is possible, she suggests, to envisage opportunities for senior judges to use their social capital and leadership and to discuss 'more adventurous solutions' which might break the diversity deadlock. If these opportunities were grasped, we would have better conversations about judicial diversity, and might move closer to making judicial diversity a reality.

Hélène Tyrrell's Chapter seven explores the expectations, behaviours, and influence of retired judges. She begins by explaining why it remains appropriate to talk about the remarks of retired judges as a type of 'extrajudicial' discourse, and outlines the limited framework for retired judges in this sphere. While the extrajudicial engagement of serving judges is captured by formal guidance, retired judges may, in theory, say what they like. In practice, however, the attitudes and behaviours of retired judges suggest that retirement does not bring total liberation. She teases the tension between the greater freedoms that retired judges enjoy and the constraints that operate in practice, challenging the justifications relating to perceptions of impartiality. She suggests that interrogating justifications for constraining the public remarks of retired judges invites a reassessment of the parameters for extrajudicial speech on the part of *serving* judges.

The final perspective considered in this section is from *beside* the bench. In Chapter eight, Jacqueline Kinghan considers extrajudicial engagement from the perspective of a judicial assistant (JA) at the UK Supreme Court, whose tasks may include writing memos on applications for leave to appeal, drafting press summaries, and conducting legal research for judgment writing and extrajudicial speeches. She suggests that having a unique and personal glimpse of the way in which judges understand and appraise their own roles serves an important educational function. In turn, JAs support the evolution of constitutional literacy activities and help to facilitate the extrajudicial discourse of the Supreme Court Justices in the wider public domain. JAs also receive a rare insight into how the Justices perceive the processes that govern how they communicate with audiences outside of the Court.

The chapters in Part II address the *practice* of extrajudicial communication. Recognising that constraints, purposes, and pitfalls vary across different mediums, this Part draws out questions of audience, both in terms of those to whom extrajudicial communication is addressed and how it is received.

Alan Paterson, in Chapter nine, focuses on academic interviews as a form of extrajudicial communication, reflecting on his experience interviewing the UK senior judiciary. He suggests that extrajudicial communications can be exercises in power, autonomy, and free speech. These exercises are influenced by a range of factors which sit along a continuum from monologues to dialogues. Interviews with academics are a comparatively modern development in the world of the law and, depending on the context and personalities, can provide some insights into the judicial process that may be inappropriate for other forms of extrajudicial communication. Interviews with academics, he argues, can foster transparency whilst reducing the mystique in judicial decision-making. A key aspect of this is the armoury they add to judicial researchers, by enabling them to have more access to the inner workings of judicial decision-making, thereby enhancing understanding and with it, accountability.

Rachel Cahill O'Callaghan's Chapter ten takes a close look at the practice of judicial speeches by UK Supreme Court Justices. She notes the importance of the individual public speech in an age where the Supreme Court has become more collective – regularly issuing unanimous decisions and with a considerable decline in dissenting judgments. With recourse to an empirical assessment of public lectures delivered by Justices between 2020 and 2025, she challenges the lack of individuality and diversity in this turn to the collective. She argues that while public lectures may present a unique opportunity for the individual voice of the judge to be established, even here we are seeing collective action in the form of dominant narratives, and shared values and principles being projected. This demise in difference and diversity, she contends, is to be lamented.

Dean Knight shifts the lens to extrajudicial discourse in small democracies, in Chapter eleven. He looks at judicial scholarship as one of the non-adjudicative functions of the judiciary and reflects on the virtue or otherwise of publication of academic articles by judges. Particular attention is paid, as an illustrative case study, to the practice and impact of judicial scholarship in Aotearoa New Zealand – a small democracy where extrajudicial scholarship is especially common-place and judicial ruminations have profound effects on legal consciousness and public thought. He characterises such scholarship as varying between a hallmark of judicial office, a hobby and, intermittently, a hazard.

In Chapter twelve, Alexander Horne explores methods of extrajudicial participation in Parliament, through the lens of the principle of the separation of powers and the changes made by the Constitutional Reform Act 2005. He argues that while extrajudicial contact between the judiciary and legislature can be perfectly appropriate, some of the formal structures in the UK remain less than transparent and could potentially benefit from some further clarification. There are also some contrasts with other forms of extrajudicial communication. Appearances may not always be entirely discretionary, and while some such communication takes place through contributions in the second chamber and via select committees, other important discourse is less transparent – achieved through backchannel dialogue with officials and parliamentarians. Much of this reflects the fact that the extrajudicial relationship between the judiciary and Parliament develops over the longer term and is likely to depend as much on habit and practice than on formal rules.

Gar Yein Ng focuses, in Chapter thirteen, on whistleblowing as a form of extrajudicial engagement. She explains that whistleblowing aligns with the justifications for any form of extrajudicial communication: promoting transparency and preserving freedom of speech. But, while other forms of extrajudicial communication may pursue a variety of aims, whistleblowing focuses entirely on exposure – reporting wrongdoing. Judicial whistleblowing therefore sits uncomfortably within frameworks which encourage extrajudicial work only insofar as it avoids harming the reputation of the judiciary. The propriety of judicial whistleblowing thus rests on the extent to which this risk is outweighed by the contribution to transparency and the operation of the rule of law. Two case studies of whistleblowing in the English judiciary provide a lens through which to assess this balance, taking into account the scope for whistleblowing and the protections for the judges involved.

In Chapter fourteen, Lewis Graham picks up on arguably the most controversial of the post-bench publications: Lord Hope's diaries. He suggests that, in modern times, we have seen nothing like the direct, and at times intensely personal, invitation to peek behind the curial veil like that provided by *Lord Hope's Diaries*. *Lord Hope's Diaries*, he argues, are also particularly helpful in shattering the stubborn and pervasive myth of absolute judicial impartiality, providing one of the strongest arguments in favour of judicial realism when it comes to the UK's highest appellate court.

James Lee's focus is on judicial life writing, in the form of the post-retirement diaries, memoirs and autobiographical writings (collectively memoirs) of former UK Supreme Court Justices. In Chapter fifteen, he offers a study of memoirs published by four retired Justices: Lady Hale, Lord Dyson, Lord Hope and Lord Brown. He examines the value of such writing, and the insights that are provided in understanding the dynamics amongst the Justices on our highest court, and how the judges conceive of, and reflect upon, their individual and collective roles serving on it. A key argument is that there should be greater engagement with, and scrutiny of, judicial memoirs as a form of 'extra-curial' communication. The issue is shown to connect to wider debates around the post-retirement activities of former judges and around public confidence in, and understanding of, the Court as an institution.

The flavour of Anurag Deb's Chapter sixteen is a little different. He looks beyond the content of extrajudicial appearances, and instead focuses on their aesthetic framing and characteristics. He considers forms of extrajudicial engagement that place judges in the public eye, whether it is interviews in national newspapers, appearances in documentaries and podcasts, or starring roles in bespoke outreach videos. He suggests that the aesthetic framing of the judge in this form of extrajudicial engagement can reveal much about the judiciary today. Despite hints of personalisation, this form of extrajudicial appearance has tended towards a strong sense of tradition and professionalism. The likely justification echoes the widely perceived risks of extrajudicial communication relating to public exposure of the institution of the court and its judges. But this, he argues, hinders judicial accessibility.

V. CONCLUSION

Key to our aims as editors has been to explore and address tensions between the behaviour of judges and core constitutional principles, including judicial independence, the rule of law and the separation of powers. The latter is frequently seen as the most relevant to this topic, since extrajudicial communication is often conceptualised as sitting on a continuum of propriety. For some, extrajudicial communication is perilous: when judges speak outside the courtroom, they run the risk of undermining the private dynamics of the bench and undercutting the mystical complexities of judicial decision-making. Depending on the subject, extrajudicial communication may threaten the public perception of the judicial system or damage the 'integrity of the court as a place in which reasoned distribution of justice is the first and highest priority'.[52] The contributions to this volume take account of these risks but also recognise the significance, value, and extensive practice of extrajudicial communication among the modern judiciary. Gone is the time when David Pannick could accurately write that the 'English judge is not a public figure'.[53] Extrajudicial communication is now

[52] WG Ross, 'Extrajudicial Speech: Charting the Boundaries of Propriety' (1989) 2 *Georgetown Journal of Legal Ethics* 589.

[53] Pannick (n 3 above) 169.

a commonly accepted practice on the part of sitting and retired judges. The motivations or purposes driving extrajudicial communication are varied. The chapters in this volume were curated to showcase that breadth and to expose the consequential value of the practice in different forms. Extrajudicial communication can be a powerful tool. Amongst other things, it can influence policy, it can support public legal education, and it can reinforce legitimacy – both of an institution and its actors. Above all, the chapters in this collection show that judges do not lose their authority by taking off their robes. Through their extrajudicial communication judges can continue to exercise considerable influence.

Our approach, coupled with the practical constraints of any edited collection, means that inevitably some topics have been left out. As noted above, in order to draw lessons across the work, we have focused on extrajudicial communication which flows from holders of high judicial office, meaning that discussion of the extrajudicial work taken on by lower court judges and magistrates is absent. Aside from the fact that most extrajudicial discourse flows from the senior judiciary, the common seniority allows us to explore synergies between forms of extrajudicial communication and across different jurisdictions. We have also drawn a temporal line which incorporates only what judges say after having been appointed (whether serving or retired), rather than exploring the role and influence of what we could term 'pre-judicial' communication. The discussion is centred on extrajudicial communication in common law jurisdictions. That the approaches of judges in civil law traditions have not been covered in dedicated chapters does not mean that we think them unimportant – no doubt an exploration of the practice from the perspective of the civil law tradition would contribute important learning. We could also see value in extended consideration of the judicial use of social media, and in a singularly focused reflection on judicial engagement in public legal education. Other possibilities could include examinations of creative outputs, as explored by the late Ruth Herz in her brilliant book, *The Art of Justice*.[54] There are numerous ways through which such outputs can, as Herz puts it, tell 'a personal judicial story … of the judge's inner world'.[55]

We hope the choices made in forming this collection serve to capture the essence of extrajudicial communication: liberations reveal constraints; a response amplifies an event; what is said makes us wonder what is not. Judges do not speak with a single voice, nor do they perform a singular function. They are, amongst other things, interpreters, educators, and commentators. These layered identities and responsibilities inspired the cover art for this volume. Finally, if we accept that extrajudicial communication can influence public understanding, shape legal discourse, and contribute to judicial accountability, then it is a further reason to give careful attention to who is speaking. Thinking about the nature and practice of extrajudicial communication provides a lens through which to see the judicial role in its full public context.

[54] R Herz, *The Art of Justice: The Judge's Perspective* (Oxford, Hart Publishing, 2012).
[55] ibid 3.

Part I

Perspectives

1

A Brief History of (Controversial) Extrajudicial Communication

TT ARVIND

I. INTRODUCTION

ON 14 NOVEMBER 1770, a letter appeared in the *Public Advertiser* under the pseudonym 'Junius'. Junius had by then established himself as an anti-regime polemicist. Since the start of the preceding year, he had written a number of scathing public letters bitterly criticising prominent figures in the government of King George III. This letter, however, was different. Its target was not Grafton, North, or the other leading Whig politicians in George III's inner circle. Instead, it was a judge who arguably remains one of the best-known judicial personages of the late eighteenth century: Lord Mansfield, Lord Chief Justice of the King's Bench.

Junius' decision to target a common law judge rather than the holder of a more obviously political office was not a departure from his usual agenda. The letter criticised Mansfield's judicial work: his 'thoughts, words, and actions', his 'contempt or ignorance of the common law of England', and his reliance on 'maxims of jurisprudence unknown to Englishmen'.[1] But by its concluding paragraphs, it had turned to Junius's principal complaint: Mansfield's extrajudicial comments and discussions. Junius accused Mansfield of pretending to be a politically neutral figure even though his extrajudicial communication revealed him to be anything but neutral. It was, Junius alleged, widely known that Mansfield would 'meanly skulk into the closet' and give secret advice to the King[2] and that, through his words and strategic silences in Parliament, he lent his support and authority to the administration's odious policies.[3] Mansfield, Junius claimed, had descended to such a 'vile practice' that, despite his talent, he was far more detested than admired and was widely viewed as wholly unqualified to preside over a court of common law.[4]

[1] Junius, *Stat Nominis Umbra*, vol 2 (London, HS Woodfall, 1772) 116–17.
[2] ibid 128–29.
[3] ibid 127–28.
[4] ibid 130.

The vehemence with which Junius criticised Mansfield will surprise modern readers more accustomed to associating Mansfield with English commercial law than the political controversies of eighteenth-century England. But Junius was not alone. Even authors more sympathetically disposed towards Mansfield had deep reservations about the positions he took in his extrajudicial communication. Sir James Mackintosh, in a biographical sketch that is generally favourable to Mansfield, noted his 'habitual & almost unconscious bias to the Cause of Government' and the absence of 'any portion of that Spirit which would have more peculiarly characterised an English judge', a failing which Mackintosh ascribed amongst other things to Mansfield's 'connexions'.[5]

Mansfield was not alone in finding himself subject to criticism. Other judges, too, faced strong criticism and opposition for politically controversial extrajudicial comments. Perhaps the best-known example is Lord Coke, whose extrajudicial writings led to the government seizing his papers, prohibiting him from publishing subsequent volumes of his *Institutes*, and for a time even committing him to the Tower of London. The extent of trouble in which Coke's writings landed him was somewhat unusual, but it was a matter of degree rather than kind. History provides plenty of examples of judges who engaged in extrajudicial communication on matters that were seen as being both political and controversial, and who came under sharp scrutiny for doing so.

In this, the past resembles the present, as the very existence of this collection evidences. In the politically polarised context of the present day, extrajudicial comments by judges again attract a heightened degree of scrutiny, particularly where they seem to touch upon politically contentious issues. The Kilmuir Rules, discussed in the Introduction to this volume, were one attempt to manage the tensions this scrutiny creates.[6] However, they were a relatively short interlude of rigid control in a more permissive tradition. This in and of itself makes the history of judges' extrajudicial communication worth studying. But there is also a second and deeper reason to study its past. The past lets us examine the motives of actors and the wider context of their actions in a way that is harder to do in relation to the present. In studying extrajudicial communications and discourse in the past, for example, we can ask questions about techniques, motives, and strategies that are less straightforward to answer in relation to the present day. The range of materials history places at our disposal lets us examine why judges in the past chose to speak and communicate extrajudicially, what they sought to achieve through their extrajudicial interventions, and how this related to their work as judges. It also lets us examine the longer-term impact of their extrajudicial action, an issue which is much more difficult to examine objectively in relation to the present day.

It is here that engaging with the history of extrajudicial communication is particularly fruitful. As this chapter will show, extrajudicial communication is not monolithic. Judges communicate with different audiences in different ways, and the effects of their communication can differ significantly depending on its form,

[5] BL Add MSS 78790, f 41.
[6] See H Tyrrell and C Mallory, 'Introduction', section I.

purpose, forum, and audience. Understanding how judges have approached extrajudicial communication in the past therefore forms a useful starting point for exploring its significance and importance.

In sections II, III, and IV, I examine the extrajudicial communications of six English judges. Three are historical figures from the seventeenth and eighteenth centuries – Lords Ellesmere, Hardwicke, and Coke – while the other three are twentieth-century judges, Lords Diplock, Denning, and Dilhorne.[7] Ellesmere, Hardwicke, and Coke lived in a time when it was reasonably common for individuals to move between politics and the bench, and all three had themselves held political office. Despite this fluidity, contemporaries had a clear sense that judicial and political roles represented different domains of activity. Junius's invective against Mansfield, for example, accused him of taking on a secret political role that was unseemly for a judge, and contemporary accounts suggest that Lord Camden, Mansfield's contemporary and rival, worried that judicial office would restrict his ability to participate in political debate.[8] Nevertheless, their political background gave them an understanding of the political dimensions of the great tensions of the day, and it also gave them access to political figures and fora. This is less true of twentieth-century judges but, as this chapter will show, there are nevertheless strong parallels between the two sets of judges, to the extent that it is possible to classify them as belonging to three broad types of extrajudicial communicators, which I term lobbyists, evangelists, and problem-solvers.

In section V, I draw on this history to argue that the UK's constitutional arrangements make it inevitable that judges will be drawn extrajudicially into deeply divisive issues, including politically controversial matters. History demonstrates that while their activity can raise genuine concerns about their reach and impact, it can also be fundamental to the effective development of the legal system. The task for law is to manage the tensions created by the judiciary's extrajudicial role, rather than seeking to avoid it altogether.

II. LEGAL ENDS, POLITICAL MEANS: ELLESMERE, DIPLOCK, AND THE JUDGE AS EXTRAJUDICIAL LOBBYIST

The early seventeenth century saw the common law courts locked in conflict with Chancery over their respective jurisdictions. The dispute began when Coke and Ellesmere (or Sir Thomas Egerton, as he was also called) headed their respective courts. Both sought to vindicate their positions not just through judicial decisions

[7] Given the historical orientation of this chapter, I have restricted myself to judges who are no longer alive at the time of writing. All six judges I discuss in this chapter held senior judicial positions. Ellesmere and Denning were both Masters of the Rolls. Hardwicke and Coke were Lords Chief Justice, in Hardwicke's case of the King's Bench, and in Coke's case of Common Pleas and King's Bench in succession. Diplock and Dilhorne sat on the Judicial Committee of the House of Lords (the predecessor of the modern Supreme Court of the UK). In addition, Ellesmere, Hardwicke, and Dilhorne also held the office of Lord Chancellor at a time when it was both a political and a judicial office, and all three heard and decided cases in that capacity.

[8] HS Eeles, *Lord Chancellor Camden and His Family* (P Allan, 1934) 67.

but also through extensive extrajudicial communication. Coke advanced his position through public statements such as legal treatises and Parliamentary debates. Ellesmere, in contrast, published very little in his lifetime. The only publication safely attributable to him is the text of the speech he delivered in the Exchequer Chamber in *Calvin's Case* (or, as he called it, the *Case of the Postnati*).[9] To advance his position in the jurisdictional conflict, he worked by seeking through private communication to persuade King James I & VI and his Privy Council to intervene.

Contemporaries were puzzled by the bitterness of the dispute between courts that had previously enjoyed good relations.[10] The cause appears to have lain in attempts by both courts to adapt their functioning to the new needs of commerce, with each disapproving of the other's attempts. Under Ellesmere, Chancery grew increasingly willing to hear cases even after a common law court had given judgment if it felt that the decision at common law was wrong, and to issue injunctions against executing common law judgments.[11] The common law courts reacted strongly, with Coke (acting judicially) playing a leading role. The common law argument was that Magna Carta required cases to be determined according to the law of the land, and statutes from the time of Elizabeth I required all cases determinable at Common Law to only be brought by due process or by writ. Chancery's proceedings violated this, and the common law courts drew on these statutes as well as the Statute of Praemunire to grant injunctions against pursuing cases at Chancery, and to grant habeas corpus to individuals arrested by order of a Chancery court.[12]

In 1615, Ellesmere moved the dispute to a new arena: the Privy Council, of which he, as Lord Chancellor, was a member. In September 1615, he prepared a paper for the Council setting out the essence of his case and seeking the King's intervention.[13] Ellesmere argued that equity was as much part of the law of the land as common law: it was 'the doeing of Right and Iustice in Cases where the Common law cannot help'. In consequence the words 'Common Law' in statutes should be construed to include equity.[14] Equally, equity proceedings should also be seen as a species of due process according to 'the auncient law of the land'.[15] Equity was not engaged in 'reversinge of the Iudgmentes given by the Iudges of the Common Law' but merely doing 'in

[9] *Calvin's Case* (1608) Co Rep 1a; 77 ER 377. Ellesmere's speech was printed as *The Speech of the Lord Chancellor of England, in the Exchequer Chamber, touching the Post-nati* (London, Society of Stationers, 1609). The issue was whether persons born in Scotland after James I & VI unified the crowns (the '*post-nati*') should be considered citizens of both England and Scotland.

[10] See eg Anthony Ben, quoted in M Lobban, *A History of the Philosophy of Law in the Common Law World 1600-1900* (Springer, 2007) 56.

[11] DC Smith, *Sir Edward Coke and the Reformation of the Laws: Religion, Politics and Jurisprudence 1578-1616* (Cambridge, Cambridge University Press, 2014) 228–32.

[12] JP Dawson, 'Coke and Ellesmere Disinterred: The Attack on the Chancery in 1616' (1941) 36 *Illinois Law Review* 127; Smith, *Sir Edward Coke* (above n 11) 234–48.

[13] Several different manuscript versions of this paper survive. I rely on a critical edition published by Louis Knafla in 1977: Lord Ellesmere, 'A breviatte or direccion for the Kinges learned Councell collected by the Lord Chauncellor Ellesmere, *mense septembris 1615 Anno Jacobi Regis*' in LA Knafla, *Law and Politics in Jacobean England: The Tracts of Lord Chancellor Ellesmere* (Cambridge, Cambridge University Press, 1977) 319–36.

[14] ibid 322.

[15] ibid 323.

equitie and conscience … which the Iudges of the Comon Law haue noe power to doe'.[16] They did not therefore contravene Magna Carta or subsequent statutes. Nor did the Statute of Praemunire apply. Even if its words were broad, it was a reaction to the 'insolent and outragious excesse' of the Pope and Church of Rome and should be read narrowly.[17]

Ellesmere then moved to a rhetorical flourish strategically calculated to appeal to James I. The courts of chancery were 'the kinges owne Courtes of equitie in England' and derived their authority directly from the King.[18] The King could suppress, alter and punish the courts and their judges at his pleasure. By preemptively taking action against Chancery, Coke and the other common law judges had in effect 'sett the kinge against himself'.[19]

In case these arguments were insufficient, Ellesmere had also privately prepared a scathing invective against Coke's reports as a way into de-legitimising the latter's legal views.[20] Here, again, his approach was calculated to appeal to James. Coke, Ellesmere argued, had in his reports systematically chosen to present the law in a way that diminished the royal prerogative and harmed the King's interests. Coke upheld acts 'whereby the King parteth with his Inheritance' while striking down acts 'by which his Maiestie would expresse his Power in dispencing with thinges forbidden, or grant his power in doeing such things as formerly had been done'.[21] The reference to the dispensing power was calculated and clever. The power's scope was deeply contested in Stuart England before its abolition following the Glorious Revolution of 1688. It was a subject on which James was unlikely to tolerate challenge. In a speech in Star Chamber on 20 June 1616, James unequivocally sided with Ellesmere.[22] Chancery, James declared, was 'vndependant of any other Court, and is onely vnder the King'. If Chancery exceeded its limits, it was for the King alone to correct it. It was 'odious and inept' for the King's Bench to grant praemunire against Chancery which, echoing Ellesmere's language, he declared akin to the King granting praemunire against himself.[23] Ellesmere's denunciation of Coke's judgments on the prerogative also had an impact: the courts were instructed henceforth not to deal with cases on the prerogative without consulting the Privy Council.[24] Coke himself was dismissed from his post as Lord Chief Justice and ordered to revise his reports of cases on the prerogative.

Ellesmere's extrajudicial communication was, in present-day terms, comparable to the actions of an extrajudicial lobbyist strategically seeking to achieve through political means what could not be achieved judicially. In this, his communication closely resembles the theory of the 'judicial politics' literature that members of the

[16] ibid 324.
[17] ibid 328, 332.
[18] ibid 335.
[19] ibid 336.
[20] Lord Ellesmere, 'The Lord Chancellor Egerton's Observacions Vpon Ye Lord Cookes Reportes' in Knafla (above n 13) 297–318.
[21] ibid 302–3.
[22] James I, 'A Speach in the Starre-Chamber' in CH McIlwain (ed), *The Political Works of James I* (Cambridge MA, Harvard University Press, 1918) 326–45.
[23] ibid 334.
[24] ibid 332.

upper judiciary engage in strategic action to reshape the law to reflect their political and ideological preferences. This requires not just persuasive judgments, but also an awareness of the institutional context and limitations of the judiciary, and a willingness to engage in strategic cross-institutional dialogue and negotiation.[25] On this approach, judicial and extrajudicial communication exist on a continuum as parts of a programme of strategic action, reflecting the fact that judges need to address a range of audiences in a range of ways to achieve their strategic goals.

Is this too bleak a reading? It is tempting to argue that Ellesmere's actions reflect early modern attitudes which have little relevance today. The historical record, however, suggests otherwise. Archival documents contain a striking example of extra-judicial lobbying in the second half of the twentieth century. The judge was Lord Diplock, and the issue was judicial review. In 1967, the Law Commission suggested the creation of a Royal Commission to inquire into how the rule of law could be balanced against the needs of administrative government.[26] The idea of an inquiry, even if not in the form of a Royal Commission, had support within government including from Shackleton, the Lord Privy Seal,[27] and Gardiner, the Lord Chancellor.[28] It was, however, opposed by Diplock.

In October 1969, Diplock privately sent a nine-page memorandum to Gardiner urging against any wider inquiry.[29] Whilst the Law Commission envisaged substantive reform, Diplock said that discussions between English and American judges had convinced him that English law's weaknesses lay not in substance but 'in the field of court procedures for judicial review'.[30] The Tribunals and Inquiries Act 1958, a product of the Franks Commission, had by abolishing 'no certiorari' clauses, given courts a greater opportunity to correct errors of law. Diplock argued that the courts had now begun using these opportunities, and should be allowed to continue to do so 'with the aid of improved and more uniform procedures'. A referral to a Royal Commission would inhibit progress for several years. A less widely based committee would be better placed to resolve what was in essence a procedural issue.[31]

Diplock's memo does not stop there. In December 1968, the House of Lords had issued their decision in *Anisminic*.[32] A key issue in the case related to the courts' power to read down privative clauses in statutes; that is to say, clauses providing that a tribunal's decision could not be reviewed by a superior court. It was well established that privative clauses would be read narrowly in certain circumstances. In *Anisminic*, the House of Lords held that these circumstances included 'errors of law going to jurisdiction', where a tribunal had exceeded its statutory jurisdiction because it had misconstrued the law. This reversed Diplock's own decision in the Court of Appeal. In his memo, without expressly revealing that he was doing so, he launched a veiled

[25] See esp L Epstein and J Knight, *The Choices Justices Make* (Washington DC, CQ Press, 1998).

[26] Law Commission, *Exploratory Working Paper on Administrative Law*, Law Com PWP No.13, 1967, para 10.

[27] TNA BA 17/261, Note of a meeting to discuss Administrative Law, 5 June 1969.

[28] TNA BA 17/261, Dobson to Armstrong, 29 July 1969.

[29] TNA BA 17/261, Administrative Law, 21 October 1969.

[30] ibid 2.

[31] ibid 2–3.

[32] *Anisminic Ltd v Foreign Compensation Commission* [1969] 2 AC 147 (HL).

attack on a key limb of the decision reversing his judgment, namely, the concept of 'jurisdiction'. Diplock argued that it was dangerous to rely on this concept. In developing administrative law, it was crucial for courts to avoid entanglement in issues of policy. Diplock believed that the US courts had been less successful at achieving this, in part because they had the power to examine the record. If English courts had access to similar material, they might 'eventually succumb to the same temptation'. He then continued: 'there are rules of substantive law about what goes to "jurisdiction" which might be used to justify such a development'.[33] Focusing on procedure would let English courts avoid being drawn into policy.

Like Ellesmere, Diplock succeeded in his goal. Gardiner abandoned the idea of substantive reform and instructed the Law Commission to consider only the narrow issue of procedure highlighted by Diplock.[34] In his judicial capacity, Diplock would subsequently play a key role in shaping the substantive doctrines that underpin the UK's administrative law and would eventually successfully abolish the concept of 'jurisdiction' that he criticised in his memo.[35] Whether this had the effect he expected, of letting the courts avoid entanglement in matters of policy, is open to question. What is not open to question is that he was only able to achieve what he did as a judge because of his own extrajudicial lobbying of the government in 1969.

III. IDEOLOGY AND DOCTRINE: HARDWICKE, DENNING, AND THE JUDGE AS EXTRAJUDICIAL EVANGELIST

Ellesmere and Diplock engaged in extrajudicial communication with political actors to bolster their own ability to develop the law in a contested direction. Hardwicke and Denning, who we will examine in this section, took a different approach. Their extrajudicial communication also concerned contested positions, but their goal was to build broader consensus for their positions.

As a politician, Hardwicke was part of the 'Court' Whigs who occupied the inner circle around George II and, subsequently, George III. As Attorney-General, Hardwicke (then Sir Philip Yorke) had marshalled arguments to support Court Whig positions on controversial matters such as slavery, whose legality he resolutely defended in the Yorke-Talbot Opinion of 1729 which he jointly authored with the Solicitor-General, Charles Talbot.[36] After his appointment to the bench, he continued to use extrajudicial comments to translate Court Whig thought into legal language and entrench it as a way of thinking about law.

Hardwicke's speech to newly appointed members of Serjeants' Inn on 5 June 1736, as Lord Chief Justice of the King's Bench, is illustrative.[37] Hardwicke began by praising Serjeants-at-Law as 'a Profession of the greatest consequence to the King

[33] TNA BA 17/261, Administrative Law, 21 October 1969, 6–7.
[34] TNA BA 17/261 Caulcott to Bancroft, 6 November 1969.
[35] *Re Racal Communications Ltd* [1981] AC 374, 383. Lindsay Stirton and I have discussed Diplock's judicial and extrajudicial history with *Anisminic* in more detail in TT Arvind and L Stirton, 'The curious origins of judicial review' (2017) 33 *Law Quarterly Review* 91.
[36] Northumberland Archives, ZMD 114/261.
[37] BL Add MSS 36115, ff 97-99.

& his People … a Profession of the highest importance to the preservation of the true Balance of our Excellent Constitution, and to the Administration of Public Justice'.[38] When the liberties of the people were threatened by the Crown, he said, the 'Professors of the Common Law have stood in the Gap' as 'the most able Champions of Public Liberty'.[39] In making this point, Hardwicke was echoing a widely held belief about the role that lawyers and the common law had played in defending liberty in the Tudor and Stuart periods. What came next, however, was more controversial. The task of a common lawyer, Hardwicke argued, was not just to defend liberty; it was also to defend the 'just Prerogative' of the King against 'Popular Fury'. A legal education should demonstrate to lawyers 'how necessary this Legal Prerogative is to the Peace & Good Order of the Kingdom' and should make them 'the most strenuous & rational Assertors of it'. Lawyers who failed to do so would be 'of all men the most inexcusable'. They would be 'acting in contradiction to the clearest light' in 'an implied Renunciation of their Profession', and perpetrating 'a kind of Degradation of themselves'.[40]

None of this was widely accepted. Opposition Whigs saw limits on the royal prerogative as a core legacy of the Glorious Revolution and would have rejected Hardwick's expansive vision outright. However, using extrajudicial speech in a quasi-evangelical way to propagate Court Whig political and juridical positions was typical of Hardwicke. His speech during a Parliamentary debate on the Habeas Corpus Bill in May 1758 provides another example. The Bill was prompted by a growth in the practice of impressment, or press ganging, which involved the forced conscription of sailors into the navy.[41] The practice was widely viewed as unconstitutional, even though the Recorder of Bristol, Michael Foster, had upheld it in *R v Broadfoot*.[42] The 1758 Bill, sponsored by Pitt and Camden, sought to give impressed sailors the right to habeas corpus. The difficulty, as they saw it, was that the courts often refused habeas corpus. They sought to make its grant obligatory.

Hardwicke, who was as strong a defender of impressment as he was of slavery,[43] opposed the Bill and delivered two speeches against it in Parliament where he defended the Court Whigs' legal ideas.[44] The problem with the Bill, he argued, was not merely that it was bad policy, nor that it confused the idea of a remedy being a matter of right (which habeas corpus already was) with it being a matter of course (which habeas corpus neither was nor should be). It also entirely misunderstood what was meant by 'liberty'. 'Law without liberty', Hardwicke conceded,

[38] ibid 97v.
[39] ibid 97–98.
[40] ibid 98.
[41] On the practice, see N Rogers, *The Press Gang: Naval Impressment and its Opponents in Georgian Britain* (Bloomsbury, 2008).
[42] *R v Broadfoot* (1743) 18 ST 1323; (1760) Fost 154, 168 ER 76. A more complete MS report of the case is available in BL Add MSS 36115, f 289.
[43] Correspondingly, there were strong links between the anti-slavery and anti-impressment movements. Individuals like Granville Sharp played a leading role in both and helped translate abolitionist tactics into the anti-impressment movement. See eg N Rogers, 'British impressment and its discontents' (2018) 30 *International Journal of Maritime History* 52, 56–64.
[44] The discussion in this section is based on Hardwicke's handwritten draft. See BL Add MSS 35878, f 37.

'is tyranny'.[45] But to treat the law as existing to protect liberty was 'a false, delusive notion'. Too much liberty would 'destroy all authority' and 'enervate the laws', thereby 'sapping the very foundations of liberty'. Law did not just defend liberty but also circumscribed it. If law without liberty was tyranny, then 'liberty without law is anarchy and confusion'.[46]

Hardwicke's extrajudicial communication, like Ellesmere's, was part of a wider strategic project, but unlike Ellesmere, his goal was to persuade a wide audience to adopt a particular view of law over others, rather than to lobby a narrow audience. His willingness to participate in debates on highly charged issues may perhaps strike a modern reader as exceptional, but here too he has modern-day counterparts. Lord Denning provides an example. In her contribution to this collection, Hélène Tyrrell gives the example of Denning's extrajudicial remarks on the 'Birmingham Six'.[47] The remarks Tyrrell cites were part of a wider defence of the legal system's treatment of the case, in which he was involved via his decision in *McIlkenny v Chief Constable of the West Midlands*.[48] Through the 1980s, he regularly defended the conviction of the Birmingham Six in parliamentary debates in the House of Lords, in which he sat as a life peer. In a debate in December 1984, for example, he asked why the men had been charged 'only with murder' and not high treason when their actions surely constituted 'levying war against the Queen in her Realm'.[49] Similarly, in 1987 when the convictions were being publicly questioned following the publication of a book by the journalist Chris Mullin, Denning insisted that he had given judgment 'upon the evidence before the court and on what I knew then' and 'would not go back on one word of it'.[50] Denning also used the case to argue for stronger criminal law measures against terrorism. In a debate on the Prevention of Terrorism (Temporary Provisions) Bill in 1984, he cited the Birmingham Six to argue against a proposal to restrict exclusion orders which, he said, protected 'the security of the lives of ordinary law-abiding citizens'.[51] He also used the IRA cases in a debate on criminalising the possession of information. Citing authorities going back to the Tudor antiquarian William Lambarde, Denning argued that the proposal would simply restore the old common law offence of misprison of felony, which had been abolished by a statutory 'side wind' but represented 'old good sense'.[52]

In these and other debates, Denning drew on his knowledge of English law to support what were often controversial positions. In a debate on abortion, he used common law ideas to argue in favour of what he claimed was the traditional doctrine that 'the unborn child has a life of its own and a right of its own', which deserved to be given 'a proper place in the vital decision that has to be made on its life'.[53] He also used these ideas to oppose the incorporation of the European Convention on

[45] ibid f 40.
[46] ibid f 47.
[47] Chapter 7: H Tyrrell, 'Extrajudicial Communication: What Changes in Retirement?'.
[48] *McIlkenny v Chief Constable of the West Midlands* [1980] 1 QB 283 (CA).
[49] HL Deb 11 December 1984, vol 458, col 122.
[50] HL Deb 20 January 1987, vol 483, cols 856–57.
[51] HL Deb 23 February 1984, vol 448, col 893.
[52] HL Deb 23 February 1984, vol 448, cols 911–912; HL Deb 8 March 1984, vol 449, cols 372–73.
[53] HL Deb 6 December 1982, vol 437, cols 75–78.

Human Rights[54] or any form of entrenched rights,[55] and to attack what he termed 'this so-called court, sitting in Strasbourg' which had taken to issuing 'most unjust' condemnations against the UK.[56]

The theme uniting Hardwicke and Denning is that both held views on law which they knew to be contested but which they firmly believed to be objectively right. They were therefore willing to insert themselves extrajudicially into highly charged and politically controversial debates, to persuade a wider audience to adopt their views. If Ellesmere and Diplock can be characterised as extrajudicial lobbyists, then Hardwicke and Denning were arguably extrajudicial evangelists.

Evangelism is a natural outgrowth of the judicial role. As Griffith pointed out, a judge asked to decide what the 'public interest' requires in a housing case cannot but be influenced by personal beliefs as to the relative importance of preventing homelessness and preserving private property.[57] Judges who regularly deal with these issues may in time come to believe that their legal expertise gives them a facility to cut through tensions and identify objectively defensible solutions to complex and controversial disputes. A judge who holds such a belief will naturally be led to use extrajudicial speech to advance and defend their views, even if those views might strike a layperson as tendentiously political.

IV. THE PRAGMATIC AND THE JURISTIC: COKE, DILHORNE, AND THE JUDGE AS EXTRAJUDICIAL PROBLEM-SOLVER

The examples we have looked at thus far involve judges using extrajudicial communication to advance strongly held views, rather than to enter into open-ended dialogue. In this section, I look to two judges, Coke and Dilhorne, who engaged in a different and less dogmatic type of communication, using their judicial experience heuristically to identify tensions that require intervention, and pragmatically to work with others to find solutions to the tensions.

Like Ellesmere and Hardwicke, Coke was both a lawyer and a politician. He had worked with Ellesmere in the government of Elizabeth I, but by the 1610s he was Ellesmere's principal opponent in the conflict between common law and Chancery. Although he made extensive use of extrajudicial communication, his approach was different from Ellesmere and Hardwicke. His communication took the form of treatises, law reports, and participation in Parliamentary debates, and reflected an incrementalism born of his general belief in the excellence of the common law's 'artificial perfection of reason', which he strongly defended in his extrajudicial writing.[58] This excellence could be affected by the ignorance of lawyers and legislators,[59] and it was to addressing this that he dedicated his efforts.

[54] HL Deb 10 December 1985, vol 469, cols 170–73.
[55] HL Deb 25 March 1976, vol 369, cols 797–801.
[56] HL Deb 16 December 1987, vol 491, cols 739–41.
[57] JAG Griffith, *The Politics of the Judiciary*, 5th edn (London, Fontana 1997) 336.
[58] Co Litt 97b.
[59] Smith, *Sir Edward Coke* (above n 11) 139.

Coke's extrajudicial work used individual cases to assess the law and devise ways of addressing its shortcomings.[60] Two examples taken from his *Institutes* illustrate his method. The first is his treatment of attainder, which appears to have been a specific response to the execution of Elizabeth Barton, a nun from Kent who had led popular opposition to Henry VIII's divorce from Catherine of Aragon.[61] After the courts refused to convict her of high treason, Henry had her convicted by a bill of attainder in Parliament. She was hanged, beheaded, and her head displayed on London Bridge. Coke criticised this as legally wrong. Attainder at law required not just words but also acts or deeds. Punishing words alone 'oftentimes trapped and snared' people who were 'minding honestly'.[62] Coke also argued, again referencing Elizabeth Barton's attainder, that Parliament's power to attaint by statute a person who could not be attainted at law should be used with care and only where high treason was specifically expressed. Parliament 'as the highest and most honourable Court of Justice' should 'give example to inferiour Courts'.[63]

Coke's target was not just attainder, but the manner in which the late Tudor and early Stuart state approached treason. Laws 'justly made for the preservation of the Common-wealth', he argued, were more often obeyed if they avoided 'great and extreme punishments'.[64] This also applied to the treatment of prisoners. Coke's writings opposed the practice of putting prisoners in irons, terming it 'an abuse' to subject prisoners to any form of torment.[65] Ellesmere had been an enthusiastic proponent of torture. He regularly deployed the rack against recusants and state prisoners, and wanted it to be available in any case where a prisoner seemed untruthful.[66] Coke took specific aim at this practice. Citing Fortescue, he said there was 'no law to warrant tortures in this land'. Nor, he argued, could they be justified on the basis of usage, being a recent innovation.[67]

Here as elsewhere, Coke sought to use his experience with the law to identify problems in emerging practices, which he sought to resolve through the law's own principles.[68] His response to the jurisdictional conflict with Chancery followed a similar pattern. His focus was on particular equitable remedies such as bills of conformity, rather than more sweeping goals like Ellesmere's. Bills of conformity forced creditors to accept a settlement of their debts and were frequently used to compel dissenting creditors to accept a composition they had rejected.[69] Whatever their objective merits, they were controversial. Ellesmere granted them frequently as did Francis Bacon who

[60] AD Boyer, *Sir Edward Coke and the Elizabethan Age* (Redwood City CA, Stanford University Press, 2003) 97–106.

[61] D Watt, 'Reconstructing the word: the political prophecies of Elizabeth Barton (1506-1534)' (1997) 50 *Renaissance Quarterly* 136; A Neame, *The Holy Maid of Kent: The Life of Elizabeth Barton, 1506-1534* (London, Hodder & Stoughton, 1971).

[62] 3 Co Inst 14.

[63] 4 Co Inst 39.

[64] 3 Co Inst 14.

[65] 3 Co Inst 34–35.

[66] Knafla (above n 13) 63.

[67] 3 Co Inst 35.

[68] Smith, *Sir Edward Coke* (above n 11) 139–44.

[69] DA Smith, 'The error of young Cyrus: The bill of conformity and Jacobean kingship, 1603-1624' (2010) 28 *Law and History Review* 307.

succeeded him as Lord Chancellor. In 1621, Parliament debated their legality. Coke, now MP for Liskeard, joined the argument, terming the bills 'a detestable and newe proiect'.[70] He believed they caused real hardship by inducing creditors to stop lending out of fear of not recovering the debt, an outcome which he said 'brings scarsity of mony'.[71] Equity could only grant relief on bonds in three situations: covin (ie fraud), accident, and breach of confidence. Bills of conformity fell within none of those categories.[72] They also violated fundamental principles of justice because they were in substance injunctions granted 'without answere or proces'.[73] Coke's arguments were persuasive. Within a fortnight, an alarmed James I addressed Parliament, declaring himself 'ashamed' at how his people had been 'vexed and polled' by these 'vile' bills.[74] By the end of the month, he issued a proclamation abolishing them, which Parliament confirmed by statute in its next session.[75]

The limitations of Coke's extrajudicial work lay in the causes he defended, such as opposing debtor relief, rather than his means. Unlike Ellesmere and Hardwicke's wider-ranging and more politically inflected programmes, Coke sought more modestly to raise awareness of specific shortcomings in the law and worked collaboratively to remedy them using the common law's own resources. If this approach seems somewhat idealised in our more political age, it has also had more recent exponents. The extrajudicial words and actions of Lord Dilhorne in the controversy that followed the decision of the House of Lords in *Anisminic* provide a particularly clear example.[76]

Anisminic was a controversial decision, and the government of the day refused to accept it. At the time, a Foreign Compensation Bill was making its way through Parliament to give effect to the Anglo-Soviet Agreement of 5 January 1968, on mutual compensation for British property that had been seized by the Soviet government in the Baltic states and Baltic gold reserves that had been seized by the UK government. To that bill, the government added a new clause 2(4) whose express purpose was to overturn *Anisminic* and clarify that the Foreign Compensation Commission's interpretations of Orders in Council were final.[77]

The clause sailed through Commons with little dissent. In the Lords, however, it ran into opposition. Denning spoke against it, arguing that it would leave the Commission 'exempt from the rule of law'.[78] Wilberforce, who had been on the panel that decided *Anisminic*, also spoke to defend the ruling and oppose the proposed amendment.[79] Dilhorne's contribution was more nuanced. Dilhorne was not at the time a Lord of Appeal in Ordinary, and would not be appointed to that role until later that year. However, he had been Lord Chancellor from 1962 to 1964, and he continued to sit to hear selected cases after ceasing that role. He participated in the

[70] *Commons Debates 1621*, vol 5 (New Haven CT, Yale University Press, 1935) 297.
[71] *Commons Debates 1621*, vol 6 (New Haven CT, Yale University Press, 1935) 63.
[72] *Commons Debates 1621*, vol 4 (New Haven CT, Yale University Press, 1935) 154.
[73] *Commons Debates 1621*, vol 5 (New Haven CT, Yale University Press, 1935) 297.
[74] *Journal of the House of Lords*, vol 3 (London, 1802) 70.
[75] 21 Jac I (c 19).
[76] *Anisminic* (above n 32).
[77] HC Deb 22 January 1969, vol 776, cols 568–72.
[78] HL Deb 04 February 1969, vol 299, cols 53–54.
[79] ibid col 38.

leading private law cases of *Suisse Atlantique*[80] and *Boardman v Phipps*[81] and was named in the 1966 Practice Statement.[82] He therefore enjoyed the standing and legitimacy of an active judge, and he drew on this to propose a compromise. Rather than make the Foreign Compensation Commission a body 'above the law ... master of its own fate and in complete control of its own jurisdiction',[83] he suggested that a better option would be to create an appeal to the Court of Appeal to be exercised during a narrow window following a provisional determination by the Commission. This, he suggested, would help not just litigants but also the Commission, which would be able to draw on judicial expertise when faced with difficult questions of construction.[84] At committee stage, Dilhorne presented a draft amendment to achieve this outcome.[85] The government initially refused to support it,[86] but once it was agreed to by the committee[87] the government capitulated, and agreed to ask Parliamentary Counsel to prepare a more thorough draft of a section creating a statutory right of appeal to the Court of Appeal.[88]

Dilhorne's successful intervention shows an understanding of the role of extrajudicial communication like Coke's, drawing attention to weaknesses in existing legal practice and identifying ways of remedying them through the common law's own intellectual resources. If Ellesmere and Diplock were extrajudicial lobbyists and Hardwicke and Denning extrajudicial evangelists, then Coke and Dilhorne arguably show a different side of extrajudicial communication, as extrajudicial problem-solvers whose intervention avoids maximalist positions and seeks to further a pragmatic plan of action or broker a workable compromise.

V. IN CONCLUSION: EXTRAJUDICIAL COMMUNICATION AND THE UK'S CONSTITUTION

Judges' discourse attracts scrutiny in a way the discourse of other officials does not. Junius's attack on Mansfield with which this chapter began declared his extrajudicial communication incompatible with his role as a judge.[89] Had Diplock's private lobbying of the Lord Chancellor on judicial review been known, it would have raised concerns that a letter by the Chief Executive of the DVLA to the Secretary of State for Transport would not. As the editors of this volume discuss more fully in their Introduction, we hold implicit expectations of judges in relation to their extrajudicial communication that we do not hold of others.[90]

[80] *Suisse Atlantique Société d'Armement SA v NV Rotterdamsche Kolen Centrale* [1967] 1 AC 361 (HL).
[81] *Boardman v Phipps* [1967] 2 AC 46 (HL).
[82] 1966 Practice Statement [1966] 3 All ER 7.
[83] HL Deb 04 February 1969, vol 299, cols 55–59.
[84] ibid cols 39–40.
[85] HL Deb 13 February 1969, vol 299, col 640.
[86] ibid col 643.
[87] HL Deb 13 February 1969, vol 299, col 653.
[88] HL Deb 11 March 1969, vol 300, cols 391–94.
[89] Junius (above n 1) 130–31.
[90] H Tyrrell and C Mallory, 'Introduction' in this volume, section III.

The discussion in this chapter has shed some light on what these expectations cannot involve. They cannot involve a separation between legal and political questions. At first sight, a separation along these lines appears an attractive basis on which to ground the limits of extrajudicial communication. History, after all, suggests that extrajudicial communication is particularly contentious when its subject-matter is of wider political interest. Junius's criticism of Mansfield's extrajudicial behaviour concentrated on questions where 'the nation is in a ferment'.[91] Were present-day judges to confine their extrajudicial discourse to topics such as the history of the Hundred Years War, it is unlikely they would attract the level of scrutiny they currently do. Likewise, extrajudicial communication tends to be contentious when a judge defends principles that are contested politically and not just juristically. Junius stressed Mansfield's extrajudicial support for policies that were regarded as 'universally odious'.[92] If a present-day reader finds Denning's comments on counterterrorism or abortion troubling, it is in part because they defend a position with which at least a subset of the wider population would disagree on ideological grounds. An extrajudicial lecture on the difficulties of the doctrine of precedent in English law, in contrast, is unlikely to attract a substantial body of critical commentary even if it supports positions that are the subject of juristic disagreement.[93]

A legal / political distinction also finds support in a new, and rapidly growing, strand of the literature that, building in part on Carl Schmitt, posits an inherent tension between the domain of the political (understood as the realm of democratic decision-making institutions) and the domain of the legal (understood as the realm of judicially-mediated elaboration of rights and conditions governing the use of power by political institutions). This literature, exemplified in the recent work of Martin Loughlin, uses this tension to argue for hard limits on judicial intrusions into political matters, which, it argues, should be left to democratic decision-making.[94] From this perspective, any increase in extrajudicial communication on matters of wider political importance (as opposed to 'lawyers' law') is symptomatic of the growth of 'juristocracy' and the 'juridical revolution',[95] and should be regarded with suspicion.

Despite its allure, this distinction sits poorly with history for at least three reasons. Firstly, as history shows, it has historically been common for judges to hold political office. This was clearly so in the time of Ellesmere, Coke, and Hardwicke, but it is not just a matter of the past. In the present day, too, senior judges in the UK are expected to discharge a range of other duties in addition to their judicial role, which draw them into questions that have a different character from those they face as judges. The requirement that the Law Commission be chaired by a judge of the High Court or Court of Appeal is a clear example.[96] But so, too, is the role judges play in public inquiries. Public inquiries are considered in greater detail by Brice Dickson in

[91] Junius (above n 1) 126–27.

[92] ibid 128.

[93] See eg Lord Leggatt, 'Precedent in English Law' (Harris Society Annual Lecture, Oxford, 26 April 2024) www.supremecourt.uk/uploads/speech_leggatt_240426_7d564b824b.pdf.

[94] For a recent example, see M Loughlin, *Against Constitutionalism* (Cambridge MA, Harvard University Press, 2022) esp 97–108.

[95] ibid 130–34.

[96] Law Commissions Act 1965, s 1(1A).

his contribution to this volume,[97] and my purpose here is narrower. Public inquiries involve not just an investigation of the past but also recommendations in relation to the future.[98] Sitting and retired judges are frequently asked to lead inquiries on politically controversial subjects. The Undercover Policing Inquiry was initially chaired by Pitchford LJ and after 2017 by Sir John Mitting, who had been on the Court of Appeal and High Court respectively, and it was tasked not just with investigating historical failures but also with making recommendations to avoid them in future.[99] The Leveson Inquiry, similarly, was chaired by Sir Brian Leveson, a sitting judge of the Court of Appeal, and tasked both with investigating the media's culture and ethics, and with making recommendations for more effective regulation and for the conduct of relations between politicians and the press.[100] Their outcomes can raise fundamental issues of constitutional doctrine and the rules of political conduct. The Scott Report is a particularly clear example. It was the result of an inquiry led by Richard Scott, a sitting judge of the Court of Appeal, and it dealt with a range of issues arising out of a controversial sale of arms to Iraq, including failures of ministerial accountability and public-interest immunity.[101] It is hard to see how these questions can be described as anything other than political. The issue is not that judges are occasionally asked to engage with these tasks; it is, rather, that it is seen as wholly natural and even necessary for them to be asked to do so, despite their politically controversial character. On the face of it, it appears difficult to see how one can erect a legal/ political separation in one area of extrajudicial communication while acting incompatibly with it in another.

Secondly, the Kilmuir Rules, which sought to erect precisely such a distinction, by most definitions did not stop public engagement by judges. In the legal imagination, the rules are closely associated with the controversy around Lord Russell's book on Nazi war crimes.[102] However, they came at a particularly tumultuous time. The expansion of the post-war state was far from uncontroversial and gave rise to numerous causes célèbres. The year before Kilmuir issued the rules, the Crichel Down affair had led to an embarrassing government climbdown and a ministerial resignation,[103] and resulted in the appointment of the Franks Committee, which overhauled the administrative system. There was widespread expectation that judges would step up to protect the citizen, and the Conservative and Unionist Inns of Court Society would later that year issue a pamphlet titled 'The Rule of Law' calling for a transformation of judicial control of government.[104] Against the backdrop of this intellectual ferment,

[97] Chapter 4: Brice Dickson, 'Extrajudicial Discourse and Legal Change'.

[98] Inquiries Act 2005, s 5(6)(a).

[99] Home Office, 'Undercover Policing Enquiry: Terms of Reference' (12 March 2015) www.ucpi.org.uk/wp-content/uploads/2016/06/Terms-of-Reference.pdf.

[100] *Report of an Inquiry into the Culture, Practices, and Ethics of the Press* (HC 2012, 780–I) 5.

[101] *Report of the Inquiry into the Export of Defence Equipment and Dual-Use Goods to Iraq and Related Prosecutions* (HC 1995-1996) 116. On its constitutional significance, see A Tomkins, *The Constitution After Scott: Government Unwrapped* (Oxford, Clarendon Press, 1998).

[102] E Russell, *The Scurge of the Swastika. A Short History of Nazi War Crimes* (Londom, Cassell, 1954) See the discussion in GR Rubin, 'Judicial Free Speech versus Judicial Neutrality in Mid-Twentieth Century England: The Last Hurrah for the Ancien Regime?' (2009) 27 *Law and History Review* 373.

[103] See I Nicholson, *The Mystery of Crichel Down* (Oxford, Oxford University Press, 1986).

[104] Inns of Court Conservative and Unionist Society, *The Rule of Law* (Conservative Political Centre, 1955).

an invitation by the BBC for current judges to discuss great judges of the past – the specific trigger for the Kilmuir Rules – was anything but innocuous. It is difficult to see how discussions about judges like Coke or Camden could have proceeded without the participants being drawn into the question of how judges should respond to the new expansion of government and the potential for abuse it brought.

Yet, the Kilmuir Rules failed, and the reason for their failure brings us to the third reason why the legal/ political distinction is not a workable basis for setting limits to extrajudicial communication. As the discussion in this chapter has shown, extrajudicial involvement in political matters has been successful. Few would assert that we would have been better off without Coke's extrajudicial work, and as I have sought to show above the same is true of modern judges like Dilhorne. The reason for this lies in the complexity of the relationship between legal and political matters. In modern constitutional theory, it is common to either completely collapse the distinction between the two or to erect a wall of separation between them. In reality, the relationship is more nuanced. Hans Morgenthau argued in his somewhat neglected book *The Concept of the Political* that 'legal' and 'political' are characteristics which can inhere in any subject-matter,[105] much as the property of being hot can inhere in any subject-matter.[106] Legal matters can therefore have either a political or a non-political character.[107] Matters are legal in nature if the considerations motivating the parties are susceptible to being resolved through a decision applying a legal rule.[108] Matters have a political character if they are concerned with maintaining, increasing, or manifesting the power of the state.[109] The legal and the political are intertwined, not least because the legal system must set conditions and limits for the maintenance, increase, and manifestation of the power of the state: power has an inherent tendency to grow and must be subject to the law to function in a predictable and prescribed way.[110] Nevertheless, Morgenthau argued, the law has its limits. He associated these limits with what he termed 'tensions': situations where there is a discordance between the needs of the state and the existing legal situation, such that the adequacy of the existing legal situation is challenged or called into question.[111] Morgenthau argued that tensions cannot be resolved within the framework of legal norms, and thus cannot be resolved by legal bodies. A legal body can re-assert or apply an existing legal norm, but it will not be able to resolve a challenge to the adequacy of the

[105] HJ Morgenthau, *The Concept of the Political* (H Behr and F Rösch (eds), M Vidal trans, London, Palgrave Macmillan, 2012). The original French text was first published in 1933: H Morgenthau, *La notion du 'politique' et la théorie des différends internationaux* (Paris, Recueil Sirey, 1933). Morgenthau's focus on its face is on international law, but the text refers throughout to examples from domestic law and it was explicitly intended to be a response to Carl Schmitt's eponymous treatise attacking Weimar democracy. See Morgenthau, *The Concept of the Political* 107–18; HJ Morgenthau, 'Fragment of an intellectual biography: 1904-1932' in K Thompson and RJ Myers (eds), *Truth and Tragedy: A Tribute to Hans J Morgenthau* (Abingdon, Routledge, 2019) 15–16.

[106] Morgenthau, *The Concept of the Political* (above n 105) 102.

[107] ibid 97–98.

[108] ibid 94.

[109] ibid 106–7, 119–20.

[110] ibid 121–22.

[111] ibid 128–29.

norm. Tensions can only be resolved within the domain of the political, and not the domain of the legal.[112]

The relationship Morgenthau describes between tensions and legally resolvable matters provides us with a helpful starting point in mapping out why judges are drawn into extrajudicial communication on contested political matters. The closer the subject-matter of a communication comes to a tension, the further it strays from the core legal domain that we associate with judges' expertise and the more it intrudes on areas that are not easily resolved by legal norms. But, as the discussion in this chapter has sought to show, judges *do* play a productive role in relation to tensions. Public inquiries are the most obvious example, but so too are some of the other interventions discussed in this chapter.

The reason for this lies in the nature of the judicial role, and the manner in which it straddles the intersection between 'tensions' and legal disputes. Although judges do not directly resolve political tensions in their judicial capacity, adjudication gives them a distinctive awareness of the tensions that exist in relation to the law at any point of time and the challenges they pose to legal norms. Extrajudicial communication is the primary vehicle through which judges can transmit their 'sense of the situation', as Llewellyn called it,[113] to other audiences, including those with the constitutional power to take measures to resolve tensions. Public inquiries represent one way in which the law channels this sense of the situation into a form that contributes to framing measures addressing the tension, but as this chapter has shown, it is not the only one.

It is this that makes history an important resource. As the discussion in this chapter has shown, senior judges in the UK have a role that is partially political in the sense of being concerned with tensions. That political aspect manifests itself in formal and informal extrajudicial communication. All six judges discussed in this chapter had views on how tensions should be resolved, and they used targeted extrajudicial discourse to bring their views into the wider conversation. These were most successful when judges used their judicial sense of the situation to work with political institutions to devise pragmatic solutions to tensions that had both legal and political dimensions, and most problematic when judges used extrajudicial communication to marshal support for their subjective views and colour them with the legitimacy of their judicial office. The real discussion to be had about extrajudicial communication is not whether judges should engage extrajudicially on controversial matters; it is, rather, how, when, through what means, and to what end they should do so if their communication is to make a productive and constitutionally sound contribution to the development of the legal system.

[112] ibid 129–30.

[113] K Llewellyn, 'Remarks of the theory of appellate decision and the rules or canons about how statutes are to be constructed' (1949) 3 *Vanderbilt Law Review* 395, 396.

2

Speaking Out: The More, The Better

ALLAN C HUTCHINSON*

'Where you see wrong or inequality or injustice, speak out'.

— Thurgood Marshall[1]

JUDGES ARE A mysterious bunch. This is not an unintended state of affairs, but is encouraged by the misplaced professional culture that surrounds the judiciary. They wrap themselves in a certain cloak of inscrutability. This involves remaining largely unknown and inaccessible to the general public. This is justified on the basis that their views and values have nothing (or, at least, very little) to do with the performance of their professional duties; law is largely an objective body of rules and principles that can be applied in an impartial and impersonal manner. As such, it is accepted that the less the public know about them, the more they will accept that the law and legal system work in that way. In the United States, the public and especially the media seem to buy into this. Reporting tends to be unduly respectable and there is almost a reluctance to say much that is critical, except in egregious cases, about them.[2] There is a compact between public and profession on not only the merit of such an approach, but also the reality of this understanding about the law and professional impartiality.

In this short chapter, I will argue that this account is not only nonsensical and unpersuasive, but also antagonistic to our supposed commitment to democratic governance. Because of judges' enormous and largely unchallenged power, it is essential that we know much more about them. If they exercise public power, then they should also be publicly known and publicly accountable for its exercise. Encouraging judges to speak out is one way to do that. And, as a necessary corollary, criticism of

*I am grateful to Jennifer Leitch and the editors of this volume for critical assistance and intellectual support.

[1] T Marshall, 'Commencement Address' (Speech at the University of Virginia, Charlottesville, 21 May 1978).

[2] But see A Orr Larsen, 'Judging "Under Fire" and the Retreat to Facts' (2020) 61(4) *William and Mary Law Review* 1083; In the UK context, see eg P O'Brien, '"Enemies of the People": Judges, the Media, and the Mythic Lord Chancellor' [2017] *Public Law* 135.

and debate about judicial performance ought to be encouraged, not discouraged. As such, I want to flip around the underlying rationale for judicial silence that judicial independence (a good thing) warrants anonymity and unaccountability (a bad thing). On the contrary, my perspective is that, while independence is an integral feature of a professional judiciary in a democracy, this does not demand judicial silence, professional anonymity, or political unaccountability. Indeed, judges should be open and candid about who they are so that their independence and accountability can be more easily and thoroughly scrutinised. 'Speaking Out' (often and candidly) is the way to go.

The chapter is divided into three sections. In the first section, I offer a very different account of the nature of law and adjudication. Rather than understanding law as an objective body of rules that can be applied impersonally and impartially, I maintain that law and its adjudicative function are an unavoidably political and partial enterprise. The second section draws out the implications of this appreciation of law and adjudication for how judges can and should go about fulfilling their duties. Finally, in the third section, I focus on what this does and does not suggest for our understanding of judicial independence and institutional accountability. Throughout the chapter, I will develop the idea that anonymity and secrecy are the blight of adjudicative integrity in a democratic society, not its blessing.

I. LAW AS A POLITICAL AND PARTIAL ENTERPRISE

The appropriate role for judges in polities that consider themselves democratic in structure and sensibilities is contested and controversial. The range of possible options is broad. There are some that loom large and extreme in the literary and popular imagination that hold little sway in more professional circles. One is Niccolò Machiavelli's young Prince, who also functioned as a judge.[3] His advice was to be worldly and hard-headed; he should countenance all manner of actions whether cynical, sly, underhand or manipulative if the ends to be achieved advanced his agenda and consolidated his position of power. Another is François Rabelais's Judge Bridlegoose.[4] After thoroughly reading the bulky pleadings, this judicial character would use his set of dice (small ones for complicated cases and larger ones for more straightforward cases) to reach a decision. When asked to explain his method of judging by Trinquamelle, the Grand President of the Court, and why he did not throw his dice without more, he replied that formalities must be observed; throwing the dice gave him honest and healthy exercise; and because time ripens all things.[5]

[3] N Machiavelli, *The Prince* (George Bull tr, London, Penguin Books, 1961 [1532]).

[4] F Rabelais, *Gargantua and Pantagruel* (Thomas Urquhart tr, Everyman's Library, 1964 [1532–64]). Bridlegoose judged for over 40 years and, in that time, had decided over 4,000 judgments. In a nice twist, the over 2000 cases appealed were all affirmed. See J Gest, 'The Trial of Judge Bridlegoose' (1924) 58 *American Law Review* 402.

[5] ibid (Book I).

These figures were, of course, meant to be satirical exemplars of what judges should *not* be doing rather than what they should be doing. As such, they were put forward as ironic and critical portrayals that sought to expose and caricature the serious, if sham practices of judges. As such, they held little appeal to professional lawyers and judges. But what they did do in drawing such an unflattering image of the judiciary was to emphasise the kind of high-minded and earnest expectations that real judges should aspire to in their exercise of official power. For these insiders, the legitimate and assumed role of the judge was to rely and reflect upon the legal resources available and the legal arguments made. After due consideration, the judge is expected to arrive at a decision and provide reasons for that decision that were principled and made in good faith. In so doing, it is taken for granted that judges will set aside their own preferences and predilections and act in a scrupulously professional and strictly honourable manner; there would be no dice, no ruses and no similar distractions involved.

The overall thrust of this continuing understanding of the judicial role is that courts must function as forums of law, not another theatre of politics. By this, it is meant that the core of the judges' work must be something separate from politics; judges must be legal professionals, not political operatives. There are, of course, different and competing accounts of how this is possible and whether it is achievable. But the connecting thread is that, as unelected and unrepresentative government officials who exercise very significant power over the polity, judges must earn and ensure their legitimacy by demonstrating that they put aside their own political leanings and follow the objective dictates and directions of the law. It is in this way, so it is argued, that courts can maintain a proper level and style of performance that will garner the approval of citizens, even if (and especially if) their decisions are regarded as unpopular and not agreed with by many citizens.

It is not surprising, therefore, that, when judges are criticised as failing to perform in a thoroughly professional and principled way, they are condemned as also being little more than Machiavellian ideologues or Rabelaisian tricksters in disguise. This criticism is therefore seen to place them in an indefensible and incorrigible role that is self-evidently unacceptable. Because each is seen as a negation of the other, there is little room to recommend that judges (and politicians) might be acting in a way that is both principled and political. This dichotomised approach is an unfortunate and unnecessary understanding of both law and politics. Consequently, critics of judicial decision-making have allowed themselves to be trapped within the same limited and limiting straitjacket. In short, they face an unnecessary Hobson's choice – judges can be principled, even if they occasionally fall short of such an exacting standard, or they can be manipulative, in that they make no attempt to be principled or honest.[6]

As regards modern jurisprudence, traditional legal theory is premised on the idea that law and political morality can be effectively and consistently kept at some distance from each other such that law does not work exclusively as a formalised site of irreducible ideological or normative contestation; adjudication *is* about morality,

[6] The locus classicus of this dichotomised view is H Wechsler, 'Toward Neutral Principles of Constitutional Law' (1959) 73 *Harvard Law Review* 1.

but it is law's own morality, not that of the judge or jurist, that wins the day.[7] As such, most traditional jurists presume that there exists a solid and detectable, if elusive, basis for judicial decision-making that can act as a realistic hedge against ideological unruliness, moral preference or personal political agendas. This is not regarded as backing jurists and judges into a formalistic corner where mechanical rule-application is the order of the day. As Ronald Dworkin summarised the modern standpoint, judges are obliged to make decisions that are 'deeply and thoroughly political … but not a matter of personal or partisan politics'.[8] Accordingly, for the modern judge and jurist, there is still a demonstrable barrier between law and politics, even if that divide is less restrictive and more permeable than earlier generations insisted.

In contrast, I insist that law and adjudication are thoroughly political. Indeed, I recommend that democracy is better served by a recognition and acceptance that judicial decisions are intrinsically and inescapably political in style, substance and outcomes. This is a strong statement, but one that can be amply and extensively defended.[9] However, there are some caveats to this sceptical and non-formalist stance:

- In insisting that adjudication is thoroughly political, politics is not reducible to the pinched range of party-politics. It embraces a much broader range of issues – the nature of the individual, the organisation of society, the relationship between an individual and society, the role of government, institutional legitimacy (including the courts' own), the distribution of power, democratic dynamics, moral pluralism and the like;
- The claim that 'law is politics' does not mean that political judging need be crudely ideological, ad hoc or unprincipled. This is a caricature of what law can become and what ordinary politics has become;
- If adjudication is an inevitable political enterprise, it can be both principled and political. Political debate might be elevated to a much more exacting and engaged standard that can enhance the quality of democracy in a modern and diverse society;
- By accepting that the law is politics, the phony war over whether law can and should be treated as something separate and different from politics can be abandoned. This will entail worrying less about the argumentative form of decisions being made and more about the substantive justice of decisions being made; and
- Once it is conceded that judges are as much political as their elected counterparts (ie, they cannot avoid taking a stand on contestable and ungroundable matters), the pressing questions become of a very different order – what is at stake is not the settled or objective quality of law, but how justice can be better achieved.

The thesis that 'law is politics' is not intended to be only a prescriptive claim (ie, that judges should begin to act in accordance with that understanding of law), but

[7] See generally A Hutchinson, *Hart, Fuller and Everything After: The Politics of Legal Theory* (Oxford, Hart Publishing, 2022).

[8] R Dworkin, *A Matter of Principle* (Oxford, Clarendon Press, 1985) 146. The idea that 'justice plays a role in fixing what the law is' was a constant theme of his work: R Dworkin, *Justice in Robes* (Cambridge MA, Harvard University Press, 2006) 35.

[9] See A Hutchinson, *Rethinking Legitimacy: Courts, Constitutions and Politics* (Oxford, Hart Publishing, 2025).

is also defended as being a valid and accurate descriptive account of what judges actually do. On both counts, the argument is that, regardless of their best efforts and good-faith intentions, judges cannot evade the conclusion that 'law is politics'. Moreover, this is not to be taken as a disabling criticism in the way that traditional commentary assumes; judges have not failed to live up to the reasonable and achievable expectations placed upon them. Indeed, once understood in the critical way that I recommend, it might also be grasped that a recognition that 'law is politics' will advance, not impair, the important need for judges to obtain and maintain democratic legitimacy. Political judges are not the threat that many assert. Indeed, it is the unwillingness to accept and hide the fact that 'law is politics' that offers the most enduring challenge to democratic politics.

II. SO WHAT?

What is entailed in terms of change if the idea that 'law is politics' is put into practice? The blunt answer to that is – not as much as many people think or fear. If the claim that law and adjudication are already political at bottom is descriptively accurate and persuasive, then no seismic shift will be required. Greater weight will be placed on the virtues of judicial frankness, institutional transparency and a reasonable sense of political engagement. What will be necessary is that judges not only come clean about the politicalness of judicial decision-making, but that they also elaborate and defend the politics that underlie and animate their decisions. Accordingly, candour will be demanded, but much more than that. The reliance on candour both promises too much (ie that candour will resolve the problems and failings of the present set-up) and promises too little (ie that candour will not need to be supplemented by other initiatives if it is to have any success). Candour will need to be supplemented by a more explicit and developed sense of 'reasoned judgement'; judges will have to address and grapple with the unavoidable presence of political values and commitments.

None of this will result in law and the adjudicative craft being discarded. While it requires a different approach to legal doctrine, it will not render such materials and arguments otiose. Under a political approach to decision-making, judges will have to run their political ideas through extant legal materials. Moreover, the rejection of the idea that there are objective legal standards or accepted principles that vouchsafe distinct forms of judicial reasoning and results does not lead to a cynical or opportunistic perspective. There will be a strong (and perhaps even stronger) demand for judges to be principled, rigorous and methodical in their work. Clearly, the shenanigans of Judge Bridlegoose and Machiavelli's Prince will be unacceptable. A badly reasoned opinion is as unlikely to garner the support and approval of the legal community as a respected precedent, whatever its political leaning or ideological appeal. But legal craft alone cannot carry the day: it will be a significant piece in a much larger and intricate puzzle about legitimate and acceptable modes of legal reasoning.

From my critical perspective, it is equally naïve to maintain that a demonstration of the inescapable politicality of legal principles would lead to any necessary progressive or ameliorating consequence. The fact is that, although candour will encourage judges and jurists to talk about political values in a more informed and direct way, candour alone is unlikely to affect any substantial progress in bridging the rift between political left and right. It will also, of course, show that the emperors really do have no legitimate clothes on; they will stand naked in their political affiliations. Further, it seems optimistic, at best, to pretend that, once judges accept the inescapable politics of law and judicial decision-making, judges will work together more reasonably and produce more reasonable results. However, this reality does not justify the continued practice of maintaining that law is not politics or that it is only so in a confined way. Democracy expects more of those entrusted with significant power; it demands honesty and openness, not dissemblance and disguise.

What will most be needed is for the judges themselves to embrace the fact that doing law is part of the same process of doing politics. Judges will need to defend their positions and decisions in political terms and not hide behind the convenient cover of some favoured interpretive theory. Indeed, a recognition of law's inevitably political nature might encourage judges to write in a more accessible and less professionalised way. It is perplexing, at best, that the resolution of some of society's most pressing challenges should be framed, phrased and reasoned in a discourse that is alien and inaccessible to most non-lawyers and even educated citizens. By adopting a more comprehensible and less obscure mode of discursive explanation, courts will become sites at which popular participation and public involvement might be more easily facilitated. At a minimum, judges would be obliged to take personal responsibility for the decisions they make; they will have to defend their substantive merit directly rather than hide behind the pseudo-doctrinal truths that their judicial methodologies claim to disclose. None of this will miraculously bring together people who have very different and often contradictory stances. But what it will do is oblige judges to stop shadow-boxing and deal with political issues directly.

One of the most common arguments against this politicised approach is that the independence and neutrality of judges will be jeopardised and perhaps fatally compromised. This is mistaken. The independence of the judiciary is extremely important. There is no mandate for the judiciary being beholden in any way to the interests of other public officials, like elected legislators and executive leaders, or to those of private actors. It is imperative that judges stand away from institutional interference or private interference, and be seen to do so; the existing concerns and standards to avoid these corrupting influences are entirely defensible. Indeed, there are good reasons for introducing 'conflict of interest' rules that are more serious and enforceable in the case of a politicised judiciary. Yet, it is unhelpful to insist that independence will be best protected by secrecy and a lack of candour; the more open and transparent the operations of judges are, the better justice and legitimacy will be served.

However, the preservation of the judiciary's independence from corrupting influences does not require that the pretence of general impartiality and apoliticalness be perpetuated.[10] While it is important to expect that judges be scrupulously impartial

[10] D Shapiro, 'In Defense of Judicial Candor' (1987) 100 *Harvard Law Review* 731 and S Altman, 'Beyond Candor' (1990) 89 *Michigan Law Review* 296.

between the interests of litigating parties who vie for their decisional favour, questions of general impartiality as regards broader values and political interests do not affect that expectation. No matter how desirable, judges are only fooling themselves (and people generally) in pretending that they do not rely on political values in fulfilling their professional roles or that they can somehow corral them adequately. This is not bad faith, but self-delusional; I am not suggesting that judges are part of a collective conspiracy to pull the wool over people's eyes. In admitting and integrating their moral and political values into their professional work, it is not that judges will simply incorporate without more their own values on any particular issue. The reasonable expectation is that they will put those values on the table (as opposed to simply hiding them) and make them available for scrutiny and reappraisal. A good judge is not a dogmatic ideologue, but a mature decision-maker, who is capable of appreciating different views and reassessing their own commitments.[11]

The received understanding about what counts as a 'great judge' is revealing; it supports the idea of a politicised judiciary that I defend. It is trite to point out that the great judge is not revered as someone who is a technician that applies established rules and principles in a sterile and apolitical manner. On the contrary, the great judge, like a Richard Atkin or a Thurgood Marshall, is applauded for their ability to put their professional craft into the service of a broader vision of social justice. It is their ability to rework those rules and principles in an imaginative and convincing way. Great judges possess technical proficiency, but they also hold a vision of what law and justice can become. As Karl Llewellyn put it, 'technique without ideals is a menace … ideals without technique are a mess'.[12] At their most innovative, these judges not only move the law forward with a persuasive break with existing tradition, but also, like artists and sportspersons, manage to transform the standards about what counts as a good performance of their professional craft. Although these persons are few and far between, they *do* symbolise and embody the idea that greatness is about blending the routine and the revolutionary in a convincing melange of law and politics.

Accordingly, the politicised judge is not some rogue figure who is dismissive of judicial traditions and who rides roughshod over other judges' responsibilities and litigants' interests. This is a scare-tactic deployed by traditional jurists and commentators. Once individual judges appreciate that they are part of a collective and politicised endeavour, they will begin to change their own self-understanding of their role and, as a result, their professional performance. Indeed, they will remain very much part of a judicial tradition, albeit a revised and reformulated one. In a manner of speaking, the account of 'law is politics' asks that judges see themselves as great judges or, at least, as great judges in the making or waiting; they will be freed from the shackles of traditional accounts of judicial decision-making. Nevertheless, they will not be given licence to do whatever they wish and however they wish. The major constraint upon them is that they must be dedicated to the idea that they are in the

[11] For a similar point but drawing on challenges for retired judges see, in this volume, Chapter 7, H Tyrrell, 'Extrajudicial Communication: What Changes in Retirement?'.

[12] K Llewellyn, 'The Adventures of Rollo' (1952) 2 *University of Chicago Law School Record* 3. For my own account of great judges and who might make the list, see A Hutchinson, *Laughing at the Gods: Great Judges and How They Made the Common Law* (Cambridge, Cambridge University Press, 2012).

privileged business of resolving disputes and developing the law in a more just and rewarding fashion. This is no small or unimportant matter.

III. GOING PUBLIC

So, this brings me to this chapter's major focus – answering the question of whether judges should or should not speak out? Hopefully, it will be obvious and understandable what the answer should and must be. It is not simply that judges should be *entitled* to speak out on a variety of issues and controversies, it is that they should be *encouraged* to do so. If judges are treated as the politicised animals that they inevitably and unavoidably are, then it is crucial that the citizenry know what their individual politics and approaches are. In short, in a democracy, it is very much a case of 'better the devil you know than the devil you don't'. Indeed, within the politicised account of law and adjudication, their devilish depiction can be abandoned and be replaced by more benign and productive portrayals: if not at all angels, then at least down-to-earth and elite justice-officials.

One of the common analogies that is used about judges is that, on appointment, they should consider themselves to have entered a priesthood and must act accordingly.[13] By this, I assume that it is meant to convey the idea that judges have left behind the freedoms and privileges of a worldly life. Henceforth, they must adopt a cloistered existence, insulate themselves from secular temptations and live a life of selfless service. As such, the judicial undertaking is an all-in affair and is understood to be one of abstinence, high-mindedness and denial; the public judge is to push aside the blandishments and associations of their private and previous professional connections. While this analogy has less of a hold on the institutional imagination today, its muted and more modernised imagery still holds considerable sway. Indeed, the 2023 UK Courts and Tribunals *Guide to Judicial Conduct* states that 'serving judges should not comment publicly on the merits, meaning or likely effect of government policy or proposals; the merits of public appointments; or the merits of individual cases'.[14] It also strongly recommends that 'judicial office holders do not talk to the media.[15] This general stance is neatly and forcefully summarised by Justice Stratas of the Canadian Federal Court of Appeal:

> Increasingly, [judges] wander into the public square and give virtue signalling and populism a go. They write op-eds, deliver speeches and give interviews, extolling constitutional rights as absolutes that can never be outweighed by pressing public interest concerns and embracing people, groups and causes that line up with their personal view of what is 'just', 'right' and 'fair' … They should not act in this way. They should stay in their proper place. Their place is not in the public square amongst the partisans and the politicians, participating

[13] See eg Lord Hailsham, HL Deb 19 November 1970, vol 312, col 1314. He also says that a judicial appointment can also be compared to 'a bridegroom approaching marriage'. Although I am not exactly sure what this means, it does not sound in any way acceptable or progressive.

[14] Courts and Tribunals Judiciary *Guide to Judicial Conduct* (2023) www.judiciary.uk/guidance-and-resources/guide-to-judicial-conduct-revised-july-2023, 16.

[15] ibid.

> in the fray. Instead, their place is inside their courthouses, hearing each side, weighing and assessing the admissible evidence and discerning and applying the relevant legal doctrine, all in a rational, open-minded and neutral way, both in appearance and actual fact.[16]

This approach – priest-like analogy – does much more harm than good. Not only does it defy any realistic sense of the judge's role (ie, that it is thoroughly political and value-laden), but it also offers a false model of what it is to be a 'good judge'. In this sense, it fits in easily with the traditional understanding of law and adjudication. But, even if the priest-like analogy is taken seriously, it is not a valid or helpful comparison. At least with priests, we know what kind of spiritual commitments they have made and what kind of values they are supposed to promote. Except in the more extreme monastic sects, priests *do* engage with the outside world and, by way of regular and pivotal sermons, *do* extol certain virtues and ways of living; it is not so much an a-ethical life, but a very particular and devoted way of ethical living.

If anything, the judiciary resemble more of a private members' club than a priesthood – largely elitist, relatively homogenous, decidedly insular and generally self-serving. Of course, even though there have been some positive changes towards a more diversely-composed judiciary, it is not at all that they do not have ethical values and political allegiances; it is that those ethical values and political allegiances are kept under wraps. Indeed, the whole approach to such matters is redolent of the idea that it is not the holding of ethical values or political allegiances that is the problem, but letting the public into what those are. The recent views of Lord Dyson, a former Master of The Rolls and Justice of the UK Supreme Court, reflect this traditional stance. Although he strives to present a more modern and sensitive approach, especially in regard to the writings and activities of retired judges, he manages to reinforce the perceived need for a remote and unknown judiciary:

> In my view, fascinating though they may be to some people, the private musings and records of what a judge thinks about his colleagues and about political issues of the day and of their deliberations when deciding cases should remain private. It can be no cause for surprise that judges have different personalities from each other and a range of political and philosophical views. It can serve no useful purpose to learn, for example, that Justice X usually votes Conservative or that Justice Y usually votes Labour.[17]

It will come as no surprise that, to me, this strikes exactly the wrong note and conveys entirely the wrong message. It defies credibility that a judge's political leanings will not influence their judicial work. Mindful that judges make and change the law, it seems particularly useful and purposeful to know such a matter; it is not a topic of idle curiosity or mere fascination. While judges are not reducible to their political views and their decisions are not robotically predictable by reference to such views, it is surely relevant to know something about their political views and leanings. In almost any other field of endeavour, it would be odd, to say the least, to ignore a person's politics when seeking to understand or appreciate her or his decision-making and actions. While those politics might not tell the whole story, they are very much

[16] *Canada (Attorney General) v Kattenburg* [2020] FCA 164, [45]–[46].

[17] Lord Dyson, 'Judicial After-Life: Should it be Subject to any Limits?' (The Birkenhead Lecture, London, 12 November 2024): www.graysinn.org.uk/events/birkenhead-lecture, para 44.

an indispensable dimension of the context that helps to determine why they went one way or another in their decision-making.

These assertions seem defensible and even demanded when the judicial task is viewed from a traditional standpoint, but they are essential when an analysis of judicial decision-making is approached form the critical perspective that I have adopted and defended. If 'law is politics', it is imperative that we know more, not less about judges and their political values. There are two obvious ways to facilitate this – a more vigorous appointment process and a more expansive sense of what should be contained in legal judgments.

As regards the first way, judges could be asked to file an account of who they are and why that should be a strong basis for their appointment; this would lift the cloak of secrecy and suspicion that presently exists. In particular, this would undercut the idea that judges were somehow neutral in their political commitments and would bring to the fore those values that animate their decision-making. None of this recommends that judges' private lives should be an open book; they are entitled to privacy like anyone else. But, when they take on the responsibilities and power of public office, they should come clean, as it were, about who they are and what makes them tick politically. Furthermore, the appointment process should be more open and have a participatory component. As I have said, independence does not mean isolation and it most certainly does not mean unaccountability.[18]

Secondly, in writing their judgments, judges should be encouraged to be open and even candid about the values that they rely on and that justify their decisions; they should not hide or claim neutrality for the values that they do espouse or rely upon. This is not the radical leap that many will assume. Legal craft will remain important, but not be an exclusive imprimatur of valid judicial decision-making. The best and most respected judges are not those who take a posited technical approach to their duties, but those who come out and stand up for those values that they believe are necessary if the law is to be just. It is the 'bold spirit', not the 'timorous soul' that should be the norm.[19] Whether staying with existing rules or changing them, judges will simply tease out and make plain what is already the case; they will bring into play what is presently left unsaid and in the wings. In doing this, judges will not be undermining the legitimacy of their actions, but will be enhancing their roles as accountable and powerful actors in a democratic society.

The recently-published diaries of Lord Hope are a good example of what my proposal does and does not recommend. I am urging that judges speak candidly about their own preferences, but this does not extend to offering a kiss-and-tell account of what is thought about other judges' views. Agreeing with Lord Neuberger that 'justice has always to be detached, almost Olympian',[20] Lord Hope is particularly critical of Lords Neuberger, Rodgers and Hale whom he maintains ought to 'put aside personal inclinations and prejudices' and not 'impose on the public the consequences of [their] own view of morality.' He also calls out Lords Steyn and Bingham

[18] See above section II. So What?

[19] See *Candler v Crane, Christmas & Co* [1951] 2 KB 164, 178 (Lord Denning MR).

[20] D Neuberger, P Riddell and C Foster-Gilbert (ed), *The Power of Judges* (London, Haus Publishing, 2018) 22.

who, while subscribing to the Olympian ideal 'on paper', did not put it into practice.[21] My own view is that he would have been better advised to turn his critical apparatus and commentary on himself. This might allow him to tease out his *own* political and moral tendencies and how they might affect, as they surely must, his own work as a judge. Indeed, Lords Kerr, Sumption and Bingham and Lady Hale have done exactly this in writing about their own style and substance of judging, even if they remain a little too cautious and guarded.[22]

Of course, while Lord Hope might well be correct (or incorrect) about the competing views on politics and morality of his judicial colleagues, he remains preposterously unpersuasive about his own lack of views on those political and moral matters that come before the Supreme Court. As I have sought to insist, this Olympian approach is not only unattainable, but it works as more of a screen than a stance. It hides the personal views and preferences that animate the professional performance and decision-making of judges; it does not do away with them. It is simply inaccurate and unhelpful to label such values and views as 'prejudices'. Indeed, a strong argument can be made that the Olympian ideal is not only unattainable, but that it is itself a political stance: a proffered detached view of morality and politics comprises a definite, if vague perspective on such matters. In short, my law-is-politics stance insists that there is no place to stand that does not itself entail a preference for some values and views over others.

IV. CONCLUSION

Accordingly, I have sought to tie the public role of judges to a defensible account of what is involved in fulfilling their judgmental responsibilities. Because, on this account, 'law is politics', and judges are perhaps the most significant architects of the law (even in a statutory age), it is essential that the public know something about who the judges are and what their political preferences are. Once it is accepted that the judges' political views affect both the creation and application of the law, it becomes apparent that the nature and thrust of those political views become a matter for public disclosure and public scrutiny. In a democracy, the views of politicians are on display and available for censure. This should be doubly so for judges. Hiding behind a contrived wall of neutrality and apoliticalness does nothing to legitimate the power and authority of unelected officials – more speaking out is required, not less.

[21] Lord Hope, *House of Lords 1996–2009: Lord Hope's Diaries Volume IV* (Avizandum, 2018), 263 and 214.

[22] See eg H O'Donoghue et al (eds), *Art, Imagination and Public Service* (London, Haus Publishing, 2021).

3

The United States Supreme Court and the Perils of Extrajudicial Speech

CHRISTOPHER W SCHMIDT

How foolish for a justice of the Supreme Court ever to venture from the bench and accept an invitation to speak …

— Justice Felix Frankfurter[1]

I. INTRODUCTION

JUDGES CHOOSE TO engage in extrajudicial speech for varied and often overlapping reasons. They may be motivated by personal interests, such as the need to explain something about themselves or a desire to connect with a particular group. They may seek to educate outside audiences about their work and the role of the courts generally. They may seek to advocate for a jurisprudential approach or defend a particular case outcome. They may be moved by institutional interests. Much extrajudicial speech aims to defend the judiciary against external criticism; sometimes they offer their own criticism of the judiciary.

The value of extrajudicial speech is that it offers an opportunity to do something that the standard mode of judicial communication, a written opinion, may not allow. By going beyond the constraints of the written opinion, a judge may reach different audiences, address different issues, speak with a different voice. There can be substantial benefits to extrajudicial speech. But there are also substantial perils. When extrajudicial speech draws attention to divisions between judges or when it makes the judiciary appear entangled in political activities, it may undermine the professional reputation of the judge and public confidence in the courts.

In this chapter, I examine the extrajudicial speech of the justices of the United States Supreme Court with the goal of illuminating its risks. I suggest that Supreme

[1] F Frankfurter, 'Personal Ambitions of Judges: Should a Judge "Think Beyond the Judicial"?' (1948) 34 *American Bar Association Journal* 656.

Court justices face the most substantial perils when they engage in speech that has the potential to produce the most substantial benefits. In other words, extrajudicial speech that is risky may also be the most rewarding. I also consider how recent changes in the politics surrounding the US Supreme Court have elevated the risks of extrajudicial speech while diminishing the rewards.

II. THE EXTRAJUDICIAL SPEECH OF UNITED STATES SUPREME COURT JUSTICES

When justices on the United States Supreme Court engage in extrajudicial speech, what are they hoping to achieve? Although the frequency and scope of extrajudicial speech have varied across the Supreme Court's history, justices have always looked for opportunities to speak about their lives and their work and to advance their views in forums beyond their written opinions.[2]

For the purposes of this chapter, I define extrajudicial speech as non-private oral or written statements made by a justice that relate to their life and work but that do not come in the form of an official written opinion, statement, or testimony. When engaging in extrajudicial speech the justice speaks in their capacity as a member of the Court, not simply as a private citizen, and they intend the speech to be heard by the public, or at least a portion of the public.[3] The forms of extrajudicial speech on which I focus are highly discretionary. Some judges avoid the practice as much as possible; some engage in it frequently and enthusiastically. There are few formal rules constraining what they say. What constraints they face are predominantly in the realm of norms and expectations.[4] The discretionary element imbues extrajudicial speech with its potential power. It also makes it particularly controversial, as a justice risks criticism not only for the content of their speech but also for their choice to speak at all.

Extrajudicial discourse by sitting Supreme Court justices comes in varied forms. Justices regularly deliver speeches or remarks at events open to the public or at closed events that are made accessible to the public by press coverage or the release of a transcript or video. Justices talk to the press, sometimes in brief targeted comments,

[2] See A Westin, 'Out of Court Commentary by United States Supreme Court Justices: Of Free Speech and Judicial Lockjaw' (1962) 62 *Columbia Law Review* 633; A Westin (ed), *An Autobiography of the Supreme Court: Off-the-Bench Commentary by the Justices* (London, Macmillan, 1963); R Wheeler, 'Extrajudicial Activities of the Early Supreme Court' (1973) *Supreme Court Review* 123; DM O'Brien, *Storm Center: The Supreme Court in American Politics*, 7th edn (New York, Norton 2005) 85–99; LB Dubeck, 'Understanding "Judicial Lockjaw": The Debate over Extrajudicial Activity' (2007) 82 *NYU Law Review* 569; CW Schmidt, 'Beyond the Opinion: Supreme Court Justices and Extrajudicial Speech' (2013) 88 *Chicago-Kent Law Review* 487.

[3] Some forms of speech are on the border between official speech and extrajudicial speech. Neha Jain has described a spectrum of 'separate judicial speech' – speech by judges other than official opinions of the court – that ranges from formal (eg written dissents) to semi-formal (eg academic articles) to informal (eg off-the-bench statements by judges on topics unrelated to judiciary). See N Jain, 'Separate Judicial Speech' (2020) 61 *Virginia Journal of International Law* 1.

[4] For an empirical analysis of how a 'shared – informal – conception of appropriate discourse in judicial office' shapes extrajudicial speech, see C Mallory and H Tyrrell, 'The Extrajudicial Voice' (2024) 44 *Legal Studies* 1. See also WG Ross, 'Extrajudicial Speech: Charting the Boundaries of Propriety' (1989) 2 *Georgetown Journal of Legal Ethics* 589.

sometimes through lengthy and wide-ranging interviews. They issue written statements or open letters. And justices have a long tradition of writing for publication, with published writings running the gamut from a brief 'letter to the editor' to a full-length book.

The purposes behind the extrajudicial speech of Supreme Court justices are also varied. Recent justices have been particularly interested in sharing their life stories. Justices in years past only occasionally published memoirs, usually only after they had left the bench.[5] It is now commonplace for justices to write books about themselves while still serving on the Court. In 2002 Justice Sandra Day O'Connor (1981–2006) published a book co-authored with her brother about their experiences growing up on a ranch in Arizona.[6] The current Supreme Court is fast approaching having a majority of published memoirists. Justices Ketanji Brown Jackson, Sonia Sotomayor, and Clarence Thomas have each produced bestselling memoirs.[7] Justice Neil Gorsuch published a book that blends autobiography, description of his jurisprudential beliefs, and constitutional history.[8] Justices Amy Coney Barrett and Brett Kavanaugh have contracts to write their own books. Supreme Court authors are generously compensated for their efforts, with some receiving multimillion dollar advances.[9] (Federal law exempts income from book contracts and sales from the limits on outside income for judges).[10] Justices typically engage in a flurry of public events and interviews promoting their books, offering many more opportunities to share their life stories.

Another common goal that justices pursue in their extrajudicial speech is to educate the public on legal issues. The Supreme Court is a powerful and often mysterious institution, and the justices regularly play the role of a civics teacher, talking and writing about the importance of the judicial system and the responsibilities of a justice. Justice Stephen Breyer (1994–2022) described one of the several books he wrote while serving on the Court as written with the goal of 'increas[ing] the public's general understanding of what the Supreme Court does'.[11] Justice O'Connor spoke about the history of women in the law and the

[5] See eg DJ Danelski and JS Tulchin (eds), *The Autobiographical Notes of Charles Evans Hughes* (Cambridge MA, Harvard University Press, 1973); E Warren, *The Memoirs of Earl Warren* (Doubleday, 1977); WO Douglas, *The Court Years, 1939-1975* (New York, Random House, 1980). Justice Douglas published the first volume of his memoirs, covering his life before he reached the Supreme Court, while still serving as a justice. WO Douglas, *Go East, Young Man: The Early Years* (New York, Random House, 1974).

[6] SD O'Connor and HA Day, *Lazy B: Growing Up on a Cattle Ranch in the American Southwest* (New York, Random House, 2002).

[7] C Thomas, *My Grandfather's Son: A Memoir* (New York, HarperCollins, 2007); S Sotomayor, *My Beloved World* (New York, Knopf, 2013); KB Jackson, *Lovely One: A Memoir* (New York, Random House, 2024).

[8] N Gorsuch, *A Republic, If You Can Keep It* (New York, Crown Forum, 2019).

[9] A VanSickle and A Alter, 'Book Deals Can Add Up to Millions of Dollars for Supreme Court Justices', *New York Times* (New York, 6 September 2024) www.nytimes.com/2024/09/06/us/politics/supreme-court-justice-book-deals.html; M Allen, 'Scoop: Justice Brett Kavanaugh plans legal memoir', *Axios* (6 June 2024) www.axios.com/2024/06/06/scotus-brett-kavanaugh-writing-book-memoir.

[10] See *Code of Conduct for Justice of the United States Supreme Court*, 13 November 2023, 12–13 www.supremecourt.gov/about/Code-of-Conduct-for-Justices_November_13_2023.pdf (*Supreme Court Code of Conduct*).

[11] S Breyer, *Making Our Democracy Work* (New York, Knopf, 2010) ix.

challenges that female lawyers have faced.[12] William Rehnquist (Associate Justice, 1972–86; Chief Justice, 1986–2005) published several books on legal history, including a history of his own court.[13] Justice Sotomayor has put her own populist spin on the educator role, publishing a line of children's books and appearing on the children's show *Sesame Street*, where she talked about careers in the law and the importance of judges.[14]

Supreme Court justices also engage in extrajudicial discourse aimed toward defending the judiciary in general and the Supreme Court in particular. A favourite theme of their public remarks is to emphasise the collegial personal relations between justices as a way of demonstrating the Court's functionality and immunisation from the endemic vitriol of American politics.[15] Justices regularly emphasise that beyond the most high-profile and divisive rulings, the justices generally agree, often unanimously, on issues they face – evidence that, according to Justice Kavanaugh, the Court operates as 'an institution of law, not of partisanship, not of politics'.[16]

The value of an independent judiciary is another popular topic for extrajudicial commentary. It was not enough for judges to 'simply undertake our own jobs as best we can', said Justice Breyer in a 2009 speech. They must also 'try to explain or to teach why [the judiciary] and independence are important, not simply to the judges or to the lawyers, but to ordinary Americans whom ultimately our institution seeks to serve'.[17] One of the most consequential instances of extrajudicial speech was the ringing defence of judicial independence that Chief Justice Charles Evans Hughes (1930–41) delivered, in the form of an open letter, in response to President Franklin Roosevelt's 1937 proposal to 'pack' the Court with six additional justices.[18] In recent years, Chief Justice John Roberts has been circumspect when it comes to extrajudicial speech, but the one topic

[12] SD O'Connor, 'Portia's Progress' (1991) 66 *NYU Law Review* 1546.

[13] WH Rehnquist, *The Supreme Court: How It Was, How It Is* (New York, William Morrow, 1987); WH Rehnquist, *Grand Inquests: The Historic Impeachments of Justice Samuel Chase and President Andrew Johnson* (New York, Knopf, 1992); WH Rehnquist, *All the Laws but One: Civil Liberties in Wartime* (New York. William Morrow, 1998); WH Rehnquist, *The Centennial Crisis: The Disputed Election of 1876* (New York, Knopf, 2004).

[14] S Sotomayor, *Turning Pages: My Life Story* (New York, Philomel Books, 2018); S Sotomayor, *Just Ask! Be Different, Be Brave, Be You* (New York, Philomel Books 2018); S Sotomayor, *Just Help!: How to Build a Better World* (New York, Philomel Books 2018); D Fontana, 'The People's Justice?', *Yale Law Journal Forum* (24 March 2014).

[15] See eg A de Vogue, 'Sotomayor and Gorsuch say they are "warm colleagues and friends" amid masking dustup', *CNN* (19 January 2022) www.cnn.com/2022/01/19/politics/gorsuch-sotomayor-masks-covid-supreme-court/index.html; AE Marimow, 'The Supreme Court seems bitterly divided. Two justices say otherwise', *Washington Post* (15 March 2024) www.washingtonpost.com/politics/2024/03/15/supreme-court-seems-bitterly-divided-two-justices-say-otherwise/.

[16] J Gerstein, 'Kavanaugh: No warring camps at Supreme Court', *Politico* (13 July 2023) www.politico.com/news/2023/07/13/kavanaugh-supreme-court-speech-partisanship-00106215.

[17] S Breyer, 'An Independent Judiciary: In Honor of the Sesquicentennial Anniversary of the Massachusetts Superior Court' (Boston MA, 22 September 2009) www.supremecourt.gov/publicinfo/speeches/viewspeeches.aspx?Filename=sp_09-22-09.html.

[18] See WE Leuchtenburg, 'Charles Evans Hughes: The Center Holds' (2005) 83 *North Carolina Law Review* 1196–98.

about which he has spoken out forcefully and directly has been the importance of judicial independence.[19]

The core message in these statements is that the Court is doing fine, that the American people should have confidence in its work, and that the political branches should leave it alone. On occasion, however, justices use extrajudicial speech to emphasise a different message: that all is not well at the Court. Justices sometimes use extrajudicial statements to criticise fellow justices. In the aftermath of the leak of a draft opinion in *Dobbs v Whole Women's Health*, the 2022 ruling that overturned the constitutional right to abortion, Justice Samuel Alito, the author of the leaked opinion, insisted that the source of the leak was someone who opposed the ruling, and not, as some suspected, someone hoping to 'lock in' the majority).[20] Justice Thomas earned headlines when he lamented the loss of trust within the Court and seemed to place blame on Chief Justice Roberts.[21] Justice Elena Kagan has recently criticised various aspects of the Court's work, including the proliferation of concurring opinions; an excessive reliance on the Court's 'emergency docket' (rulings on cases via an expedited process that does not include full oral arguments or written opinions); and inconsistency and opportunism by her conservative colleagues – particularly when, in her view, they put aside their claimed fidelity to originalist and textualist methodologies in order to achieve their preferred conservative rulings.[22]

Another category of extrajudicial commentary seeks to explain and defend a judge's approach to their work. This can range from an explanation about particular tendencies or quirks (such as when Justice Breyer talked about his decision not to use footnotes) to full-blown defences of a theory of constitutional interpretation.[23] In the middle decades of the twentieth century, several justices used lectures and interviews to defend their jurisprudential views.[24] In the 1980s, Justice William Brennan (1956–90) critiqued the originalist approaches to constitutional interpretation that were gaining currency in conservative legal circles.[25] Justice Thurgood Marshall (1967–91) also attacked originalism, criticising conservatives for holding an unjustified reverence for the Founding era and for a Constitution that was, in Marshall's controversial

[19] See, eg A Liptak, 'Chief Justice Defends Judicial Independence After Trump Attacks "Obama Judge"', *New York Times* (New York, 21 November 2018) www.nytimes.com/2018/11/21/us/politics/trump-chief-justice-roberts-rebuke.html.

[20] J Taranto and DB Rivkin Jr, 'Justice Samuel Alito: "This Made Us Targets of Assassination"', *Wall Street Journal* (New York, 28 April 2023) www.wsj.com/articles/justice-samuel-alito-this-made-us-targets-of-assassination-dobbs-leak-abortion-court-74624ef9.

[21] J Bravin, 'Clarence Thomas Criticizes Supreme Court Leak of Draft Opinion on Roe v. Wade', *Wall Street Journal* (New York, 14 May 2022) https://www.wsj.com/articles/clarence-thomas-criticizes-supreme-court-leak-of-draft-opinion-on-roe-v-wade-11652508439?mod=article_inline.

[22] J Gerstein, 'Kagan repeats warning that Supreme Court is damaging its legitimacy', *Politico* (14 September 2022), https://www.politico.com/news/2022/09/14/kagan-supreme-court-legitimacy-00056766; D Cole, 'Justice Elena Kagan says Supreme Court's code of conduct needs an enforcement plan', *CNN* (25 July 2024), https://www.cnn.com/2024/07/25/politics/kagan-supreme-court-ethics-sacramento-conference/.

[23] 'In Justice Breyer's Opinion, A Footnote Has No Place', *New York Times* (New York, 28 July 1995) 18.

[24] See eg 'Justice Black and First Amendment "Absolutes": A Public Interview' (1962) 37 *NYU Law Review* 549; WO Douglas, 'The Bill of Rights is Not Enough' (1963) 38 *NYU Law Review* 207; AJ Goldberg, 'Equality and Governmental Action' (1964) 39 *NYU Law Review* 205; HL Black, *A Constitutional Faith* (New York, Knopf, 1968).

[25] See eg S Taylor Jr, 'Brennan Opposes Legal View Urged by Administration', *New York Times* (New York, 13 October 1985).

assessment, 'defective from the start'.[26] Justices Antonin Scalia (1986–2016) and Breyer were notably active in talking about their contrasting approaches to constitutional interpretation – sometimes together in staged public debates. Among current members of the Court, Justice Gorsuch has been the most vocal in advancing his jurisprudential views through off-the-bench writings, interviews, and speaking engagements.

On occasion a sitting Supreme Court justice expresses their views involving issues not directly about the Court, the law, or themselves. These statements may have no relation to the work of the justice and thus fall outside the definition of extrajudicial speech used in this chapter. But sometimes a justice ventures opinions or observations on topics that are not directly about law or their role as a judge but that observers nevertheless understand as meaningful because of the speaker's position as a Supreme Court justice. No justice of the past century was more outspoken off the bench than Justice William O Douglas (1939–75), who wrote and lectured on issues ranging from foreign affairs to environmentalism to the perils of cultural conformity. One of the most controversial episodes of extrajudicial speech in recent memory was in 2016 when Justice Ginsburg gave a series of interviews in which she criticised Republican presidential nominee Donald Trump.[27] On the current Court, Justice Alito has been outspoken about the role of religion in American society, lamenting that religious liberty 'is fast becoming a disfavored right'.[28] Justice Thomas has aired his views about the ideological landscape in modern America, chastising liberal commentators and the media for what he sees as unwarranted attacks on those holding conservative views.[29]

III. WHO BENEFITS FROM EXTRAJUDICIAL SPEECH?

Although the central concern of this chapter is the risks associated with extrajudicial speech, these risks cannot be assessed without also considering the benefits that extrajudicial speech may offer. In this section I identify three primary categories of beneficiaries of extrajudicial speech: the public, the judiciary, and the judge.

A. The Public

Members of the Supreme Court often justify forays into extrajudicial speech as responding to the needs of the American people. These benefits are most obvious

[26] T Marshall, 'Reflections on the Bicentennial of the United States Constitution' (1987) 101 *Harvard Law Review* 1.

[27] J Biskupic, 'Justice Ruth Bader Ginsburg calls Trump a "faker," he says she should resign', *CNN* (12 July 2016) www.cnn.com/2016/07/12/politics/justice-ruth-bader-ginsburg-donald-trump-faker/index.html.

[28] See eg 'Address by Justice Samuel Alito' (Federalist Society National Lawyers Convention, 12 November 2020) www.youtube.com/watch?v=tYLZL4GZVbA. See also 'U.S. Supreme Court Justice Samuel Alito delivers keynote address at 2022 Notre Dame Religious Liberty Summit in Rome', (Notre Dame Religious Liberty Summit, Rome, 28 July 2022) https://law.nd.edu/news-events/news/2022-religious-liberty-summit-rome-justice-samuel-alito-keynote/.

[29] J Bravin, 'Clarence Thomas Criticizes Supreme Court Leak of Draft Opinion on Roe v. Wade', *Wall Street Journal* (New York, 14 May 2022) www.wsj.com/articles/clarence-thomas-criticizes-supreme-court-leak-of-draft-opinion-on-roe-v-wade-11652508439?mod=article_inline.

and direct when justices seek to expand public understanding of the Court. Justice Breyer recalled that when he arrived on the Court, Justice Harry Blackmun (1970–94) told him that 'the American public has an unquenchable thirst to find out what this institution is', and he should find opportunities to 'tell people what you do' – advice Justice Breyer took to heart.[30] Extrajudicial speech can be a particularly powerful vehicle for explaining to the public how courts work, the role of the courts in a constitutional democracy, and the value of an independent judiciary. As one advocate for a more robust judicial role in educating the public has written,

> judges can raise the level of debate if they invest their prestige and learning in an effort to educate the public about the laws they administer, the boundaries of their authority, and the handicaps, both avoidable and unavoidable, under which they function.[31]

Responding to the public interest is also a motivation behind the rapidly expanding shelf of justice memoirs; their impressive sales figures attest to the popular demand for information about the lives of the members of the Court.

The public may also be the intended beneficiary of more controversial forms of extrajudicial speech, such as warnings about the direction of the Court or commentary on current events. When justices criticise their colleagues or opine on a public policy issue, they assumedly see themselves as fulfilling a responsibility to the broader public – or at least the segment of the public that might be swayed or energised by their words.

B. The Judiciary

The judiciary as an institution is another beneficiary of extrajudicial speech. Justices often reference a desire to promote the interests of the judiciary as their motivation for engaging in extrajudicial speech.[32] When faced with a challenge to the judiciary, a direct response from one of its members may be the most effective way to ensure that a robust defence of the courts is part of the public discussion. This was what moved Chief Justice Roberts to speak out against Donald Trump's attacks on judges.[33] This was why when the Court came under fire for the questionable ethical practices of some of its members, several made statements insisting that the Court was taking the issue seriously.[34]

[30] S Breyer, 'In Conversation with Jeffrey Rosen and Paul Holdengräber' (New York Public Library, 20 September 2010) www.nypl.org/events/programs/2010/09/20/justice-stephen-breyer-conversation-jeffrey-rosen-paul-holdengräber?nref=121031.

[31] MS Tucker, 'The Judge's Role in Educating the Public about the Law' (1982) 31 *Catholic University Law Review* 206.

[32] See C Mallory and H Tyrrell, 'The Extrajudicial Voice' (above n 4) 15.

[33] M Sherman, 'Roberts, Trump Spar in Extraordinary Scrap Over Judges', *Associated Press* (21 November 2018) https://apnews.com/article/north-america-donald-trump-us-news-ap-top-news-immigration-c4b34f9639e141069c08cf1e3deb6b84.

[34] See eg R Barnes, 'Justice Kavanaugh says ethics changes may be coming to Supreme Court,' *Washington Post* (7 September 2023) https://www.washingtonpost.com/politics/2023/09/07/justice-kavanaugh-ethics-supreme-court/.

In response to outside criticism that a justice feels is unfair or inaccurate, justices on occasion have used extrajudicial forums to defend the substance of the Court's work. In the mid-1960s, in response to growing public criticism of the Court's expansion of the rights of criminal defendants, several justices engaged in a modest public relations campaign on behalf of the Court. Chief Justice Earl Warren (1953–69) and Justice Brennan publicly defended the Court against accusations that it was dismissive of State-level authority.[35] Justice Arthur Goldberg (1962–65) wrote a *New York Times* article refuting 'myths' about the Court that he felt were misleading the American people.[36] In the 1970s, when the Court faced criticism from frustrated liberals who believed the Court was abandoning the Warren Court's[37] commitment to individual rights, several justices came to the Court's defence.[38] In the aftermath of *Dobbs*, Chief Justice Roberts urged the American people not to allow disagreement with the Court's rulings to turn into skepticism toward the legitimacy of the Court itself.[39] Across United States history, protecting the courts against perceived threats has frequently motivated extrajudicial speech.

C. The Judge

Judges can benefit from engaging in extrajudicial speech. A 'man or woman who becomes a Justice should try to stay alive; a lifetime diet of the law alone turns most judges into dull, dry husks', wrote Justice Douglas, a man who had a particularly active, and often controversial, life beyond the bench.[40] Talking to outside audiences may cause a judge to learn something relevant to their work or to think differently about issues in ways that make them a better judge. Public engagement informs the judicial mind by exposing the judge to the viewpoints, experience, and passions of an outside audience. Most forms of extrajudicial speech involve some degree of interaction between the judge and the public. Public events often include audience questions; they may feature sharp criticism and sometimes acts of protest. Interviewers confront judges with questions that they believe would be of interest to the general public. Even the isolated act of writing a book, essay, or speech may encourage a judge to expand their perspective beyond the narrower confines of the bench and bar that is the primary audience for their written opinions. For those who

[35] J Langguth, 'Warren Defends the High Court', *New York Times* (New York, 26 September 1963) 29; J Langguth, '50 Justices Hear Plea By Brennan', *New York Times* (New York, 8 August 1964) 46.

[36] A Goldberg, 'The Court Sits in the Center of the Storm', *New York Times Magazine* (8 November 1964).

[37] The Warren Court refers to the period in US Supreme Court history when Earl Warren served as Chief Justice, from 1953 to 1969. The era is recognised for its significant expansion of individual rights and liberties through judicial interpretation.

[38] L Oelsner, 'High Court Record on Individual Rights Defended by Burger', *New York Times* (New York, 9 April 1976) 1; L Oelsner, 'Powell Finds High Court Showing "Sounder Balance"', *New York Times* (New York, 12 August 1976) 18.

[39] R Barnes and M Karlik, 'Roberts says Supreme Court will reopen to public and defends legitimacy', *Washington Post* (10 September 2022) www.washingtonpost.com/politics/2022/09/10/supreme-court-roberts-legitimacy/.

[40] Douglas, *Go East* (above n 5) 469.

believe that the justices are too closed off to the world around them, spending too much time with admiring clerks and speaking to sympathetic audiences, a steadier diet of public appearances may have the benefit of broadening their perspective.[41]

Judges may also benefit personally from extrajudicial speech in ways that are more direct and immediate. Writing books can have substantial financial benefits, and the adulation that Supreme Court justices typically receive at their public appearances surely has psychological benefits. Extrajudicial speech can also serve as a tool of crisis management. A famous example is a speech that Hugo Black (1937–71) gave soon after his appointment to the Court in which he defended himself against press reports that as a young politician he had joined the Ku Klux Klan. Black told a national radio audience that he had been a Klan member but was no longer, and he pointed to his record in public life and his personal relationships with racial and religious minorities as evidence that he was not a bigot. The storm over his appointment soon passed, and Black went on to serve on the Court for over three decades. In the late 1960s, Justices Douglas and Abe Fortas (1965–69) made public statements defending themselves against accusations of impropriety relating to payments they had received from businessmen with questionable interests. In recent years, Justice Samuel Alito has spoken out to defend himself against various accusations of impropriety involving his expenses-paid vacation travels and flags flown outside his homes that have been associated with the Republican effort to overthrow the 2020 presidential election.[42] Although no justice wants to fend off accusations of impropriety, several have concluded that it was in their best interest to speak out directly in their own defence.

IV. THE RISKS OF EXTRAJUDICIAL SPEECH

The risk of extrajudicial speech boils down to a single overriding concern: that what a judge says or writes off the bench will undermine public confidence in the judiciary. This confidence is generally understood to depend on a belief that judges should be fair minded and motivated by a commitment to the law rather than personal bias or partisan preferences – an image the justices encourage. 'Judges wear black robes because it doesn't matter who they are as individuals', explained John Roberts at his confirmation hearings.[43] The 2023 Supreme Court Code of Conduct reflects this assumption when it tells justices to avoid 'extrajudicial activities that detract from the dignity of the Justice's office, interfere with the performance of the Justice's official duties, [or] reflect adversely on the Justice's impartiality'.[44]

[41] See eg DR Stras, 'Why Supreme Court Justices Should Ride Circuit Again' (2007) 91 *Minnesota Law Review* 1710–51.

[42] S Alito Jr, 'ProPublica Misleads Its Readers', *Wall Street Journal* (New York, 20 June 2023) www.wsj.com/articles/propublica-misleads-its-readers-alito-gifts-disclosure-alaska-singer-23b51eda?mod=article_inline; SA Alito Jr to RJ Durbin and S Whitehouse, *Washington Post* (24 May 2024) www.washingtonpost.com/documents/ae3feb5a-13a4-4f0f-9046-b61a530c40fb.pdf?itid=lk_inline_manual_4.

[43] Confirmation Hearing on the Nomination of John G Roberts, Jr, to be Chief Justice of the United States, 109th Cong., 1st Sess. (13 September 2005) 178.

[44] *Supreme Court Code of Conduct* (above n 10) 4.

For most of the extrajudicial speech in which Supreme Court justices regularly engage, potential harms to the judiciary are relatively small. Speech aimed at educating the public about the courts is one of the most common forms of extrajudicial speech by a Supreme Court justice, and it's not particularly controversial. When a judge talks to the public about the history of their court or when they explain the logistics of how they select and decide cases or when they laud the benefits of an independent judiciary, it's hard to see their words harming the judiciary in any meaningful way. Some might question the propriety of a Supreme Court justice talking to puppets on a children's show. A justice's discussion of the Court's history may on occasion touch on some point of current controversy. But the content of this speech is often downright banal, and central goal of this kind of extrajudicial speech is to cultivate faith in the judiciary. Indeed, the commentary to the Model Judicial Code of Ethics notes, 'Judges are uniquely qualified to engage in extrajudicial activities that concern the law, the legal system, and the administration of justice, such as by speaking, writing, teaching, or participating in scholarly research projects'. Such activities can bolster the public's 'understanding of and respect for courts and the judicial system'.[45] The prestige and even celebrity that attach to their positions mean that Supreme Court justices have a uniquely influential platform from which to serve this educational role.[46]

A riskier variant of this category of extrajudicial speech is when a justice reveals something about the internal operations or dynamics of the Court that is not generally known. Pulling back the curtain on the Court in this way may be innocuous; it may even have the goal of bolstering public confidence in the Court, such as when the justices talk about how well they get along, their respect for one another, or the apolitical nature of Supreme Court decision-making.[47] But revealing information about the Court risks undermining the carefully cultivated image of the Court as an institution whose integrity is integrally linked to the closed nature of the justices' deliberations.

The insider knowledge revealed may be low stakes. Justice Blackmun, for instance, liked to gossip about his colleagues' personal eccentricities.[48] But insider information about the Court can sometimes be more substantive, more purposeful – and more controversial. In 1946, Justice Robert H Jackson (1941–54) believed that other justices had schemed to block his elevation to Chief Justice, and he responded with an open letter accusing Justice Black of unethical behaviour on the bench.[49] Rumblings of discontent with Chief Justice Warren Burger (1969–86) seeped into the press and turned into a scandal when several justices leaked information to the authors of a

[45] American Bar Association, Center for Professional Responsibility, *Model Judicial Code of Ethics*, Rule 3.1, Comments [1]–[2].

[46] See S Polak and S Stroband, 'The Notorious RBG: The Discursive Power of Celebrity in Defense of the Supreme Court' (2023) 56 *Journal of Popular Culture* 635.

[47] See eg S Breyer, *The Authority of the Court and the Peril of Politics* (Cambridge MA, Harvard University Press, 2021); 'A Conversation with Justice Stephen Breyer' (Bolch Judicial Institute, Duke Law School, 26 January 2022) https://judicialstudies.duke.edu/2022/01/justice-stephen-breyer/.

[48] 'Justice Gives Details on the Inner Workings of the High Court', *New York Times* (New York, 5 December 1982) 49; Associated Press, 'Blackmun Has Sharp Opinions Of Colleagues', *New York Times* (New York, 18 July 1988) 10.

[49] DJ Hutchinson, 'The Black-Jackson Feud' (1988) *Supreme Court Review* 203.

bestselling 1979 exposé of the Court.[50] The leak of the *Dobbs* opinion brought a flood of warnings about the harms of this kind of exposure and the dangers of losing the longstanding norms protecting the internal workings of the Court. (It's still unknown whether the leak emanated from a justice, a law clerk, or someone else.) Although a justice who reveals insider information about the Court to the outside world likely believes they are acting with the best interests of the Court in mind, these exposures invariably spark concerns about the Court's dysfunctionality. They get a lot of attention but don't make anyone look good in the end.

Despite the growing frequency of justices speaking in an autobiographical register, from an institutional perspective there may still be risks to this kind of extrajudicial speech. Norms surrounding public figures and their personal lives have changed so that it has become more acceptable, and even expected, for public figures to talk about their backgrounds. Biography has become a centrepiece of how nominees present themselves to the Senate and the public in their confirmation hearings; much of the biographical writing and speaking that a sitting justice does is an extension of and elaboration on themes they introduced to the public during the confirmation process. Norms that may have previously existed about justices avoiding drawing attention to their individual stories have dissipated. Yet the extensive attention some justices give to telling their own stories – including the recent trend of heavily marketed autobiographies – has been criticised for drawing too much attention to the distinctive personal experiences of members of the Court, which detracts from the ideal of judging as a depersonalised act of legal analysis.[51] If the task of legal interpretation aspires, or should aspire, to transcend the individual beliefs and commitments of the interpreter, then writing books aimed a highlighting the distinctive lives of the judge may send mixed messages to the public. If justices were solely concerned with protecting the Court from criticism, Judge Richard Posner has suggested, they would adopt a posture of 'dignified silence' in which:

> the justice is appointed, and then disappears into the Court's marble palace … refusing to speak to journalists at any time, in any place, on any subject. Remote, wrapped in mystery, the justice committed to the pose of dignified silence issues opinions that present the Court's decisions as impersonal products compelled by 'law' regarded as external to the justices, as the Ten Commandments were external to Moses – handed to him, not written by him.[52]

These concerns gain more traction when we see certain justices becoming public celebrities, their celebrity status built upon their personal stories (often bolstered by the publication of bestselling autobiographies and author tours) as much as their contribution to the law.[53] Critics of the rise of celebrity justices have expressed various concerns. Some worry that the adulation of 'cult-like' fans can make the justices too sure of themselves. Some worry that it makes judges more interested in promoting their personal 'brand' than in protecting and promoting the Court as an institution.

[50] B Woodward and S Armstrong, *The Brethren: Inside the Supreme Court* (New York, Simon & Schuster, 1979).

[51] See eg J Rosen, 'Judicial Exposure', *New York Times* (New York, 29 January 2006).

[52] RA Posner, 'The Court of Celebrity', *New Republic* (4 May 2011) https://newrepublic.com/article/87880/supreme-court-burger-blackmum-media-celebrity.

[53] See RL Hasen, 'Celebrity Justice: Supreme Court Edition' (2016) 19 *Green Bag* 157.

Critics worry that 'celebrity-seeking by Supreme Court justices raise[s] the suspicion that their actions are self-serving rather than evidence of a commitment to impartial judging and the rule of law' and that justices are behaving less like 'traditional judges' and more like 'publicity-hungry politicians or impassioned polemicists'.[54]

The risks of extrajudicial speech escalate quickly when justices go beyond the educational and autobiographical. A justice who defends the judiciary in the context of rebutting a challenge to the courts, for example, ventures onto fraught terrain. The situation always presents the risk of getting dragged, willingly or not, into a public debate with people outside the judiciary. Chief Justice Hughes' strategically savvy rebuttal of Roosevelt's Court-packing plan in the 1930s, for instance, still earned him criticism for having transgressed the boundaries of his judicial office.[55] A judge who engages in public debate with politicians, public figures, or academics, will rarely get the last word – as Donald Trump made clear when Chief Justice Roberts sought to counter Trump's attacks on the courts.[56] Particularly at times like the present, when the Supreme Court has become such a fraught issue on the American political scene, simply engaging in public debate risks undermining the perceived detachment and stature of the Court.

Speaking out on jurisprudential issues or on recently decided cases also comes with clear risks. If a justice voices a position on an issue that then comes before the Court, they may feel the need to recuse themselves from the case. Demands that justices recuse themselves because of something they said or did have increased in recent years. Supreme Court justices make their own decision about whether to recuse;[57] they ignore most recusal requests, but on occasion they will recuse in a case involving an issue on which they expressed a position in an extrajudicial context. This occurred in 2003, for example when Justice Scalia recused himself from a case involving a constitutional challenge to the reference to God in the Pledge of Allegiance after he had made public remarks in which he discussed his views on the issue.[58]

Statements that elaborate on or defend a justice's written opinions bump into a longstanding belief that a judge's decisions should, as Justice Goldberg once explained, 'speak for themselves'.[59] Supplementing written opinions with unofficial commentary may dilute, confuse, or detract from the written opinion, and justices have generally – but not always – steered clear of substantive commentary on recently decided cases.[60] When a justice *does* talk about recent Court rulings, they usually offer nothing more than generic summaries that add little to what is contained in the opinion itself.

[54] S Sherry, 'Our Kardashian Court (and How to Fix it)' (2020) 106 *Iowa Law Review* 188; CS Lerner and N Lund, 'Judicial Duty and the Supreme Court's Cult of Celebrity' (2010) 78 *George Washington Law Review* 1269.

[55] Leuchtenburg, 'Charles Evans Hughes' (above n 18) 1197.

[56] Sherman, 'Roberts, Trump Spar' (above n 33).

[57] *Supreme Court Code of Conduct* (above n 10) 2–4.

[58] L Greenhouse, 'Supreme Court to Consider Case On "Under God" in Pledge to Flag', *New York Times* (New York, 15 October 2003).

[59] Hearings on Nonjudicial Activities of Supreme Court Judges and Other Federal Judges, before the Subcommittee on Separation of Powers, 91st Congress, 1st Session, 162 (1969) (Statement of A Goldberg).

[60] For examples of justices discussing decided cases, see Schmidt, 'Beyond the Opinion' (above n 2) 506–8.

Justices airing their views on political, social, or cultural issues brings considerable risks. For instance, Justice Douglas, who in the 1960s gave speeches and wrote articles on a range of social, cultural, and political issues, ran into criticism for an article in which he denounced a government agency's plans to build a new dam. The agency director charged Douglas with making 'downright false statements', which he saw as 'a grave violation of the personal ethics which a Supreme Court Justice is presumed to have'.[61] Justices expressing their partisan opinions – particularly when they attack individual politicians – are on particularly dangerous ground, often earning criticism even from their usual allies. When Justice Marshall criticised President Ronald Reagan's record on civil rights, even the editors of the *New York Times*, who normally sided with Marshall over Reagan, chastised the justice for his 'gratuitous' comments, which were 'hardly worth the cost'.[62] Similarly, Justice Ginsburg had few defenders when she spoke out against Donald Trump during the 2016 election. Her comments were unusual enough in their timing and bluntness that she soon made a strategic retreat, issuing a public apology and then refusing to talk further about the matter. Starkly partisan remarks or commentary on public policy disputes are among the most perilous forms of extrajudicial speech.

V. THE RISK–REWARD RELATIONSHIP IN EXTRAJUDICIAL SPEECH

In this section I consider the relationship between the risks and rewards of extrajudicial speech by Supreme Court justices. Some common forms of extrajudicial speech may be categorised as low risk and low reward. Educational and autobiographical speech, for instance, pose little threat to the courts, and their contributions to public discourse or advancing the interests of the judiciary are modest. Less common is high-risk, low-reward extrajudicial speech – speech that is widely condemned as improper and offers little benefit to the public, courts, or judge. This category would include commentary on contentious political topics and criticism of fellow justices. The normative implications for low-reward speech are relatively straightforward: justices would do well to steer clear of high-risk, low-reward speech; they should engage educational and autobiographical speech if moved to do so, but steering clear of this form of extrajudicial speech is also an option with little harm to the judiciary or public.

Harder questions arise when we turn to extrajudicial speech with more substantial potential benefits. When the rewards are higher, the lure of extrajudicial speech is stronger; a justice may even feel a responsibility to speak out. The challenge is that speech with higher rewards also tends to come with higher costs. In many cases the two are connected: the rewards derive from the risks.

Consider, for example, speech defending the judiciary. Standing up for the integrity of the courts and the value of judicial independence is encouraged by judicial ethical

[61] P Gailey, 'Douglas Branded a Violator of Ethics in TVA Attack', *Atlanta Constitution* (23 May 1969).

[62] S Taylor Jr, 'Marshall Puts Reagan at "Bottom" Among Presidents on Civil Rights', *New York Times* (New York, 9 September 1987) 1; S Taylor Jr, 'Complacency and the Constitution', *New York Times* (New York, 14 September 1987) 18.

guidelines and generally doesn't raise substantial questions of judicial propriety. The judiciary benefits from prominent public reminders of these principles, and urging these principles poses minimal risks for the justice or the Court. This speech becomes more controversial, however, when a justice's defence of the Court includes – or is seen as implying – a critique of individuals or groups who the justice believes are unfairly attacking the Court or undermining its independence. Now the concern arises that the justice is stepping too far from their role as an impartial adjudicator of legal disputes. The justice is walking the fine line between defending institutional prerogatives and becoming an advocate in a policy dispute. The justices walk this line when they attack the press for what they see as unfair or misleading coverage of the Court.[63] Chief Justice Hughes walked this line when he rebutted Roosevelt's case for Court-packing. Chief Justice Roberts did the same when he spoke out against Trump's criticism of the courts, as did Justice Alito in his wide-ranging counter-offensive against recent criticism of him and the Court.

More directed and thus more controversial efforts to defend the judiciary can be uniquely powerful. A justice who wants to defend the Court can offer familiar platitudes about the importance of judicial independence; they may offer some historical anecdotes to illustrate the point. But if they want to raise the possibility of getting the public's attention, if they want to convey the urgency the feel about this particular issue, they might offer a defence that takes a more combative posture. The press pays attention, politicians respond, commentators comment, and the American people are far more likely to hear the justice's words. The potential risks produce the potential rewards.

We can see similar dynamics at play with other categories of potentially high-reward speech. Justices have a long history of giving speeches and writing articles and books that describe their views on the law. This form of extrajudicial speech can serve to advance important ideas about the role of the courts and the challenges of legal interpretation. What controversy this speech produces is generally based on the substance of the views expressed, not the propriety or otherwise of a justice speaking out on this topic. But the instances of jurisprudential speech that do the most to spark and shape public debate are when the justices framed their contributions as criticism – of particular rulings, of other justices, or of the general direction of the Court. Since justices are not supposed to offer substantive comments on the Court's decisions, nor are they supposed to criticise fellow justices, these kinds of comments ring out like an alarm bell.

Risky extrajudicial speech brings headlines. Regardless of the merits of the comments themselves, they are news events simply because the justice chose to push against the norms of propriety in speaking out in certain ways. It is the risk of transgression that draws attention to extrajudicial speech, that tells the audience that

[63] See eg 'Address by William J. Brennan' (1979) 32 *Rutgers Law Review* 173, 175; 'Scalia: Abortion cases are "easy"', *Politico* (5 October 2012) www.politico.com/story/2012/10/scalia-says-abortion-gay-rights-are-easy-cases-082060; M Ramsey, 'Justice Amy Coney Barrett argues US Supreme Court isn't "a bunch of partisan hacks"', *Louisville Courier Journal* (12 September 2021) https://www.courier-journal.com/story/news/politics/mitch-mcconnell/2021/09/12/justice-amy-coney-barrett-supreme-court-decisions-arent-political/8310849002/.

what the judge is saying is worth listening to, that it contains special insights, inside information – that the speaker believes the importance of the information justifies the risks.

VI. POLARISED POLITICS, CELEBRITY JUSTICES AND THE FUTURE OF EXTRAJUDICIAL SPEECH

Just over a decade ago, in assessing the trend toward more frequent 'public intellectual activity' by Supreme Court justices, Richard Posner concluded that the trend was bad for the Court but ultimately inconsequential: bad because such activities tended to undermine the dignity of the office; inconsequential because 'there's very little dignity in public life these days' and because the legitimacy of the Court was secure.[64] Judge Posner's assessment about the level of dignity in public life may still hold true, but his dismissal of concerns with the Court's legitimacy does not. Political maneuvering over appointments to the Court, divisive and unpopular rulings, and exposures of the ethically questionable behaviour of several justices have undermined public confidence in the Court. The legitimacy of the institution and its rulings has become a major issue of public concern.

In response to the fraught political environment surrounding the Court, its members have not followed Posner's recommendation of dignified silence. If anything, they've responded by speaking out more often. Justice Kagan charged the conservative majority with transforming the Court from an institution of law to one of politics. Justice Sotomayor discussed her personal frustrations with the direction of the Court. Justices Alito and Thomas lashed out against the Court's critics, and even the normally reticent Chief Justice joined in some of these efforts. Justice Alito offered blunt rebuttals against accusations of judicial impropriety. Justice Thomas has lamented the loss of trust among the justices following the leak of the *Dobbs* opinion. Justices Jackson and Gorsuch recently completed publicity tours promoting their new books, and we are now awaiting the release of books by Justices Kavanaugh and Barrett. In the not too distant past it was something of a novelty for a justice's off-the-bench statements to become news stories. Today it's a regular occurrence.

These two trends – the heated politics surrounding the Court and the ever-growing willingness of the justices to engage in extrajudicial speech – are producing a new landscape of risks and rewards relating to the justices' extrajudicial speech, in which the risks are becoming more pronounced as the rewards diminish.

Today, more than at any other point in the Court's modern era, a justice who ventures from the bench to offer substantive, possibly controversial, remarks about issues of public concern will encounter more criticism than praise. In the current climate of polarisation and partisan tribalism, justices are readily sorted into two camps, conservatives and liberals, and whatever they say will be filtered through partisan and ideological lenses. Much extrajudicial speech lately seems designed to energise their fan base, with the predictable and perhaps intended effect of amplifying

[64] RA Posner, 'The Supreme Court and Celebrity Culture' (2013) 88 *Chicago-Kent Law Review* 303, 305.

the polarisation of attitudes toward the Court. But even when their comments are intended to defend the Court, to locate common ground among the justices – when, for example, Justice Barrett insists that the justices are not 'partisan hacks', or when Justice Breyer urges that the Court not be considered just another political institution, or when Chief Justice Roberts defends the Court against charges that its rulings are illegitimate – the reception is similarly divisive. A smattering of applause for defending the integrity of the Court is drowned out by a cascade of criticism of the justices' naïveté and disingenuousness.[65]

As extrajudicial speech becomes more commonplace, and the norm of judicial reticence is further eroded, the distinctive value of extrajudicial speech diminishes. The value of extrajudicial speech has been the unique insights that judges offer and the potential for extrajudicial speech to spark and contribute to a public discussion about the law. That value was premised in large part on the novelty of extrajudicial speech. Because it was assumed that a justice who engaged in extrajudicial speech was doing something unusual, perhaps even transgressive, their words were amplified and given greater significance. It was the existence of the ideal of the judge as separated from society, as reclusive, as a monk operating in a monastery of the law, that made the occasional entry of the judge into public discourse powerful.

Today, memoirs, interviews, speeches, and statements that signal a justice's allegiance with outside constituencies have become commonplace. Justices still get a good deal of press coverage for their extrajudicial statements, although today this likely has less to do with the rarity of extrajudicial statements and more to do with the heightened public interest in the Court. There is nothing exceptional today about a justice speaking out about their life, about the Court, about legal issues, even about matters of general concern. What notice these statements receive is attributable more to the constant swirl of controversy surrounding the Court than to the transgressive nature of extrajudicial statements.

Although today, more than ever, a posture of dignified silence may be the best way to protect the institutional interests of the Court, the justices continue to write and speak. They do so because their celebrity status ensures a public eager to buy their books and watch them on late-night television shows; because they have crowds of admirers who are ready to fill auditoriums and ballrooms to see them; because they feel unfairly criticised for their rulings and their off-the-bench activities and they want to defend themselves. The lure of extrajudicial speech as a way to advance the individual interests of the judge is more powerful than ever. Less clear is its continued value for advancing the institutional interests of the Court.

[65] See eg D Lithwick, 'Amy Coney Barrett Should Just Judge Without Bias Before Writing a Book on Judging Without Bias', *Slate* (20 April 2021) https://slate.com/news-and-politics/2021/04/amy-coney-barrett-book-deal.html; LM Litman, 'Hey Stephen' (2022) 120 *Michigan Law Review* 1109.

4

Extrajudicial Discourse and Legal Change

BRICE DICKSON

I. INTRODUCTION

IN ALL LEGAL systems the main function of judges is to decide disputes in accordance with the law of the legal system in question. For various reasons they may be encouraged, or inclined, to reduce the number of decisions they have to make by nudging litigating parties to reach a settlement based on their own negotiations or having received assistance from a conciliator, mediator or arbitrator. In those situations the judges are helping people to solve their differences, but they are not themselves, strictly speaking, interpreting or applying the law. Any change to the position of the parties resulting from the resolution of their dispute is not, therefore, a legal change brought about by the judge. Likewise, in those instances when judges *do* decide disputes by issuing some sort of judgment, they may simply be applying the existing law and not in any way changing it – except in so far as they may change the reach of the law by extending it to a context where it was not previously thought to apply. It is only in rare cases, even in common law legal systems, that a judge's decision in a dispute will actually alter the substance of the law in the way that the commencement of a new piece of legislation will do.

But judges also have occasional opportunities to change the law through their extrajudicial work. Indeed, the opportunities may be more frequent in that sphere because, outside of the courts, judges are not trammelled in their thinking by the pressures exerted by having to establish facts and consider the specific arguments put by the parties. In their extrajudicial work judges can still command respect and find an audience, yet can be freer in their thinking and more imaginative in their problem-solving. This chapter explores the extrajudicial role of judges as agents of change by focusing on three species of that role: their work as writers of textbooks for practitioners; their work as writers of courses of lectures; and their work as chairs of official commissions and inquiries.

II. EXTRAJUDICIAL WRITING FOR LEGAL PRACTITIONERS

Nearly all judges have spent some time practising law, usually as a barrister.[1] Occasionally an enthusiastic practitioner, usually a successful one, will decide to write a guide on how to practise the field of law in which they have become a specialist, and in due course their book may become rather influential in the field in question. The practitioner may in turn be offered a place on the bench, at which point they may or may not continue to be involved in producing further editions of their practitioners' guide. Over the years there have been many instances of distinguished judges being able to look back on their publishing career with a distinct sense of pride that they have affected the course of a legal field's evolution. Mallory and Tyrrell say that 'education for those practising or studying towards a career in law, is perhaps the most common and least contentious form of extrajudicial communication'.[2] It certainly serves a valid purpose and is 'proper' to the extent that it is the expression of a view rather than the assertion of a truth.

There are numerous examples of practitioners' manuals written by people who later became judges but continued their involvement with the publication. They include two major books on arbitration. *Foskett on Arbitration*, first published in 1980 and now in its 10th edition (2024) was the brainchild of Sir David Foskett, a High Court judge from 2007 to 2019. Michael Mustill, who served as a High Court judge from 1978 to 1985, a Lord Justice of Appeal from 1985 to 1992 and a Lord of Appeal in Ordinary from 1992 to 1997, was the co-author, alongside Stewart Boyd QC, of *Mustill and Boyd on Arbitration*, first published in 1982 and credited with earning Mustill election as a Fellow of the British Academy.[3] A third edition appeared in 2024. Both books are regularly cited in legal disputes arising from arbitrations and no-one seems ever to have had any reservation about the propriety of doing so.

Other judges have written expository textbooks for use not just by practitioners but also by students.[4] Robert Goff (another commercial judge who was elected a Fellow of the British Academy) started his working life as a Fellow in Law at Lincoln College, Oxford, between 1951 and 1955. During that period he developed an interest in what was then called the law of quasi-contract and when he moved to the commercial bar in 1955 he teamed up with Gareth Jones, a Fellow at Trinity College, Cambridge to write a book on the topic.[5] After many years of collaboration they produced *The Law of Restitution* in 1966. Goff was appointed to the High Court

[1] There are exceptions to this rule, such as when academics are appointed to a constitutional court even though they have no previous experience of adjudicating litigation.

[2] C Mallory and H Tyrrell, 'The Extrajudicial Voice' (2024) 44 *Legal Studies* 1, 10.

[3] For more on Lord Mustill see this account on the website of the Commercial Court of England and Wales: www.commercialcourt.london/mj-mustill#:~:text=Michael%20Mustill,%20exhibiting%20characteristic%20good%20humour. This observes, wryly, that 'the book's intellectual calibre helped contribute to the modern myth that arbitration is an area of substantive law in its own right, rather than a particular means of resolving substantive disputes'.

[4] See too Chapter 11: D Knight, 'Judicial Scholarship (in a Small-ish Democracy): Hallmark, Hobby and/or Hazard?'.

[5] Apparently an earlier attempt to collaborate with Ronald Maudsley ran into the sands: see J Beatson, 'Lord Goff' in R McCabe et al, *Biographical Memoirs of Fellows of the British Academy, XVIII* (British Academy, 2019) 241–73 www.thebritishacademy.ac.uk/documents/925/Memoirs_18-12-Goff.pdf, 251–56.

in 1975, to the Court of Appeal in 1982 and to the House of Lords in 1986, serving as the senior Lord of Appeal from 1996 to 1998, when he retired. He continued his involvement in the second and third editions of the book in 1978 and 1986, but not in the fourth in 1993, by which time his work as a Lord of Appeal and other extra-judicial activities were too onerous to allow him to continue as an editor.[6] Another distinguished judge, Jack Beatson, penned a long tribute to Lord Goff for the British Academy.[7] He mentions that Lord Goff was 'pivotal in the authoritative acceptance by the House of Lords in *Lipkin Gorman v Karpnale Ltd* of restitution as an independent branch of law founded on the principle of unjust enrichment'.[8] There can be little doubt that Robert Goff's championing of the principle of unjust enrichment is one of the clearest instances of a judicial figure bringing about legal change through their extrajudicial research and writing, whether before or after becoming a judge.

Robert Megarry obtained a third-class degree in law from Cambridge in the early 1930s but qualified as a solicitor and then as a barrister before being appointed a Fellow in Law at Trinity College, Cambridge in 1945 and a Reader at that University in 1967. He had a strong academic side to him, serving as an assistant editor of the *Law Quarterly Review* from 1944 to 1967 and as President of the Society of Public Teachers of Law (now the Society of Legal Scholars) for the academic year 1965–66. He, too, became a Fellow of the British Academy, in 1970. He was appointed a High Court judge in 1967 and remained in that role until his retirement in 1985, living on until 2006. In the extrajudicial arena Sir Robert is best known for *The Law of Real Property*, which he co-authored with William Wade in 1957; a 10th edition was published in 2024, edited by Martin Dixon, Janet Bignell and Nick Hopkins. Between 1939 and 1988 Megarry also published 11 editions of a handbook to the Rent Acts. For good measure he was an editor of *Snell's Equity* for the 23rd to the 27th editions, published between 1947 and 1973. Even more so than in the case of Robert Goff, Robert Megarry can be credited with having had a seminal influence on a host of legal questions, on which his books were cited as reliable authorities. That does not necessarily mean that he *changed* the law, but he certainly chaperoned its development.

These few examples of judges who wrote primarily for practitioners (or advanced students) illustrate how committed some judges have been to their educative role. Their books will not just have been pored over by avid readers: the views expressed in them will have been quoted to judges in countless cases as authoritative statements of the current law. Judges' reliance on such books is naturally all the greater if the subject-matter is a novel or niche one, as is the case with the books on arbitration and unjust enrichment already mentioned. Other examples (out of many) include Sir Thomas Scrutton's book on *Charterparties and Bills of Lading*, first published in 1886, edited by Scrutton up to the 11th edition in 1923 and now in its 25th edition;[9]

[6] ibid 259.

[7] Beatson, 'Lord Goff' (above n 5).

[8] ibid 1. *Lipkin Gorman v Karpnale Ltd* [1991] 2 AC 548. Today the book is in its 10th edition but with a different title: C Mitchell, P Mitchell and S Watterson (eds), *Goff and Jones on Unjust Enrichment*, 10th edn (London, Sweet & Maxwell, 2022).

[9] D Foxton, H Bennett, S Berry and C Smith (eds), *Charterparties and Bills of Lading*, 25th edn (London, Sweet and Maxwell, 2024). Scrutton was a High Court judge from 1910 to 1916 and a Lord Justice of Appeal from 1916 to 1934.

Sir Mackenzie Chalmers' book on *Bills of Exchange and Cheques*, now published as *Chalmers and Guest on Bills of Exchange and Cheques* and in its 19th edition;[10] and *Law of Guarantees* by Geraldine Andrews and Richard Millett, first published in 1993 and currently in its 7th edition.[11] Perhaps the best known instance of a recent judge maintaining their involvement in a leading legal textbook even while serving as a judge is that of Brenda Hale, who retained principal authorship of her book on *Mental Health Law* from its first edition in 1975 to its sixth edition, the most recent, in 2017.[12]

It is important not to confuse specialist practitioners' books with more generalist works. The multi-volume encyclopaedia, *Halsbury's Laws of England*, now in its fifth edition, has traditionally had an 'editor-in-chief' who is a former Lord Chancellor. While this undoubtedly adds lustre and prestige to the publication, it does not mean that these former judges play a 'hands-on' role in the editing process. They rather advise at a higher level. The five editors-in-chief to date have been the Earl of Halsbury, Lord Hailsham (senior), Viscount Simonds, Lord Hailsham (junior) and, since 1998, Lord Mackay.

III. EXTRAJUDICIAL COURSES OF LECTURES

Another chapter in this book is looking at the extrajudicial work which judges carry out when delivering public lectures.[13] Here I want to focus not on one-off lectures but on series of lectures, in particular the Hamlyn series. Before doing so I should note that one of the greatest repositories of extrajudicial writings on a particular field of law is the Collected Courses of the Hague Academy of International Law. These courses are replete with insights into the achievements and defects of public and private international law and with recommendations for change. Few UK judges have delivered such courses in recent years, but in the 101-year history of the courses UK judicial contributions have been far from insignificant.[14] Many lectures were given by international law scholars or practitioners who in later life served as judges on international courts: Arnold McNair and Hersch Lauterpacht are but two of the prominent names. Other British 'judicial' lecturers at The Hague include Sir Gerald Fitzmaurice, who lectured in 1973 at the end of his 13-year stint as a judge at the International Court of Justice and just before beginning his six-year period as a judge at the European Court of Human Rights, Sir Humphrey Waldock, Dame Rosalyn

[10] S Gleeson (ed), *Chalmers and Guest on Bills of Exchange and Cheques* (London, Sweet & Maxwell, 2024). Sir Mackenzie Chalmers served as a county court judge as well as the Acting Chief Justice of Gibraltar before retiring from the bench and becoming a draftsman; he is most famous for drafting the Bills of Exchange Act 1882, the Sale of Goods Act 1893 and the Marine Insurance Act 1906.

[11] G Andrews and R Millett (eds), *Law of Guarantees*, 7th edn (London, Sweet & Maxwell, 2015). An 8th edition is due in 2026. Geraldine Andrews was appointed a High Court judge in 2013 and a Lady Justice of Appeal in 2020.

[12] B Hale, *Mental Health Law*, 6th edn, (London, Sweet & Maxwell 2017). The sixth edition was prepared with the help of P Gorman, R Barrett and J Jones. Lady Hale was a senior judge from 1994 to 2020.

[13] See Chapter 10: R Cahill-O'Callaghan, 'The Individual Voice in a Collective Court: Insights from Judicial Lectures'.

[14] For a list of the courses that have been given since 1923 (all 439 volumes to date) see https://referenceworks.brillonline.com/browse/the-hague-academy-collected-courses?lang=en.

Higgins and Lord Lawrence Collins, who lectured in 2007 just after being promoted from the role of High Court judge to that of Lord Justice of Appeal and who later served in both the House of Lords and the Supreme Court from 2009 to 2011.[15]

Miss Emma Hamlyn, the daughter of a solicitor in Devon, died in 1941 and in her will left money 'for the furtherance by lectures or otherwise among the common people of the United Kingdom of the knowledge of the comparative jurisprudence and the ethnology of the chief European countries, including the United Kingdom'. It took some time to put her wishes into effect, with the first lectures occurring in 1949. Of the 77 series of lectures which have been given since then (up to and including the series for 2025), 23 have been given by judges.[16] Of those judges, 17 were still serving at the time; the other six were retired. Fifteen of the 23 were or had been judges in the UK, five had served in Commonwealth countries (Australia, Canada, New Zealand or South Africa), one in both the UK and New Zealand, one in the European Court of Justice in Luxembourg, and one in both the UK and the ECJ. Two further lecturers were not judges at the time but became so later.[17]

Taken collectively, the Hamlyn lectures delivered by judges are an outstanding example of the value of extrajudicial work. As the lecturer is asked to deliver a series of three, or sometimes four, lectures around a theme of their choosing, they provide an excellent opportunity not just to 'fly a few kites' but to construct a broader argument relating to the theme in question. There is additional pressure on the lecturers because they know that what they say will then need to be written up and footnoted for publication as a book.[18] While it is often difficult to draw a direct link between ideas discussed in the lectures and subsequent changes to legislation or case law, it is undeniable that the lectures have almost invariably ruffled some feathers and gently pushed the envelope on legal reform. From the very start the judicial lecturers have displayed an outspokenness which even today can seem rather daring.

The first three sets of Hamlyn lectures authored by judges were by Sir Alfred Denning (*Freedom under the Law*), Sir Patrick Devlin (*Trial by Jury*) and Lord MacDermott (*Protection from Power under English Law*). They exhibited four features in common: a focus on the history of their subject-matter; an acknowledgement that in the past judges have sometimes been unduly restrained or taken wrong turnings; an assumption (shared by Emma Hamlyn) that English law is the best in the world; and a commitment to the concepts of freedom and liberty. In relation to the last feature, for example, Lord Denning asserted that:

> Our procedure for securing our personal freedom is efficient, our procedure for preventing the abuse of power is not. Just as the pick and shovel is no longer suitable for the winning of coal, so also the procedure of mandamus, certiorari, and actions on the case are not

[15] For a *Festschrift* in Lord Collins' honour, see J Harris and C McLachlan (eds), *Essays in International Litigation for Lord Collins* (Oxford, Oxford University Press, 2022).

[16] Videos of some of the most recent lectures are available at https://law.exeter.ac.uk/about/thehamlyntrust/lectures/.

[17] Robert Megarry gave the 1962 lectures and became a High Court judge in 1965; Andrew Burrows gave the 2017 lectures, having served as Deputy High Court judge since 2007, but he became a full-time judge only when appointed to the Supreme Court in 2020.

[18] These were initially published by Stevens & Sons and then by Sweet & Maxwell from 1996, but since 2005 the task has fallen to Cambridge University Press.

> suitable for the winning of freedom in the new age. They must be replaced by new and up to date machinery, by declarations, injunctions and actions for negligence ... This is not a task for Parliament ... The courts must do this. Of all the great tasks that lie ahead this is the greatest.[19]

In the 1960s the judicial lecturers were Lord Kilbrandon (a Scot), Oliver Schreiner (a South African) and Bora Laskin (a Canadian). Lord Kilbrandon (in *Other People's Law*) canvassed the idea of no-fault liability for accidents, suggesting that an insurance system be set up so that victims of accidents could recover compensation whether or not fault for the injury could be attributed to anyone. He noted too that while most prosecutions in England were still brought by the police, in Scotland, France and Germany most prosecutions were in the hands of salaried state officials.[20] In *The Contribution of English Law to South African Law; and the Rule of Law in South Africa* Judge Schreiner, regrettably, missed his opportunity to argue for legal change in South Africa; instead he deployed some mental gymnastics to try to demonstrate that apartheid was not a breach of the rule of law because that was not a legal rule but only a statement of principle.[21] For his part, Bora Laskin (*The British Tradition in Canadian Law*) also avoided revealing his personal views on controversial legal issues. This was a pity because, as a founding member of the Canadian Civil Liberties Association, Laskin was always known for his liberalism. He had also experienced considerable antisemitism when he first set out on his legal career.

In *The English Judge* (1970), the judge-cum-novelist, Henry Cecil justified solicitors not being appointed to the High Court on the ground that there were too many of them to ensure that someone with dubious integrity would not be selected.[22] On the other hand, he innovatively suggested that judges ought not to sentence offenders for serious crimes: he thought this should be done by a special (presumably non-judicial) panel.[23]

Perhaps the most reformist Hamlyn lectures were those delivered by Sir Leslie Scarman in 1974 (*English Law – The New Dimension*). Exercising amazing foresight, he considered whether the common law would be able to cope with five upcoming challenges, namely, the international challenge to secure human rights and the Common Market; the social challenge regarding family life and social security; the challenge of the environment; the industrial challenge; and the regional challenge. He maintained that it would, provided that 'a new dimension' were added to the common law. This needed to consist of a new constitutional settlement (including devolution), one which placed some restrictions on the powers of Parliament (eg requiring a two-thirds majority for certain decisions), enshrined a Bill of Rights, and created a Supreme Court with power to declare legislation unconstitutional. It would also require more codification of laws, reform of administrative law, additional interpretative and remedial powers for judges and a more systematic approach to law reform

[19] A Denning, *Freedom under the Law* (London, Stevens & Sons Ltd, 1949) 126.

[20] Lord Kilbrandon, *Other People's Law* (London, Stevens & Sons Ltd, 1966) 49–56 and 69–72.

[21] OD Schreiner, *The Contribution of English Law to South African Law; and the Rule of Law in South Africa* (London, Stevens & Sons Ltd, 1967) 77.

[22] H Cecil, *The English Judge* (London, Stevens & Sons Ltd, 1970) 13–15.

[23] ibid 82.

through Law Commissions. Overall, the lectures are a paradigm of radicalism mixed with respect for tradition, a wonderful mixture of idealism and pragmatism. They were, in many ways, prophetic. By way of contrast, in 1977 Lord Mackenzie-Stuart, the first UK judge on the European Court of Justice, was careful not to be too speculative in *The European Communities and the Rule of Law*. He warned against the (then) European Court of Justice (ECJ) going beyond its judicial function[24] and, practising what he preached, he then refused to suggest how much further the European integration process should go, for fear, as he put it, of 'baptising outside my parish'.[25]

In 1983 Lord Hailsham became the first Lord Chancellor to take up the Hamlyn baton (*Hamlyn Revisited: The British Legal System Today*). In what was really a reverse approach to that of Lord Scarman, he explained how the legal system had, to its credit, responded well to six major challenges during the previous 40 years. These included supra-national institutions, the growth in the power of central government (what he called 'the elective dictatorship') and the increase in crime and delays in dealing with it.[26] He maintained that the British legal system was accommodating these challenges satisfactorily, but he warned against complacency. He could not resist concluding, somewhat pompously perhaps, that 'what this nation needs is ballast and cement, a renewed sense of unity and purpose, a revived recognition of objective moral principle and respect for authority'.[27]

In his 1986 lectures, *The Fabric of English Civil Justice*, Sir Jack Jacob lauded the principles of orality, publicity, finality and specialisation, but he admitted that the adversarial system does lead to delays and increased costs. He therefore emphasised the need for what today is termed judicial case management and he proposed both a Ministry of Justice and a Council on Civil Justice, both of which did eventually emerge.

Sir Harry Woolf's lectures, three years later (*Protection of the Public – A New Challenge*), focused on administrative law, building on what Lord Denning had said in 1949. His reasoning is not always convincing when he defends some of the procedural restrictions on judicial review applications, nor when he sides with Lord Diplock after the latter famously drew a fairly rigid line between public law and private law in *O'Reilly v Mackman*.[28] But he rightly regretted that courts and tribunals were not able in most instances to award compensation to people who were treated unjustly by public bodies.[29] He also advocated training for judges on how to bring domestic law into line with the European Convention on Human Rights (ECHR) – this almost 10 years before the Human Rights Act 1998 was enacted.[30]

[24] Lord Mackenzie Stuart, *The European Communities and the Rule of Law* (London, Stevens & Sons Ltd, 1977) 25, 34, 42, 70 and 81.

[25] ibid 115.

[26] The others were the development of education and the growth of the welfare state, the need to maintain the independence and integrity of the judiciary, and the decline in the importance of contract coupled with the rise in the importance of status (looking in turn at tenants, employees and taxpayers).

[27] Lord Hailsham, *Hamlyn Revisited: The British Legal System Today* (London, Stevens & Sons Ltd, 1983) 85.

[28] *O'Reilly v Mackman* [1983] 2 AC 237.

[29] H Woolf, *Protection of the Public – A New Challenge* (London, Stevens & Sons Ltd, 1989) 56–62.

[30] ibid 121.

There were no fewer than five judicial lecturers during the 1990s. In 1991 the then UK judge at the ECJ, Gordon Slynn, gave a very positive portrayal of European Community law (in *Introducing a European Legal Order*) but observed that reforms would be necessary when the size of the Community expanded beyond what was then just 19 Member States.[31] In 1993 Lord Mackay became the second Lord Chancellor to deliver the lectures, entitled *The Administration of Justice*. Controversially, like Cecil in 1970, he staunchly defended the current system for appointing judges, but, like several of his other predecessors, he also strongly supported the principle of judicial independence, pointing out that in 1987 he had made it known that judges no longer needed to abide by the so-called Kilmuir Rules of 1955, which required the Lord Chancellor's consent before a judge intervened in public discussion of some issue.[32] Lord Mackay was also instrumental in moving the Courts Service away from the control of the Lord Chancellor's Office, turning it instead into an independent Executive Agency – an example, perhaps, of how a judge who is also a member of government can more easily bring about change. Today, of course, such a role for a judge would not sit at all well with the ECHR.[33]

Dame Brenda Hale became the first female judge to deliver the Hamlyn lectures in 1995 (*From the Tube to the Coffin: Choice and Regulation in Private Life*). It was no surprise that she chose as her theme the regulation of family and private life, since she was an academic expert in those fields and, as a Law Commissioner, had been one of the progenitors of both the Children Act 1989 and of what ultimately became the Family Law Act 1996. She includes a section on gay relationships and intimates that in her view there is no good reason why same-sex couples should not be able to marry.[34] We now know from her autobiography that Lady Hale's own daughter is in a same-sex relationship,[35] a fact that may well have influenced her when she sat in the case of *Bellinger v Bellinger* on the legal definition of a 'spouse'.[36]

Lord Cooke's 1996 lectures, *Turning Points of the Common Law*, explored how leading cases in four different legal fields had subsequently fared both in the UK and in other Commonwealth countries, especially his native New Zealand.[37] In 1998 Sir Stephen Sedley was more ambitious. This being the 50th anniversary of the series, he agreed to the Trustees' suggestion that he re-visit Lord Denning's theme under the title *Freedom, Law and Justice* (even though Sir Harry Woolf had also chosen to build on Lord Denning's lectures less than a decade earlier).[38] Sedley very much stressed the importance of 'a positive ideal' of access to rights and to equality and he tried to demonstrate that 'the true concern' of the common law has been,

[31] G Slynn, *Introducing a European Legal Order* (London, Stevens & Sons Ltd, 1991) 171–72.

[32] Lord Mackay, *The Administration of Justice* (London, Stevens & Sons Ltd, 1993) 25–26.

[33] Article 6 of the ECHR protects the right to a fair trial. When judging what is fair the European Court of Human Rights looks askance at any national court which is staffed by judges who simultaneously play a legislative or executive role within the state.

[34] B Hale, *From the Tube to the Coffin: Choice and Regulation in Private Life* (London, Stevens & Sons Ltd, 1995) 84–85.

[35] B Hale, *Spider Woman – A Life* (London, Bodley Head, 2021) 170.

[36] *Bellinger v Bellinger* [2003] UKHL 21; [2003] 2 AC 467.

[37] Lord Cooke, *Turning Points of the Common Law* (London, Sweet & Maxwell, 1997).

[38] Lord Justice Sedley, *Freedom, Law and Justice* (London, Sweet & Maxwell, 1999).

and always should be, the control of abuse of power, whether exercised privately or publicly.

The 2003 lectures (*Judicial Activism: Authority, Principle and Policy in the Judicial Method*) were delivered by Michael Kirby,[39] who by then had been a member of Australia's highest court for seven years. He himself had already acquired a reputation for judicial activism. He argued that a judge was not being partial just by supporting fundamental rights and he stressed that international law could be a productive source for consistent judicial decision-making where there is a gap to be filled in the common law or an ambiguity in legislation. Kirby ended his lectures by emphasising that at times judges must take policy considerations into account, as when they are asked to extend the duty of care concept to new 'neighbourhood' situations.

After a six-year gap Lord Bingham stepped up to the plate in 2009 with *Widening Horizons: The Influence of Comparative Law and International Law on Domestic Law*.[40] Like Kirby, he was of the clear view that it was a good thing for national judges to interact with international law, yet he made a veiled criticism of his erstwhile colleague Lord Hoffmann, who in a recent lecture had suggested that national courts should be free to apply universal human rights principles at the national level as they thought fit.[41]

In 2013 Sir John Laws chose as his title *The Common Law Constitution*. He lauded the common law as a phenomenon which helps to unify the UK and he argued that it was strong enough to withstand threats from extremism of various kinds (including arbitrary governments) and from Europe (by which he meant the EU and the European Court of Human Rights). In a section headed 'The Constitutional Balance' (later expanded into a book)[42] he wrote:

> The sovereignty of Parliament itself only has life by means of the common law's methods … This meeting of Parliament and judges is the constitutional balance. It is at the core of my thesis … by force of the common law, efficacy is allowed but oppression is forbidden to the power of the state, and this is achieved by a benign *continuum* of developing law.[43]

Another titan of New Zealand's legal system, Dame Sian Elias, was the Hamlyn lecturer in 2016. Her theme, *Fairness in Criminal Justice: Golden Threads and Pragmatic Patches*, allowed her to examine whether procedural safeguards in criminal justice were 'being eroded in a way that undermines fundamental values in the legal order'.[44] In her first and second lectures she stresses that the procedural law of criminal justice protects those who are not popular, and that the presumption of innocence and the right to remain silent are crucial safeguards. In her third lecture she tells the cautionary tale of how the New Zealand Court of Appeal devised a

[39] M Kirby, *Judicial Activism: Authority, Principle and Policy in the Judicial Method* (London, Sweet & Maxwell, 2003).

[40] TH Bingham, *Widening Horizons: The Influence of Comparative Law and International Law on Domestic Law* (Cambridge, Cambridge University Press, 2010).

[41] L Hoffmann, 'The Universality of Human Rights' (2009) 125 *Law Quarterly Review* 416.

[42] J Laws, *The Constitutional Balance* (Oxford, Hart Publishing, 2021).

[43] J Laws, *The Common Law Constitution* (Cambridge, Cambridge University Press, 2014) 18.

[44] S Elias, *Fairness in Criminal Justice: Golden Threads and Pragmatic Patches* (Cambridge, Cambridge University Press, 2016) xvi.

scheme in the late 1980s (when Robin Cooke was its President) to speed up the delivery of justice, only to have it subsequently struck down by the Privy Council as being 'extra-legal'.[45]

Kate O'Regan, a Justice of the Constitutional Court of South Africa from 1994 to 2009, gave the Hamlyn lectures in 2022 under the title *Courts and the Body Politic*.[46] She examined the growth in, and opposition to, judicial constitutionalism, explored the boundaries between appropriate judicial power and appropriate executive power (especially during emergencies and in the context of corruption), and supported the claim that courts have a duty to protect human rights, this last issue being particularly germane at a time when elements within Britain's then Conservative government were calling for the country's withdrawal from the European Convention on Human Rights and the repeal of the Human Rights Act 1998.

The most recent of the Hamlyn lectures delivered by a judge are those in 2023 by Lord Thomas of Cwmgiedd, the Lord Chief Justice of England and Wales from 2013 to 2017 (*Laws for a Nation and Laws for Transnational Commerce. Where is the line drawn?*). While he sets out some of the challenges currently facing English commercial law (such as those presented by digital assets like crypto currencies and non-fungible tokens) he is careful not to suggest what legal changes should be made to accommodate those challenges. He does, however, credit judges who to date have allowed commercial law to develop in ways which have suited those who are actually involved in trade, and he acknowledges that in the nineteenth century judges such as Lord Blackburn used their knowledge of civil legal systems to enhance the effectiveness of English law.[47]

Summing up this section, we can see that the Hamlyn Lectures have presented an enviable platform for judges to express extrajudicial views about numerous aspects of the law. Mostly the judicial lecturers have stood back from the fray and allowed themselves the luxury of ruminating more broadly about what changes still need to be made to the law to keep it modern as well as just. They have (almost always) stressed how crucial is the rule of law and the role of judges in maintaining it. Naturally some lecturers have been more adventurous than others. Not all of their suggestions for reform have been heeded and those that have been have not always been traced back to the Hamlyn lecture in question. But, taken collectively, the series represents extrajudicial thinking and writing at its very best. When senior judges – and committed law reformers – such as Lord Scarman and Lady Hale take up their pen to write such series of lectures you can be sure that they will keep one eye firmly on the influence their words could have on future law-makers, whether elected or unelected. They usually cover their backs in that regard by making it clear that they are committed adherents to the rule of law and the separation of powers, but they understandably recognise that when they speak of the need for change their views will be given careful attention at the highest levels.

[45] ibid 155–56.

[46] K O'Regan, *Courts and the Body Politic* (Cambridge, Cambridge University Press, 2025).

[47] Lord Thomas, *Laws for a Nation and Laws for Transnational Commerce. Where is the line drawn?* (Cambridge, Cambridge University Press, 2025).

IV. EXTRAJUDICIAL CONTRIBUTIONS THROUGH INQUIRIES AND COMMISSIONS

While legal change may on occasions be linked *indirectly* to something written by a judge primarily for practitioners or for a more general readership, changes occurring after reports have been issued by commissions or inquiries chaired by judges can at times be *directly* attributed to those individuals. Judges, especially if retired, are commonly asked to chair inquiries into incidents that have led to a number of deaths or to possible miscarriages of justice.[48] It seems undeniable that governments like to appoint judges to chair inquiries, because relevant stakeholders can usually be relied upon not to query the credentials and objectivity of a judge.[49]

Judges are eminently qualified for such tasks because they are familiar with the niceties of taking evidence from people and with establishing facts on that basis. They are less qualified to undertake inquiries which are looking at major policy issues, where the conclusions and recommendations are expected to relate less to holding people to account for the past and more to setting out what policies should be adopted for the future. When judges are sitting in courts they understandably steer clear of interfering in the economic and social policy choices made by governments.[50] Notoriously, judicial review applications challenging such policy choices are limited to assessing how and why they were chosen; the merits of the various choices are not considered to be within the judges' domain, even if on some matters it is extremely difficult to distinguish clearly between issues of process and issues of substance.[51]

A. Royal Commissions

Until quite recently governments resorted to Royal Commissions in order to obtain a 'neutral' opinion on some troubling issue. Traditionally they comprise a body of people and a prominent chairperson. In the past 60 years there have been three Royal Commissions chaired by a serving or recently retired judge.

The first of these was the Royal Commission on Trade Unions and Employers' Associations, chaired by Lord Donovan from 1965 to 1968 during the time when he was a serving Lord of Appeal (1964–71).[52] Although the then Labour government was hoping for recommendations which would reduce trade union power,

[48] Eg Sir John May, shortly after retiring as a Lord Justice of Appeal, chaired an inquiry into the quashing of the 'Guildford Four' and 'Maguire Seven' convictions. His interim report was published on 12 July 1990 and his final report on 3 December 1992: *Report of the inquiry into convictions arising out of the bomb attacks in Guildford and Woolwich* (HC 296).

[49] See P O'Brien and B Yong, *Work in Judicial Retirement – A Policy Report* (June 2023) https://drive.google.com/file/d/1facLKhFKmi6MLiqI921P9lDIbs5tKONO/view, 14 and 29.

[50] See eg Lord Neuberger, 'Judges and Policy: A Delicate Balance' (Institute for Government, London, 18 June 2013) www.supremecourt.uk/speeches/lord-neuberger-at-the-institute-for-government-uk.

[51] Consider the split decisions of the Supreme Court in the social security cases of *R (on the application of SG) v Secretary of State for Work and Pensions* [2015] UKSC 16; [2015] 1 WLR 1449 and *R (on the application of DA) v Secretary of State for Work and Pensions* [2019] UKSC 21; [2019] 1 WLR 3289.

[52] *Report of the Royal Commission on Trade Unions and Employers' Associations 1965-1968* (Cmnd 3623, 1968).

the Commission suggested instead that changes should be made to the collective bargaining system and to the rules on dismissals. A controversial National Industrial Relations Court was established but was shortly afterwards abolished by the Trade Union and Labour Relations Act 1974, which put in place what are now called employment tribunals.

The Royal Commission on the Constitution was chaired initially by Lord Crowther (1968–72) until he died, and then by Lord Kilbrandon (1972–73), the latter having been a judge in Scotland from 1959 to 1971 and a Lord of Appeal from 1971 to 1975.[53] The Commission could not reach a unanimous agreement on whether there should be devolution of powers to Scotland and Wales but it was fully agreed that there should be no devolution within England. After issuing a White Paper on devolution in 1974,[54] the Labour government held referenda on the issue but the required majority was not reached in either region; it took a further 20 years for new referenda to be successful, leading to the Scotland Act 1998 and the Government of Wales Act 1998. Two of the Commission's recommendations *did* lead to constitutional changes: the number of MPs elected from Northern Ireland to Westminster was raised from 12 to 17[55] and committees in the House of Commons were reorganised (following a further review by a Select Committee on Procedure in 1978) so as to align them with the functions of government departments.

Thirdly, the Royal Commission on Civil Liability and Compensation for Personal Injury (1973–78) was chaired by Lord Pearson, who had been a judge in the High Court (1951–61), the Court of Appeal (1961–65) and the House of Lords (1965–74); one of the other 16 members of the Commission was a Scottish judge, Lord Cameron, who had earlier written an important report on civil unrest in Northern Ireland.[56] The main recommendation of the Pearson Commission was that a no-fault insurance scheme should be established for accidents at work and on the roads (a throwback to Lord Kilbrandon's 1966 Hamlyn lectures) and a strict liability scheme in the realm of consumer protection. The Labour government of the day, however, was not willing to implement the recommendations and nor were any of Mrs Thatcher's governments between 1979 and 1990.

B. Public Inquiries

Public inquiries can be statutory or non-statutory; the statutory ones will be established either by a distinct piece of legislation or under the Inquiries Act 2015, which

[53] *Royal Commission on the Constitution, Report: 1969-1973* (Cmnd 5460, 1973) Kilbrandon Report.

[54] *Democracy and Devolution: Proposals for Scotland and Wales* (Cmnd 5732, 1974).

[55] House of Commons (Redistribution of Seats) Act 1979; for the background to this legislation see G Walker and G Mulvenna, 'Northern Ireland Representation at Westminster: Constitutional Conundrums and Political Manoeuvres' (2015) 34 *Parliamentary History* 237. An 18th seat was later created by the Parliamentary Constituencies (Northern Ireland) Order 1995 (SI 2992).

[56] *Disturbances in Northern Ireland: Report of the commission under the chairmanship of Lord Cameron appointed by the Governor of Northern Ireland* (Cmd 532, 1969). Two of this report's recommendations led to the establishment of an improved system for dealing with complaints against the police in Northern Ireland and to a more independent process for appointing senior officials to local councils.

repealed and replaced the Tribunals of Inquiry (Evidence) Act 1921. Again, serving or retired judges are frequently appointed to chair such inquiries.

Of the public inquiries chaired by judges which have been completed this century, perhaps six have been particularly prominent (the first two were conducted under the 1921 Act, the last four under the 2015 Act): the inquiry into the murders committed by Harold Shipman (2000–05) by Dame Janet Smith (a High Court judge from 1992 and a Lady Justice of Appeal from 2002 to 2011); the inquiry into the events on 'Bloody Sunday' in Derry/Londonderry on 30 January 1972 (1998–2010) by Lord Saville (a High Court judge from 1985 and a serving Lord of Appeal/ Justice of the Supreme Court while conducting the inquiry);[57] the inquiry into the culture, practices and ethics of the press (2011–12) by Sir Brian Leveson (a High Court judge from 2002 and a Lord Justice of Appeal while conducting the inquiry); the inquiry into the deaths in the Manchester Arena bomb attack of 2017 (2019–23) by Sir John Saunders (a judge of the High Court from 2007 to 2016); the Infected Blood Inquiry (2017–24) by Sir Brian Langstaff (a High Court judge from 2005 to 2018); and the Grenfell Tower Inquiry (2017–24) by Sir Martin Moore-Bick (a High Court judge from 1995 and a Lord Justice of Appeal from 2005 to 2016). Since 2000 several other judge-led inquiries – less high-profile – have been completed.[58]

At the time of writing 17 public inquiries are in full swing, four of which are being led by a serving judge and a further eight by a retired judge. They include the heavily publicised inquiries into undercover policing by Sir John Mitting, the UK Covid-19 Inquiry by Baroness Hallett, the Post Office Horizon IT Inquiry by Sir Wyn Williams and the Lucy Letby inquiry by Lady Justice Thirlwall. It is too early to say whether any legal changes will result from the outcome of these inquiries, but the very fact that judges seem to be more trusted than ever to undertake such public service indicates the value which the government, and the public, place on this type of extrajudicial activity. Judges have skill sets, and a reputation, which make them ideal individuals to take on such very challenging tasks. It is not least their experience in listening to, collating and assessing large amounts of evidence which equips them for the role.

As to pinpointing specific legal changes which have been brought about by inquiries chaired by judges, we again have to exercise caution. While it is occasionally possible for the conclusions of an inquiry to be immediately fully accepted by the government, as occurred when Prime Minister David Cameron responded to Lord

[57] This was the second inquiry into those events, the first one, chaired by Lord Widgery, the then Lord Chief Justice of England and Wales, having been deemed to have been very poorly and partially conducted in the early months of 1972.

[58] These included Lord Penrose's two inquiries into the financial difficulties of the mutual life assurance company Equitable Life, 2001–04, and into contaminated blood in Scotland, 2008–15; Sir Brian Keith's inquiry into the murder in youth custody of Zahid Mubarek, 2004–06; Sir Edwin Jowitt's inquiry into the sectarian murder of Robert Hamill in Northern Ireland, 2004–10; Lord Ranald MacLean's two inquiries into the murder of Billy Wright in the Maze Prison, 2005–10, and into the occurrence of clostridium difficile infection at the Vale of Leven Hospital, 2009–14; Lord Gill's inquiry into the explosion at the ICL plastics factory in Glasgow on 11 May 2004, 2008–09; Sir William Gage's inquiry into the death of Baha Mousa in British Army custody in Iraq, 2008–11; Sir Anthony Campbell's inquiry into fingerprint evidence in a Scottish case, 2008–11; and Sir John O'Hara's inquiry into hyponatraemia-related deaths in hospital, 2004–18 (Sir John became a High Court judge in 2013).

Saville's report on the Bloody Sunday killings,[59] it is more usual for implementation of an inquiry's recommendations to be a drawn out process, thereby attenuating the direct link to the inquiry. Many other voices may have influenced the implementation process in the interim. That said, it is clear that the Shipman Inquiry, for example, led to changes to the rules on death certification, to the powers of the General Medical Council and to the record-keeping of doctors' prescription habits. There have also been changes made to the law as a consequence of recommendations made by judicially-led inquiries held under specific statutes. Thus, the Macpherson Report into the 1993 murder of Stephen Lawrence (where the Metropolitan Police were adjudged to be 'institutionally racist') led to the establishment of the Independent Police Complaints Commission and ultimately to new laws which allow for an acquitted person's retrial if fresh evidence of their apparent guilt comes to light.[60] Likewise, the Historical Institutional Abuse Inquiry conducted by Sir Anthony Hart in Northern Ireland between 2014 and 2016 led to the creation of a special compensation scheme for the victims of such abuse and to the appointment of a Commissioner for Survivors of Institutional Child Abuse.[61]

V. CONCLUSION

This chapter has aimed to show that there has been a distinct purpose and value in the extrajudicial activities of judges in three separate spheres – the writing of legal textbooks, the delivery of courses of public lectures, and the chairing of important inquiries. In each of them judges have been influential in 'moving the dial' of the law's development, even if it is sometimes difficult to point to specific legal changes which have been an obvious consequence of their extrajudicial work. The activities have nonetheless contributed substantially to respect for the rule of law and, in nearly every instance, to admiration of the judges' independence, objectivity, insightfulness and fairness.

[59] In apologising for the killings, Cameron said they were 'unjustified and unjustifiable': HC Deb 15 June 2010, vol 511, col 739. His words were later endorsed by the then head of the army, General Sir David Richards. The Ministry of Defence has subsequently paid out hundreds of thousands of pounds in settling civil claims brought by families of the victims on Bloody Sunday. See eg A Erwin, 'Almost £1m compensation awarded for Bloody Sunday victims', *Belfast Telegraph* (Belfast, 25 October 2018).

[60] The inquiry was held under the Police Act 1996. Sir William Macpherson was a High Court judge from 1983 to 1996; he conducted the Lawrence Inquiry between 1997 and 1999. The new laws were contained in the Criminal Justice Act 2003, Pt 10.

[61] The inquiry was held under the Inquiry into Historical Institutional Abuse Act (Northern Ireland) 2013. Sir Anthony Hart was a High Court judge in Northern Ireland from 2005 to 2012. The Redress Board and Commissioner were established under the Historical Institutional Abuse (Northern Ireland) Act 2019.

5

Extrajudicial Rhetoric and the International Judge

CONALL MALLORY*

I. INTRODUCTION

THE EXPANDING INFLUENCE of international institutions has seen a proliferation of in-roads into sovereign state autonomy.[1] The judges at the courts and tribunals which oversee this international system inhabit different worlds to their domestic counterparts. While ascension to international office may result in ostensibly greater authority, personal prestige and recognition, the positions they occupy are often more contested. When compared to their domestic counterparts, the international judge may endure more robust criticism and from a wider range of detractors. Slurs directed at them include that they are, inter alia, interventionist, activist, foreign, elitist, out of touch and unqualified. These criticisms are both directed personally, and at the regimes for which they act. The result is that international judges experience something of an inherent 'legitimacy deficit' when compared to their domestic counterparts.[2]

Existing scholarship then tells us that a core motivating factor behind extrajudicial communication by the international judge is in response to this deficit. International judges speak so as to enhance and sustain their legitimacy. Scholarship also tends to note how, rather than speaking directly to the public like domestic judges, international judges' principal audience is a series of key constituencies upon whose approval their existence is dependent.[3] These constit-

*My thanks to Hélène Tyrrell, Brice Dickson and Adam Ramshaw for their comments on early drafts of this chapter. Any errors are my own.

[1] RP Alford, 'The Proliferation of International Courts and Tribunals: International Adjudication in Ascendance' (2000) 94 *American Society of International Law* 160.

[2] A Føllesdal, 'The Legitimacy Deficits of the Human Rights Judiciary: Elements and Implications of a Normative Theory' (2013) 14 *Theoretical Inquiries in Law* 339. See also: J Gomes Garcia de Moraes and P Alvarado, 'Game Theory and the Legitimacy of International Adjudicative Bodies' (2019) 16(1) *Brazil Journal of International Law* 147, 157.

[3] T Squatrito, 'Judicial diplomacy: International Courts and Legitimation' (2021) 47(1) *Review of International Studies* 64; S Steininger, 'Creating loyalty: Communication Practices in the European and Inter-American Human Rights Regimes' (2022) 11(2) *Global Constitutionalism* 161.

uencies comprise the actors with the greatest sway over the reputation of the respective institution, its authority and legitimacy. We therefore have accounts of *why* international judges engage in extrajudicial communication and *who* they are speaking to. In this chapter, I add to this a reflection on *what* international judges say, and what this means for the role of the international judge. I use the practice of the President of the European Court of Human Rights (ECtHR) as a case study to demonstrate how judges at international courts will sometimes depart from the sanitised and measured tone of most extrajudicial oration, instead adopting a more political position, deploying rhetoric, in order to argue in favour of their institution.

This argument is established in four sections. In section II below, I start by unpacking how international organisations broadly, as well as international judges specifically, use communication to narrow the legitimacy deficit within which they exist. In section III, I outline how this communication is strategically directed at a series of constituencies whose approval is required for the international court to act effectively. In section IV, I position this practice in respect of the ECtHR and the role of the President to act as the system's chief diplomat. In section V, I demonstrate this performance in action by unpacking how the President of the ECtHR deploys traditional models of rhetoric – *pathos, ethos* and *logos* – to argue in favour of the ECtHR's legitimacy and authority when facing its key constituencies at the annual 'solemn hearing' to open the judicial year. To make this case, I use examples from the Presidential addresses given between 2001 and 2025 to demonstrate that extrajudicial communication from the international bench sees judges depart from their traditional cloak of legal interpreter and translator and become robust advocates for their institution.[4]

II. USING COMMUNICATION TO CLOSE INTERNATIONAL COURTS' LEGITIMACY DEFICIT

Institutions which have been created by states and empowered to fulfil specified roles within the international order are dependent on being perceived as legitimate to fulfil their mandates. Legitimacy, however, is a complex concept which covers several elements,[5] some of which are both contingent and evasive.[6] In the specific context of international courts and the international judiciary, legitimacy is often linked to the wielding of authority and the perception that the authority exercised is justified.[7] The higher the degree of legitimacy an international institution holds, the more likely it is that its rulings and judgments will be adhered to, even when they are unpopular.[8] The aspiration of an international court is to establish a degree of legitimately recognised authority which can engender 'diffuse support' from state

[4] This set comprises 26 speeches as it includes one from Judge Wildhaber shortly after his retirement from the Court.

[5] N Grossman, 'The Normative Legitimacy of International Courts' (2013) 86 *Temple Law Review* 61, 65.

[6] Garcia de Moraes and Alvarado (above n 2) 154.

[7] Grossman (above n 5) 122.

[8] TM Franck, 'Why a Quest for Legitimacy' (1988) 21 *UC Davis Law Review* 535, 547.

parties;[9] that is, sufficient support that secures deference and compliance, even when a party does not necessarily agree with all of its rulings and legal interpretations.[10]

The challenge for international courts is that not only are they critically dependent on legitimacy to function, but their legitimacy is fragile. That fragility begins with the basic challenge that all judges and courts face in generating support when compared to the domestic executive and legislature.[11] Yet, unlike domestic courts, international courts do not enjoy the 'presumption of legitimacy' which is commonly associated with national institutions.[12] Instead, their challenge is amplified by the contestable nature of democratic legitimacy for a supranational body to review the actions and inactions of a state.[13] International courts and judges then look to a host of explanations to justify their legitimacy. The principle of consent from a national state to cede a degree of oversight to an external body[14] has traditionally served as the bedrock to an international institution's legitimacy.[15] The increasing number of states party to treaties and the practice of evolutive interpretations by international judges, however, have rendered this foundational claim to legitimacy somewhat contested.[16] Bodies applying evolutive interpretations, in particular, may appear overly dynamic.[17] The geographic distance of most international institutions from the audiences that they serve can increase a sense that judges are out of touch. In the era of a populist backlash against international institutions, they are intermittently framed as politicised, foreign, interfering and unjust.[18] Human rights bodies, whose remit it is to assess the standards of treatment by states of individuals normally located within their own sovereign territorial borders, particularly attract vitriol and criticism.[19]

To counter these attacks, international institutions – not just courts – have become adept at using communication to sustain and develop their legitimacy. They may become proactive in the construction (and reconstruction) of their purpose and image, explaining and justifying their actions, and describing their contributions.[20]

[9] D Easton, 'A Re-assessment of the Concept of Political Support' (1975) 5 *British Journal of Political Science* 435.

[10] A Føllesdal, 'The Legitimacy of International Courts' (2020) 28(4) *The Journal of Political Philosophy* 476, 481.

[11] C Tibi Weber, 'Latin American Courts Going Public: A Comparative Assessment' (2024) 44(1) *Revista de Ciencia Polítca* 109, 113.

[12] Squatrito (above n 3) 71. See also: Y Shany, 'Stronger Together? Legitimacy and Effectiveness of International Courts as Mutually Reinforcing or Undermining Notions' in N Grossman, H Cohen, A Føllesdal, and G Ulfstein (eds), *Legitimacy and International Courts* (Cambridge, Cambridge University Press, 2018) 354.

[13] A von Staden, 'The Democratic Legitimacy of Judicial Review Beyond the State: Normative Subsidiarity and Judicial Standards of Review' (2012) 10(4) *International Journal of Constitutional Law* 1023.

[14] Follesdal (above n 10) 481.

[15] Grossman (above n 5) 78.

[16] K Dzehtsiarou, 'Keep Me in the Loop: Feedback Exchange between the European Court of Human Rights and States' (2023) 22 *The Law and Practice of International Courts and Tribunals* 591, 596.

[17] K Wojtyczek, 'The European Court of Human Rights and Judicial Law-Making' in M Florczak-Wątor (ed), *Judicial Law-Making in European Constitutional Courts* (London/ New York, Routledge, 2020) 227.

[18] E Posner, 'Liberal Internationalism and the Populist Backlash' (2017) *University of Chicago Public Law & Legal Theory Paper Series*, No 606.

[19] N Torbisco-Casals, 'The Legitimacy of International Courts: The Challenge of Diversity' (2021) 52 *Journal of Social Philosophy* 491, 492.

[20] For commentary see Steininger (above n 3) 167.

When they face criticism, they may publicly respond to justify their behaviour. When faced with protests or scandals they adopt communication strategies to control the narrative.[21] In recent decades, these communication strategies have been professionalised with the intention of reaching wider public support.[22] Chaudoin, for instance, identifies a strategic attempt made by international organisations to affect national media coverage so as to cut through to domestic audiences.[23] Steininger identifies how the Inter-American Court of Human Rights (IACtHR) focuses on intermediaries such as journalists to convey its messages.[24] For the most part, however, the primary audience of international courts has not been the public, but a set of key constituencies.

III. STRATEGIC COMMUNICATION

In an age of populism and democratic backsliding, as Ginsburg states, 'courts need allies'.[25] As Judge Pere Pastor Vilanova of the ECtHR notes, '[g]iven that judges are not usually elected by citizens, they may be tempted to look elsewhere for some form of legitimacy or social acceptability'.[26] International judges, then, look to the individuals and institutions with the greatest leverage to shape and sustain state support for them. This constituency will be diverse so as to include both sub-state and non-state actors,[27] be national and international in focus, and include a wide range of demographics, from legal trainees and students, through to apex court judges.[28] A list would include, inter alia, domestic political elites, judges, civil servants, bar associations, lawyers, academics, journalists, law students, legal activists, researchers and members of civil-society organisations.[29] The work conducted by judges in engaging with these constituencies is a direct form of judicial diplomacy. Courts and judges 'emulate and practise statecraft' in a manner similar to a sovereign state.[30] The international judge can use their office to target their key constituencies in order to build and sustain their legitimacy.[31] Steininger notes how both the ECtHR and the IACtHR orient their judicial diplomacy towards interested stakeholders and compliance constituencies,[32]

[21] M Ecker-Ehrhardt, 'International Organizations "Going Public"? An Event History Analysis of Public Communication Reforms 1950–2015' (2018) 62 *International Studies Quarterly* 723, 733.
[22] ibid 723.
[23] S Chaudoin, 'How International Organizations Change National Media Coverage of Human Rights' (2023) 77 *International Organization* 238, 257.
[24] Steininger (above n 3) 186.
[25] T Ginsburg, 'Demographic Backsliding and the Rule of Law' (2018) 44 *Ohio Northern University Law Review* 351, 368.
[26] Judge Pere Pastor Vilanova, 'Accountability of the Judiciary: Shared Responsibility of Judges and the State' in ECtHR, Judicial Seminar, 'The Authority of the Judiciary 1. Challenges to the authority of the judiciary 2. Responses to the challenges' (Strasbourg, 2018) 23.
[27] Squatrito (above n 3) 68.
[28] ibid 64.
[29] ibid 169; AF Tatham, '"Off the Bench but Not off Duty": The Judicial Diplomacy of the Court of Justice' (2017) 22 *European Foreign Affairs Review* 303, 304 and Squatrito (above n 3) 68.
[30] ibid Tatham 304.
[31] Squatrito (above n 3) 65.
[32] Namely, domestic mechanisms and groups that influence and enforce compliance with international agreements and domestic laws.

especially when they fear there is a legitimacy deficit with these audiences.[33] As Squatrito notes, judicial diplomacy will include presenting 'norm-referential narratives of their processes and outcomes' at the institution.[34]

Such extrajudicial communication brings perils along with potential. The legitimacy deficit experienced by the international judiciary means that criticism of missteps and misbehaviour in extrajudicial communication can be amplified, and institutions may risk losing authority on account of the behaviour of only one individual. As former ECtHR judge Helen Keller notes, '[j]udges must observe a reasonable degree of self-discipline when exercising their freedom of expression'.[35] Some judges may therefore be more fearful and hesitant to engage in such judicial diplomacy, with an apprehension that their comments may risk politicising the institution.[36] For others, language may be an obstacle to effective communication.[37] There are also inevitable concerns about 'neutrality, impartiality and the authority of the office' which may engage scepticism towards accepting invitations and speaking out.[38] Individual responsibility in extrajudicial affairs is therefore a core component of life for the international judge.

These concerns about the perils of extrajudicial discourse shape the ethics and conduct guides that exist for international judges. The Burgh House Principles on the Independence of the International Judiciary note in their preamble the 'special challenges facing the international judiciary in view of the non-national context in which they operate'.[39] On judicial freedom of expression, the principles encourage 'appropriate restraint' and chart that expression 'must be exercised in a manner that is compatible with the judicial function and … may not affect or reasonably appear to affect judicial independence or impartiality'.[40] The Bologna and Milan Code of Judicial Ethics similarly notes this freedom of expression, but adds the qualification that a judge 'shall always conduct himself or herself in such a manner as to preserve the dignity of the judicial office and the impartiality and independence of the judiciary'.[41]

The Code of Ethics for the ECtHR notes that adherence to conduct rules 'sustains and enhances public confidence in the Court'.[42] On extrajudicial expression and activity it is stated that judges 'shall refrain from any activity, expression and association that may be considered to affect adversely public confidence in their impartiality'.[43] This provision of the code is then embedded in the Practice Directions of the Court,

[33] Squatrito (above n 3) 83.

[34] ibid 65.

[35] H Keller, 'How to Improve Independence and Impartiality of Judges of the European Court of Human Rights' (2023) *European Convention on Human Rights Law Review* 1, 1.

[36] Squatrito (above n 3) 65.

[37] Steininger (above n 3) 182.

[38] ibid 170–71.

[39] P Sands, C McLachlan and R Mackenzie, 'The Burgh House Principles on the Independence of the International Judiciary' (2005) 4(2) *The Law & Practice of International Courts and Tribunals* 247. Preamble. Available at: https://docs.pca-cpa.org/2020/04/ef1f0fb6-burgh-house-principles.pdf.

[40] ibid 7.1–7.3.

[41] *Bologna Milano Global Code of Judicial Ethics* (2015) Principle 5.2.6.

[42] ECtHR, 'Resolution on Judicial Ethics' (January 2025) Preamble.

[43] ibid.

which connect the obligation to the recusal of a judge from a particular case.[44] Similarly, the IACtHR imposes an obligation on judges to 'act with loyalty towards the institution',[45] and thereby 'exercise their freedom of expression in a manner compatible with their functions, dignity of office and reputation of the Court'.[46] Likewise, the International Criminal Court Judicial Ethics Code restrains freedom of expression so as not to 'affect or appear to affect judicial independence or impartiality'[47] and 'avoid expressing views which may undermine the standing and integrity of the Court'.[48] Similar to domestic judicial codes, conduct and ethics guides in respect of the international judge speak to protecting the legitimacy and authority of the judicial office. And yet, their legitimacy deficit requires the international judge, particularly those in leadership roles, to run the gauntlet of extrajudicial communication to construct the support needed for their institution. We see this with the President of the ECtHR.

IV. MAKING THE ARGUMENT FOR THE EUROPEAN COURT OF HUMAN RIGHTS

The ECtHR operates as the permanent judicial body within the Council of Europe (CoE). The Court is the principal supervisory body for the European Convention on Human Rights (ECHR), an international human rights treaty created in the aftermath of the Second World War, largely by Western European states. It has since grown to cover the entire continent of Europe, with the notable exceptions of Belarus and the Russian Federation. The Court has long received individual applications against states, making it a frenetically active judicial body. Its caselaw is both sophisticated and developed, and with state parties demonstrating a high degree of acceptance of its rulings, it is globally renowned as one of the most effective human rights adjudicative bodies.[49]

The Court is composed of one judge nominated by each of the contracting parties to the treaty, and so currently has 46 members of its judicial bench.[50] A plenary meeting of all of the judges elects the President of the Court whose responsibility it is to direct its work and administration, as well as to engage with the authorities of the CoE.[51] With the extrajudicial work of the Strasbourg judges equating to judicial diplomacy, the President is in effect the ECtHR's chief diplomat. Since its creation in 1953, there have been 18 Presidents. For the period covered in this study the respective Presidents were: Luzius Wildhaber of Switzerland

[44] ECtHR (Strasbourg, 24 March 2024) Rule 28.
[45] Inter-American Court of Human Rights, *Code of Ethics for Judges of the IACtHR* (December 2022), 6.
[46] ibid 7.1–7.2
[47] International Criminal Court, *Code of Judicial Ethics* (2022), Art 10.1. https://www.icc-cpi.int/sites/default/files/2022-10/A5-09.Code%20of%20Judicial%20Ethics-EN-v.3.pdf
[48] ibid Art 10.2.
[49] Nowak refers to the ECtHR as the 'most sophisticated individual complaints mechanism'. M Nowak, 'The Need for a World Court of Human Rights' (2007) 7(1) *Human Rights Law Review* 251, 257.
[50] Article 20 ECHR.
[51] European Court of Human Rights, Rules of Court (Strasbourg, 15 September 2025) Rule 9, Rules of Court 2025. https://www.echr.coe.int/documents/d/echr/rules_court_eng.

(1998–2007); Jean-Paul Costa of France (2007–11); Sir Nicolas Bratza of the United Kingdom (2011–12); Dean Spielmann of Luxembourg (2012–15); Guido Raimondi of Italy (2015–19); Linos-Alexandre Sicilianos of Greece (2019–20); Robert Spano of Iceland (2020–22); Síofra O'Leary of Ireland (2022–24); and Marko Bošnjak of Slovenia (2024–25).

Judicial diplomacy by the President spans a broad spectrum of activities. The President regularly conducts visits to Member States, meeting with both governmental representatives and domestic judicial officers. They are also active in engaging with the CoE's Committee of Ministers, the official state representatives within the organisation. As Dzehtsiarou notes, at these meetings the role of the President is to 'demonstrate that the Court is not an "enemy" of the states'.[52] In certain circumstances, this emphasis will see the President go beyond the bench to address criticism levelled at the Court from influential individuals. For example, when retired British Supreme Court Justice Jonathan Sumption used his Reith Lectures to criticise the democratic legitimacy of the ECtHR, then President, Judge Spano, visited London to give a direct response.[53] The President's diplomacy extends to engaging not only with state agents and public authorities, but also with constituencies who actively rely on the Court for their own work. Thus, they are active in engaging with civil society organisations, human rights defenders and victims. These engagements take place across a variety of mediums and at different moments within the year. One of the most important events within the judicial calendar takes place in the final week of January with the annual solemn hearing which marks the opening of the judicial year.[54] The event is attended by an array of key constituency members, from senior judges and Presidents of the Constitutional and Supreme Courts of Member States, to parliamentarians, permanent representatives and senior officers of the CoE, and on to ambassadors, as well as an array of both United Nations and other regional human rights body representatives.[55]

When the President speaks at the opening of the judicial year, they deploy rhetoric. That is, they use the opportunity to persuade their audience. Rhetoric, after all, involves modes of persuasion.[56] In engaging in rhetoric, the President is not venturing into new territory. Judges engage in rhetoric on an ongoing basis within the courtroom and in their judgments. We have long since departed from a view that the law itself is an emotionless, neutral field, in which judges act as scientists relying on 'reduction and certainty in order to resolve disputes with finality'.[57] There is now wide acceptance that judges use rhetoric in their judgments so

[52] K Dzehtsiarou, 'Between a Rock and a Hard Place: The Role of the President of the European Court of Human Rights' (2023) 4(1) *European Convention on Human Rights Law Review* 1, 4. See also R Spano, '*Primus Inter Pares*, but More *Pares* than *Primus*! – Recollections of a Former President of the European Court of Human Rights' (2023) 4 *European Convention on Human Rights Law Review* 7.

[53] R Spano, 'The Democratic Virtues of Human Rights Law – A Response to Lord Sumption's Reith Lectures' (The Old Hall, Lincoln's Inn, London, 20 February 2020).

[54] The annual meeting is now accompanied by a judicial seminar.

[55] It was moved in 2021 and 2022 due to the ongoing response to the COVID-19 pandemic.

[56] Aristotle, *The Art of Rhetoric* (London/ New York, Collins Classics, 2012) 5–6.

[57] D Coulson, *Judicial Rhapsodies: Rhetoric and Fundamental Rights in the Supreme Court* (Amhurst MA, Amhurst College Press, 2023) 25; FJ Mootz III, 'Rhetorical Knowledge in Legal Practice and Theory' (1998) 6 *Southern California Interdisciplinary Law Journal* 491, 568.

as to enliven, legitimise and frame their opinions.[58] Nonetheless, there has been limited research to date on *extrajudicial* rhetoric as a constituent part of judicial diplomacy.[59]

Often dismissed as 'mere rhetoric' and characterised as 'a superficial play of surfaces that misleads and distracts audiences rather than informs them',[60] there has been a tendency to frame rhetoric in a pejorative way. Those who engage in it, particularly politicians, are accused of conjuring 'mirages in the desert'.[61] I do not seek to use the term rhetoric here in a disparaging way. Indeed, in order to execute effective judicial diplomacy, the ECtHR President *must* engage in forms of rhetoric. They are the leading voice of an organisation whose authority is consent based. As Squatrito states, 'we would expect the content of judicial diplomacy to express validity claims and persuasive arguments about the substantive provisions of law while targeting public officials'.[62] Such is the manner in which the President engages with the core constituencies at the solemn hearing to open the judicial year. When doing so, they do not speak like judges with the fine-tuned expressions of court judgment. Instead, it is closer to a form of political rhetoric: a style with less 'rational, sober discourse, but one in which the character of the speakers and the emotions they incite are equally as important as their substantive arguments'.[63] Their appeals are then made in the triad of classical rhetoric identified by Aristotle, the earliest authority on persuasive discourse: *pathos* and *ethos*, as well as the more traditionally fine-tuned *logos* of the courtroom.[64] Australian judge Fleur Kingham accurately summarises these:

> Logos targets the brain; it is the logical, rational aspect of argument. Pathos is about the heart; moving the listener to *want* to accept your proposition. Ethos appeals to the gut – the instinctual response to a person – that sense of whether we can trust what we are being told.[65]

For the various Presidents of the ECtHR, these appeals are used to convey a common message: that the ECHR is an essential instrument, and that the ECtHR is a legitimate body to render authoritative interpretations and judgments in respect of it.

[58] See eg Coulson, ibid; T Jacobi and E Mascia, 'Alternative Facts: The Strategy of Judicial Rhetoric' (2023) 73 *Emory Law Journal* 363; R Nelson, *Judges: A Critical and Rhetorical Commentary* (London, T&T Clark, 2017).

[59] Dzehtsiarou, (above n 52) 5 and Spano (above n 52) 19.

[60] A Finlayson and J Martin, 'Introduction: Rhetoric and the British Way of Politics' in J Atkins, A Finlayson, J Martin, and N Turnbull, *Rhetoric in British Politics and Society* (London/ New York, Palgrave, 2014) 1.

[61] N O'Shaugnessy, 'The Rhetoric of Rhetoric – Political Rhetoric as Function and Dysfunction' in Atkins et al, ibid, 20.

[62] Squatrito (above n 3) 68.

[63] J Atkins and N Turnbull, 'Rhetoric, British Identity and Interdisciplinarity' in Atkins et al (above n 60) 174.

[64] KC McCormack, 'Ethos, Pathos, and Logos: the Benefits of Aristotelian Rhetoric in the Courtroom' (2014) 7 *Washington University Jurisprudence Review* 131, 132.

[65] F Kingham, President of the Land Court of Queensland, 'Maximising your Impact as an Advocate: A view from the Bench' (2 March 2017, QLS Modern Advocate Lectures Series) 1. https://archive.sclqld.org.au/judgepub/2017/kingham020317.pdf.

V. THE APPEALS OF RHETORIC

The deployment of each appeal – *logos*, *ethos* and *pathos* – is used for different purposes in conveying the Presidents' principal message at any given time. When on the back foot and defending the Court from its critics, Presidents appear to deploy *logos* to rationalise and justify the existence of the Court and its actions. As Dzehtsiarou noted above, this is where the President reminds the constituencies that they are not enemies.[66] When mustering support for the Court and making the case for its ongoing work, the Presidents' appeal is one of *ethos*, to their own character, and more commonly to that of their fellow judges. Finally, when inspiring the constituencies and landing their argument for the necessity of the Convention, they use *pathos* to draw emotional connections and energise the constituencies. I take each in turn.

A. *Logos*

The first practice of rhetoric to consider is *logos*. For judges, this is the safest territory. In the courtroom *logos* requires that the advocate's argument takes the 'audience step by step along a smooth path that leads inexorably to [their] conclusion'.[67] Then, in their decisions, judges adopt this 'clear and understandable argumentation' in application of the law to justify the result.[68] Judges are therefore experienced as both the audience of *logos* in legal argumentation, and the authors of it, in judgment writing.

At the solemn hearing *logos* is deployed by the respective Presidents as a defensive practice, to explain to their constituencies that the occasional tension that exists between them – principally states, domestic authorities and courts – and the ECtHR, is simply a natural by-product of the Court's existence. Spano articulates this most clearly:

> [T]his is the logic of the system to which the Member States have signed up, based on their own sovereign choice. The Court has demonstrated in recent years an acute awareness of the role of national authorities under the principle of subsidiarity, but sometimes the Court's rulings must draw a line in the sand. Indeed, that is the whole point of why the system was put in place more than 70 years ago. This role can be unpopular with the government in question or even sometimes with the majority of a country's population, if the outcome is not to their liking.[69]

Several of the components in this passage are repeated across different judicial speeches. The first part of the structured argument is creation; that is, that the Court itself is a product of the Contracting Parties. As Costa reminds his audience: '[t]he Court did not spring into existence spontaneously; it was called into being

[66] Dzehtsiarou (above n 52) 4.

[67] Kingham (above n 65) 1.

[68] MV Yakutina, LX Milyaeva, LY Tarasova, and PP Rostovtseva, 'Rhetorical Categories of Ethos, Logos and Pathos: Sounding Judicial Speech of Lawyers' (2020) 25(7) *Utopía y Praxis Latinoamericana* 111, 113.

[69] R Spano, 'Speech by Robert Spano, President of the European Court of Human Rights, on the Occasion of the Opening of the Judicial Year' (Strasbourg, 24 June 2022) 5.

by the Convention (and therefore by the States)'.[70] Costa would further note three years later that the Court's actions are entirely dependent on states. He remarks that '[i]t is only at that price, and under those conditions, that the Court – a creation of the States – can play the role that they themselves conferred on it: it must ensure the observance of their engagements'.[71] Spielmann positions the Court in this interaction, noting that 'legitimacy is conferred on us by the States that we find against, and our position is therefore far from easy'.[72] Thus, a reminder is served to the state officials that the Court and system are of their creation. The second part to this structured argument is to then position the Court in relation to the states. In this respect, Presidents have repeatedly focused on the principle of subsidiarity. That is, to quote Wildhaber: the principle that '[t]he primary level of protection has to be the domestic one. Only where that first level of protection has failed to operate effectively does the European supervision by the Court come into play'.[73] Costa prefers to characterise this relationship not as 'subsidiarity, but as solidarity between national systems and European supervision'.[74] This domestic line of protection, however, has its limits. And it is the extent of those limits that the Court must consider.

This gives rise to the third line, that when it acts, the Court may have to do things that states do not like. It may have to create the law which is thereafter applied. As Wildhaber notes:

> [o]ur Court is to a certain extent a law-making body. How could it be otherwise? How is it possible to give shape to Convention guarantees such as the prohibition of torture, equality of arms, freedom of expression or respect for private and family life, if – like Montesquieu – you see in the judge only the mouthpiece of the law?[75]

This use of rhetorical questioning is intended to amplify the power of the point. Is it not obvious that judges must breathe meaning into the Convention? After all, the ECHR is populated by a series of notoriously 'generic terms',[76] all of which require meaning to be provided by its interpreters.[77]

[70] JP Costa, 'Speech Given by Mr Jean-Paul Costa, President of the European Court of Human Rights, on the Occasion of the Opening of the Judicial Year' (*Dialogue between judges*, 19 January 2007) 45.

[71] JP Costa, 'Speech Given by Mr Jean-Paul Costa, President of the European Court of Human Rights, Solemn Hearing of the European Court of Human Rights on the Occasion of the Opening of the Judicial Year' (*Dialogue between judges*, 29 January 2010) 35.

[72] D Spielmann, 'Speech Given by Mr Dean Spielmann, President of the European Court of Human Rights, Solemn Hearing of the European Court of Human Rights on the Occasion of the Opening of the Judicial Year' (*Dialogue between judges*, 31 January 2015) 45.

[73] L Wildhaber, 'Speech Given by Mr Luzius Wildhaber, President of the European Court of Human Rights, on the Occasion of the Opening of the Judicial Year' (Registry of the European Court of Human Rights, Strasbourg, 21 January 2005) 37.

[74] JP Costa, 'Speech given on the Occasion of the opening of the judicial year' (*Dialogue between judges*, Strasbourg, 25 January 2008) 54.

[75] L Wildhaber, 'Speech Given by Mr Luzius Wildhaber, President of the European Court of Human Rights, on the Occasion of the Opening of the Judicial Year (*Dialogue between judges*, Strasbourg, 21 January 2006) 36.

[76] LA Sicilianos, 'Speech Given by Mr Linos-Alexandre Sicilianos, President of the European Court of Human Rights, on the Occasion of the Opening of the Judicial Year' (Strasbourg, 31 January 2020) 5.

[77] Wojtyczek (above n 17) 233.

They may also have to bring the law up to speed with modern developments. Sicilianos used his speech in 2020 to defend the evolutive doctrine of the living instrument. He notes that the Convention's 'indeterminate duration, suggest[s] that the parties wished the text to be interpreted and applied in a manner that reflects contemporary developments'.[78] Even further, the Court may have to advance the Convention to read that there are positive obligations upon a state to act in order to *prevent a violation*, along with the more commonly understood negative obligations to *refrain from violating* an individual's rights. Judge Costa in 2011 explained this development with reference to the Convention text, noting that '[c]ontrary to what is sometimes said, positive obligations are not a concept deriving purely from judicial interpretation. Significant traces of them can be found in the Convention itself'.[79] To round this off, the point is further made that these are not necessarily interpretative developments which judges wish to push. As Costa contends, despite the fact that judges may not want to address every issue, the responsibility to do so is something they 'cannot refuse, otherwise we would be accused of shirking responsibility or denying justice'.[80] The speech thus serves as a reminder that judges are thrust into the position of addressing contentious issues.

The construction of this argument all builds to a core point: that states created a system of human rights protection in Europe which is premised on subsidiarity, but which requires ECtHR oversight. At times, this will lead to a very natural tension. Wildhaber draws the conclusion that the Court will 'not always be able to please everybody, and it will not always be popular with governments. But that is unavoidable, and accepting that is an inescapable part of belonging to the community of democratic States'.[81] For Costa, the resistance which the Court experiences from some states is 'understandable', and indeed he is 'happy to note that it fades over time'.[82] For Spielmann, the inevitably of instances of conflict derives from the fact that the mission of the Court 'is not to be popular. Sometimes it is even necessary to cause displeasure'.[83] In sum, the Presidential speech has tended to be used as an annual reminder to the Court's principal stakeholders that the tension that sometimes exists between them and the judges is not grounded in malice, or misunderstanding, but is an entirely natural by-product of an international system of supervision with such an important mandate.

[78] Sicilianos (2020) (above n 76) 5.

[79] JP Costa, 'President of the European Court of Human Rights, Solemn Hearing of the European Court of Human Rights on the Occasion of the Opening of the Judicial Year' (*Dialogue between judges*, Strasbourg, 28 January 2011) 45.

[80] Costa (2010) (above n 71) 32.

[81] L Wildhaber, 'Former President of the European Court of Human Rights, on the Occasion of the Opening of the Judicial Year' (*Dialogue between judges*, Strasbourg, 19 January 2007) 39.

[82] JP Costa, 'President of the European Court of Human Rights, Solemn Hearing of the European Court of Human Rights on the Occasion of the Opening of the Judicial Year' (*Dialogue between judges*, Strasbourg, 28 January 2011) 40.

[83] D Spielmann, 'President of the European Court of Human Rights, Solemn Hearing of the European Court of Human Rights on the Occasion of the Opening of the Judicial Year' (*Dialogue between judges*, Strasbourg, 31 January 2014) 34.

B. *Ethos*

The second rhetorical appeal deployed by Presidents in their speeches is that of *ethos*. Marked by some as the most important of the three appeals, the deployment of *ethos* is critical for ECtHR Presidents.[84] Logic may explain to their key constituencies why there is natural tension in the system, and yet demonstration of their own character is vital to sustain their trustworthiness to administer a system which presents such tension.[85] Both the inherent legitimacy deficit experienced by the ECtHR, and the personal criticism of the judges, means that there is an onus on them to 'arouse the audience's trust' when the opportunity presents.[86] Demonstrating *ethos* is a pathway towards doing so. It is described as a 'general ability to deal with a communication situation', and thus it requires cognisance of the surroundings and what the audience expects.[87] To Aristotle, it required the expression of three characteristics: (i) practical intelligence, (ii) goodwill, and (iii) a virtuous character.[88] All three are exhibited by Presidents in their annual speeches.

First, practical intelligence is demonstrated by Presidents in explaining to their constituencies that they understand the major issues of the day which are facing them. The period under consideration (2001–2025) was one marked by security and policy challenges across the continent. While cases would arrive relating to the fallout from the global financial crisis of 2008, and a growing refugee crisis, the one continuous theme throughout this period was the persistence of terrorist attacks, particularly in Western European states. In the aftermath of the 9/11 attacks on the USA, Wildhaber was emphatic in his message that it must

> be possible for democratic States governed by the rule of law to protect themselves effectively against terrorism; human rights law must be able to accommodate this need. The European Convention should not be applied in such a way as to prevent States from taking reasonable and proportionate action to defend democracy and the rule of law.[89]

Over a decade later, in the shadow of further terrorist attacks on the French public, Raimondi lauded the fact that the Convention had a derogation clause to allow states to lower fundamental rights protection standards when addressing threats.[90] He later advocated that collective action to address challenges of the day was necessary, and that the Convention obligations could be read in harmony with such responses: '[t]errorism, economic crisis, the mass arrival of migrants: Europe must square up to

[84] Yakutina et al (above n 68) 113.

[85] F Baetens and R Bismuth, 'Face á Face: Interview with Angelika Nussberger – Professor and Former Judge and Vice-President of the European Court of Human Rights' (2021) 20 *The Law and Practice of International Courts and Tribunals* 225, 228.

[86] Yakutina et al (above n 68) 113.

[87] ibid 113.

[88] Aristotle (above n 56) 80. See also M Frost, 'Ethos, Pathos & Legal Audience' (1994) 99 *Dickinson Law Review* 85, 99.

[89] L Wildhaber, 'President of The European Court of Human Rights, on The Occasion of the Opening of The Judicial Year', in European Court of Human Rights, Annual Report 2001 (ECtHR Registry, Strasbourg, 31 January 2002) 20.

[90] G Raimondi, 'President of the European Court of Human Rights, Solemn Hearing of the European Court of Human Rights on the Occasion of the Opening of the Judicial Year' (*Dialogue between judges*, Strasbourg, 29 January 2016) 38.

all of these challenges simultaneously'.[91] And from this, a wider message is communicated: that the Convention itself is not a panacea for all injustices. It was not, for Wildhaber, 'intended to cure all the planet's ills and indeed cannot effectively do so'.[92] Nor was it, for Raimondi, 'created to solve all problems'.[93]

The second component for Aristotle was goodwill. This can be demonstrated through a multitude of ways, with one of the most effective being the quality of candidness. By levelling with one's audience and appearing to speak with them both plainly and honestly, the advocate builds trust. Through their speeches, Presidents are candid with their core constituencies about the problems which their institution has faced. In the early years, there was considerable focus by Presidents on the delays in implementing a proposed restructuring of the ECtHR system.[94] Other vulnerabilities ranged from the backlog that the Court was faced with, to the eroding commitment to the rule of law across Europe, and on to financial challenges resulting from a waning of state commitment. These themes are encapsulated by Costa in his 2008 address:

> At the end of my first year in office, I cannot hide, and have not hidden from you, the fact that our Court is running into difficulties. Perhaps one can say without exaggeration that the crisis it faces is without precedent in its already long history.[95]

Candid reflections on the position of the judge and their own weaknesses can also demonstrate goodwill, by showing the audience that they do not consider themselves to be perfect. In his first speech, Bošnjak notably conveyed that 'Judges cannot remain in their perceived ivory towers'.[96] Elsewhere, Costa accepts that the 'Court is no more infallible than any other',[97] while he later reflects that judges are simply trying their best in their 'very honest labours' when dealing with the 'essentially subjective concept' of law.[98]

The third component of *ethos* is then of a virtuous character. Presidents have tended to convey this in two ways. While rare, Presidents will occasionally appeal to their own character to demonstrate their credibility in this regard. Bratza refers to his lengthy association with the Convention system, noting that his involvement ran to 'forty years, as counsel, member of the Commission and a judge of the Court itself'.[99]

[91] G Raimondi, 'President of the European Court of Human Rights, Solemn Hearing of the European Court of Human Rights on the Occasion of the Opening of the Judicial Year' (*Dialogue between judges*, Strasbourg, 27 January 2017) 58.

[92] Wildhaber (2002) (above n 89) 23–24.

[93] Costa (2010) (above n 71) 32.

[94] This challenge was provoked by the withholding of consent by the Russian Federation to sign Protocol 14 of the ECHR.

[95] JP Costa, 'Speech given on the occasion of the opening of the judicial year' (*Dialogue between judges*, 25 January 2008) 55.

[96] M Bošnjak, 'President of the European Court of Human Rights, on the Occasion of the Opening of the Judicial Year 2025' (Strasbourg, 31 January 2025) 6 https://www.echr.coe.int/documents/d/echr/speech-20250131-bosnjak-jy-bil.

[97] JP Costa, 'Speech given on the occasion of the opening of the judicial year' (*Dialogue between judges*, Strasbourg, 25 January 2008) 52.

[98] Costa (2007) (above n 70) 45.

[99] N Bratza, 'President of the European Court of Human Rights, Solemn Hearing of the European Court of Human Rights on the Occasion of the Opening of the Judicial Year' (*Dialogue between judges*, 27 January 2012) 28.

In doing so, he foregrounds his experience to demonstrate why his reflections are worth hearing. Elsewhere, personal *ethos* is more implicitly communicated. Raimondi for instance, relates his credibility to his age and life experience in commencing a point: 'Allow me to add that, for someone of my generation who was born when the horror of the Holocaust was still a recent memory, and for those of us who have known the survivors'.[100] Spano reminds the audience of his independence by summarising a case against his own state, Iceland, in which he led the Court to hold unanimously in favour of the applicants.[101]

For the most part, however, Presidents prefer instead to make appeals through *ethos* in respect of the Court itself as a renowned judicial body. The 'genius' of the Court is lauded.[102] Frequent references are made by Presidents to the 'quality of our judgments'.[103] These outputs are due to the work of 'judges of high quality and great dedication',[104] 'who are profoundly devoted to the Court'.[105] Wildhaber, a particular champion of the Court, refers to it as 'the most productive of all international tribunals'[106] and 'an incredibly successful institution, known and respected across the whole world'.[107] This external validation is a common trait in speeches. It establishes that the prestige is not merely the opinion of the President, but a widely held one. Raimondi discusses how the Court's judgments are used elsewhere, citing it as 'proof that our case-law is a source of inspiration even beyond the continent of Europe'.[108] Examples are also given, with Bošnjak highlighting how the blockbuster climate-change decision of *Verein KlimaSeniorinnen* 'provided crucial inspiration for a recent judgment of the South Korean Constitutional Court'.[109] Having visited Contracting States throughout his period in office, Costa vouched that 'the authority and prestige of the Court remain intact'.[110]

In sum, through demonstrating appreciation for the challenges faced by the principal stakeholders, showing candidness in reflection of the Court's own position, and echoing the widely held view of the quality of the Court, Presidents seek to sustain the confidence of core constituencies in their operation of the system.

[100] G Raimondi, President of the European Court of Human Rights, Solemn Hearing of the European Court of Human Rights on the Occasion of the Opening of the Judicial Year (*Dialogue between judges*, 26 January 2018) 55.

[101] R Spano, 'President of the European Court of Human Rights, on the Occasion of the Opening of the Judicial Year' (Strasbourg, 10 September 2021) 3: *Guðmundur Andri Ástráðsson v Iceland* (Application no 26374/18) (ECtHR, GC, 1 December 2020).

[102] Raimondi (2017) (above n 91) 60.

[103] Spielmann (2014) (above n 83) 32. See also: Speech Given by Raimondi (2017) (above n 91) 58.

[104] S O'Leary, 'President of the European Court of Human Rights, on the Occasion of the Opening of the Judicial Year' (Strasbourg, 27 January 2023)

[105] Raimondi (2016) (above n 90) 38.

[106] Wildhaber (2005) (above n 73) 39.

[107] ibid 39.

[108] G Raimondi, 'President of the European Court of Human Rights, Solemn Hearing of the European Court of Human Rights on the Occasion of the Opening of the Judicial Year' (Strasbourg, 25 January 2019) 3.

[109] Bošnjak (2025) (above n 96) 4.

[110] Costa (2008) (above n 95) 50.

C. *Pathos*

The final practice of rhetoric to consider is *pathos*. This is the style of appeal which tends to obtain the primary focus in scholarship and practice.[111] It is the style that stirs the audiences' 'emotions',[112] grasping their attention and – when successful – carrying them to a destination of sentiment which the orator has predetermined. For the most part, the appeals to *pathos* made by the ECtHR Presidents fall late in their speeches, where three themes emerge.

First, there is a clear intention to rouse the audience as a collective in their shared endeavour. The Convention is referred to as 'part of our common heritage',[113] 'our common responsibility'[114] and 'our common system'.[115] It is a joint endeavour between states and the Court: '[t]ogether and collectively we protect human rights'.[116] Thus, states have a responsibility to act to make the Convention system a success. The audience is told that the future of the Court 'depends on you, the representatives of the States'.[117] That responsibility extends beyond the Court 'to the Contracting States themselves',[118] and further to others, like national judges, legal practitioners and NGOs, who 'in often difficult, and sometimes dangerous, conditions make a major contribution … for which they should be given credit'.[119] To them all: 'Without you, there can be no common area of protection of rights and freedoms. Without you, there is no rule of law'.[120] The Convention's successes and celebrations are therefore shared.

A second, and interrelated theme is to build this into a wider image of enlightened Europeans which binds the core constituencies together.[121] In this respect, emotion is invigorated as a shared sense amongst the audience.[122] Just as '[n]ational identity, as membership of an imagined community, is often created and recreated through pathos', so *pathos* can be used to fortify the identity of the 'European imaginary'.[123] One effective way to construct an imagined community between disparate groups of individuals is to remind them of the common history they share. As Macmillan notes, history 'creates the collective memories that help to bring the nation into being. The shared celebration of the nation's great achievements – and the shared sorrow at its defeats – sustain and foster it'.[124] Rather than using rhetoric here to enforce a

[111] N O'Shaugnessy, 'The Rhetoric of Rhetoric – Political Rhetoric as Function and Dysfunction' in Atkins et al (above n 60) 17.

[112] Aristotle, *The Art of Rhetoric* (London/ New York, Collins Classics, 2012) 9.

[113] Wildhaber (2005) (above n 73) 40.

[114] Wildhaber (2006) (above n 75) 37.

[115] Spielmann (2014) (above n 83) 34.

[116] Raimondi (2018) (above n 100) 56.

[117] Costa (2007) (above n 70) 46.

[118] Bratza (2012) (above n 99) 27.

[119] JP Costa, 'President of the European Court of Human Rights, on the Occasion of the Opening of the Judicial Year' (*Dialogue between judges*, Strasbourg, 30 January 2009) 40–41. On national judges see: O'Leary (above n 104) 7.

[120] Raimondi (2018) (above n 100) 56.

[121] B Anderson, *Imagined Communities* (London/ New York, Verso, 1983).

[122] S Leith, *You talkin' to me? Rhetoric from Aristotle to Obama* (London, Profile Books, 2011) 67.

[123] B Byrne, 'Rhetoric and Multiculturalism – David Cameron's "King James" Speech and the Crisis of Multiculturalism' in Atkins et al (above n 60) 126.

[124] M Macmillion, *The Uses and Abuses of History* (London, Profile Books, 2010) 81.

single European state, it is used to reinforce the shared European imaginary.[125] Thus, Presidents have a tendency to hark back to the dark events in 1930s and 1940s Europe which preceded the creation of the ECHR, to position the shared suffering of the continent. To Wildhaber, the Convention was 'the legacy of the twentieth century, with its battlefields and its camps, to the twenty-first century, with its new challenges and fears. The rights and freedoms it guarantees are both timeless and universal'.[126] O'Leary developed this: 'Let us not forget why the Convention was conceived'.[127] The responsibility of the past weighs heavily on contemporary European societies. As Costa noted, '[w]e must ensure that at least we Europeans use the law to reduce that suffering and to prevent it recurring'.[128]

From the memory of the tragic past, Presidents speak of celebrating the accomplishments of Europe since the Second World War and under the Convention. Raimondi is particularly effective with this point, stating that 'the rule of law is what sets Europe apart: it is one of the achievements of *our* civilisation, a rampart against tyranny'.[129] For both Spano and Sicilianos separately, it is 'no doubt one of the greatest peace projects in the history of humanity'.[130] For Wildhaber, 'it is the ultimate expression of the capacity, indeed the necessity, for democracy and the rule of law to transcend frontiers'.[131] Moreover, this 'is what Europe represents: a part of the world where the rules of the democratic game have been laid down, and where compliance with these rules is guaranteed by the Constitutional and Supreme Courts'.[132] For Wildhaber, this is not something to be modest about. The Convention is 'an outstanding testimony to European ethical and legal culture, and we have every reason to be proud of it'.[133] After all, it is 'a model for an international community bound together by respect for common standards and their collective enforcement'.[134] This is stirring material to an audience whose combined success is being celebrated. It denotes Aristotle's advice on the use of rhetoric, to always 'take into account the nature of our particular audience when making a speech of praise; for, as Socrates used to say, "it is not difficult to praise the Athenians to an Athenian audience"'.[135]

A third and final use of *pathos* to energise the core constituencies is by deploying imagery, idioms and analogy. *Pathos* invites the 'dramatization and visualization of details and motives of actions'.[136] This can be representative of the Court and the relationship between the Court and the constituencies it is working with. On the Court, a much-repeated idiom is that it is the 'jewel in the Crown' of the CoE system for human

[125] PM Lützeler, 'The European Imaginary in the Discourse on Peace' in F Kläger and G Bayer (eds), *Early Modern Constructions of Europe: Literature, Culture, History* (Abingdon, Routledge, 2016).
[126] Wildhaber (2006) (above n 75) 37.
[127] O'Leary (2023) (above n 104) 7.
[128] Costa (2009) (above n 119) 41.
[129] Raimondi (2017) (above n 91) 58.
[130] Sicilianos (above n 76) 4. Echoed by Spano (2022) (above n 69) 2 and O'Leary (2023) (above n 104) 3.
[131] Wildhaber (2006) (above n 75) 34.
[132] Raimondi (2017) (above n 91) 58.
[133] Wildhaber (2005) (above n 73) 40.
[134] Wildhaber (2006) (above n 75) 37.
[135] N O'Shaugnessy, 'The Rhetoric of Rhetoric – Political Rhetoric as Function and Dysfunction' in Atkins et al (above n 60) 25–26.
[136] Yakutina et al (above n 68) 113.

rights protection. This has provoked reflections from Presidents that the 'the Crown must remain strong for the jewel to continue to shine' in discourse around enforcing the Court's judgments.[137] It is also set as a standard to exceed. More than merely a jewel, it is described as a

> symbol, and indeed the practical expression, of an ideal, an aspiration for a society in which the marriage of effective democracy and the rule of law provides the basis for political stability and economic prosperity, while allowing the self-fulfilment of individuals.[138]

Elsewhere, Bošnjak neatly describes the Court as 'the brightest lodestar for States which falter on the path of democracy. Those States will always find our Human Rights building to guide them back'.[139] Thus, the constituencies are elegantly reminded of the success, prowess and esteem of the institution.

The imagery is even more effective in respect of the relationship between the Court and the constituencies. In this regard, Spielmann was highly effective in using musical analogies to represent the sophistication of the ongoing inter-relationship between the Court and its domestic counterparts. On the dialogue, he reflects:

> I sometimes see our courts as the soloists in the Concerto for Two Violins in D minor of Johann Sebastian Bach. In that Concerto the two soloists are intertwined, sometimes alternating the melodic line, carrying different tunes and rhythms, yet ultimately – and this is the important point – joining together and combining to produce a particularly harmonious piece. What a splendid example of musical dialogue![140]

Thus, through *pathos,* the judges seek to stir in their constituencies a shared cause for celebration in the success of the system, in its achievements and in what they continue to build for their shared societies of individuals within their Europe.

VI. CONCLUSION

In response to the challenges they face, judges at international courts will occasionally practise extrajudicial rhetoric as a discrete form of communication. Their legitimacy deficit can compel them into action; to use their voice to justify their position. As outlined, when they do communicate, they often speak strategically and directly to a series of key constituencies upon whom their legitimacy is dependent. In so doing, as with all extrajudicial speech, they run the risk of upsetting key audiences. Indeed, in the aftermath of his 2018 Opening Speech, Azerbaijani authorities raised an objection as to the impartiality of President Raimondi and the Court as a whole, in a subsequent case.[141] While this complaint was dismissed, it serves as a reminder of the fine line which the international judge must walk in their extrajudicial communication.

[137] Spano (2022) (above n 69) 2.
[138] Wildhaber (2007) (above n 81) 37.
[139] Bošnjak (2025) (above n 96) 6.
[140] Spielmann (2014) (above n 83) 35.
[141] Proceedings under Article 46 § 4 in *Ilgar Mammadov v Azerbaijan* (Application no 15172/13) (ECtHR, GC, 25 May 2019) [6].

In this chapter, I have outlined how leadership judges at the ECtHR effectively use rhetoric in their communications. They do so in an express and unabashed way and deploy a judicial voice that simply would not sit naturally within the courtroom. Through appeals to *logos* they defend the Court, through *ethos* they attempt to build trust with their constituencies, and through *pathos* they seek to stir in their audience a pride in their collective endeavour. Their efforts reaffirm that a primary purpose of extrajudicial communication from the international bench is related to legitimacy. They also demonstrate the prowess and competence of the judges in responding to the prevailing environment that their institution faces and make the case for its future.

6

Uncomfortable Truths, Clichés and Real Dilemmas: Extrajudicial Discourse on Judicial Diversity

ERIKA RACKLEY*

I. INTRODUCTION

JUDICIAL ENGAGEMENT WITH (the question of) greater diversity in the judiciary is long-standing. Whether it is discussing why we've not got a more diverse judiciary, how we might get one or even why we might want one in the first place, judicial diversity is a topic on which judges have many and differing views. And rightly so. Judges, particularly those who are themselves 'diverse' and/ or occupying leadership positions, are uniquely placed to offer a view not only on why judicial diversity is important but, vitally, about how we might get it.

However, despite the regularity and authority with which senior judges speak on the subject, judicial diversity, in the UK at least,[1] remains some way off. Progress toward a judiciary that is truly diverse – particularly at its senior levels – has for some time now been 'glacial'.[2] Where there is progress, it comes in fits and starts and, in the interim,

*Thanks to Kate Malleson, Conall Mallory, Hélène Tyrrell and Charlie Webb for their comments and insights. The usual caveats apply.

[1] In 2023, the UK was ranked last out of 24 OECD (Organization for Economic Co-operation and Development) countries for gender representation in the judiciary (OECD, 'Gender equality in the judiciary' in *Government at a Glance 2023* (OECD Publishing, 2023).

[2] See eg House of Commons Justice Committee, Oral evidence: Pre-appointment hearing: Chair of the Judicial Appointments Commission, HC 925, Q29 (6 December 2022) (Q29, Maria Eagle). The fact that the same language was used over 20 years earlier underlines the point (Leading Article: 'Our white, male, upper-middle-class, snail-paced judiciary', *The Independent* (London, 10 October 1997)).

gains – if they are made at all[3] – are often lost.[4] Why is this? After all, greater diversity among our judges has been seen as – all things being equal – 'A Good Thing' for some time now.[5] Few would – publicly at least – agree with Lord Tebbit that 'there should be no more talk of … diversity among judges than among Olympic athletes'.[6] Quite the opposite. Arguments for greater diversity – typically legitimacy (including public confidence), equality and quality – and reasons for why we've not got it are well-rehearsed: the absence of sustained political will and leadership,[7] ongoing discrimination within the appointments process, inadequacies in the judicial pipeline, the apparent amorphousness of merit.[8] And yet, at the same time, this familiarity and predictability in the debates about diversity in England & Wales are part of the problem. Conversations about judicial diversity have become stale and pedestrian, populated, to use Lord Sumption's words, by 'received clichés' and 'bedevilled by an unthinking resort to sterile formulae and an unwillingness to ask awkward questions or address real dilemmas'.[9]

Extrajudicial discourse on the topic is no exception. Each new speech or video posted on social media for Black History Month, Pride or International Women's Day, every taskforce or five-year 'diversity and inclusion' strategy addressing the ongoing lack of representation in the judiciary and plans for reform brings with it a nagging sense that we've heard it before. Because often we have. With notable exceptions, senior judges – like others involved in the diversity debates – have been talking and thinking publicly about diversity, in much the same way, at least since the early 1990s.[10] Little wonder extrajudicial conversations about diversity are exhibiting signs of diversity fatigue.[11]

[3] No Justice from a visible minoritised ethnic background, for example, has been appointed to the UK Supreme Court. If all current members serve until 75, the next vacancy is expected to arise in June 2026 by which time the Court will be somewhat short of the 'reasonable and achievable target' set by JUSTICE in 2017 'of at least two non-white Justices and a maximum of seven white men by 2026' (JUSTICE *Increasing Judicial Diversity* (2017) [3.22]).

[4] The representation of women on the UK Supreme Court is a good example here. For a period of 14 months between October 2018 and January 2020, three women Justices on the Court (Lady Hale (President), Lady Black and Lady Arden), since then there have been two periods (January–April 2021 and January 2022–November 2023) where there has only been one woman Justice. There are currently two women on the Court: Lady Rose and Lady Simler.

[5] See eg K Malleson almost 25 years ago: *The New Judiciary: The Effects of Expansion and Activism* (Aldershot, Ashgate, 1999) 106.

[6] Lord Tebbit, 'Supreme Court: President' HL Deb 16 November 2011 Vol 732, col 681, 682. He is wrong on both counts. See further A Topping, 'Team GB still too white and suburban, says Sport England board member', *The Guardian* (London, 9 August 2021).

[7] There was, eg, no mention of judicial diversity in the Labour 2024 manifesto, nor in the Lord Chancellor's swearing in speech, delivered at the Royal Courts of Justice in London on 16 July 2024.

[8] See eg B Hale, 'Equality and the judiciary: why should we want more women judges?' [2001] *Public Law* 489; E Rackley, *Women, Judging and the Judiciary: From Difference to Diversity* (Abingdon, Routledge, 2013); Lord Burnett, 'A Changing Judiciary in a Modern Age' (Treasurer's Lecture 2019, London, 18 February 2019); J Barton-Crosby et al, *Judicial diversity: Barriers and initiatives. Rapid evidence assessment* (National Centre for Social Research, 2023).

[9] Lord Sumption, 'Home Truths about Judicial Diversity' (Bar Council Law Reform Lecture, London, 15 November 2012).

[10] The judiciary is not alone in this. The same point, and indeed many of the criticisms made in this chapter, might also be levelled at the Judicial Appointments Commission, parliamentarians, government departments and academics.

[11] This insight is attributed to Linda Dobbs, though in her interview she does not use this exact phrase: Anon, 'Linda Dobbs: "Diversity fatigue is the greatest challenge at the moment"' (first100years.org.uk, 5 July 2016); 'First 100 Years: Dame Linda Dobbs Biography' (*YouTube*, 13 March 2019) www.youtube.com/watch?v=pwigUfQ0SDs&ab_channel=First100Years.

This chapter considers the role judges have played, as individuals and through their occupancy of institutional leadership roles,[12] in shaping and inhibiting diversity debates in England & Wales. Drawing on public extrajudicial interventions across a wide range of formats, including lectures, select committee evidence, taskforce reports, social/media contributions,[13] it argues that extrajudicial discourse about diversity is stuck on repeat: characterised by an over-reliance on personal testimony and a reluctance (again with notable exceptions) to address 'uncomfortable truths',[14] confront received clichés and real dilemmas. This reluctance on the part of (many, though not all) judges engaging in this debate to use their social capital and leadership and to discuss 'more adventurous solutions'[15] which might break the diversity deadlock is significant, not least because senior judges are *the* key gatekeepers to change. And, in the meantime as we are seeing, progress toward a judiciary that is truly reflective of the society it serves will continue to be too slow, inevitably fragile, and overly risk averse.

II. ANOTHER 'UNCOMFORTABLE TRUTH'

In 1924 Florence Allen, a Justice on the Supreme Court of Ohio, visited England. Her trip was reported in the *Manchester Guardian* where Allen is described as 'a youngish woman with a quiet, rather reserved manner', and a 'fine musician'.[16] By the time of her visit, Allen had already accumulated a number of 'firsts': first woman attorney to appear before the National War Labor Board, first woman in the world to preside in a first-degree murder trial and first woman to sit on a State Supreme Court (Ohio).[17] To the women (and possibly some men) readers, Allen would have been something of an icon. Women in England & Wales, having only been able to (formally) join the legal

[12] Lord/ Lady Chief Justice, all members of the UK Supreme Court, Heads of Division, Senior Presiding Judge, members of the Judicial Diversity Committee of the Judges Council, and Diversity and Community Relations judges. This is not to suggest that important contributions to the diversity initiatives are not being made by judges outside these formal roles. I also recognise that judges, particularly but not only those in leadership roles, are often constrained in what they can say publicly. This chapter is not intended to offer any views on their personal or private commitment to equality, diversity and inclusion.

[13] My source material here is inevitably partial, but I hope it is also to be representative and inclusive of material that is publicly available. There are, of course, many conversations and interventions both within and without the judiciary which take place in private and which may – or may not – reflect these public statements.

[14] In 2013 Lady Hale, in a lecture responding to Lord Sumption's *Home Truths* lecture the previous year (above n 9), noted a number of 'uncomfortable truths' about judicial diversity including the fact that not only was the lack of diversity in the judiciary out of step with much of the rest of the world but that, notwithstanding this, it continued to be 'very widely admired in the outside world' and 'better paid than almost any in Europe' (the latter particularly in contrast to judiciaries where there are more women judges than men): Lady Hale, 'Equality in the Judiciary' (Kuttan Menon Memorial Lecture, London, 21 February 2013).

[15] G Vos, 'Judicial diversity and LawTech: Do we need to change the way we litigate Business and Property Disputes?' (Speech to Chancery Bar Association Annual Conference, London, 18 January 2019) para 37.

[16] Anon, 'From music critic to the Bench: US Woman Supreme Court Judge', *The Manchester Guardian* (Manchester, 18 July 1924).

[17] Allen would go on to be the first woman to be shortlisted for the US Supreme Court. Though she was nominated a further 11 times, she was never appointed to the Court: R Knake Jefferson and H Brenner Johnson, *Shortlisted: Women in the Shadows of the Supreme Court* (New York, NYU Press, 2020).

profession five years earlier, were yet to join the judiciary – though they were beginning to make their mark as magistrates.[18] Longstanding calls from members of the Women's Freedom League and National Council for Equal Citizenship for the appointment of women judges were on the cusp of gaining some momentum.[19] Conservative MP Alfred T Davis had raised the possibility of women's appointment to the High Court in Parliament in 1922.[20] He would be joined by others throughout the 1930s, including Helena Normanton, the first woman to join one of the Inns of Court,[21] the Bishop of Birmingham, Earnest Barnes,[22] and playwright and author Edgar Middleton, who wrote in the *Daily Mail*

> In science there are women professors; women doctors run hospitals. The Government has thought fit … to appoint them chairmen of Parliamentary committees. There has even been a woman Cabinet Minister … Why should there not be women stipendiary magistrates, county court judges and, for that matter, women judges of the High Court?[23]

Just over 100 years later, the *Manchester Guardian*'s report of Florence Allen's visit continues to feel familiar. One reason for this may be because, like many modern-day media interviews with judges from under-represented backgrounds,[24] it follows a recognisable pattern: a comment on the subject's appearance, or 'different' attribute, usually accompanied, or perhaps off-set, by a list of their accomplishments; an example of how they have been 'lucky' and/ or have triumphed over adversity or some form of discrimination (often as a means of demonstrating that such attitudes or barriers no longer exist or at least are now significantly reduced); and, finally, their view on the importance of a diverse judiciary or, more specifically, the difference more judges 'like them' may or may not make to public confidence in the justice system generally.

Compare, for example, references to Allen's achievements and her relative youth – she was 40 years old at the time of her visit – with references to Victoria McCloud's (the youngest person appointed master of the King's Bench Division of the High Court) 'faint blue-tinged' hair,[25] or discussion of the much commented on decision of Mota Singh (the first person from a minoritised ethnic background to be appointed as a circuit judge) to wear a white turban in court,[26] references to immigration tribunal

[18] In 1926 nearly 1500 women were serving as magistrates in England & Wales: A Logan, *Making Women Magistrates: Feminism, Citizenship and Justice in England and Wales 1918–1950* (PhD thesis, University of Greenwich, 2002).

[19] See eg Anon, 'The Law of Divorce', *The Times* (London, 30 June 1910); Anon, 'Women Judges!', *The Nottingham Evening News*, 30 June 1910; L Ross Clyne, 'We need Women judges', *Derby Daily Telegraph* (Derby, 8 November 1929).

[20] Anon, 'Women Judges. Equal Opportunities with Men', *Daily Mail* (London, 19 May 1922).

[21] H Normanton, 'Helena Normanton, Senior Woman Barrister, demands – Women Judges NOW', *Daily Mail* (London, 2 December 1937).

[22] P Cater, 'Bishop calls for Women Judges', *Daily Mail* (London, 29 June 1937).

[23] E Middleton, 'Why shouldn't women be judges?', *Daily Mail* (London, 1 February 1939).

[24] In this chapter I refer to 'non-traditional' and 'under-represented' judges interchangeably and in preference to prioritising and isolating some identity characteristics over others.

[25] C Baksi, 'Toilet politics and death threats: why transgender judge Victoria McCloud quit', *The Times*, 15 April 2024.

[26] Associated Press, 16 August 1982. It was still a talking point in his obituary 34 years later: V Singh, 'Sir Mota Singh obituary', *The Guardian* (London, 4 December 2016).

judge, Siew Ying Loke's youth ('her sprightly age') and martial arts training,[27] and the continuing fascination with Lady Hale's (former President of the UK Supreme Court) brooches.[28] Other comparisons are more chastening. The expectation, articulated by Florence Allen, that she 'not only do her job as well as a man, but … do it better',[29] for example, which has been echoed by women judges across the decades.[30] And while the prejudice underlying the expectation of exceptionality is most visible and objectionable in judges' accounts of their experiences of explicit racism, sexism, ableism and homophobia,[31] it is no less invidious in the subtler tales of exclusion and silencing – often re-told for laughs or as part of the narrative that things are better now.[32]

Finally, we can hear echoes of Allen's response to the now familiar question of whether women judges might be more 'critical' than (read: 'judge differently to') their male counterparts, that women judges' eyes are perhaps 'a little more open to human questions than those of the men'[33] in *Will Women Judges Really Make a Difference?*, a lecture by Bertha Wilson (the first woman appointed to the Supreme Court of Canada) over half a century later. She concluded:

> If … women judges through their differing perspective on life can bring a new humanity to bear on the decision-making process, perhaps they *will* make a difference. Perhaps they will succeed in infusing the law with an understanding of what it means to be fully human.[34]

We see the same, more recently, in former President of the UK Supreme Court, Lord Neuberger's counsel to all judges to 'approach the task of judging in a manner which embraces, rather than eschews, our humanity'.[35]

Of course, views differ on whether and how a non-traditional judge's 'difference' may impact on the quality and content of their decision-making. Compare, for example, the view of former Chief Justice of New Zealand, Sian Elias, that 'we should expect women judges to make a difference',[36] or US Supreme Court Justice, Sonia Sotomayor's, now-famous assertion – 'I would hope that a wise Latina woman with the richness of her experiences would more often than not reach a better conclusion

[27] T Connelly, 'From black belt to the bench: Martial arts expert, 37, appointed to judiciary', *Legal Cheek* (15 January 2018).

[28] K Youde, 'My Favourite Pieces: How Lady Hale's brooches livened up more than her attire', *Financial Times* (London, 8 July 2022).

[29] In Anon (above n 16).

[30] See eg H Xue, Judge at the International Court of Justice in 'Women in justice: three trailblazing judges send a powerful message' (UN Regional Information Centre for Western Europe, 9 March 2023).

[31] See eg Anon, 'Linda Dobbs' (above n 11); Anon, 'Lady Justice Hallett: "I was given a promotion by a senior judge – and then he sexually propositioned me"', *The Standard* (12 April 2012); H Siddique, '"I became Billy No-Mates": a disabled magistrate in an inaccessible court', *The Guardian* (London, 19 June 2023); Mr Justice Fulford, 'Diversity Speech' (Middle Temple Hall, 20 January 2009).

[32] See eg Lady Hale in conversation with Supreme Court Justice Ruth Bader Ginsburg in 2008 ('The British and United States Legal Systems', Georgetown University Law Center, 24 January 2008).

[33] Anon (above n 16).

[34] B Wilson, 'Will Women Judges Really Make a Difference?' (1990) *Osgoode Hall Law Journal* 507, 522.

[35] Lord Neuberger, '"Judge not, that ye be not judged": judging judicial decision-making' (FA Mann Lecture 2015, London, 29 January 2015).

[36] S Elias, 'JUSTICE for One Half of the Human Race? Responding to Mary Wollstonecraft's Challenge' (Address to the Canadian Chapter of the International Association of Women Judges Conference, Vancouver, Canada, 10 May 2011).

than a white male who hasn't lived that life'[37] – with that of fellow US Supreme Court Justice Elena Kagan, who has commented that 'in general, I think that being a woman does not much affect the kind of decision-making I do, or even the way I speak or think about certain issues'.[38] Sandra Day O'Connor, the first, and at the time, only woman Justice on the US Supreme Court, put her views more bluntly: 'we must not allow the "New Feminism" complete sway … asking whether women attorneys [and one assumes judges] speak with a "different voice" than men do is a question that is both dangerous and unanswerable'.[39]

Other non-traditional judges, while rejecting suggestions that their background or 'difference' impacts on their judicial role directly, nonetheless recognise that it can be an important and often visible manifestation of equality and legitimacy arguments for judicial diversity. Former Lord Justice of Appeal Adrian Fulford, for example, is on record as saying that 'I don't think the fact I am a gay man has very much, if anything, to do with the way I perform my job as a judge. It is almost entirely irrelevant'.[40] However, his decision early on in his career to be 'honest and up front' about his sexuality, 'not preaching from the rooftops in a proselytising sort of way but simply being honest and making sure people knew',[41] resonates with Mary Morgan's (the first 'out' lesbian to be appointed as a judge in the United States) founding membership of BALIF (Bay Area Lawyers for Individual Freedom) – a campaigning group established in 1980 to encourage then lesbian and gay, and now LGBTQI, lawyers to apply to become judges – prior to her appointment to the San Francisco Municipal Court in 1981.[42] Of course, not all judges are willing to be 'representatives' of a particular group or community in this way – and nor should they be expected to. David Tatel, who recently retired as a judge from the DC Circuit Appeals Court, for example, throughout his career asked people when introducing him, including Bill Clinton when nominating him to the court, not to mention to the fact he was blind.[43]

Without doubt many of these comments and responses are jurisdiction-specific and/ or a product of a time when the judicial bench was even less diverse. A time when understandings of the judge as 'supra-human'[44] – 'anonymous, dehumanised, impartial, authoritative – [and]… intrinsically male'[45] – prevailed and it was indeed dangerous (or at very least job-threatening) for judges to acknowledge any 'difference' to the superhuman norm.[46] A time when being seen as a 'woman judge' risked

[37] S Sotomayor, 'A Latina Judge's Voice' (2002) 13 *Berkeley La Raza Law Journal* 87, 92.

[38] E Kagan in conversation with JL Mnookin, 'US Supreme Court Justice Elena Kagan Visits UCLA Law', UCLA School of Law, *YouTube*, 29 September 2018, 1:02:32 www.youtube.com/watch?v=3BoJrlaZIvY.

[39] S Day O'Connor, 'Portia's Progress' (1991) *New York University Law Review* 1546, 1557.

[40] L Moran, 'Judicial diversity and the challenge of sexuality: some preliminary findings' (2006) 28(4) *Sydney Law Review* 565, 587.

[41] ibid.

[42] 'A History of BALIF's Activism (Part 1)', BALIF, *YouTube*, no date www.youtube.com/watch?v=PFGOiJjkebY.

[43] He also ensured that references were removed from his Wikipedia page (Interview between David Tatel and Ari Shapiro on Boise State Public Radio, Idaho, 11 June 2024).

[44] E Rackley, 'Representations of the (woman) judge: Hercules, the little mermaid, and the vain and naked Emperor' (2002) *Legal Studies* 602, 614,

[45] Hale (above n 8) 489, 497.

[46] See further E Rackley, 'Judicial diversity, the woman judge and fairy tale endings' (2006) *Legal Studies* 74.

also being seen as a contradiction in terms.[47] In the UK, this is not so much the case today. Lady Rose, for example, has commented:

> I no longer feel that I have to disguise any part of my personality, or temper what I do and say. There is less of an assumption that everything I do is gender-directed, and less concern about whether and how being a woman might influence my decisions.[48]

But it is clearly still the experience of some judges. In her resignation letter, published in *The Times*, former High Court judge, Victoria McCloud, spoke of having 'reached the conclusion that in 2024 the national situation and present judicial framework is no longer such that it is possible in a dignified way to be both "trans" and a salaried, fairly prominent judge in the UK'.[49]

Moreover, taken out of context, there is a risk that such comments are presented as fixed or as overly determinative of an individual's view, rather than what they are: partial soundbites clipped from a more nuanced or complex narrative. After all, judges – like all of us – can change their minds. Take, Lady Hale, for example:

> I too used to be sceptical about the argument that women judges were bound to make a difference, but I have come to agree with those great women judges who think that sometimes, on occasions, we may do so. That is the result of the lived experience of being a judge for 19 years now and a Law Lord for nine.[50]

Whatever view is expounded, these personal extrajudicial contributions are a vital and valuable component in discussions about judicial diversity. For well over a century,[51] judges have informed, buttressed and, at times, under-cut arguments and conversations about diversity. Judges speak with considerable power – both on and off the bench.[52] Their views are essential to public understandings not only of diversity, but of the judiciary and what judges do more generally. Without doubt, these first-hand examples play a key role in providing an authoritative account of the value and impact of judicial diversity. After all, judges know and understand what they do – the job of judging – best.

And yet, to speak, to adapt Sandra Berns' words, as a judge, unbracketed[53] – in other words to speak not as a (woman) judge or even as a woman (judge) but as a woman judge, blind judge, Asian judge, working-class judge and so on – requires courage. To reveal your 'self' – whether through choice or lack thereof – in the performance of your judicial role, to face the repeated questions, challenges of bias, intrusions into your private life, comments on your appearance. To feel 'that perhaps you're not

[47] Rackley (above n 44) 603.

[48] A Inglese, 'The chain of reasoning: Lady Rose of Colmworth', *Counsel* (13 February 2023).

[49] C Baksi, 'Judge's exit triggers trans debate', *The Times* (London, 29 February 2024).

[50] Hale (above n 14).

[51] Beginning perhaps with US Supreme Court Justice Benjamin Cardozo: 'The eccentricities of judges balance one another. One judge looks at problems from the point of view of history, another from that of philosophy, another from that of social utility; one is a formalist, another a latitudinarian, one is timorous of change, another dissatisfied with the present; out of the attrition of diverse minds there is beaten something which has a constancy and uniformity and average value greater than its component elements': *The Nature of the Judicial Process* (first published 1921) (New Haven CT, Yale University Press, 1961) 177.

[52] RM Cover, 'Violence and the Word' (1986) 95 *Yale Law Journal* 1601, 1609.

[53] S Berns and P Baron, 'Bloody Bones: A Legal Ghost Story and Entertainment in Two Voices – To Speak as a Judge' (1994) 2(1) *Australian Feminist Law Journal* 125, 127.

one of the chaps, you don't quite fit in'[54] – is, at least for some, uncomfortable, often exhausting and at times lonely. Judicial difference does not come without cost. Being Ms, Mx or even Mr Diversity is hard work,[55] especially when those previously considered to be 'beacons' become lightening-rods for our disappointment and collective failings.

Moreover, it is an(other) uncomfortable truth that, judicial leadership roles aside, making the case for diversity, and maintaining momentum, as well as day-to-day engagement with diversity initiatives fall predominantly on under-represented judges. It is women judges, judges from a minoritised ethic background, who are living with a disability, who are LGBTQI+, or from a working-class background, who are engaged in grassroots diversity activities, who participate in roadshows, sit on diversity panels, who engage in training and mentoring, who support colleagues, who talk to school children, who record videos for social media,[56] who 'volunteer' to be Diversity and Community Relations judges (DCRJs), while at the same time continuing with their 'day job' and pushing against internal institutional structures and processes. Clearly this is not to suggest that this work is *only* done by judges from these groups, nor that all non-traditional judges choose to do so. But it is surely no coincidence that around 22 per cent of DCJRs are from a minoritised ethnic background, compared to just 11 per cent of judges in the courts and tribunals overall; nor that Lady Hale – who sat alone in the Appellate Committee of the House of Lords and then Supreme Court for almost 14 years – spoke on the topic of judicial diversity more often than her colleagues.[57]

This not only puts undue pressure on a relatively small group of judges, who are already expending a large amount of time and emotional labour, but also reinforces the view that diversity is *only* important to, or the responsibility of, those who are in some way themselves 'diverse' or different to 'the norm'. It contributes to a sense of 'diversity fatigue', a term coined in the US in the late 1990s, whereby those seeking to push for change and/or support others in doing so – often against institutional inertia – are often left emotionally exhausted, frustrated by the lack of progress and feeling that diversity measures are just for show.[58]

[54] Anon 'Linda Dobbs' (above n 11) at 8.23 mins.

[55] L Peacock, 'Britain's most senior female judge, Baroness Hale: "My biggest fear ... When am I going to be found out?"', *The Telegraph* (London, 18 April 2014).

[56] The Judiciary of England & Wales posted 45 videos about being a judge or magistrate on its *Facebook* page in 2023.

[57] R Hunter and E Rackley, 'Judicial leadership on the UK Supreme Court' (2018) *Legal Studies* 191; R Hunter and E Rackley, 'Lady Hale – The challenges of being a feminist court president' in E Delaney and R Dixon (eds), *Elgar Companion to Female Chief Justices in Comparative Perspective* (Cheltenham, Edward Elgar, forthcoming). Since 2000 Lady Hale has spoken and written about diversity on many occasions. In her autobiography she comments that: 'I considered it my duty, when I became the most senior woman judge in the country, to speak out. I could not be accused of furthering my own ambitions. Other women judges might be deterred, fearing either that accusation or the inevitable unpopularity that speaking out would bring': B Hale, *Spider Woman: A Life* (London, Bodley Head, 2021) 98. Certainly, at times, this commitment has been to her professional detriment: Joshua Rozenberg, 'An insider's account of the "Brenda agenda"', *Law Society Gazette* (3 February 2020); Hale, *Spider Woman*, 177.

[58] See eg Po Bronson with Ashley Merryman, who suggest that 'The idea of diversity seems to have worn out its welcome. It is now like a house guest who has stayed too long': 'Are Americans Suffering Diversity Fatigue?', *Time* (31 May 2006); H Hsu, 'The Year in "Diversity Fatigue"', *The New Yorker* (New York, 26 December 2017).

It also risks under-cutting the strongest argument for judicial diversity. In other words, the (perhaps understandable) focus on under-represented background and identity characteristics when making the case for greater judicial diversity, risks reinforcing the assumed irrelevance of those of qualities in 'traditional' judges. This is out-of-step with understandings of judging more generally. As Lady Rose has argued,

> there is … increasingly a recognition that … male judges are not completely neutral in their own views and the experience they bring to the office. So, when women are appointed, it does not mark the first occasion on which a subjective life experience is brought to bear on the daily work of the judge.[59]

That the background and experiences of *all* judges will, on some occasions, inform their decision-making – that who the judge is – their background and experiences – will sometimes make a difference to how the case is decided – is increasingly (though not completely) uncontroversial. So, too, is the acceptance that, if this is the case (and there is no reason to think otherwise), then, as US Supreme Court Justice Benjamin Cardozo noted in 1921,[60] the more varied and diverse the background and perspectives that those judges bring, the better. After all, a diverse judiciary is a stronger judiciary, one better able to do its job: to deliver justice. Lady Hale, in the conclusion to her first speech on judicial diversity in 2001, put it rather more bluntly:

> A system of justice will be the richer for diversity of background and experience. It will be the poorer, in terms of appreciating what is at stake and the impact of its judgments, if all its members are cast in the same mould.[61]

If this is the case (and again there is no reason to think it is not), then *all* judges – whatever their backgrounds – but particularly those in leadership positions, with the ability to effect change, should not only be making the case for greater judicial diversity, but doing so effectively and as often as possible. The difficulty is that, often, they're not.

III. CLICHÉS AND DILEMMAS

In 1930 Lord Dickinson, long-term supporter of women's suffrage and a member of the Liberal Party, optimistically predicted that women barristers would in a 'very short time rise to positions of distinction … [and] … before long we shall find women judges on the bench'.[62] In fact, it would be another 19 years until Rose Heilbron and Helena Normanton would become the first women KCs, and a further 16 years after that until Elizabeth Lane's ground-breaking appointment to the High Court. It would take until 2003 for women to make it onto the (then) Appellate Bench of the House of Lords (now the UK Supreme Court) – some 73 years after Dickinson's initial comment.

[59] Lady Rose, 'Oxford Union' (Oxford Union Talk, Oxford, 4 May 2022) para 29 https://supremecourt.uk/uploads/oxford_union_4_may_2022_lady_rose_01a9c8e1c5.pdf.

[60] Cardozo (above n 51).

[61] Hale (above n 8) 504.

[62] Membership of The House: Position of Women, HL Deb 16 July 1930, vol 78 col 515.

Over the years, Dickinson has not been alone in predicting substantial change on the horizon, only to later find it has failed to materialise. In 1989, the Solicitor General, Nicholls Lyell, suggested that the bench would look 'very different' in the next 10 or 20 years.[63] A few years later, Thomas Legg, former Permanent Secretary in the Lord Chancellor's Department, told the Home Affairs Select Committee that it would be 'just a matter of time' before there were 'quite a lot of women judges'.[64] He was followed in 2005 by Lord Falconer who, as Lord Chancellor, set his sights somewhat lower: five years to ensure under-represented candidates were being appointed 'in proportion to their presence in the pool'.[65] More recently, Lord Chancellors have refused to be drawn on when judicial diversity might be secured and the predictions challenge has been taken up by others. The results are rather less upbeat. Alan Paterson and Chris Paterson predicted in 2012 that it would take almost 100 years, on the current rate of progress, to achieve gender parity.[66] 10 years later, the Law Society reduced this dramatically, predicting that on the then current rate of progress it would take until just 2037 for the proportion of women judges to match estimates for the general population, though somewhat longer – 127 years – for the proportion of the judiciary who are black to do the same.[67]

Nor are judges immune from engaging in a spot of extrajudicial forecasting. In 1992, Lord Taylor, then Lord Chief Justice, looked forward to a 'substantial number' of appointments of women and judges from a minoritised background 'within the next five years'.[68] He was followed in 1998 by Lord Bingham who suggested it would be a 'very short time' before a woman was appointed to the position of Lord Chief Justice.[69] In 2012, former UK Supreme Court Justice Lord Sumption predicted it would take another 50 years for there to be gender parity in the judiciary.[70] This figure was repeated by Linda Dobbs (first non-white judge to be appointed to the High Court) in 2016.[71] A few years later, Lady Hale was slightly more optimistic, suggesting that gender parity should be achieved in less than the 50 years usually stated.[72]

And yet, despite these gloomy predictions, extrajudicial discourse on progress toward a diverse judiciary remains largely upbeat. Since the Judicial Appointments Commission (JAC) started work in 2006, and the changes to the offices of Lord Chancellor and Lord Chief Justice, senior members of the judiciary, and particularly those in leadership or diversity and community liaison roles, have largely remained 'on message'. In essence it is this: there has been progress; we know it is not enough,

[63] Judges, HC Deb 21 December 1989, vol 164 col 670.

[64] 'Judicial Appointments' Home Affairs Committee 3rd Report 1995-1996 (HC 52).

[65] Lord Falconer, 'Increasing Judicial Diversity: The Next Steps': Speech for the Commission for Judicial Appointments (Institute of Mechanical Engineers, London, 2 November 2005).

[66] A Paterson and C Paterson, *Guarding the Guardians? Towards an independent, accountable and diverse senior judiciary* (London, CentreForum, 2012) 37.

[67] Law Society, 'Over 100 years before the judiciary reflects the Black population in our society' (26 October 2022).

[68] Lord Taylor, 'The Judiciary in the Nineties' (The Richard Dimbleby Lecture, 30 November 1992).

[69] Lord Bingham, HC Home Affairs Committee – Minutes of Evidence, 17 March 1998, Q125. It would in fact take another 25 years. Lady Carr became the first Lady Chief Justice in October 2023.

[70] Sumption (above n 9).

[71] Anon 'Linda Dobbs' (above n 11).

[72] Legal Action Group, 'Lady Hale answers your questions' (21 October 2019).

but we are trying our best within various unmoveable parameters (there is a limited pool; appointment is made on merit; the pool depends on who chooses to apply, and so on) to make sure it happens soon (though maybe not as soon as we'd all like). Extrajudicial speeches read like a bingo-card of stock-phrases and cliché. We are told both that 'change is coming'[73] and that the judiciary has 'changed beyond all recognition'.[74] And even if there is 'no quick fix',[75] with progress limited by 'the pool' of potential candidates,[76] there is no need to be down-heartened: change will not happen 'overnight … [but it] need not take decades'.[77] Progress is being made. And depending on your view, it is either 'better than people might think'[78] or 'too slow'.[79] Either way, there is still 'much to do':[80] 'work remains for all of us to make our judiciary as diverse and as inclusive as it should be',[81] but that work is being done – look, see this list of diversity and inclusion outreach activities![82]

This narrative has been repeated across a variety of formats. We see it not only in judicial speeches, but also in judges' social media presence, traditional media interviews, in their evidence to government select committees, as well as in updates to various diversity strategies. See, for example, the Judiciary of England and Wales *Judicial Diversity and Inclusion Strategy: Update 2023*, which states: 'Progress has been made, but there is no room for complacency. We must continually learn from what works, and what does not work, and look for new opportunities to make further improvement'.[83] And the UKSC's *Judicial Diversity and Inclusion Strategy 2021–2025*:

> Progress is being made, but the Court recognises that barriers are entrenched in our society as well as the legal profession, and the solutions to eliminating them are complex and multifaceted. The Court will continue to play its role in removing those barriers and promote equal access to opportunities.[84]

[73] Barbara Mensah, 'The Law Society's Black History month' (London, 2 October 2009).

[74] Inglese, 'Lady Rose' (above n 48).

[75] Lord Justice Goldring, 'Improving Judicial Diversity' (Westminster Legal Policy Forum Keynote, London, 23 May 2012) referring to the conclusion of *The Report of the Advisory Panel on Judicial Diversity 2010* [2].

[76] Goldring, ibid; Lord Judge, 'Equality in Justice Day' (Royal Courts of Justice, London, 24 October 2008); Lord Thomas, 'Speech to the Temple Women's Forum and the Association of Women Barristers' (Leeds, 29 April 2015).

[77] Burnett (above n 8).

[78] Lord Burnett Annual evidence session with the Lord Chief Justice, House of Lords Constitution Committee, 18 May 2022, Q12.

[79] Lady Simler, Chair of the Judicial Diversity Committee of the Judges' Council, foreword to the *Diversity and Inclusion Strategy 2020–2025* (Judicial Office, 2020) 5.

[80] Lady Carr, '75th Anniversary Event to celebrate the first women being appointed Silk' (London, 30 September 2024) para 5.

[81] Geoffrey Vos speaking at the swearing in of Dame Sue Carr as Lady Chief Justice, *YouTube*: www.youtube.com/watch?v=y8wsa-Z9wY4 [5:29].

[82] See eg Goldring (above n 75) and Thomas (above n 76).

[83] Lady Justice Carr, Foreword, *Judiciary of England and Wales, Judicial Diversity and Inclusion Strategy Update 2023*, 1.

[84] Lord Reed foreword to *The Supreme Court of the United Kingdom and the Judicial Committee of the Privy Council, Judicial Diversity and Inclusion Strategy 2021–2025 Annual Update 2024*, 3 https://www.supremecourt.uk/uploads/2024_Annual_Update_Final_6bc6eb8bc6.pdf.

But what's the problem? After all, no one is saying things are ideal.[85] Moreover, it is clear that Lady Carr, as Lady Chief Justice, is committed to spearheading change. Making her first appearance before MPs at the House of Commons Justice Select Committee in January 2024, Lady Carr commented: 'Diversity is the day job for me; it is always there'.[86] And, what is more, some progress *has* been made. The judiciary in many respects is more diverse than, say, 10 years ago, let alone 20 or 30 years ago. And it is likely to become even more so, even without the enormous amount of extrajudicial energy and effort that continues to be expended to ensure the success of diversity and inclusion outreach activities. Perhaps, as Lord Sumption has pointed out, we simply need to be 'patient'.[87]

The difficulty is, as is often the case with clichés, the suggestion that we simply need to wait is beginning to wear a bit thin. Suggestions that 'change is coming' and that progress is 'better than we think'[88] – however well meant – are beginning to ring increasingly hollow. Take, for example, the increase in the proportion of 'judges from Black, Asian and other minority ethnic backgrounds', celebrated (with the usual caveats of needing to do better) in the *Judicial Diversity and Inclusion Strategy 2020–2025*.[89] In fact, the appointment of black judges has stagnated: none of the 161 judges in the senior judiciary are black, and just one per cent of the judiciary in England & Wales – the latter remaining unchanged since 2014.[90] Similarly, the comforting refrain that we have 'the best judiciary in the world'[91] sits at odds with the uncomfortable truth, noted by Lady Hale in 2013, that, at least in relation to the gender of our judges, the judiciary in England & Wales actually is out of step with the rest of the world.[92] Over a decade later, England & Wales is in exactly the same place as it was: 42nd out of 46 countries in the Council of Europe, followed only by Scotland, Armenia and Azerbaijan – something which has remained unchanged since 2012.[93]

This resort to platitudes is compounded by an apparent unwillingness to engage directly with awkward questions and real dilemmas. Quotas and targets, for example,

[85] Lady Hale, '"When there are 12": Legal Education and a Diverse Judiciary' (Lord Upjohn Lecture, online, 25 May 2021): published in (2021) *The Law Teacher* 425, 428.

[86] Lady Carr, Oral evidence: Work of the Lady Chief Justice, HC 466 House of Commons Justice Committee, 16 January 2024, [Q9].

[87] Sumption (above n 9). Not least because men make up less than one-third of applicants for undergraduate law programmes: M Fouzder, 'Women outnumber men two to one in law studies', *Law Society Gazette* (8 February 2023).

[88] Burnett (above n 78).

[89] In Lady Simler's foreword (above n 79) 5.

[90] By way of comparison. judges from a minoritised ethic background make up just over 11% of the courts and tribunal judiciary in 2024, up from 7% in 2014: Ministry of Justice, 'Diversity of the Judiciary: 2024 Statistics' (12 November 2024); K Monteith et al, *Racial Bias and the Bench: A Response to the Judicial Diversity and Inclusion Strategy (2020-2025)* (November 2022) 8.

[91] See eg the opening paragraph of the Courts and Tribunal Judiciary's description of the judiciary: 'The English and Welsh legal system has evolved over more than a 1,000 years and is still changing to meet the needs of modern society. It is widely regarded as one of the best and most independent in the world' (Courts and Tribunal Judiciary, 'Overview of the Judiciary', Courts and Tribunal Judiciary website, no date).

[92] Hale (above n 14). While the representation of women in the judiciary overall has improved since Hale's remark, it remains true in relation to the senior judiciary.

[93] Council of Europe Commission for the Efficiency of Justice, 'Gender Equality in Courts and Public Prosecution Services' (9 September 2024).

are typically dismissed out of hand,[94] despite, as Lord Sumption and others have argued, these being 'the only thing that is likely to accelerate the rate of progress significantly'.[95] Nor is there much appetite for measures that would dramatically widen the pool of potential applicants, such as targeted judicial training to allow lawyers who are not professionally qualified, most obviously academics, to learn the skills of judge-craft.[96] Similarly, the touchstone of appointment on merit continues with no little sustained discussion as to what this really means, or if it is happening.[97] So too arguments for diversity are cited by rote with little or no recognition that they pull in different directions and require different responses.[98] At the same time judicial responses to the presence and impact of discrimination or bias within the appointments processes or judicial culture more broadly, at least in public, have been muted at best.[99]

Clearly not all these options may be palatable or even desirable.[100] But, to use Lord Sumption's words, they should 'at least be on the menu'.[101] Judges should at least be open to discussing them, if only to prevent themselves, and others committed to greater judicial diversity, from being caught in a Sisyphean nightmare: destined to repeat the same cycle of reports, dismay, reform, and regress.[102] It's time we started to call out stale clichés, to challenge institutional inertia, and to confront difficult dilemmas and ask awkward questions.

IV. REAPPRAISING EXTRAJUDICIAL DISCOURSE ON DIVERSITY

So where does this leave us? What might progressive extrajudicial discourse on diversity look like?

[94] See eg Sarah Asplin, '100 years of Women in the Law: Women in the Judiciary' (Meeting Minds Weekend in Oxford, 21 September 2019); Burnett (above n 78); Lord Judge, 'Diversity Conference' (Canary Wharf, London, 11 March 2009).

[95] Sumption (above n 9); K Malleson, 'The Disruptive Potential of Ceiling Quotas' in G Gee and E Rackley (eds), *Debating Judicial Appointments in an Age of Diversity* (Routledge, 2018) 259; G Bindman and K Monaghan, *Accelerating Diversity* (2014); M Fouzder, 'Labour conference: quotas needed to improve judicial diversity', *Law Society Gazette*, 20 September 2019; E Rackley, 'A Short History of Judicial Diversity' (2023) *Current Legal Problems* 265.

[96] See eg Mrs Justice Dobbs, 'Diversity in the Judiciary – Lecture' (Queen Mary, University of London, 17 October 2007).

[97] cf Lord Clarke, 'Selecting Judges: Merit, Moral Courage, Judgment & Diversity' (2009) 5 *High Court Quarterly Review* 49.

[98] E Rackley and C Webb, 'Three models of diversity' in G Gee and E Rackley (eds), *Debating Judicial Appointments in an Age of Diversity* (Abingdon, Routledge, 2017) 283–98.

[99] K Monteith, '"Racial Bias and the Bench": one year on', *Counsel*, 20 March 2024 (discussing the Racial Bias and the Bench report (above n 90)). Though see Lord Leggatt's welcoming remarks at the launch of the Association of Black Judges: 'we are well aware of the statistics which show that, although the diversity generally of the judiciary and of the legal profession has been improving very gradually over recent years, that has not been true for black lawyers. It is a shameful state of affairs'. ('Launch of the Association of Black Judges', UK Supreme Court, 1 July 2025). It also appears that there have been some modifications of the Equal Treatment Bench Book in line with the Report's recommendations: M Fouzder, 'Equal Treatment Bench Book: racism chapter "tighter and full of practical guidance"', *Law Society Gazette* (23 January 2024).

[100] With the obvious exception of recognising and acknowledging institutional racism embedded within the justice system, including the judiciary.

[101] Sumption (above n 9).

[102] See further E Rackley and C White, 'Judicial diversity: a Sisyphean endeavour?' in J Bourne (ed), *Research Handbook on Gender and the Legal Profession* (Cheltenham: Edward Elgar Publishing, forthcoming).

One of the most innovative recent extrajudicial interventions in this context has not been focused on diversity all, but rather has taken the form of a series of speeches considering what might broadly be termed 'judging in the 21st century', delivered by Sir Geoffrey Vos since he became Master of the Rolls in January 2021.[103] Through these speeches Vos has explored the benefits of Artificial Intelligence, digital justice and technological reform as part of his ongoing commitment to 'a radical revision of the way we provide justice for every single member of our society'.[104]

But what's this got to do with judicial diversity? Quite a lot – at least according to Vos:

> [M]y thesis is that, in the context of the technological developments that are affecting every aspect of what we do, we may need to consider changing our approach to court-based dispute resolution. If we do so, we may be able to kill at least two birds with one stone. We may be able to create a dispute resolution system truly fit for the middle part of the 21st century, and we may be able finally to complete the creation of a judiciary and a legal profession that is really representative, in terms of gender and ethnicity, of the society that they serve.[105]

The creation of a digital justice system would, Vos argues, allow for 'a "win-win" outcome … a new system for a new era, with the essential requirements of justice and the diversity of the judiciary in mind'.[106] It would, for example, provide greater flexibility for both judges and lawyers as to when and where particular work takes place, allowing work to be completed asynchronistically within shorter deadlines at times convenient to all parties. A shift to digital working may also support the implementation of what are often called 'family and carer friendly working patterns', which may in fact benefit *all* workers' health and well-being, would allow case management and preparation to be completed outside 'normal court hours', and potentially improving retention rates within the legal profession, as well as the attractiveness of a judicial career. Vos continues,

> as more and more cases are resolved without lengthy face-to-face court hearings the process becomes more acceptable and intuitive to a younger generation of more diverse lawyers. At the moment, becoming a judge, particularly a senior judge, is perhaps most attractive to a cohort of small 'c' conservative lawyers, who are often disproportionately white and male. The paraphernalia of judging – specifically the contentious process in the courtroom – is hard-wired into that section of our legal community. But once we put the process online … I can see women lawyers and lawyers from all communities being more attracted to the flexibility of online judicial working … [and] there would be … a real likelihood that the composition of the pool from which judges are chosen would come closer to its natural and representative diversity.[107]

[103] See eg Vos (above n 15); G Vos, 'How Judges Work: A Reappraisal for the 21st Century' Justice' (Tom Sargant Lecture, online, 4 November 2021); G Vos, 'The legal profession: its three most pressing issues for 2022' (The Legal Services Board: Reshaping Legal Services Conference 2022, London, 13 October 2022).

[104] Vos (2021) ibid, para 43.

[105] Vos (above n 15) para 4.

[106] Vos (2021) (above n 103) para 40.

[107] Vos (2021) (above n 103) para 37.

Rosemary Hunter has made a similar point. She argues that changes to the judicial role already taking place further down the judicial hierarchy, and in particular the expectation that the judge be 'part administrator and part service worker', already require judges to have a more 'feminised' skill set that utilises problem-solving and interpersonal and therapeutic techniques over 'traditionally masculine judicial authority'.[108]

While there may be disagreement and pushback both on the substance and articulation of Vos's vision for the future,[109] he is without doubt right that the technological and digital changes he is talking about 'will come quicker and be more radical than probably any of us can imagine'.[110] And insofar as it is, at the very least, plausible that some of these changes will provide the impetus for the 'breakthrough' which has so far eluded advocates seeking diversity across the judiciary, we should embrace and support them.[111] 'The time has come' to use Vos's words, 'to consider somewhat more adventurous solutions' in order 'to square the circle of appointing only the very best candidates and trying to achieve a fully diverse judiciary for the benefit of the society is serves'[112] – and the promise of AI and digital justice may well be part of this.[113]

V. A FINAL (NOT SO) UNCOMFORTABLE TRUTH

There is a broader point to be made here. Vos's exploration of digital judicial futures provides a model as to how extrajudicial discourse might be reinvigorated going forward. It demonstrates the gains to be made from finding different ways of talking about judicial diversity: by widening the net not only in terms of who gets to speak about diversity, relieving pressure on non-traditional candidates, but also in relation to who gets to hear it, the reach of the arguments about diversity might be more effectively mainstreamed.

For Vos this involves talking about diversity in the context of technology and justice. But this is not the only example. Access to justice, legal aid, family justice, climate change, migration, global governance, and civil litigation might be other contexts. For just as the twenty-first-century use of AI in legal disputes is not an end in itself – but is rather a means through which to secure a given end, that is, 'the need for independent and accountable judges and justice systems to deliver fair and

[108] R Hunter, 'Judicial Diversity and the 'New' Judge' in H Sommerlad, S Harris-Short, S Vaughan and R Young (eds), *The Futures of Legal Education and the Legal Profession* (Oxford, Hart Publishing, 2015) 79, 83–84.

[109] Vos has acknowledged that his 2019 Chancery Bar Association speech was not 'universally well-received' (Vos (2021) (above n 103) para 40).

[110] Vos (2021) (above n 103) para 43.

[111] Vos (above n 15) para 5.

[112] Vos (above n 15) para 37.

[113] As Conall Mallory noted in his comments on my chapter, there is of course, something deeply dispiriting but perhaps not surprising about the fact change – if it comes (and it is not clear it will and, if so, that it will reach all echelons of the judiciary) – will have been a response to an external and unrelated stimulus rather than a result of judicial recognition and determination to right historic and traditional disparities. See also Hunter (above n 108).

transparent, affordable, and most of all timely justice for our citizens'[114] – neither is judicial diversity.[115] A diverse judiciary is not an end in itself (though this is important); nor is it simply a means of securing better justice for society as a whole (though this too is important). Rather, campaigns for greater judicial diversity are better seen – and presented – as part of a wider political equality project, seeking to secure and protect fairness and justice across our institutions, culture and society.[116] This allows diversity to be placed at the heart of efforts to secure judicial strength, unity and quality,[117] as opposed to separated off as a distinct topic or initiative. Put another way, we might have better conversations about diversity – and we might make stronger arguments for it – if we talked a little less about the details of how and when we might get it and why we might want it, and a bit more about where and how a judiciary that is representative of the society it serves fits into wider conversations about justice, fairness and equality. Moreover, more judges might be willing to harness their authority, visibility and political capital to make these arguments and to get involved in the discussion. And if this were the case, not only would we have better conversations about judicial diversity – conversations that demonstrate the need for bolder steps and that confront awkward dilemmas and uncomfortable truths – but we might, finally, move closer to making judicial diversity a reality.

[114] Vos (2021) (above n 103) para 43.
[115] See further Rackley (above n 95).
[116] Malleson (above n 95) 272.
[117] Carr (above n 86) [Q6].

7

Extrajudicial Communication: What Changes in Retirement?

HÉLÈNE TYRRELL*

I. INTRODUCTION

IN THIS CHAPTER I explore the parameters for extrajudicial communication, focusing on the way that these change between serving and retired judges. I begin with why it is appropriate to describe the discourse of former judges as 'extrajudicial', accepting that a former judge is a former *judge*. Nevertheless, there is an obvious perception that retired judges enjoy greater freedom than serving judges in terms of their public remarks. This is plain from differences in the formal guidance written for serving and retired judges, and the fact that some former judges may engage in legislative business. Retired judges also make popular interview subjects and public speakers in part because of a sense that they may be able to speak more freely than serving judges. But unpacking these liberations reveals that there remain constraints. Many former judges continue to be influenced by the guidance, conventions and institutional culture that had regulated their speech when on the bench. Even those whose activities suggest that constraints dissolve almost entirely in retirement identify limits.

Absent any significant framework governing the public discourse of retired judges, these constraints are generally self-imposed.[1] The most obvious constraints stem from lingering fears about damage to judicial reputation (individual and collective) or to public perceptions about the integrity or independence of the judiciary. These are reasonable fears but do not, I suggest, always provide strong justifications for constraining the speech of retired judges. Solutions which do not require

*I thank Francesco de Cecco, Alexander Horne, Ruth Houghton, Conall Mallory, and Colin Murray for comments and suggestions on earlier drafts. Remaining errors are my own.

[1] A 'Guide to Conduct for Retired Judges' of the UK Supreme Court and Judicial Committee of the Privy Council was published in 2025: *The Supreme Court of the United Kingdom and the Judicial Committee of the Privy Council Guide to Conduct for Retired Justices* (June 2025) https://www.supremecourt.uk/uploads/Guidance_for_retired_justice_3858fbeb7b.pdf. At the time of writing, this guidance runs to seven paragraphs and does not make significant additions to pre-existing judicial conduct guides.

extrajudicial silence are available. Further, the public utterances of retired judges on matters normally attracting circumspection have the potential, counterintuitively, to promote confidence in the judiciary. Finally, I suggest that interrogating justifications for constraining the public remarks of retired judges invites a reassessment of the parameters for extrajudicial speech on the part of *serving* judges.

II. 'EXTRAJUDICIAL' AND THE EX-JUDICIAL

Describing what judges say in retirement as 'extrajudicial' deserves explanation. After all, retirement normally marks the end of formal duties and, with it, a liberation from professional constraints. Former judges may continue to sit on supplementary panels and can take on judicial work elsewhere,[2] but otherwise can no longer be considered to speak *judicially*. Nevertheless, it is difficult to forget that a retired judge was once, indeed, a judge. Guides to Judicial Conduct recognise that retired judges 'may still be regarded by the general public as representatives of the judiciary'.[3] This public perception makes it likely that the comments of retired judges will attract public attention.[4] This is especially so for senior judges, who are commonly invited to talk on the basis of their judicial experience, or whose former role will underpin the legitimacy of a report. When Lord Bingham gave his 2008 Grotius Lecture,[5] criticising the then Attorney General's defence of the 2003 invasion of Iraq, it was reported in the press as his 'first major speech since retiring as the senior law lord'.[6]

Former judges may also continue to work in judge-like roles in their retirement, taking on trusted roles in public life, such as chairing public inquiries.[7] In fact, when inquiries are not led by a judge, they are often criticised as a lesser form of investigation,[8] even if parliamentarians might not always be inclined to treat chairing an

[2] It is well known that a number of the UK senior judiciary have, in retirement, joined the Hong Kong Court of Final Appeal (albeit that it is not universally agreed that they should): J Rozenberg, 'What retired judges do really matters' (*The Law Society Gazette*, 15 November 2024) www.lawgazette.co.uk/commentary-and-opinion/what-retired-judges-do-really-matters/5121545.article.

[3] Courts and Tribunals Judiciary *Guide to Judicial Conduct* (July 2023) www.judiciary.uk/guidance-and-resources/guide-to-judicial-conduct-revised-july-2023/, 6; *Statement of Ethics for the Judiciary in Northern Ireland* (2nd Revision, August 2011) www.nijac.gov.uk/statement-ethics-judiciary, 10.2; *The Supreme Court of the United Kingdom and the Judicial Committee of the Privy Council Guide to Conduct for Retired Justices* (June 2025) (above n 1), para 2.

[4] P O'Brien and B Yong, 'Work in Judicial Retirement: A Policy Report' (June 2023) sites.google.com/brookes.ac.uk/the-judicial-afterlife, 29.

[5] Lord Bingham, 'The Rule of Law in the International Order' (Grotius Lecture at the British Institute of International and Comparative Law, London, 17 November 2008).

[6] R Norton-Taylor, 'Top judge: US and UK Acted as "Vigilantes" in Iraq Invasion', *The Guardian* (London, 18 November 2008) www.theguardian.com/world/2008/nov/18/iraq-us-foreign-policy.

[7] '68% of inquiries launched since 1990 [have been] chaired by a judge or former judge. Of the 18 ongoing inquiries with an appointed chair, 13 are chaired by a current or former judge': S Sangha and R McKee, 'Public Inquiries' (13 February 2025) www.instituteforgovernment.org.uk/explainer/public-inquiries. Indeed, it is possible that the mere prospect of one day being called upon to, for example, lead a public enquiry might act as a constraint on extrajudicial speech for both serving and retired judges. I thank Francesco de Cecco for this excellent observation.

[8] S Cooper and O Thomas, 'Judge-led Public Inquiries in the UK: The Gold Standard?' in S Prasser (ed), *New Directions In Royal Commissions & Public Inquiries: Do We Need Them?* (Queensland, Conor Court, 2023).

inquiry as the performance of a judicial function.[9] These sorts of roles led O'Brien and Yong to conclude that retired judges 'are normally still considered to be "judges" in the public mind'.[10]

III. THE SPACE FOR EXTRAJUDICIAL COMMUNICATION IN RETIREMENT

The parameters and risks relating to the public utterances of *serving* judges have been subject to extensive consideration, both in this volume and elsewhere:[11] comments revealing the internal dynamics of panel deliberations might compromise future processes and undermine decision-making, while discussion of decided cases might undermine 'the finality of judgments'.[12] Extrajudicial engagement with matters of political controversy might be made at some risk to the public perception of judicial independence and impartiality, or may 'tarnish the reputation of the judiciary'.[13] Depending on the context, such remarks might also give rise to a real possibility of bias so as to require recusal or a re-trial.

> [J]udicial office holders should, so far as is reasonable, avoid extra-judicial activities that are likely to cause them to have to refrain from sitting because of a reasonable apprehension of bias or because of a conflict of interest that would arise from the activity.[14]

But not all of these considerations apply in the same way to retired judges. Some of these considerations do not apply at all.

The Kilmuir Rules, which applied between 1955 and 1987, and strongly discouraged judges from speaking in public beyond their official duties,[15] never applied to retired judges. Guides to Judicial Conduct provide a steer in relation to the extrajudicial engagement of serving judges, but offer very little guidance on the public remarks of former judges. For example, while serving judges are given explicit guidance on the substance of acceptable public comments – avoiding comment 'on the merits, meaning or likely effect of government policy or proposals; the merits of public appointments; or the merits of individual cases' – the *Guide to Judicial Conduct* only goes so far as to recognise that retired judicial office holders should 'exercise caution' on the basis that they 'may still be regarded by the general public as representatives of the judiciary'.[16] Retired judges are merely 'encouraged' rather than required to refer to the guidance.[17] The 2025 Guide to Conduct created explicitly for retired Justices of the UK Supreme Court and Judicial Committee of the Privy Council

[9] J Beatson, 'The New Model Judiciary and the Other Two Branches of the State' [2015] *Judicial Review* 63, 71.

[10] O'Brien and Yong, 'Work in Judicial Retirement' (above n 4) 2.

[11] See eg C Mallory and H Tyrrell, 'The Extrajudicial Voice' (2024) 44(1) *Legal Studies* 1.

[12] *Guide to Judicial Conduct* (above n 3) 16.

[13] ibid.

[14] ibid 9.

[15] Letter from Lord Kilmuir to Sir Ian Jacob KBE of 12 December 1955, reprinted in AW Bradley, 'Judges and the Media – the Kilmuir Rules' [1986] *Public Law* 383, 385.

[16] *Guide to Judicial Conduct* (above n 3) 6. *Statement of Ethics for the Judiciary in Northern Ireland* (above n 3) 10.2.

[17] ibid.

reinforces these themes but goes only as far as suggesting that retired Justices 'exercise discretion' with respect to their retirement activities, keeping in mind the possibility that these could compromise the Court's independence or impartiality.[18] Neither are retired judges subject to formal coercive measures for non-compliance, and it is made explicit that '[t]here is no prohibition on retired judges, engaging in political activity and wider public debate' (provided that they are no longer sitting).[19] Whatever the public perception, retired judges are no longer members of the judiciary and it is inevitable that retirement will open up the space for extrajudicial speech.

Some former judges may engage in legislative business. When the apex court sat in the House of Lords, appointment as a new Law Lord meant the grant of life peerage,[20] making participation in parliamentary debate a well-established forum for extrajudicial speech in retirement. In practice, there was a convention that the sitting Law Lords did not become involved in politically contentious issues and retired Law Lords, who retained membership of the House of Lords, generally adhered to that tradition. But, as noted by Shetreet and Tureene, even 'the convention that Law Lords would not become involved in politically contentious issues was less and less observed towards the end of the twentieth century'.[21] This shift flowed into retirement – perhaps amplified by the separation of the senior judiciary from the second chamber, following the Constitutional Reform Act 2005 (CRA). The CRA included a provision to prevent serving judges from sitting or voting in the House of Lords,[22] but did not prevent retired judges from engaging in legislative debates, insofar as they held a peerage. In this setting, some retired judges have taken on influential roles: Lord Hope acted as convenor of the Cross-bench peers between 2015 and 2019; Lord Woolf chaired the Sub-Committee on Lords' Conduct and became a member of the Joint Committee on Human Rights; Lord Phillips made significant contributions to the Joint Committee on the Draft Voting Eligibility (Prisoners) Bill; Lord Thomas sat on the House of Lords European Union Committee and its Financial Affairs Sub-Committee; Lord Brown and Lord Mance were both members of the House of Lords European Union Select Committee, and both acted as Chair of its Sub-Committee on European Law and Institutions.[23]

Those arrangements recognised that retired judges could offer an unparalleled vantage point and that political engagement by retired judges could be considered to be in the public interest.[24] Lord Hennessy recounts that Lord Judge was 'an antidote to the view … that crossbenchers are the political wing of the British establishment. … he always brought something of considerable value to whatever the business was'.[25] 'His speech in the second reading [of the Rwanda Bill] would have been the one that

[18] *The Supreme Court of the United Kingdom and the Judicial Committee of the Privy Council Guide to Conduct for Retired Justices* (June 2025) (above n 1), para 7.

[19] *Guide to Judicial Conduct* (above n 3) 16.

[20] Appellate Jurisdiction Act 1876, s6.

[21] S Shetreet and S Turenne, *Judges on Trial* (Cambridge, Cambridge University Press, 2014) 248.

[22] Constitutional Reform Act 2005, s 137(3).

[23] For discussion see, in this volume, Chapter 12: A Horne, 'Methods of Extra-Judicial Participation in Parliament'.

[24] Shetreet and Turenne (above n 21) 268.

[25] The University of Law Podcast, 'The Judges: Power, Politics and the People' www.youtube.com/playlist?list=PLIr_gf3NNn2jvMHVS4oFnGTigu8mroujy, Episode 9: Lord Judge, (4 April 2024).

we all hang on'.[26] The inescapability of 'Henry VIII clauses' and the well-recognised deficiencies of the democratic process in respect to legislative debate in the Commons made such participation especially valuable.[27] There is evidently 'a real public interest in knowing what retired judges, especially senior retired judges, have to say' on legislation or on an important decision of the courts.[28] However, while the CRA did not prevent retired judges from engaging in legislative debates, it did eliminate automatic life-peerages for the senior judiciary. As such, the CRA made no automatic provision for future parliamentary participation on the part of retired judges and there is a consequent disparity in the potential for extrajudicial participation in the House of Lords.

A number of judges might take up academic posts, which, as Stephen Sedley put it, offer the 'opportunity and stimulus to confront the incuriosity' met in the profession, as well as to satisfy personal curiosity.[29] Others will contribute to practitioner or student texts,[30] or publish journal articles with a view to 'stirr[ing] … points, which wiser heads in time may settle'.[31] Retired judges may feel able to respond to a greater number of invitations, giving public interviews or appearing on podcasts – in 2024 a number of retired senior judges gave interviews to Frances Gibb, journalist and former legal editor of *The Times*.[32] Many judges take the time to reflect on their life and career, publishing diaries or memoirs.[33] A few will offer their thoughts in shorter works, writing newspaper columns, contributing articles to magazines, or speaking on the radio.[34] Most of the contributions will be related to the law. Others will talk about golf.[35]

While appearing as a television food critic or allowing a public view into one's home life might be viewed in some quarters as undignified,[36] these activities are not normally likely to draw the judiciary into 'the controversies of the day'.[37] At most,

[26] ibid (Lord Hennessey).

[27] The University of Law Podcast (above n 25) Episode 5: Lord Phillips (10 January 2024). 'Henry VIII clauses' are legislative provisions allowing the executive to amend or repeal primary legislation without further parliamentary approval.

[28] Lord Dyson, 'Judicial after-life: should it be subject to any limits?' (Birkenhead Lecture, London, 12 November 2024) www.graysinn.org.uk/events/birkenhead-lecture/, para 34.

[29] S Sedley, *Lions under the Throne: Essays on the History of English Public Law* (Cambridge, Cambridge University Press, 2015) ix.

[30] Eg Lord Collins of Mapesbury and Professor Jonathan Harris (eds), *Dicey, Morris & Collins on the Conflict of Laws*, 16th edn (London, Sweet & Maxwell Publishing, 2025).

[31] Lord Bingham of Cornhill, 'The House of Lords: its future?' [2010] *Public Law* 261, 274. Citing *Coggs v Bernard* (1703) 2 Ld Raym 909, 920; 92 ER 107 (KB).

[32] The University of Law Podcast (above n 25).

[33] Non-exhaustive examples include: The Rt Hon Lord Woolf, *An Uncommon Lawyer* (Oxford, Hart Publishing, 2022); Lord Dyson, *A Judge's Journey* (Oxford, Hart Publishing, 2019); Lady Hale's *Spider Woman: A Life* (London, Bodley Head/ Penguin, 2021); *Lord Hope's Diaries* volumes I–V (Edinburgh, Avizandumm, 2018–19); In this volume, Chapter 14: L Graham, 'Learning from Lord Hope's Diaries' and Chapter 15: J Lee, 'Judging Memoirs: Life-Writing as Extra-Judicial Communication'.

[34] Baroness Hale of Richmond, 'Desert Island Discs' (*BBC Radio 4*, 19 September 2021) www.bbc.co.uk/sounds/play/m000zt7b.

[35] S Brown, 'Taking the smooth with the rough…' (2021–22) 22 *Golf Quarterly* 38–39; Lord Brown, *Playing off the Roof & Other Stories: A Patchwork of Memories* (London, Marble Hill, 2020) and *Second Helpings* (London, Marble Hill, 2021).

[36] Lord Neuberger, 'Where Angels Fear to Tread' (Holdsworth Club Presidential Address, London, 2 March 2012) www.judiciary.uk/wp-content/uploads/JCO/Documents/Speeches/mr-speech-holdsworth-lecture-2012.pdf, para 8.

[37] Bradley (above n 15) 384.

an interest in these types of communication reflects the personage that some judges acquire.[38] Such outputs can also help to humanise judges, which must be at least part of the motivation behind some judicial retrospectives. Lady Hale, for example, begins *Spider Woman* with 'imposter moments', carving out her aim to tell the story of 'that little girl from a little school in a little village in Northern Yorkshire' and how 'she found that she could cope. And how all those other people who feel they are imposters can learn to cope too'.[39] Along with accounts of early life and personal influences, many retired judges reveal insights into personal-professional experiences. Lord Woolf describes his time as a newly appointed Law Lord and the 'intimidating' practice of the post-hearing discussion, in which judges spoke in reverse order of seniority.[40] Lord Dyson writes about the pressures he felt under upon his appointment to the Supreme Court, with a candid account of his 'impression that at least some [of the Justices] wrote judgments to impress each other and to win colleagues over to their point of view', admitting that he 'may have been guilty of this' himself.[41]

Few doubt the propriety of serving or former judges discussing topics relating to the justice system. It is unsurprising when even serving judges, especially those in leadership positions, come forward to defend against threats to the justice system or attacks on the judiciary. This is especially important if and when the constitutional actors with responsibility for defending the independence of the judiciary abdicate their role. When, following the first *Miller* judgment (concerning the legal mechanism for triggering 'Brexit') and the infamous 'Enemies of the People' headline,[42] the then Lord Chancellor, Liz Truss, dragged her feet in defending the judiciary against unwarranted media attacks, it was not surprising that the then Lord Chief Justice spoke out.[43] This much is anticipated by the *Guide to Judicial Conduct*, which, while generally advising against serving judges communicating with the media, *does* envisage circumstances justifying 'cautious engagement'.[44] Retired judges are not subject to that advice and so the relative freedom enjoyed by retired judges allows them to 'play an important role in voicing the judiciary's concerns'.[45] A month after his retirement, for example, Lord Kerr spoke in defence of judges and lawyers, following criticisms from the then Prime Minister and then Home Secretary of legal work which had

[38] Explored further in this volume, Chapter 16: A Deb, 'Ermine Trims and Marmite Toast: Judicial Portraits from Extrajudicial Aesthetics'.

[39] Lady Hale, *Spider Woman* (above n 33) 1.

[40] Lord Woolf, *An Uncommon Lawyer* (above n 33) 74.

[41] John Dyson, *A Judge's Journey* (above n 33) 130.

[42] J Slack, 'Enemies of the people: Fury over "out of touch" judges who have "declared war on democracy" by defying 17.4m Brexit voters and who could trigger constitutional crisis' (*Daily Mail*, 4 November 2016) www.dailymail.co.uk/news/article-3903436/Enemies-people-Fury-touch-judges-defied-17-4m-Brexit-voters-trigger-constitutional-crisis.html.

[43] O Bowcott, 'Lord chief justice attacks Liz Truss for failing to back article 50 judges', *The Guardian* (London, 22 March 2017); *BBC News*, 'Attacks on Judges Undermine Law – Supreme Court President' www.bbc.co.uk/news/uk-38986228. See further P O'Brien, '"Enemies of the People": Judges, the Media, and the Mythic Lord Chancellor' [2017] *Public Law* 135.

[44] *Guide to Judicial Conduct* (above n 3) 16.

[45] Shetreet and Turenne (above n 21) 359; the 2025 *Guide to Conduct for Retired Judges* notes that retired Justices of the UK Supreme Court have, among other things, given media interviews and that these activities do not run counter to the guidance. It is merely restated that such activities are capable of presenting risks to public confidence, independence and impartiality (above n 1), paras 5–6.

obstructed immigration controls.[46] Across the Atlantic, retired US Supreme Court Justice, Justice Sandra Day O'Connor defended Iowa's system of merit-based selection of judges when three of its Supreme Court Justices were facing retention elections because of their votes in favour of same-sex marriage.[47] Into this category we could also place Lord Sumption's remarks about aspects of Supreme Court reform,[48] or Lord Brown's publications relating to the backlog of untried Crown Court cases.[49]

IV. LIBERATIONS

Retirement also appears to open up topics of discussion that would have been inappropriate for a serving judge. Lady Hale has explained that retired judges could be 'a little more candid'.[50] In a number of his post-retirement speeches, Lord Judge was explicit about being able to speak more freely than when a serving judge: 'I can … say something that I could not perhaps have said [prior to retirement] two months ago';[51] '[s]ince leaving office I have become less inhibited in the expression of my views'.[52]

Retired judges are generally more willing to comment on matters of public controversy or to give their view of legislative and political decisions. In *An Uncommon Lawyer*, Lord Woolf argues that repeal of the Human Rights Act 1998 would be a 'retrograde step'.[53] Sir Stephen Sedley's *Lions Under the Throne* reveals cynicism about initiatives in relation to the development of judicial review,[54] and a 'growing unease among the higher judiciary at evidence that both ministers and Parliament itself are prepared to manipulate or even abandon constitutional norms for short-term ends'.[55] Recall too that Lord Bingham was retired at the point of his 2008 Grotius Lecture, in which he criticised the legality of the Iraq war – a point that he later confirmed that he had consciously refrained from making in lectures while a serving judge.[56] Contributing to Lord Bingham's obituary, Henry Porter reported that

> [f]reed from the constraints that went with being Britain's first senior law lord, Tom Bingham was able to be more open in public about the deep commitment to liberty and

[46] O Bowcott, 'UK Needs Judges to Limit Government Power, says Lord Kerr', *The Guardian* (London, 19 October 2020) www.theguardian.com/law/2020/oct/19/uk-needs-judges-to-limit-government-power-says-lord-kerr? Unfortunately, Lord Kerr's post-retirement contributions were cut short by his death in December 2020, just two months after his retirement.

[47] R Boshart, 'Former Justice Backs Judicial Independence', *Quad-City Times* (Davenport IA, 8 September 2010) qctimes.com/news/state-and-regional/iowa/5e26167a-bb53-11df-966d-001cc4c03286.html.

[48] House of Lords Select Committee on the Constitution, Lord Sumption, Constitutional implications of COVID19 (2 December 2020); J Ames, 'Supreme Court Reforms are "Cheap Revenge", Lord Sumption says', *The Times* (London, 16 November 2020).

[49] Mallory and Tyrrell (above n 11) 14.

[50] Lady Hale, interview with the authors: Mallory and Tyrrell (above n 11) 14.

[51] Lord Judge, 'The Evidence of Child Victims' in *The Safest Shield: Lectures, Speeches and Essays* (Oxford, Hart Publishing, 2015) 229.

[52] Lord Judge, 'Constitutional Change: Unfinished Business' in *The Safest Shield*, ibid 3.

[53] Lord Woolf, *An Uncommon Lawyer* (above n 33) 74.

[54] Sedley, *Lions under the Throne* (above n 29) 108.

[55] ibid 115.

[56] Interview with Lord Bingham, conducted by A Macfarlane (31 March 2009) www.youtube.com/watch?v=fEp4pAnoRoc&ab_channel=cephalite.

> rights … notably those concerning the internment of foreign terror suspects at Belmarsh prison, south-east London, and the use of information gained by torture.[57]

These were points that he picked up in a chapter of his 2010 book, *The Rule of Law*.[58]

A number of judges have entered, or accepted an invitation to participate in, debates about the UK's relationship with international bodies. Various examples can be drawn from the ongoing discussion about membership of the European Convention on Human Rights (ECHR). Lord Burnett revealed that he had not been persuaded that withdrawal was 'remotely necessary',[59] and Lord Dyson has argued against those who believed that the UK had no need for the European Court of Human Rights, suggesting that their view was 'born of the arrogant belief that we know best and have nothing to learn from foreigners'.[60] A year after retirement from the presidency of the UK Supreme Court, Lord Phillips was happy to say in a public lecture that he sympathised with those who were dismayed about the hostile treatment given to the Strasbourg Court and the Convention, while also agreeing that the Strasbourg Court had probably enlarged the reach of the Convention in a way that had gone beyond what the parties anticipated when they subscribed to it.[61] Lord Sumption has made numerous forceful contributions to the debate, not least via his 2019 Reith Lectures,[62] in which he was critical of the European Court of Human Rights' approach to the interpretation of human rights law. He later advocated leaving the ECHR.[63]

Another apparent liberation relates to the general principle against discussion of decided cases. In a post-retirement interview, Lord Neuberger said: 'I've always said that … once you've given the decision, you should never say whether it was right or wrong'.[64] It was 'particularly' important, he thought, not to say a case was wrongly decided: 'Somebody cites your judgment to a high court judge. And the other side says "but Lord Neuberger has just said in public he thought he was wrong"'. Similarly, judges who have chaired an inquiry may consider it improper to be 'drawn into discussion of the merits of the substantive proposals or conclusions

[57] P Sands, 'Lord Bingham of Cornhill Obituary', *The Guardian* (London, 11 September 2010) www.theguardian.com/law/2010/sep/11/lord-bingham-of-cornhill-obituary (quoting Henry Porter). See also F Gibb, 'Freed from his Judicial Shackles, Lord Bingham Delivers his Judgment on the Iraq war', *The Times* (London, 19 November 2008) www.thetimes.com/article/07afa3b5-7a26-4747-838e-2fcbe3f43d09.

[58] T Bingham, 'The Rule of Law in the International Legal Order' in *The Rule of Law* (London, Penguin, 2010) 110–29; Shetreet and Turenne (above n 21) 366.

[59] The University of Law Podcast (above n 25) Episode 9: Lord Burnett (14 March 2024).

[60] J Dyson, *A Judge's Journey* (above n 33) 137; Lord Dyson, 'What is Wrong with Human Rights?' (Hertfordshire University, 3 November 2011), supremecourt.uk/uploads/speech_111103_85c8e61696.pdf, 20.

[61] Lord Phillips of Worth Matravers, 'The Impact of Human Rights on Domestic Courts' (FW Guest Memorial Lecture, University of Otago New Zealand, 6 March 2013) www.youtube.com/watch?v=aWBO5I6RQws&ab_channel=FacultyofLaw%2CUniversityofOtago%2CDunedin%2CNewZealand.

[62] J Sumption, 'The Reith Lectures 2019: Law and The Decline of Politics'.

[63] C Hymas, 'Lord Sumption Backs Calls for Britain to leave European Convention on Human Rights', *The Telegraph* (28 September 2023) www.telegraph.co.uk/news/2023/09/28/lord-sumption-backs-britain-to-leave-echr/.

[64] The University of Law Podcast (above n 25) Episode 2: Lord Neuberger (9 November 2023).

drawn'.[65] What a judge later says might diminish confidence in the outcomes of the inquiry in the same way as ex post discussion of cases might raise questions in relation to a judgment.[66] But it is obvious that retired judges have considered themselves to enjoy at least a little freedom to make 'general observations' about decided cases.[67]

Lord Woolf was willing to reflect on his sentencing decision for *Venables and Thompson*.[68] Lord Neuberger was willing to reveal that his 'heart' in *Nicklinson* had been 'with Brenda [Hale] and Brian [Kerr]' (dissenting) who would have issued a declaration that the blanket ban on assisted suicide in section 2(1) of the Suicide Act 1961 was incompatible with Article 8 of the European Convention on Human Rights.[69] Lord Judge wrote of his personal regret about the law in this context, 'ventur[ing]' a view on the appropriate legislative response to *Nicklinson*: 'now that the issue of incompatibility has been raised, our sovereign Parliament really cannot, and should not, ignore the pleas by the courts for the issue to be addressed'.[70] Others have gone further. Notable examples include Lord Hoffmann, who retired as a Law Lord in 2009 but who has been an active speaker on a number of subjects since then. In 2023 Lord Hoffmann was drawn into giving 'second thoughts' on decided cases. The decision in *Fairchild* (a case about liability for damages regarding asbestos-induced mesothelioma),[71] Lord Hoffmann thought, 'was a disaster': 'we [the House of Lords] invented an exception' to the established rules, and that had been 'a great mistake'. He went on to explain 'what [the court] should have said'.[72] Remembering *Sheldrake v DPP* (a case about the reversal of the burden of proof),[73] Lord Phillips revealed that, perhaps 'pusillanimously' he had been 'persuaded to suppress [his] reservations about the constitutionality' of an approach to statutory interpretation that seemed deliberately to depart from the clear intention of the parliament that enacted the legislation.[74] And while criticism of judicial colleagues, especially those still serving, is normally considered off-limits, this did not stop Lord Bingham from revisiting *Jackson v Attorney General* and criticising the comments made by Lord Steyn, Lord Hope, and Lady Hale on the limits of parliamentary sovereignty.[75]

[65] Beatson (above n 9) 70.

[66] Such discourse on the part of *serving* judges might also have an impact on the formal relationship between the judiciary and other branches of state: ibid, 65.

[67] WG Ross, 'Extrajudicial Speech: Charting the Boundaries of Propriety' (1989) 1 *Georgetown Journal of Legal Ethics* 589, 603.

[68] The University of Law Podcast (above n 25) Episode 1: Lord Woolf (24 October 2023).

[69] *R (Nicklinson) v Ministry of Justice (CNK Alliance Ltd intervening)* [2014] UKSC 38; [2015] AC 657.

[70] Lord Judge, 'Assisted Suicide: Moral and Constitutional Issues' in *The Safest Shield* (above n 51) 118.

[71] *Fairchild v Glenhaven Funderal Services Ltd* [2002] UKHL 22; [2003] 1 AC 32.

[72] BCLP LLP, 'An Interview with Lord Hoffmann: In Conversation with a Reasonable Man' (7 February 2023) www.youtube.com/watch?v=jDjYNmiIxH4&ab_channel=BCLP.

[73] *Sheldrake v Director of Public Prosecutions* [2004] UKHL 43; [2005] 1 AC 264.

[74] Lord Phillips of Worth Matravers, 'The Impact of Human Rights on Domestic Courts' (University of Otago New Zealand, FW Guest Memorial Lecture 2013, Dunedin, 6 March 2013) www.youtube.com/watch?v=aWBO5I6RQws&ab_channel=FacultyofLaw%2CUniversityofOtago%2CDunedin%2C-NewZealand.

[75] Bingham, *The Rule of Law* (above n 58) 166–67. *Jackson and Others v HM Attorney General* [2005] UKHL 56.

V. CONSTRAINTS

Unpacking these liberations also reveals constraints. While, in retirement, Lord Judge said that he was 'no longer constrained by the principle that serving judges do not discuss political questions'; he also explained that it would have been 'a breach of this soundly based principle to have ignored it altogether'.[76] He could not, for example, 'breach confidences' or discuss matters which were 'entrusted to [him] when in office'.[77] In fact he was 'determined' not to speak on matters which 'might enable anyone to suggest or even imply that I may have been in breach of confidences'.[78] That others in the judicial community agree can be read into the reaction to the publication of Lord Hope's diaries, wherein he disclosed previously unknown information in relation to candidates for judicial appointments and made various comments on the politics or nature of his colleagues.[79] Lord Hope also recounted details of what had been said during some informal post-hearing panel deliberations. The impact of extrajudicial revelations, particularly about panel deliberations, may be very significant:

> If judges know or believe that what they say to their colleagues when they are discussing how a case should be decided is likely to be published, that is bound to have a seriously inhibiting effect on what they say during their discussions.[80]

It is for that reason that Lord Dyson suggested that, in relation to retired judges, these are points about which the *Guide to Judicial Conduct* should be explicit.[81]

It is possible, of course, for discussion of decided cases to stop short of drawing the judiciary into political debate, with the accompanying risks to the perception of impartiality. These constraints operate informally. As Lord Sumption explained in his interview with Francis Gibb, discussion of a decided case does not necessarily entail discussing politics: 'by saying, for example, that the prorogation decision was right, you are [not] necessarily endorsing remaining [in the EU] or the opposite' – there is 'a world of difference' between reflecting on the judgment concerning procedure and saying that it was a sound decision and saying that the UK ought never to have left the EU.[82] Many legal issues are issues with political implications, but that does not mean that the judges deciding them are being political or are politically motivated. The Supreme Court judgment in *Miller* opened with the disclaimer that the question was not about whether or not the UK should exit the European Union.[83] This case had nothing to do with [the political] issues relating to the UK's exit from or future relationship with the European Union: 'Those are all political issues which are matters

[76] Lord Judge, 'Constitutional Change: Unfinished Business' in *The Safest Shield* (above n 51) 73.
[77] ibid 80.
[78] Lord Judge, *The Safest Shield* (above n 51) 3.
[79] Mallory and Tyrrell (above n 11) 17 text from fns 186–194; in this volume, see Chapter 14: L Graham, 'Learning from Lord Hope's Diaries' and Chapter 15: J Lee, 'Judging Memoirs: Life Writing as Extra-Judicial Communication'.
[80] Lord Dyson, 'Judicial after-life' (above n 28) para 44.
[81] ibid para 45. The 2025 *Guide to Conduct for Retired Judges* relating to the UK Supreme Court and Judicial Committee of the Pricy Council made no such addition (above n 1).
[82] The University of Law Podcast (above n 25) Episode 6: Lord Sumption (25 January 2024).
[83] *R (Miller) v Secretary of State for Exiting the European Union* [2017] UKSC 5; [2018] AC 62 [3].

for ministers and Parliament to resolve' and the duty upon judges was 'to decide issues of law'.[84]

The discussion of past decisions might also be carefully balanced to avoid undermining legal certainty. Lord Neuberger's willingness to comment on *Nicklinson* flowed from his feeling that, despite the lack of clarity in the judgment, the right decision had been reached.[85] Similarly, his reflections on *Miller and Cherry* amounted to an explanation of why he felt the Supreme Court had got their decision right.[86] When Lady Hale was drawn into comment on the controversial Supreme Court decision in *For Women Scotland* at the Charleston literary festival (concerning the definition of a 'woman' for the purposes of the Equality Act 2010),[87] she was reported to have said that the last thing she wanted now that she had retired was to 'undermine the court and its authority by being critical of its decisions' but she was willing to be 'critical of the way it has been received'.[88] Lord Sumption, too, seems to have focused his remarks on the misinterpretations of the Supreme Court's ruling.[89] Others have suggested temporal constraints. Lord Brown articulated such a limit in an interview, thinking about retired judges who had 'become so out of touch that what they say doesn't have contemporary relevance'.[90] Although that principle seemed to evade Lord Denning, whose controversial remarks in retirement in the 1980s included suggestions that immigrants might not be suitable as jurors and that the Birmingham Six ought to have been hanged.[91]

Such examples might explain the lingering fears about damage to judicial reputation (individual and collective). Lord Kilmuir discouraged serving judges from extrajudicial communication partly on the basis that: 'so long as a Judge keeps silent *his reputation* for wisdom and impartiality remains unassailable' (emphasis added).[92] Bound up in such anxiety is a sense of collective identity: '[T]he current judiciary will look upon the past judiciary – whether alive or dead – just in a similar way that a child will look at their parents or their grandparents'.[93] Judges bear a responsibility 'to the entire judicial family as a whole'.[94] When former judges speak, they also risk *their* familial reputation: a judge 'may have a very good reputation at some point in

[84] ibid.

[85] The University of Law Podcast (above n 25) Episode 2: Lord Neuberger (9 November 2023).

[86] ibid. *R (on the application of Miller) v Prime Minister; Cherry and Others v Advocate General for Scotland* [2019] UKSC 41.

[87] *For Women Scotland v The Scottish Ministers* [2025] UKSC 16.

[88] L Knight, 'Court Ruling on Legal Definition of a Woman "Misinterpreted", Lady Hale Says', *The Guardian* (London, 22 May 2025) www.theguardian.com/law/2025/may/22/court-ruling-legal-definition-of-a-woman-misinterpreted-lady-hale.

[89] Lord Sumption, 'PM' (*BBC Radio 4*, 18 April 2025).

[90] Lord Brown interview with authors in Mallory and Tyrrell (above n 11) 14.

[91] eg C Dyer, 'Lord Denning, Controversial "People's Judge", Dies Aged 100', *The Guardian* (London, 6 March 1999) www.theguardian.com/uk/1999/mar/06/claredyer1. A Denning, *What Next in the Law* (London, LexisNexix, 1982).

[92] Bradley (above n 15) 384–85. See further: G Rubin, 'Judicial Free Speech versus Judicial Neutrality in Mid-Twentieth Century England: The Last Hurrah for the Ancien Regime?' (2009) 27(2) *Law and History Review* 373.

[93] Anonymous interview with authors, in Mallory and Tyrrell (above n 11) 14.

[94] Lord Judge, 'Induction Seminar: Welcome' in *The Safest Shield* (above n 51) 356.

his career, which is subsequently significantly diminished by what he or she says in retirement'.[95]

Some have criticised Lord Sumption's public remarks in retirement on these grounds. When Lord Grabiner KC expressed his view that it is 'quite damaging for senior retired lawyers to participate in controversial public debate, and indeed to lead that debate', he had Lord Sumption 'well in mind'.[96] A chapter could be written on Lord Sumption's public remarks in retirement alone. It may be that Lord Sumption's prolific and ongoing contributions to public debate are a stand-out example, flowing from an unusual career path, encompassing publication as a historian and culminating in appointment straight to the Supreme Court.[97] But Lord Sumption, too, has identified limits. Owing to his public criticism of the government in respect of Brexit and the handling of the COVID-19 pandemic, for example, Lord Sumption suggested that his name be withdrawn from the supplementary list.[98] In a post-retirement interview he explained that while he did not consider there to be limits to what may legitimately be discussed, 'one has to stay within a very broad notion of the range of – for want of a better word – acceptable opinion'.[99] And in an interview for *The Times*, Lord Sumption is quoted as having recognised '[t]he conventional view' that retired judges should refrain from commenting on politically controversial issues, while also recognising that his own activities have done exactly that: 'I actually approve of that convention although I have been an egregious breaker of it'.[100] His reasoning comes through in interview with Francis Gibb: there were issues, like COVID, on which judges should, 'in principle… not speak out even after retirement' but 'there are exceptions to every rule':[101]

> there are some issues which are so fundamental that they are much more important than any convention about what a judge should or shouldn't say after retirement … on those issues you have to stand up and be counted.[102]

On this Lord Sumption is not alone – he is one of a number of former judges, including other retired Justices of the UK Supreme Court, to sign letters concerning the conflict in the Middle East and its impact on the population in Gaza.[103]

Retired judges, it seems, do not become uninhibited but 'less inhibited' in the expression of their views.[104] There remains some 'self-imposed reticence', albeit that where individual judges draw the line varies.[105] The absence of any significant

[95] Anonymous interview with authors, in Mallory and Tyrrell (above n 11) 14.

[96] The University of Law Podcast (above n 25) Series Finale (30 May 2024).

[97] For an insight, see eg Lord Sumption, 'The Historian as Judge' (Rolls Building, 6 October 2016) supremecourt.uk/uploads/speech_161006_347600ce1f.pdf.

[98] Freedom of Information Request, Emails relating to Lord Sumption's resignation from the supplementary panel available at www.supremecourt.uk/docs/foi-2021-29-recorded-information-12-7-21.pdf.

[99] Lord Sumption interview with authors, in Mallory and Tyrrell (above n 11) 18.

[100] D Jones, 'Jonathan Sumption on War with France, Brexit and Cancel Culture', *The Sunday Times* (London, 27 August 2023).

[101] The University of Law Podcast (above n 25) Episode 6: Lord Sumption (25 January 2024). www.youtube.com/watch?v=raA40Y190Hs&ab_channel=TheUniversityofLaw.

[102] ibid.

[103] See, in particular, letters of 3 April 2024 and 26 May 2025 lawyersletter.uk/.

[104] Lord Judge, 'Constitutional Change: Unfinished Business' in *The Safest Shield* (above n 51) 73.

[105] ibid.

framework governing the public discourse of retired judges allows this. Some have argued for more detailed guidance,[106] but this depends on a prior acceptance that it is appropriate to apply formal constraints in retirement, and that is not itself obvious. Or, at least, eroding a retired judge's right to freedom of expression 'requires particularly cogent and clear justification'.[107]

VI. JUSTIFICATIONS: CONFIDENCE AND IMPARTIALITY

A clear justification for restraint in relation to the extrajudicial speech of serving judges is that it may reveal partiality: 'a speech on a subject which may become the subject of judicial determination … could compromise judicial independence';[108] 'if the issue on which they had spoken came up in litigation, they could not approach it with an open mind'.[109] As a justification for constraining extrajudicial communication on the part of *retired* judges, however, this is less convincing. Concerns relating to any perception of bias and the risk of recusal from a future case are not relevant to retired judges (unless forming part of a supplementary panel), who have left the bench and so have no future cases to worry about.[110]

More interesting is the claim that the extrajudicial speech of retired judges may do retrospective harm to perceptions of judicial impartiality or that it might 'create a risk to the legitimacy or reputation of the judiciary by association'.[111] When Yong and O'Brien conducted interviews for their project on work in judicial retirement, they were told by one former judge that coming out with 'strong or extreme political views' in retirement would be likely to feed a 'natural conclusion … that you'd held them the whole time'. That interviewee continued by explaining that it was 'not a very good idea to hold them, and … certainly not a very good idea to tell everyone that you hold them'.[112] Although Yong and O'Brien consider the risk to be 'diffuse', they believe that airing such views might lead to a perception that those views may be shared by retirees' former colleagues,[113] recommending that invitations for extrajudicial comment should be rejected if 'likely to draw the serving judiciary or the courts into political controversy, or if comment on a matter of controversy may reasonably lead members of the public to believe that serving judges hold contentious viewpoints'.[114]

[106] O'Brien and Yong, 'Work in Judicial Retirement'(above n 4) 24.
[107] Lord Dyson, 'Judicial Afterlife' (above n 28) para 11.
[108] Lord Neuberger, 'Where Angels Fear to Tread' (above n 36) para 20.
[109] ibid.
[110] Aside from the possible appointment to a supplementary panel, there was a brief moment during which retired judges might be re-appointed. Such was the case for Lord Lloyd-Jones, who stepped down as a Justice of the UK Supreme Court in January 2022 upon reaching the then mandatory retirement age of 70 but was re-appointed in March 2022 subsequent to a legislative increase in the judicial retirement age to 75. Sir David Richards, too, retired from the Court of Appeal upon reaching the mandatory retirement age in June 2021 but was appointed as a Justice of the Supreme Court in August 2022.
[111] O'Brien and Yong, 'Work in Judicial Retirement' (above n 4) 23.
[112] ibid 23 (interview).
[113] ibid 24.
[114] ibid 31–32.

Perceptions matter. Recall Lord Hewart's well-worn maxim in *Ex parte McCarthy*: 'justice should not only be done but should manifestly and undoubtedly be seen to be done'.[115] That is reflected in the leading case. By shifting the emphasis from avoiding a 'real danger' of bias,[116] to avoiding a 'real possibility', *Porter v Magill* focused the mind less on the actual circumstances and more towards how they are seen (by the public):[117] the relevant question is 'whether the fair-minded *observer*, having considered the facts, would consider that there was a real possibility that the tribunal was biased' (emphasis added).[118] For a serving judge, this means recognising not only 'when [their] independence is at risk, but when the perception of [their] independence may be at risk … [and] however ill-founded a perception may be in fact, perception itself is a fact'.[119]

This was an obvious motivation behind removing the senior Law Lords from the House of Lords. Having expressed an opinion on the operation of legislation in Parliament, a judge, sitting judicially, 'might subconsciously strive to avoid reaching a conclusion which would undermine the very clear assurances he had given to Parliament'.[120] But there is something uncomfortable about constraining the extrajudicial speech of *retired* judges on this basis. It hinges either on the façade of absolute judicial impartiality,[121] or upon a view that anything threatening to undo that façade must be concealed. Yet it is not news that judges hold personal views on a range topics, including matters of public debate or political allegiance.[122] 'If … "bias" and "partiality" be defined to mean the total absence of preconditions (in the mind of the judge), then no-one has ever had a fair trial and no-one ever will'.[123] We do not expect, or imagine, that judges will forget their history or humanity when they come to decide cases:[124] 'judges and other decision makers are human beings and not robots [and] they are inevitably, to some extent, the product of their own upbringing, experience and background'.[125]

[115] *R v Sussex Justices, ex parte McCarthy* [1924] 1 KB 256, 259; *Davidson v Scottish Ministers* [2004] UKHL 34 [7] (Lord Bingham).

[116] *R v Gough* [1993] AC 646; [1993] 2 WLR 883, 670 (Lord Goff).

[117] *Porter v Magill* [2001] UKHL 67; [2002] 2 AC 357 [103] (Lord Hope).

[118] ibid; the public perception is 'the key': *Lawal v Northern Spirit Ltd* [2003] UKHL 35 [14].

[119] Lord Judge, 'Judicial Independence and Responsibilities' in *The Safest Shield* (above n 51) 278; see also the *2025 Guide to Conduct for Retired Justices*, urging retired Justices of the UK Supreme Court to 'exercise discretion as to whether their retirement activities might compromise the Court's independence or impartiality, *actual or perceived*' (above n 1) para 7 (emphasis added).

[120] *Davidson (above n 115)* [17] (Lord Bingham).

[121] See also, in this volume, L Graham (above n 33).

[122] AC Hutchinson has taken this as far as to argue, in this volume, that 'judges are only fooling themselves (and people generally) in pretending that they do not rely on political values in fulfilling their professional roles or that they can somehow cabin them adequately': In this volume, Chapter 2: AC Hutchinson, 'Speaking Out: The More the Better'.

[123] *Re JP Linahan Inc*, 138 F.2d 650 (1943), cited in L Blom-Cooper, 'Bias: Malfunction in Judicial Decision-Making' [2009] *Public Law* 199, 204.

[124] M Kirby, 'A Darwinian Reflection on Judicial Values' in J Lee (ed), *From House of Lords to Supreme Court: Judges, Jurists and the Process of Judging* (Oxford, Hart Publishing 2011) 18; T Etherton, 'Liberty, the Archetype and Diversity: a Philosophy of Judging' [2010] *Public Law* 727, 743; J Bell, *Policy Arguments in Judicial Decisions* (Oxford, Oxford University Press, 1983) 247.

[125] Bingham, *The Rule of Law* (above n 58) 93.

What judges *are* expected to do is apply themselves to the law, rather than be steered by concerns which find their basis in personal or political outlook.[126] This is reflected in the fact that the prior expression of a view which could have adverse implications for one of the parties in a dispute will not necessarily indicate bias: even 'adherence to an opinion expressed judicially in an earlier case does not of itself denote a lack of open-mindness'.[127] Similarly, it is not a given that judges will feel pressured by public hostility – the 'judge's responsibility is to be impervious to it'.[128] Some extrajudicial speech on the part of retired judges might even serve to illustrate this. What other conclusion could be drawn when hearing, for example, from a judge who was part of a judicial majority declining to make a declaration that the law prohibiting assisted dying was incompatible with the European Convention on Human Rights, that he has 'personal regret' about the decision. Recall that Lord Neuberger admitted that his 'heart' in hearing *Nicklinson* in the Supreme Court had been with the minority, who would have made a declaration of incompatibility – '[t]hat's what I would like to have done. But I felt that wasn't right for us to do it then'.[129] Similar sentiments have been expressed by Lord Dyson:

> My view as a private citizen is that assisted suicide should be permitted, subject to stringent safeguards. But that did not influence my conclusion [in *Nicklinson* in the Court of Appeal] that, as a matter of law, decriminalising assisted suicide was not a matter for the judges.[130]

Judges, after all, swear an oath to set aside 'fear or favour, affection or ill-will'.

Of course, even a decision-maker who is 'truly independent of all influences extraneous to the case to be decided is likely to be impartial, but may nonetheless be subject to personal predilections or prejudices which may pervert his judgment'.[131] Indeed, the scholarship advocating for greater diversity in the judiciary is predicated on the idea that judicial individuality matters.[132] Being honest about these limits might bring both liberation (for judges in respect of their extrajudicial speech) and transparency. While in post as President of the Supreme Court, Lord Neuberger expressed (albeit 'parenthetically') similar ideas:

> If Lord Hoffmann and Lord Scott had not voted on the Foxhunting Bill, or if Justice Scalia had not expressed his opinion on the Pledge of Allegiance, presumably they would have been entitled to hear the appeals in question. But, if anything, it could be said that that would have been more pernicious than their hearing the appeals after expressing their views. If they had kept quiet or not voted, their views, or prejudices, would have been no

[126] *Locobail (UK) Ltd v Bayfield Properties Ltd* [2000] QB 451.

[127] *Davidson* (above n 115) [10] (Lord Bingham).

[128] Lord Judge, 'Judicial Independence and Responsibilities' in *The Safest Shield* (above n 51) 277; Lord Woolf concludes his autobiography by reflecting on problems with the press, writing that they 'have not diverted me from doing what I believe is right': Lord Woolf, *An Uncommon Lawyer* (above n 33) 150.

[129] The University of Law Podcast (above n 25) Episode 2: Lord Neuberger (9 November 2023).

[130] J Dyson, *A Judge's Journey* (above n 33) 188.

[131] Bingham, *The Rule of Law* (above n 58) 93.

[132] E Rackley, *Women, Judging and the Judiciary: From Difference to Diversity* (Abingdon, Routledge, 2013): Further, B Hale, 'Equality and the Judiciary: Why Should we Want More Women Judges?' [2001] *Public Law* 489; R Hunter, 'More than just a Different Face? Judicial Diversity and Decision-Making' (2015) 68(1) *Current Legal Problems* 119 and, in this volume, Chapter 6: E Rackley, 'Uncomfortable Truths, Clichés and Real Dilemmas: Extrajudicial Discourse on Judicial Diversity'; Chapter 10: R Cahill-O'Callaghan, 'The Individual Voice in a Collective Court: Insights from Judicial Lectures'.

> different but they would have been secret. There is, therefore obvious force in the argument that the presently accepted approach discourages transparency and encourages hypocrisy, or, to put the point another way, the present system seems to value justice being seen to be done above justice actually being done.[133]

After all, it was Lord Hoffmann's publicly-*undeclared* association with Amnesty International which caused the first House of Lords judgment in the *Pinochet* extradition case to be set aside.[134] Just as important as the expectation that serving judges would 'alert themselves to, and so neutralize, any extraneous considerations which might bias their judgment' is the expectation that 'if [serving judges] are conscious of bias, or of matters which might give rise to an appearance of bias, they must decline to make the decision in question'.[135]

VII. CONCLUSIONS

While apparent that retired judges do regard themselves as enjoying greater freedom in respect of their extrajudicial remarks, retired judges are not remotely unconstrained. Former judges continue to be influenced by the guidance, conventions, and institutional culture that regulated their speech when on the bench. Even those whose activities suggest that constraints dissolve almost entirely in retirement identify limits. Absent any significant framework governing the public discourse of retired judges, these constraints are generally self-imposed, and subject to individuality.

Some have argued for more detailed guidance to former judges about speaking on public issues.[136] But this depends on a prior acceptance that it is appropriate to apply such constraints in retirement – and that is not itself obvious. The justifications for constraining the extrajudicial speech of serving judges do not always apply to retired judges, or do not apply in the same ways. Even to the extent that extrajudicial speech on the part of retired judges might cause damage to judicial reputation (individual and collective) or to public perceptions about the impartiality and independence of the judiciary, solutions which do not require extrajudicial silence are available. This might be as simple as incorporating explanations of the judicial role, along with the rules and expectations that regulate serving judges.

In warning serving judges off extrajudicial communication, Lord Kilmuir in the mid-twentieth century recognised that 'there are positive advantages to the public when serious and important topics are dealt with through the medium of broadcasting by the highest authorities' and that it was likely, for example, that the public would 'get a better assessment of the qualities of some eminent Judge of the past through an existing member of the Judiciary than from anyone else'.[137] This might even apply

[133] Lord Neuberger, 'Where Angels Fear to Tread' (above n 36) para 23.
[134] *R v Bow Street Metropolitan Stipendary Magistrate and Others, ex parte Pinochet Ugarte (No 2)* (*In re Pinochet*) [1999] UKHL 1; [1999] All ER 577; For discussion see K Malleson, 'Judicial Disqualification and Bias after Pinochet (No 2)' (2000) 63(1) *Modern Law Review* 119.
[135] Bingham, *The Rule of Law* (above n 58) 93.
[136] O'Brien and Yong, 'Work in Judicial Retirement' (above n 4) 24.
[137] Bradley (above n 15) 385.

to matters of public controversy and in relation to decided cases, whereupon the remarks of retired judges might offer tangible examples of judges separating legal analysis from personally held beliefs. In other words, public utterances on matters normally attracting circumspection might sometimes, counterintuitively, promote confidence in the judiciary.[138]

The difficulty is not specific to the UK, and the conundrum is always the same: how to balance the value to be had from hearing what judges have to say, 'against the need to protect our collective faith in the institution that cannot exist when that faith is annihilated'?[139] Perhaps the answer is that it ought not to be possible for retired judges to annihilate that faith. On that basis, thought might be given to the principles governing the extrajudicial speech of *serving* judges – ideally, the remarks of retired judges would not then come as a surprise.

[138] For a similar paradox in the context of dissenting judgments, see H Mistry, 'A Performative Theory of Judicial Dissent' (2023) 86(3) *Modern Law Review* 729.

[139] D Lithwick and S West, 'Unplugged: When Do Supreme Court justices Need to just Sit Down and Be Quiet?', *SLATE* (14 December 2010) slate.com/news-and-politics/2010/12/when-do-supreme-court-justices-need-to-just-sit-down-and-be-quiet.html.

8

Beside the Bench: Education, Outreach and the Role of Judicial Assistants in Extrajudicial Discourse

JACQUELINE KINGHAN

I. INTRODUCTION

THE EXTRAJUDICIAL PRACTICE of UK Supreme Court Justices extends to their roles as educators and mentors. One important way in which they perform this role is in their mentorship and oversight of judicial assistants (JAs), and yet, the role of JAs has been subject to only limited study to date. Every year a small number of early career lawyers take up this invaluable opportunity to work alongside judges in the UK's highest courts.[1] In this chapter, I draw upon my own experience as a JA in the final year of the House of Lords and first months of the UK Supreme Court (UKSC). While the tasks of JAs may depend in some part on the approach taken by the Justice to whom a JA is allocated, they perform a number of consistent roles. These include writing memos on applications for leave to appeal, drafting press summaries and conducting legal research for judgment writing and extrajudicial speeches. Having a unique and personal glimpse of the way in which judges understand and appraise their own roles serves an important educational function. This occurs at multiple levels, both by JAs helping to support the Court in meeting its objectives in outreach and literacy and, in turn, through experiential learning about the everyday culture and practice of the Court by way of immersion.

[1] The High Court, Court of Appeal and UKSC in London recruit judicial assistants usually on an annual fixed-term basis. Fixed-term law clerks (2 years with an option to extend for a third year) are also appointed in Scotland to assist the Lord President, the Lord Justice Clerk and other judges of the Inner House of the Court of Session. In Scotland and Northern Ireland, a related role also exists whereby qualified lawyers act as Legal Secretary to the Lord President and Lady Chief Justice respectively but on a more permanent basis.

II. THE FUNCTION OF EXTRAJUDICIAL OUTREACH

In this chapter I reflect upon the way in which the relationship between a JA and their Justice(s) helps to facilitate the extrajudicial communication of the Court. As discussed elsewhere in this collection, how judges communicate to different audiences is critical to ensuring the accessibility of the courts, and also in helping us to better understand wider judicial functions related to the promotion of law.[2] The literacy and outreach function rests in part upon the theory of reputation: for the public to have confidence in a court's decision making they must also have confidence in its judges. It is obviously difficult to have confidence in an institution and its actors, if the latter are largely unknown. Some scholars have sought to define outreach activities as part of 'judicial leadership' by framing, for example, extrajudicial speeches, overseas engagements and academic publications as part of a wider conception of leadership connected to 'community' rather than simply leading the jurisprudential development of the UKSC.[3]

More generally, De Visser observes that courts have a role to play in 'advancing constitutional literacy'.[4] He points to the fact that individual judges 'remain plausible role-models of constitutional ethics', especially given their impartiality as compared to other government actors.[5] Drawing upon McKay's definition, he considers the literacy role of the Federal Constitutional Court in Germany to be related to its extrajudicial function and describes it as 'quasi-judicial' in nature.[6] This is because activities relate to the judicial function of the court by informing audiences 'about the nature of law or the substance of its component parts' and therefore helping to develop public discourse.[7] This engagement serves an important function in supporting public understanding of the Court's role in a democratic society. Notable examples of literacy internationally include reporting on the Court and its case law to ensure their accessibility to wider audiences, even through the use of infographics and cartoons (in Mexico and Korea), as well as the use of digital technology (*YouTube*, social media) to spread awareness of the Court's decision making.[8] De Visser also notes the value of 'immersion' through open days, guided tours and school visits as part of civic education.[9]

III. HOUSE OF LORDS TO UK SUPREME COURT (2008–10)

In the UKSC, the JAs sit behind the Justices during hearings, whereas, in the House of Lords' Appellate Committee Rooms, they could usually be found slightly to the front

[2] N Garoupa and T Ginsburg, 'Judicial Roles in Nonjudicial Functions' (2013) 12 *Washington University Global Studies Law Review* 755, 760.

[3] R Hunter and E Rackley, 'Judicial leadership on the UK Supreme Court' (2018) 38(2) *Legal Studies* 191.

[4] M de Visser, 'Promoting Constitutional Literacy: What Role for Courts?' (2022) 23(8) *German Law Journal* 1121.

[5] ibid 1124.

[6] ibid 1133 (citing RB McKay, 'The Judiciary and Nonjudicial Activities' (1970) 35(1) *Law & Contemporary Problems* 9, 20).

[7] ibid.

[8] ibid 1128.

[9] ibid 1131.

and beside them. For the purposes of this chapter, I have chosen to describe the JAs role as being *beside* the bench, as it can accurately be thought of as a role working alongside or at the side of the Justices, in a way that affords a unique learning experience.

Lord Hope was known to analogise the allocation of JAs to putting together a football team.[10] We were only five in number during my time at the House of Lords (2008–09) although this later increased to up to 11 JAs per year at the UKSC. Assigning JAs requires delicately balancing individuals who will work well with particular Justices as well as complementing one another as a team. As a graduate of Scots Law originally from Northern Ireland, I was an obvious candidate for Lord Rodger and Lord Kerr, and was also assigned to Lord Collins. I spent most of my time working for Lord Rodger. He was extremely proactive in overseeing the work of his JAs, and it is largely this experience that I draw upon in this chapter.

Sitting alongside the Law Lords (as they then were) features strongly in my own memory of the role. Having spent many years studying the decisions of the Law Lords, the shift from 'law in books' to 'law in action' by being so close to the frontline of high-level judicial decision making was nothing short of intriguing. Lord Rodger allowed us the opportunity to see the intricacies of his judicial practice and the position 'beside' the Law Lords even afforded close enough proximity to receive hand-written notes during hearings. More often than not, these were simply humorous observations on the case (or counsel) and brought some lightness to proceedings. As Lord Hope observed of Lord Rodger, '[the] notes were typical of Alan's acute sense of the ridiculous, and of his unique ability to maintain his intense concentration on a case while making fun of it at the same time'.[11]

Much has been written about the social interactions and perspectives of those final days of the Appellate Committee of the House of Lords. Paterson describes well the culture of the Law Lords' corridor and the personalities within it, which accords with my own experience.[12] By far, my preferred part of the day was my daily morning meeting with Lord Rodger to which, as another former JA put it, he had an 'almost religious adherence'.[13] Every morning at 8.30 am he would lean back in his chair and ask with a quizzical look whether the lower court 'got it right'. We would then have a lively discussion about the case and how it might be decided. The perspective of a JA was not a recommendation, nor was it likely to be influential in terms of the final decision, as compared to the US practice where law clerks have a role in drafting opinions. Rather, it was part of Lord Rodger's commitment to putting arguments to the test and helping his JAs to develop their own advocacy skills. Over the course of the year, I would begin to learn and predict what Lord Rodger might think about the issues before him as he provided unique training in how to 'think like a judge'. Aside from discussion and engagement on cases, my tasks were varied and sometimes unpredictable. They included not only supporting Lord Rodger and my other

[10] T Nesterchuk, 'The View from Behind the Bench: The Role of Judicial Assistants in the UK Supreme Court' in A Burrows, D Johnston and R Zimmermann (eds), *Judge and Jurist: Essays in Memory of Lord Rodger of Earlsferry* (Oxford, Hart Publishing, 2013) 98, 102.

[11] Lord Hope of Craighead, 'Lord Rodger's Notebooks' in Burrows et al (above n 10) 83.

[12] A Paterson, *Final Judgment: The Last Law Lords and the Supreme Court* (Oxford, Hart Publishing, 2013).

[13] Nesterchuk, 'The View from Behind the Bench' in Burrows et al (above n 10) 107.

assigned Law Lords (and later, Justices) in their day-to-day work but also in their wider extrajudicial outreach in a myriad of ways, which I explore further below.

A. Memos and Press Releases

When considering the literacy and outreach of the UKSC, it is important to consider who constitutes 'the Court'. In addition to the judges, the communications team, court reporters, registry office personnel and senior management all have roles to play. However, it is perhaps not well known in the UK context that a large amount of the work in communicating the UKSC's decision making to the wider public falls to its JAs. This was not always the case and changed markedly even in my own short time in the role. At the House of Lords, press releases about recent judgments of the Court were not the norm.[14] Indeed, as Cornes notes, the work of the Appellate Committee was not known for its transparency:

> The Appellate Committee had no annual reports, and no articulated strategic objectives, relevant to communications or otherwise. It had no separate institutional identity; it was a 'court' yes, but a court which sat as a committee of Parliament. One consequence of the Appellate Committee's form was that it carried out its work in a relatively un-self-aware fashion. It did not, indeed it could not, as a sub-part of a larger constitutional body, present a distinct face to the world.[15]

Against this background, I recall in the Spring of 2009 being given the task of drafting my first press summary by Jenny Rowe who was to be the new Chief Executive of the UKSC. We were asked to look at different models for press summaries[16] and to draft examples from cases we were working on that might be used to inform the structure and approach for the first cases to be heard at the UKSC. In fact, Lord Rodger was notoriously skeptical and largely opposed to the use of press summaries, and I recall having to be somewhat circumspect about spending any time on the task. He strongly believed that the Court did not necessarily need to be open to public view and that a judgment should speak for itself.[17] He commented, with his usual wry charm, that if a legal journalist was unable to distill the key points of a judgment then they simply needed to rethink their choice of career.

Of course, much has changed over the last 15 years. The move to the UK Supreme Court was underpinned by a drive to be more open, accessible and

[14] To the best of my knowledge, there were a few occasions when particularly long judgments of the Appellate Committee were summarised for ease of understanding but this only happened rarely.

[15] R Cornes, 'A Constitutional Disaster in the Making? The Communications Challenge facing the United Kingdom's Supreme Court' [2013] *Public Law* 266.

[16] Lord Hope directed us to look at examples in Scotland where he had, during his time as Lord President, encouraged press summaries in cases where there was a wider public interest.

[17] As Lord Phillips writes in relation to the documentary being filmed at the House of Lords in 2009 in anticipation of the move to the UKSC: 'Television cameras should be permitted within the court and press notices issued explaining the effects of the judgments given by the court. Alan was not persuaded that any of this was necessary or even desirable. Even less was he persuaded that it was desirable for the public to learn anything about the personalities or the private life of individual Justices'. Lord Phillips of Worth Matravers, 'Strasbourg has Spoken' in Burrows et al (n 10) 111, 111.

transparent.[18] This was embedded into the early practices of the Court, including in its mission statement, and supported by the establishment of a separate communications office.[19] The way in which courts generally engage with the public, and communicate their decision making to different audiences aside from in the judgment itself, forms an important part of extrajudicial practice. To that end, drafting press releases, together with memos on applications for leave to appeal, now forms a large bulk of the work that JAs do. A summary of the facts and key legal issues in the written case for leave to appeal is given in a memo.[20] That memo is used as a guide for the Justices before and during the leave-to-appeal meeting, which JAs also attend. The summary provided in the memo is directly lifted onto the UKSC website when giving details to the public about the upcoming court hearings, outlining the issues, facts and judgments of the lower courts. It is also printed in a short document handed to members of the public or parties in the case when attending a hearing.[21] The webpage of the case will usually retain the case summary when linking to the Court's decision and the associated press release when judgment is eventually handed down. Usually, a JA keeps a case from the point of writing the memo through to drafting the press release, although this may change depending on who the lead judge writing the judgment turns out to be.

Therefore, while tasks related to media relations rest with the communications team, it is the JAs who summarise the legal substance of the everyday decision making of the Court. The aim is to promote literacy and public engagement, but the JAs' approach has not been without criticism. The legal journalist Joshua Rozenberg finds press summaries dry and observes that they are 'written by lawyers, for lawyers'.[22] Moran similarly observes that the provision of press summaries is 'not a service that meets the needs of contemporary audiences'.[23] However, to produce a news report 'would stray too far into the territory of journalism and potentially compromise journalistic independence'.[24]

We were certainly aware that we should only ever summarise the judgment and that there should never be any form of added gloss or opinion. That said, there was not a great deal of oversight for the task of writing memos and press releases during my own time as a JA. We were largely trusted to be able to distill key issues in the appeal and provide an accurate summary. This became challenging when there was a longer, more complex decision on appeal which had to be summarised within a short word count (we were encouraged to keep memos to roughly a few pages), or where

[18] L Moran, 'Judicial Institutional Change and Court Communication Innovations: The Case of the UK Supreme Court' in R David and D Taras (eds), *Justice and Journalists: The Global Perspective* (Cambridge, Cambridge University Press, 2017) 255, 256.

[19] Cornes, 'A Constitutional Disaster in the Making?' (above n 15) 268.

[20] These were formerly called 'petition memos' referring to the practice of petitioning the House of Lords for leave to appeal.

[21] This document typically also includes the names of counsel and a small diagram of the Bench to show where each Justice is sitting.

[22] J Rozenberg, 'The Media and the UK Supreme Court' (2012) 1 *Cambridge Journal of International and Comparative Law* 46.

[23] Moran, 'Judicial Institutional Change' (above n 18) 265.

[24] ibid 266.

there were multiple opinions to consider for a press summary and it was necessary to carefully distinguish the different lines of reasoning in each, as well as in any dissent. I note that in more recent years a more permanent 'Head Judicial Assistant' has been recruited to have oversight responsibilities for the annually appointed JAs, which may also provide some supervision for tasks assigned.

B. International Exchange

The former High Court of Australia judge Justice Kirby observed that 'a distinctive feature of the present age has been the increase in dialogue between judges and other lawyers across national boundaries'.[25] Justices at the UKSC are often visited by scholars and judges from other jurisdictions and may themselves participate in judicial visits to other countries. JAs might be tasked with conducting international research either at the request of their Justice, or in relation to a request for information from another jurisdiction about a UKSC matter. They can also support the hosting of judicial visitors by accompanying them to hearings or attending meetings.

The international exchange opportunities available at the UKSC also extend to the JAs. For example, during my time as a JA we had a funded exchange to the US Supreme Court in 2009 and spent time with US law clerks. We attended a court hearing and had a meeting, pre-arranged by Lord Rodger, with Justice Antonin Scalia. I recall that Justice Ruth Bader Ginsburg also joined the meeting and we had a lively discussion about, amongst other topics, the role of international jurisprudence in domestic courts. As Justice Ginsburg outlined in the more recent documentary about her life and work, while on opposite sides of the political spectrum she and Justice Scalia were great friends; she would often attend engagements together with him to provide a balanced perspective of the US Supreme Court's decision making.[26]

The American Inns of Court support the JAs' visit to Washington and, by way of reciprocation, the UKSC hosts a visit of the annual Temple Bar Scholars. The Temple Bar Foundation was created in 1991 by Lord Denning and Chief Justice of the United States, Warren E Burger, to 'strengthen ties between leading members of the English and American Bars and to advocate that greater attention be paid to the professional ethical standards of both establishments'.[27] Experience as a law clerk in the US is one of the main selection criteria for appointment as a Temple Bar Scholar. Four scholars come to London for a month-long visit in October every year and, as well as shadowing barristers in court, they have the opportunity to spend time with Justices of the UKSC and to shadow the JAs. Further engagement between JAs in the UK and law clerks in the US is promoted through annual receptions and events.

[25] Justice M Kirby, 'Transnational Judicial Dialogue, Internationalisation of Law and Australian Judges' (2008) 9 *Melbourne Journal of International Law* 171, 171.

[26] 'RBG', directed by B West and J Cohen (Magnolia Pictures, 2018).

[27] The Temple Bar Scholarship Program, 'What is the Temple Bar?' www.innsofcourt.org/TempleBarScholarships/.

International exchange therefore relates to extrajudicial communication in two important ways. Firstly, it helps JAs to refine their own practices in facilitating and delivering the extrajudicial work of the Court (eg, drafting of memos, press releases and speeches, and / or conducting comparative research). For example, while the role of the US law clerk is different in some important respects, interaction between US law clerks and UK JAs can nonetheless facilitate shared learning around similar aspects of best practice. Secondly, the JAs might even be seen as an extension of the literacy and outreach role of the Court by themselves communicating aspects of its work and decision-making to different audiences. These international exchange opportunities have positive impacts in terms of facilitating communication about different approaches to the practicalities of judicial decision making. Relatedly, the role of international exchange seems to test the limits and extent of a shared understanding about the role of the courts – and those of actors working within them – through comparative discussion, observation and immersion.

C. Public Outreach

Over the years, JAs have supported the wider outreach of the Court. For example, during my own time as a JA we were asked to design and draft the legal content for the 'Be A Justice' exhibition for the new UKSC. The exhibition, which still exists in the education space in the basement of the Court, allows members of the public to work through different cases on a digital display and choose how they might decide the case. Moving through a number of options, the display will tell you how the case was decided and whether your own decision would have accorded with that of the Justices, with a brief explanation as to why. These cases are researched and updated by JAs to include recent landmark cases of both the UKSC and Judicial Committee of the Privy Council.

Other outreach events might include: supporting Justices in judging moots involving school and University students; helping to train students in advocacy skills; delivering short talks to visiting groups; and hosting visitors as requested by Justices on an ad hoc basis. Notably, JAs might also observe or participate in meetings with academics conducting research interviews.[28] Some JAs have also travelled to sit in hearings across the UK, given that the outreach of the UKSC has more recently included visits to the devolved nations. Hearings took place in Edinburgh in 2017, in Belfast in 2018, and in Cardiff in 2019; and there has recently been a series of lectures across the UK to mark the 15th anniversary of the Court. As discussed above in relation to de Visser's analysis of constitutional literacy, these regional sittings are intended to help spread awareness of the Court's constitutional role across the UK and build confidence in its decision making.

Finally, conducting research and assisting with drafting extrajudicial speeches also forms a part of a JA's role and serves an important outreach function of the

[28] For an account from a methodological perspective, see eg H Tyrrell, *Human Rights in the UK and the Influence of Foreign Judgments* (Oxford, Hart Publishing, 2018) 35.

Court. The extent to which a JA might be tasked with this work of course depends on how active one's assigned Justice is in giving extrajudicial speeches, and this can vary widely. Some Justices heavily rely on their JAs and their contributions are usually noted with an acknowledgement in the speech itself.[29] Topics can be interesting and wide-ranging. These sometimes also afford exposure to the work of the wider communications team, who may have to manage any fallout in the press should messages be misconstrued or deemed to have a political message. Mallory and Tyrrell note that extrajudicial speeches reveal a 'shared conception among the judicial community of what is appropriate', motivated by a common desire to maintain public confidence in judicial office.[30] The drafting of speeches certainly seemed to be governed by unwritten rules that informally regulate much of the extrajudicial conduct of the Court. I observed first-hand that some Justices would be more reticent than others and that, aside from the judicial values set out in the Code of Conduct,[31] their approach seemed to be determined more by their own personality and perspective rather any form of strict regulation. In conducting research and supporting the drafting process, JAs could therefore get a glimpse of how the Justices perceive issues highly relevant to their judicial practice and the processes that govern how they communicate with audiences outside of the court.

D. Mentorship

Paterson has long observed that the decision-making in the UK's highest court is a 'social and collective' process.[32] For JAs, intensive immersion in the day-to-day practice of the UKSC provides an insight into the social and cultural processes that influence its decision making. For early career lawyers, this can be an experience that is both formative and influential in terms of shaping their future careers. In describing the role of a JA, Lord Sales observes:

> Being a judicial assistant in the Supreme Court is a once in a lifetime opportunity to see the inside workings of the court other than being a Supreme Court Justice. You see how law is made at the highest level, how we debate cases and think about the law; and you see the best advocates in the country arguing cases in front of us, which is hugely instructive.[33]

To 'see' the law being made at the highest level is to begin to understand not only the occupational culture of the Court but also how judges see themselves and appraise their own roles. This affords an experiential learning process whereby the JAs begin to understand the sources of legitimacy in the Court's judicial practice.

[29] See eg B Hale, 'Judgment Writing in the Supreme Court' (First Anniversary Seminar, London, 30 September 2010) 2, www.supremecourt.uk/uploads/speech_100930_4593dcd53c.pdf.

[30] C Mallory and H Tyrrell, 'The Extrajudicial Voice' (2024) 44(1) *Legal Studies* 1, 3.

[31] *United Kingdom Supreme Court Guide to Judicial Conduct* (UKSC, 2019) www.supremecourt.uk/uploads/uksc_guide_to_judicial_conduct_a456af62f8.pdf.

[32] A Paterson, 'Decision-making in the UK's top Court' (Second annual BAILII Lecture, London, 9 December, 2013) www.bailii.org/bailii/lecture/02.html.

[33] UK Supreme Court, Lord Sales: JA Recruitment Video www.supremecourt.uk/about/ja-recruitment.html.

Arguably, many Justices also make legitimacy clear through their mentorship of JAs and by offering day-to-day opportunities to engage in reflective learning, as the mentorship role naturally involves transferring knowledge, skills and attitudes. It is well accepted that mentorship is associated with wide-ranging positive outcomes including attitudinal, relational, motivational and career-related ones.[34] Drawing from my own experience, by working through how a case might be decided and asking me to reflect on the implications (in law, policy and practice), Lord Rodger helped me to develop a rich insight into both the possibilities and limitations of the law, as well as the constraints placed upon judges in their decision making. For him, mentorship also brought an interest in my own future career path and, again, gentle encouragement to reflect upon my own choices and decisions. Looking back, it often seemed as if my own perspective, and my future career, was of as much interest to Lord Rodger as his day-to-day work was to me. Similarly, Nesterchuck observes:

> Lord Rodger felt that the young lawyers who came to spend a year as judicial assistants with the Supreme Court were an invaluable addition to the court. Whilst at times my contribution to Lord Rodger's heavy workload felt incredibly meagre, we were throughout encouraged, and perhaps even trained, by him to think like a judge. He clearly took delight in seeing the progress his charges made over the course of the year in the Supreme Court and beyond.[35]

I have argued elsewhere that opportunities for inter-generational exchange offer the possibility to develop a social identity relevant to one's future career.[36] For JAs, working so closely beside the Justices day-to-day facilitates rich learning that can be later communicated in different forums and might be conceived of as part of the extrajudicial practice of the Court. Since the time of the Appellate Committee, there have been over 200 JAs who have worked in this capacity at the highest UK court with others at the Royal Courts of Justice; the Court of Session in Scotland and the Court of Appeal in Northern Ireland. They are each informed and shaped by their experiences and by the mentorship of their respective judges, which they carry into their professional lives as lawyers.

IV. CONCLUSION

The UK Supreme Court has developed over the last 15 years to become a more transparent and open institution than its predecessor. JAs undertake wide-ranging tasks, which have supported the evolution of constitutional literacy activities and, in turn, helped to facilitate the extrajudicial discourse of the Justices in the wider public domain. The expanding role of JAs gives rise to questions in terms of regulation and oversight of their work, as well as the need for further research to better

[34] LT Eby et al, 'Does Mentoring Matter? A Multidisciplinary Meta-Analysis Comparing Mentored and Non-Mentored Individuals' (2008) 72(2) *Journal of Vocational Behaviour* 254.

[35] Nesterchuck (above n 10) 99.

[36] J Kinghan, 'Lifetimes of Commitment to Law and Social Justice' in D Newman and F Gordon (eds) *Leading Works in Law and Social Justice* (Abingdon, Routledge, 2021) 7–17.

understand their influence. There is also rich potential for a comparative study of JAs across different courts and in the devolved nations to interrogate the similarities and differences in each setting, as well as determine best practice for the many tasks they undertake relevant to literacy and outreach. As part of this analysis, we should not, however, overlook the two-way process of influence that occurs in the Justice–JA relationship and the valuable mentorship role that has lasting impacts on the JAs' lives and future careers.

Part II

Practice

9

Judicial Interviews

ALAN PATERSON

I. INTRODUCTION

COMMUNICATIONS BY THE judiciary are of significance because of the position judges occupy in the justice system. They are a key branch of government, particularly since they have the power to curb the activities of the other, elected branches of government. This in turn gives rise to accountability problems.[1] Electing judges might be a theoretical solution but few jurisdictions have embraced it, because of its downsides, and politicians appointing judges in the expectation that they will reflect the appointer's political stance tends nowadays to bring the independence of the judiciary into disrepute as can be seen in the US Supreme Court (USSC) and its decisions on the Bush / Gore election,[2] the reversal of the *Roe v Wade* decision on abortion[3] and, most recently, the decisions on the immunity of President Trump from prosecution for criminal acts.[4] Instead, constitutional commentators rely on transparency and reasoned judgments by the judges as the principal form of accountability. So, what role might extra-judicial communications play to bolster accountability – especially if, as in the UK, it is generally frowned on for judges to elaborate on their judgments in public? In this chapter I will discuss three related questions concerning interviews with senior judges and indeed extra-judicial communications more generally. First, what can judges say in interviews and other extra-judicial communications that they cannot say in judgments? Secondly, what is the value and purpose of such contributions? Lastly, what is the propriety of judicial interviews (and other extra-judicial communications) – and does this depend on what is being discussed and when?

[1] See A Paterson, *Final Judgment. The Last Law Lords and the Supreme Court* (Oxford, Hart Publishing 2013) 304 ff.

[2] *Bush v Gore* 531 US 98 (2000).

[3] *Dobbs v Jackson Women's Health Organization* 597 US 215 (2022).

[4] *Trump v United States* 603 US 593 (2024).

II. A ROLE FOR JUDICIAL INTERVIEWS AND EXTRA-JUDICIAL COMMUNICATIONS

Turning to the first question, even a cursory glance at judicially authored books in the publishing catalogues or the judicial lectures on court or Inns of Court websites shows that judges feel relatively uninhibited today in addressing a wide range of contemporary topics on the justice system. The discussion of important constitutional principles such as the rule of law or the separation of powers is a 'hardy perennial' form of public legal education provided by senior judges, which enhances transparency and accountability. As befits an arm of government – judges' extra-judicial pronouncements on the justice system cast light on them as wielders of state power in a democracy. Such contributions, whether in private interviews or in the shape of responses to Executive consultations on judicial review, the future of court structures, the need for a UK Human Rights Bill, or the levels of court fees, enable the judiciary to make policy observations (which are not *ex-cathedra* pronouncements of the law contained in a judgment), whilst not obviously entering the political arena. Similarly, the senior judiciary, by appearing before parliamentary committees or delivering conference presentations or giving background interviews with trusted commentators, can support (and, sometimes, resist) Executive policies without underlining that that is what is happening, eg pushing for more judicial diversity or supporting the place of the English courts and common law on an international stage. Individual forays like these may reflect the considered views of the leaders of the court, but sometimes they come from Justices who know they are propounding a view which some, perhaps a majority of colleagues on the court, do not hold – these are akin to judicial dissents, appealing to the wisdom of future judges. Equally idiosyncratic are the offerings in our final category of extra-judicial contributions – attacks on, or defences of, court judgments, without this being apparent to the casual reader.[5] However, in my experience, senior judges in the UK are slow to criticise their colleagues or contemporary judgments of their court in interviews, even with trusted commentators.

III. THE VALUE OF EXTRA-JUDICIAL COMMUNICATIONS – AND JUDICIAL INTERVIEWS IN PARTICULAR

Judicial interviews and extra-judicial communications have a value to, and serve the purposes of, *both* the judges and their audiences. For judges they can provide vehicles to get messages across that they may not be able to communicate through judgments. This is especially true for the apex courts like the UK Supreme Court (UKSC) where, increasingly, single judgments have replaced the former multi-judgment format of the

[5] See, eg, Chief Justice Mason's defence in the media of decisions of the Australian High Court when he was presiding. G Appleby and A Lynch, 'Sir Anthony Mason: Towering Over the High Court of Australia' in R Abeyratne and I Porat (eds), *Towering Judges: A Comparative Study of Constitutional Judges* (Cambridge, Cambridge University Press, 2021) 74–75.

Court – and its predecessor the Appellate Committee of the House of Lords,[6] thus reducing the number of opportunities for judges on these courts to demonstrate their individuality in the judgments of the Court. Further, apex judges whose court has been under attack in recent times from other branches of government, eg in Poland, Hungary, Israel, the USA and the UK, may well feel there is merit in extra-judicial engagements with their attackers, without overtly appearing to do so. Similarly, senior judges may use judicial interviews or judicial monologues to lament the decline of legal aid or to deplore media attacks on the judiciary without appearing to be involved in politics. These same judges frequently espouse other causes that, by their nature, cannot so easily form part of a judgment, eg support for judicial diversity, a general critique of judicial activism, or speaking out in favour of concurring judgments.[7] Indeed for modern leaders in apex courts, pronouncing on the limits of judicial law-making, the bindingness of precedents from the apex court or the merits of dissenting judgments seems little short of a rite of passage.

Clearly, then, extra-judicial communications can be exercises in power, autonomy and free speech. These exercises are influenced by several factors, eg content, context, timing[8] and interactivity. The last of these reminds us that extra-judicial communications range along a continuum from monologues to dialogues. The out-and-out monologue, such as a diary, podcast, lecture or monograph, maximises the autonomy of the judge over the content and the context in which it appears as well as the timing of the communication. True, the instigator of the lecture (if it is not the judge) or podcast or the publisher of the diaries or monograph will have an input into the topic and timing of the communication, but this will rarely constitute much of a fetter on the judicial autonomy.[9] Judicial monologues have a value to judges precisely because of their control over the content of the communication. They enable judges to target their message to the audiences they wish. On the other hand, however, Q & A sessions at the end of lectures, questions after the launch of a publication, letters, emails, interactive videos, phone / face-to-face conversations, appearances before parliamentary committees[10] and judicial interviews are more dialogues than monologues and hence encroach to some extent on judicial autonomy. The remaining focus of this chapter is on the judicial interview, which is amongst the most dialogical of

[6] In 1990, nearly 90% of HL cases had more than one judgment. In the last five years (to 2025) the corresponding figure has been around 25% of UKSC cases. In the Australian High Court there has been a similar development in the last decade.

[7] See Justice Heydon, 'Threats to judicial independence: the enemy within' (2013) 129 *Law Quarterly Review* 205.

[8] Lord Sumption, a Justice of the UKSC from 2013–18, timed his extra-judicial communications criticising the growing scope of the European Convention on Human Rights to come out just before taking up his post on the Court, eg 27th Sultan Azlan Shah lecture, Kuala Lumpur, 20 November 2013, or just after he stepped down – the Reith Lectures for 2019.

[9] UK Supreme Court Justices receive many invitations to give speeches/ lectures, thus allowing them to pick and choose which invitations to accept, although their job description encourages them to give some lectures. While timing and topic are negotiated, such invitations provide an opportunity for the Justices to address issues they are interested in or wish to provide leadership on.

[10] The judiciary may seek to influence the content of these by indicating in advance what topics and issues they are willing to discuss and which – eg discussion of particular cases – are off limits. The appearances of US Justices before Congress when the budget of the USSC is being debated seem to include references to actual cases.

the extra-judicial communications.[11] Here I am drawing largely on my experience of the 75 interviews that I have had with Law Lords and Justices of the Supreme Court since 1972.[12] At least in my experience, content, context and timing reflect, in part, the desires of the interviewer in contradistinction to judicial monologues[13] – the more so if there is no expectation that the questions will be shared with the judge in advance,[14] all of which leads to a shared or negotiated autonomy.

How can timing issues affect judicial dialogues?[15] At the simplest level, letters, written questionnaires and emails entail a time lag which affords the judicial interlocutor more scope for a measured response than more immediate forms of communication. Again, there are situations when the context and timing of the interview can influence the value of the judicial interview as a fact-gathering exercise. Thus when an apex court is tentatively embracing greater transparency in its internal operations,[16] or when a new Justice in the apex courts of the UK, the US or Australia is being introduced to the legal community, the questions can be relatively benign, eg 'What do you see the role of the Supreme Court as being, both within the judiciary and the public at large?', 'What do you view as the greatest risks to our justice system at the moment?', 'What is the main difference between being a lower court judge and one in the apex court?' In a different context, the forthright defences given by members of the UKSC of the UK apex court's cases on terrorism, the rule of law and the

[11] Elite judges retain a strong measure of autonomy in judicial interviews. Tyrrell records that in her interviews 'there was a general tendency among the judges to steer the focus of the interviews towards topics that they felt comfortable discussing'. H Tyrrell, *Human Rights in the UK and the Influence of Foreign Jurisprudence* (Oxford, Hart Publishing, 2018) 33.

[12] See A Paterson, *The Law Lords* (London/ New York, Macmillan, 1982) and A Paterson, *Final Judgment* (above n 1). Although I have read the work of numerous other scholars who have also interviewed members of the House of Lords and/ or the UK Supreme Court in the same period, unfortunately, I have not been able to do justice to the insights they gleaned from their interviews, in this short chapter. See, eg D Roberston, *Judicial Discretion in the House of Lords* (Oxford, Oxford University Press, 1998); P Darbyshire, *Sitting in Judgment* (Oxford, Hart Publishing, 2011); E Mak, *Judicial Decision-Making in a Globalised World* (Oxford, Hart Publishing, 2013), Tyrrell, *Human Rights in the UK* (above n 11), as well as several interviews on the *UKSC blog* (www.ukscblog.com).

[13] One exception to this was Lord Reed's decision to mark the 15th Anniversary of the UKSC with two interviews with journalists: F Gibb, 'What is a woman?', *The Times* (London, 5 October 2024) and J Rozenburg, 'Putting MPs in their place' (28 October 2024) https://rozenberg.substack.com/p/putting-mps-in-their-place.

[14] In over 100 judicial and counsel interviews, spread over 40 years, I have only been asked to provide my questions in advance on two or three occasions. Prior intimation of questions is said to lead to more considered answers. If the purpose of the interview is to elicit factual items, that would reinforce the case for such a practice. Where the focus is primarily on judicial perceptions and opinions, then the intuitive answer may be more revealing than the more considered one. As a protection for the judges against an unguarded response to an unexpected question, all of my interviews are 'off the record' until the Justice, having viewed the transcript, has approved aspects of it for publication. There is no uniformity between interviewers of UK apex court judges. Some have provided their questions in advance; some have offered anonymity; some not only clear the transcript with the judges but also the chapters in which their interview is quoted; some have not used tape recordings.

[15] It might be thought that retired judges will be more revealing than sitting ones. Intuitively, that makes sense, but in my interviews being retired didn't seem to affect the judge's candour or willingness to trust the interviewer. It might have had an effect on their ability to recall the details of 'routine' appeals.

[16] Eg in 2009 when the USSC first acceded to televised interviews with its Justices. B Lamb, S Swain and M Farkas (eds), *The Supreme Court. A C-SPAN Book Featuring the Justices in their Own Words* (Public Affairs / C-SPAN National Cable Satellite Co, 2010). Yet, the UKSC documentary in 2011 was rather more revealing, and did involve a discussion in general terms of individual cases.

Executive when interviewed for television in 2011[17] might have been more nuanced had the programme been made in 2022, when the very existence of the Court was being threatened by the Johnson Government. Times had changed.

Televised judicial interviews in a documentary on the Court are a subset of judicial interviews as a whole and will not have gone ahead without the agreement of the President of the Court. As such there are likely to be understandings as to what might be discussed and which parts of interviews may be broadcast. The encroachment on judicial autonomy in these dialogues will be minimised, whilst the public impact will exceed that of most monologues.[18] That said, it would be surprising if Justices with a message to convey were to prefer a judicial interview in place of a lecture, book or other form of monological extra-judicial communication, since dialogues tend to involve an element of loss of autonomy of the judge over the content and path of the dialogue. At any rate, lectures by judges remain more commonplace than judicial interviews, even in common law countries. On the other hand, one can understand why a judicial researcher would prefer the interview over other forms of extra-judicial communication. Its dialogical nature offers the researcher the opportunity to focus the interaction on aspects of the internal judicial decision-making process that have hitherto been largely hidden from analysis, eg collegiality and teamwork in the Court, the operation of the 'judicial hunch', judicial motivation in citing foreign precedents, changes of mind or the lead judgment switching hands, the nature and content of judicial discussions over the text of the judgment, and the subtle art of influencing one's judicial colleagues.[19] To commentators concerned with the Court and the judiciary as a branch of government, lifting the veil in this way helps with transparency, accountability and democracy, even if they lack the power of the political interview.[20]

IV. CANDOUR AND COMPLETENESS

The value of the judicial interview as a method for studying aspects of judicial decision-making that are not easily visible to external observers turns, in part, on the candour or completeness of the answers given by the judges and, secondly, on the accuracy of their recall. In terms of candour and completeness, context, content and timing can again have a role to play. A gentle interview with a new member of an apex court by a blog or journal is unlikely to elicit much as to the operation of the Court, since the interviewee is so new to the position. An exit interview with a retiring Justice will generally prove more fruitful, since there will be several years of relevant experience and cases to reflect on, provided the interviewer has a reasonable knowledge of the work of the Court in those years *and the trust of the interviewee*. Yet, whenever the interview takes place, some issues, eg inter-collegial relations or judicial illnesses, will

[17] In a TV documentary on the UKSC: BBC, 'The Highest Court in the Land: Justice Makers' (*BBC Four*, 27 January 2011).

[18] Some monologues, eg the Reith lectures, also have dialogical elements in the Q & A at the end.

[19] See *Final Judgment* (above n 1) ch 1.

[20] Examples include Emily Maitlis's interview with Prince Andrew (2019) or David Frost's interviews with Richard Nixon in 1977.

be more sensitive than others. Similarly, if the interview is given in the context of a lecture theatre of academics, as has happened to Lady Hale on several occasions, the public nature of the interview may sometimes lead to more guarded responses.

Context, content and timing, then, are relevant to candour or completeness in the judicial interview, but the key factor is undoubtedly trust by the Justice in the interviewee. When I interviewed the Law Lords in 1972 I was a young, naïve, doctoral student whom there was no reason to trust with judicial confidences, only protected from judicial impatience by my foreignness (I was from Scotland and therefore not required to be an expert in the English legal system) and my links to Oxford academics through whom the interview had been obtained.[21] I was told later that one or two Law Lords had given less than complete answers to some of the questions.[22] I think this was less of a problem in my interviews for *Final Judgment* in 2009. By then I was a more established academic with a reputation to protect, who had demonstrated through *The Law Lords*[23] that I could be trusted not to traduce the Court or its members.[24] That applies even more to me as a senior scholar today, who has made a career through interviewing the judges of the apex court.[25] True, some Justices are more guarded in their answers than others, but a refusal to discuss individual cases is the exception rather than the rule – the more so when the interviews are off the record unless the Justice decides otherwise.[26]

As we saw earlier, there are some topics on which the Justices will be more guarded in their responses than others, eg collegial relations. Equally, there is a range of topics where experience suggests that interviews will be less rewarding, not because of caution but simply because of a lack of information on the part of the interviewee. This is not restricted to new appointees to apex courts. Inquiring how often a Justice has voted with one colleague or another, how often in split cases the Justice has been on the winning or the losing side, what is the average length of the post-hearing judicial conference, or in how many, and what type of cases there have been follow up judicial conferences, rarely produces precise data. These are not matters that the Justices typically take note of and, unless the issues have become the subject of management statistics,[27] are not ones where the judicial guestimates can always be relied on. Indeed, sometimes the primary purpose for including such questions in an interview is to gauge whether the judge's behaviour can be influenced by the judge's perceptions of what the actual statistics are.

[21] See *The Law Lords* (above n 12).

[22] This may have been due also to the novelty of the exercise, since the Law Lords had not been interviewed before.

[23] *The Law Lords* (above n 12).

[24] Attaining a trusted status with the Court is a two-edged sword. It gives access to internal confidences, but contains tacit understandings as to the interviewer's continuing ability to write critically of the Court.

[25] In the last 20 years I have had the privilege of interviewing (often on more than one occasion) the great majority of judges to have sat in the apex court during that period.

[26] Too much candour can make for painstaking negotiations over what may be published and with what attribution. Understandably, the interviews produced some information – usually relating to other judges or counsel – which fell into the 'cannot be used in its current form' category.

[27] In the last five years the CEO's office has been producing statistics on workload, outstanding judgments, dissent rates and the like, which are shown to the Justices several times a year and to presiders, in every case.

In today's post-modern society we accept that in the complex cases reaching the apex court there are many competing versions of the truth. Judge A's experience of a seminal case may be quite different from Judge B's. One solution to this is triangulation – interviewing both judges, and collecting whatever objective data can be gleaned from other sources to provide a composite jigsaw of the case.[28] Judicial interviewers need, therefore, to maintain a balance between questions designed to elicit information of a factual sort and those that are trying to reach deeper into perceptions, eg as to the operation of the judicial hunch, the limits to judicial activism on the apex court or assessing the judges' concerns as to the consequences of their decisions.

One final reason why judicial responses in an interview may need to be tested is that they are human beings – granted, very clever ones – but ones like the rest of us, who occasionally find their memories to be at fault or lacking. In a career as a Justice lasting five or six years, the typical UK Justice will have sat in over 200 cases (in the UKSC and the Privy Council) not to mention an even larger diet of applications for permission to appeal. Although my experience is that Justices have remarkably high levels of recall, it would be surprising in that context if a Justice did not occasionally forget the name of a case, or transpose it with that of another case, or fail to recall an aspect of a case, especially if it was several years ago. If access is not a problem, there is something to be said for restricting one's questions to relatively recent cases in which the judgments have been handed down. Ironically, a few Justices may be more open to discussing matters not usually in the public domain, only when some years have elapsed, but by then their memory may have become selective. More often, Justices will discuss some of these matters even while the case is being decided, but place embargoes or limits on what may be published.

V. PROPRIETY

Extra-judicial communications by judges have existed since judging began, but that has not prevented them from being a source of concern from time to time. First, senior judges are expected to exercise caution in discussing, even in a textbook, legal issues which might come before them at a later date for decision in an appellate or apex court. It is not, as is sometimes thought, because of a potential conflict of interest; rather it is to guard against a perception of bias in the eyes of the parties. Here the legal test was set out by Lord Hope in *Porter v Magill*: 'whether the fair-minded and informed observer, having considered the facts, would conclude that there was a real possibility that the tribunal was biased'.[29] One celebrated example was Lord Steyn and the *Belmarsh case*,[30] on the compatibility with the Human Rights Act 1998 of indefinite detention without trial of foreign nationals suspected of terrorism. Lord Steyn had written on this matter in his FA Mann lecture[31] but

[28] Eg, judicial notebooks, spreadsheets and judicial statistics.

[29] *Porter v Magill* [2001] UKHL 67.

[30] *A and Others v Secretary of State for the Home Department* [2004] UKHL 56.

[31] Lord Steyn, 'Guantanamo Bay: The Legal Black Hole' (27th FA Mann Lecture, 25 November 2003). Published in (2004) 53(1) *International and Comparative Law Quarterly* 1.

was taken aback when the Government legal team wrote to Lord Bingham as senior Law Lord, requesting that Lord Steyn recuse himself from the appeal. He was even more dismayed when Lord Bingham took the view that he should do so.[32] Despite this example, any attempt by a party to recuse a Justice in the UKSC on the grounds that she had taken part in an earlier case and expressed a view on a legal issue would receive short shrift.[33] Somehow extra-judicial communications are seen as more problematic. That said, UKSC Justices are expected to give lectures on legal matters as part of their job description and to take part in semi-private conclaves with legal academics and foreign apex court judges on a regular basis, discussing legal issues that are coming up in a range of jurisdictions across the common law world, including the UK.[34]

What about judicial interviews? Are they different from extra-judicial communications more generally? After Lord Mackay had rescinded the Kilmuir Rules on judicial statements to the media (in 1987), the propriety of judicial interviews was less of a problem, especially if the interview was private or embargoed within certain limits. The dialogical aspect of such interviews affords enough protections for the judicial interviewee to minimise the risk of embarrassing matters, eg personal reflections on other members of the Court, receiving a public airing. A century ago, it was not done for senior judges to discuss the mechanics of judicial decision-making or their decisions in particular cases in an appellate court in the UK. Indeed, there remains to this day a convention in both the UK and US Supreme Courts that Justices should not discuss, other than generally, the reasoning of cases they have sat in, in extra-judicial communications, lest it be seen as some kind of official gloss on the ratio of the case. The judgment of the Court is expected to speak for itself. However, that objection applies less clearly to discussions of the internal operation of the Court, in an interview. There, the stumbling block was simply that it had never been done before. At the time of my DPhil research in the early 1970s into judicial decision-making in the House of Lords, nothing had been published on the internal working of the Appellate Committee and not much more concerning the Canadian Supreme Court or the Australian High Court. The USSC was the outlier, even in pre-*The Brethren* days.[35] However, whilst access to lower court judges by researchers was controlled by the Lord Chief Justice, access to the Law Lords was in their own hands. This enabled me to persuade more than half the Law Lords in the 1970s to be interviewed about their role as final decision-makers.[36] When I returned to judicial interviews in the apex court for the UK in 2009 and thereafter to the current date, the great majority of Law Lords and Justices of the UKSC have been willing to discuss past and even ongoing cases with me in judicial interviews – though not always for publication – with varying degrees of caution, but that is perhaps because the

[32] *Final Judgment* (above n 1) 294.

[33] To entertain such a challenge would make it harder for the Court to reconsider a recent precedent of the Court.

[34] Examples of these can be found on the Supreme Court website and in the Annual Reports of the UK Supreme Court, see www.supremecourt.uk.

[35] B Woodward and S Armstrong, *The Brethren: Inside the Supreme Court* (New York, Simon and Schuster, 1979).

[36] *The Law Lords* (above n 12).

questions have been about the judicial deliberations in the case, rather than whether the Court had got the decision correct.[37]

The willingness of most UK Justices to discuss the decision-making process in some cases in interviews is in sharp contradistinction with most appellate courts in Europe, including the Federal Constitutional Court in Germany, where it is a criminal offence to report what happened in the judicial conferences after the hearing of the case.[38] In many of them it is not even permitted to discover whether the decision of the apex court was unanimous or, if there were dissents, who the dissenters were.[39] This preference for the confidence of the conference seems to be due, in part, to an unwillingness to admit to the public that judicial perceptions of 'the right answer in law' in a case may vary, and also due to a belief that the 'right answer in law' is what the majority of the judicial conference says it is. Supporters of the civilian approach claim that it promotes candour and transparency – within the Court[40] – though not, ironically to external observers. Which is more desirable in a democracy remains a debated question.

A third objection which is sometimes heard to extra-judicial communications and interviews which involve discussion of judicial deliberations, is the concern that 'going behind the judicial curtain' harms the mystique of judicial decision-making.[41] This objection has its roots in a belief that if the legal community or the public were aware of the content of the judicial deliberations during significant cases it might undermine their respect for the judiciary. As Bismark is alleged to have said, 'Laws are like sausages – it is best not to see them being made'.[42] The counter to this argument – as set out at the beginning of this chapter – is that transparency is now widely considered to be an essential element in judicial accountability. The current President of the UK Supreme Court, Lord Reed of Allermuir, has several times spelt out the importance which he attaches to judicial transparency in relation to the operation of the Court.[43] In truth, all of the Presidents of the Court have been strong supporters

[37] See *Final Judgment* (above n 1). For an extended account of three cases which came to the Lords in 1998 relating to the extradition of General Pinochet, and of the reasoning in them, based largely on interviews with the relevant judges, see D Sugarman, 'The hidden histories of the Pinochet case' (2024) 51(4) *Journal of Law and Society* 459. For Lord Hoffmann's views, see P Sands, *38 Londres Street* (London, Weidenfeld and Nicolson, 2025) 159–61. It is perhaps relevant that publication of the contents of the judicial interviews on the Pinochet cases did not come until 25 years after the cases.

[38] Much of the discussion of judicial decision-making in *The Law Lords* (above n 12) and *Final Judgment* (above n 1) would be struck at in these jurisdictions.

[39] See B Hacker and W Ernst, *Collective Judging in Comparative Perspective* (Cambridge, Intersentia, 2020) 16–17 and 324–35.

[40] ibid 7.

[41] For such an argument, see M Dan-Cohen, 'Decision Rules and Conduct Rules' (1984) 97 *Harvard Law Review* 625.

[42] See Lord Neuberger, 'Sausages and the Judicial Process: the Limits of Transparency' (Address to the Annual Conference of the Supreme Court of New South Wales, Sydney, 1 August 2014) https://supremecourt.uk/speeches/lord-neuberger-at-the-annual-conference-of-the-supreme-court-of-new-south-wales-sydney. Ironically, Lord Neuberger was, and remains, very committed to transparency in relation to the operation of the UK Supreme Court.

[43] See eg Lord Reed of Allermuir, 'Timely, Inclusive and Transparent Justice' (22nd Ibero-American Judicial Summit, Dominican Republic, 15 May 2025); Lord Reed, 'Trust in the Courts in an Age of Populism Speech to the Inner Temple' (Peter Taylor Memorial Address 2025, London, 12 June 2025) and Lord Reed, 'Judicial Transparency and Communication' (Keynote speech, Supreme Court of Montenegro 80th anniversary and AIRE Centre's conference, 'From Traditional to European Judiciary', Podgorica, Montenegro, 20 June 2025) https://supremecourt.uk/uploads/speech_lord_reed_200625_9ae0fdf1f1.pdf.

of transparency in relation to aspects of the Court, from live streaming of the hearings and judgment delivery to opening up the Court building and the provision of case papers on the Supreme Court website. For all of them the judicial interview has become a way of building public trust and confidence in the Court.[44]

VI. CONCLUSION

Judicial interviews are a comparatively modern development in the world of the law. They add a further string to the senior judge's bow – which fosters transparency whilst reducing the mystique in judicial decision-making. Interviews are but one of a range of judicial communications which augment public legal education and boost trust in appellate and apex courts, which are more heavily scrutinised than 20 years ago. Senior judges in the UK have certainly become more willing to be interviewed.[45] Indeed, engagement with the media and the wider public is now part of the job descriptions of senior judges. Equally importantly for judicial researchers, judicial interviews add considerably to their toolkit, by enabling them to have more access to the inner workings of judicial decision-making and thereby enhancing understanding and with it, accountability. If democracy dislikes secret exercises of state power, judicial interviews may provide some small steps to a more open society.

[44] All of the UKSC Presidents have granted me interviews on several occasions.

[45] Ranging from television and radio interviews with current or retired judges to answering the questions of early career academics.

10

The Individual Voice in a Collective Court: Insights from Judicial Lectures

RACHEL CAHILL-O'CALLAGHAN

I. INTRODUCTION

DEBATES SURROUNDING THE importance of judicial diversity, have two main strands. The first focuses on the importance of representation and a judiciary that reflects the society it serves and the second, grounded in psychology, recognises that a diversity of experiences, perspectives and identities in the decision-making process improves the quality of the final decision.[1] Both recognise the central importance of the individual judge and judicial difference. Many international systems of judicial appointment to the highest courts require judges to declare who they are and the factors that shape their decision making. It is acknowledged in those courts that who the judge is matters.[2] This premise is the foundation of the US jurimetrics studies which explore how facets of individual decision makers shape legal outcomes.[3] In a collegiate court, the influence of an individual judge extends well beyond their decision making: influential judges may shape the decision making of others.[4] This may be related to their expertise, their personality, or as Paterson suggests in the UK Supreme Court (UKSC), their office location in relation to the coffee pot.[5] Regardless of the foundation of the

[1] See eg R Hunter, 'More than just a different face? Judicial diversity and decision-making' (2015) 68(1) *Current Legal Problem* 119; G Gee and E Rackley (eds), *Debating Judicial Appointments in an Age of Diversity* (Abingdon, Routledge, 2017).

[2] JG Gimpel and RM Wolpert, 'Opinion-holding and public attitudes toward controversial Supreme Court nominees' (1996) 49(1) *Political Research Quarterly* 163.

[3] See eg C Zorn and BJ Barnes, 'Ideological influences on decision making in the federal judicial hierarchy: An empirical assessment' (2010) 72(4) *The Journal of Politics* 1212.

[4] A Paterson, 'Creating a group oriented Supreme Court – Lord Neuberger's legacy' (2021) 28(1) *International Journal of the Legal Profession* 107; A Paterson, *Final Judgment: The Last Law Lords and the Supreme Court* (Oxford, Hart Publishing, 2013).

[5] ibid *Final Judgment*.

influence, the individual identity of the judge has a significant impact on their decision making and the decision making of others. A diverse judiciary should reflect differences in individual identity.[6]

There is increasing recognition that institutions require both overt and cognitive diversity, and an institutional commitment to recruiting diverse candidates requires external evidence of diversity at both levels (surface or overt, and cognitive difference).[7] The UKSC is committed to appointing diverse candidates, yet there is very limited evidence of overt diversity and we know very little about those who sit on the bench. Unlike the US, there are no confirmation hearings, and although the new Supreme Court is committed to transparency, very little is known about the Justices and the factors that influence their decision making.[8] Concurring and dissenting judgments have provided some insight into judicial difference, but since the opening of the Court there has been a significant rise in shared decision making and joint judgment writing with an associated decrease in individual judgments.[9] As such, the individual voice of the judge and the differences they may espouse is starting to slip from view. In this context, judicial public lectures offer an opportunity to hear an individual UK Supreme Court Justice. Individuals shape and are shaped by the institution, and the analysis of judicial public lectures offer a lens by which to view the influences, norms and values that members of the court espouse and an opportunity to detect expressions of cognitive diversity.

This chapter presents the results of analysing a database of public lectures (n = 80) delivered by the UKSC Justices between July 2020 and January 2025. This is a significant period for the UKSC. It represents the first four years of Lord Reed's tenure as President. Lord Reed will be (if he does not step down early) the longest-serving President of the UKSC, serving twice the duration of any other President, and he will have been on the selection commission for the majority of the UKSC bench. As such, evidence of a commitment to displaying overt and cognitive diversity during this time may shape the diversity of the UKSC bench.

It is argued that the selected audiences for judicial public lectures may serve to perpetuate a bias towards those who are traditionally viewed as judicial 'material', distancing those who may be different, and thus limiting diversity. Analysis of the content of the speeches identifies evidence of cognitive difference, but this difference is subordinate to the evidence of cognitive similarity and the shared values that are prioritised by the Court and are espoused by members of the Court. The limited overt

[6] See eg AN Johnson, 'Intersectionality, life experience & judicial decision making: A new view of gender at the Supreme Court' (2014) 38 *Notre Dame Journal of Ethics & Public Policy* 353; JP Kastellec, 'Racial diversity and judicial influence on appellate courts' (2013) 57(1) *American Journal of Political Science* 167; DR Songer and KA Crews-Meyer, 'Does Judge Gender Matter? Decision Making in State Supreme Courts' (2000) 81(3) *Social Science Quarterly* 750.

[7] For a review of judicial diversity see 'More than just a different face?' (above n 1) 119–41. For a psychological/business meta-analysis of the complex influence of cognitive diversity in small group decision making see AL Mellow and JR Rensch, 'Cognitive diversity in teams: A multidisciplinary review' (2015) 46(6) *Small Group Research* 623.

[8] One example of this commitment is BBC, 'The Highest Court in the Land: Justice Makers' (*BBC Four*, 27 January 2011).

[9] 'Creating a group oriented Supreme Court' (above n 4).

diversity, the dominance of the collective Court narratives and the cognitive similarity displayed poses a significant risk to enhancing the diversity of the UKSC.

The chapter is set out as follows: it opens with a brief review of the importance of judicial cognitive diversity and the relationship to decision quality, and the central importance of difference in collective decision making. Drawing on social identity theory, the chapter sets out the two strands required to improve diverse applications, an overt commitment to diversity and evidence of difference (overt and cognitive) within the institution. The UKSC's overt commitment to improving diversity is not the focus of this chapter, rather the chapter draws on empirical data from public lectures to examine how diversity is displayed by the institution.[10] Displayed diversity is explored at two levels, the first examines diversity through the lens of those that speak for the Court and the audience they choose. The second level draws on the content of the speeches, to identify evidence of cognitive diversity. The limited evidence of cognitive difference and the strength of dominant narratives underpins the central argument that whether by accident or design, these narratives obscure individual difference and limit the potential to enhance the diversity of the Court.

II. THE CHANGING COURT – INDIVIDUAL TO COLLECTIVE

Since the opening of the UKSC in October 2009, the Court has failed to achieve gender diversity, and there is no evidence of other forms of overt diversity. Notwithstanding a brief high of three female Justices, the Court is largely constituted by white, Oxbridge-educated, male Justices. Despite very limited overt diversity on the UK Supreme Court bench, it has long been accepted that judicial diversity is imperative.[11] The many arguments supporting a more diverse judiciary are well rehearsed elsewhere and not the focus of this chapter.[12] But it is important to highlight the strand of debates which centres on the decision making of the Court and that highlight the importance of cognitive difference. Empirical studies of the impact of a limited number of demographic characteristics on judicial decision making have had very mixed results.[13] This in part is because of the assumption that surface-level diversity (overt demographic diversity) is a proxy for deep-level cognitive diversity (values, attitudes, opinions and information diversity). Whilst surface-level diversity is essential for legitimacy, it is deep-level cognitive diversity that is the focus of this chapter. It is this form of diversity that is required to ensure high-quality decision making.[14]

[10] See, eg, the variety of strategies adopted by the Court: for example, 'Diversity and Inclusion at the Supreme Court of the United Kingdom': UK Supreme Court www.supremecourt.uk/corporate-information/diversity-and-inclusion.

[11] ibid.

[12] See eg *Debating judicial appointments in an age of diversity* (above n 1). In this collection see Chapter 6: Erika Rackley, 'Uncomfortable Truths: Extrajudicial Discourse on Judicial Diversity'.

[13] For reviews see 'More than just a different face?' (above n 1); JJ Rachlinski and AJ Wistrich, 'Judging the judiciary by the numbers: Empirical research on judges' (2017) 13(1) *Annual Review of Law and Social Science* 203.

[14] See eg C Nemeth, 'Dissent, group process and creativity' (1985) 2 *Advances in Group Processes* 57; KW Phillips and DL Lloyd, 'When surface and deep-level diversity collide: The effects on dissenting group members' (2006) 99 *Organizational Behaviour and Human Decision Making Processes* 143.

A. The Value of the Individual

Much of the research exploring how cognitive diversity improves decision making takes place in the context of business management studies and the study of team effectiveness and performance.[15] Panel decision making is broadly divided into two stages. The first is the 'surfacing' or identification of the cognitive resources (knowledge, etc) that each person brings to the decision, and the second stage – the cognitive processing stage – is 'combining' (aggregating, pooling, transforming) this knowledge to produce the final outcome.[16] In the context of panel judicial decision making in the UKSC, these phases are reflected in the processes of decision making. The first phase, the gathering of opinions, knowledge, expertise occurs in the post-hearing conference where each Justice presents their initial position. The combining of knowledge and expertise happens in the dialogues that follow, and in the processes which underpin the final decision and judgment.[17]

An excellent meta-analysis of 125 studies by Martins and Sohn starts to make sense of the extensive data which addresses the role of cognitive diversity (resources and structures) in both of these phases of decision making.[18] The first phase requires a diversity of cognitive resources, including task-relevant knowledge, skills and experience. This diversity of resources increases the range of inputs and expands the problem-solving and creative capacity of the team and the epistemic motivation of the panel, resulting in more effort. The second phase requires a diversity of cognitive structures – the values, perspectives, beliefs and educational/ functional biases that serve as lenses through which members view the task. A diversity of cognitive structures results in more divergent thinking and alternative approaches, and reinforces team coordination. Whilst diversity of cognitive structures and resources is not without disadvantage, since it is a challenge to developing a shared understanding and may also result in representational gaps (inconsistencies), there is nevertheless clear evidence that cognitive diversity improves decision making.[19] As such a diverse judiciary should reflect both a diversity of cognitive resources and structures. In a judicial context, the cognitive resources reflect in part the education and professional training and practice of the judge. It is notable, therefore, that half of the Justices in this study, practised at the commercial Bar, and four served on the bench at the Chancery division of

[15] For a nuanced meta-analysis see AL Mellow and JR Rensch, 'Cognitive diversity in teams: A multidisciplinary review' (2015) 46(6) *Small Group Research* 623.

[16] VB Hinsz, RS Tindale and DA Vollrath, 'The emerging conceptualization of groups as information processors' (1997) 121(4) *Psychological Bulletin* 43; VB Hinsz, 'Group decision making with responses of a quantitative nature: The theory of social decision schemes for quantities' (1999) 80(1) *Organizational Behavior and Human Decision Processes* 28.

[17] For detail on the process see *Final Judgment* (above n 5).

[18] LL Martins and W Sohn, 'How does diversity affect team cognitive processes? Understanding the cognitive pathways underlying the diversity dividend in teams' (2022) 16(1) *Academy of Management Annals* 134.

[19] See eg AL Mello and LA Delise, 'Cognitive diversity to team outcomes: The roles of cohesion and conflict management' (2015) 46 *Small Group Research* 204; E Mannix and MA Neale, 'What differences make a difference? The promise and reality of diverse teams in organizations' (2005) 6 *Psychological Science in the Public Interest* 31.

the High Court. It maybe that many of the Justices thus share similar cognitive resources. This is important when reflecting on recruitment of diverse candidates to the UKSC.

Many of the initiatives which seek to encourage diverse applicants and enhance judicial diversity are grounded in social identity theory, which recognises that an individual, when deciding whether to join an institution, draws on situational clues to determine their potential status within that institution.[20] As such, organisations who wish to recruit diverse candidates display and signal their diversity-related attitudes, and in doing so offer opportunities for the applicant to recognise identity contingency cues.[21] Traditionally, this has focused on overt – surface-level – diversity, with a focus on demographic diversity. Whilst important, psychological experiments suggest that these interventions have significant limitations.[22] Indeed, Nichols et al have demonstrated the limitations of the focus on surface-level diversity, arguing that evidence of deeper cognitive difference is required to encourage diverse applicants.[23] Traditionally, displays of this cognitive difference in a court would be identified through the publication of concurring and dissenting judgments, however the collective decision-making practices of the UKSC have significantly reduced the number of individual written judgments.[24] From the outset a climate of collegiality and co-operation in plurality judgments was encouraged in the Court. This has developed into what Paterson refers to as 'group orientated court'.[25]

The focus of this chapter is the first four years of the tenure of Lord Reed as President. Paterson has drawn our attention to the significant role of the President in shaping the decision making of the Court, not least in the selection of the panel members to hear the case and determining which Justice will deliver the lead judgment.[26] Indeed, Paterson's work suggests that the influence of the President extends beyond the administrative role and that the President plays a significant role in shaping the culture of the Court. As such, the sample frame of this study is very important. By the time of Lord Reed's retirement (if he serves a full term), he will be the longest-serving President of the Court (11 years) and he will have played a role in the appointment of the majority of Justices on the bench. Lord Reed has continued the process of collective decision making, noting: 'Single judgments, or at least a single majority judgment, are favoured where possible, so that the reasoning of

[20] For an excellent review of social identity theory see E Stets and PJ Burke, 'Identity Theory and Social Identity Theory' (2000) 63(3) *Social Psychology Quarterly* 224.

[21] For eg V Purdie-Vaughns, CM Steele, PG Davies, R Ditlmann and JR Crosby, 'Social identity contingencies: How diversity cues signal threat or safety for African Americans in mainstream institutions' (2008) 94 *Journal of Personality and Social Psychology* 615.

[22] See LM Brady, CR Kaiser, B Major and TA Kirby, 'It's fair for us: Diversity structures cause women to legitimize discrimination' (2015) 57 *Journal of Experimental Social Psychology* 100; TL Dover, CR Kaiser and B Major, 'Mixed signals: The unintended effects of diversity initiatives' (2020) 14(1) *Social Issues and Policy Review* 152; FF Chen and DT Kenrick, 'Repulsion or attraction? Group membership and assumed attitude similarity' (2002) 83 *Journal of Personality and Social Psychology* 111.

[23] AD Nichols, J Jordan, E Gosnell and D Ariely, 'A field study of the impacts of workplace diversity on the recruitment of minority group members' (2023) 7 *Nature Human Behaviour* 2212.

[24] 'Creating a group oriented Supreme Court' (above n 5).

[25] ibid.

[26] See *Final Judgment* (above n 5).

the majority is expressed in a single text, so as to assist lower courts and legal practitioners'.[27]

The collective processes of decision making and judgment writing have resulted in a significant decrease in the visibility of the individual voice. In the first year of the court between 2009 and 2010, only 38 per cent of cases resulted in a single collective published judgment, whether a single judgment of the court or a single lead judgment agreed by the other Justices. This increased to an average of 78 per cent of cases in the four years of the Court that are a focus of this chapter, with, on average, a Justice delivering an individual judgment in six per cent of cases (Table 1).[28] These are not evenly distributed and it is clear that the voice of some Justices is rarely heard in public. Whilst dissenting judgments and concurring judgments have not disappeared, their significant reduction limits the opportunity to observe deep-level cognitive difference.[29] In this context, the judicial public lecture offers an alternative opportunity to hear the individual voice of the Justice and explore the deep-level similarity and difference espoused in this forum.

B. Identifying the Individual

The analysis of judicial public lectures is located within the judicial biography tradition.[30] The ambitions of judicial biographies are diverse, and detailed biographies of individual judges often seek to reflect on upon the 'judicial approach' to decision making. This chapter does not aim to detail the life and career of an individual, but rather it draws on the judicial speech as an element of a judicial biography and to use the data contained within it to characterise the individual in a collective court.[31] Although extrajudicial speeches have been the subject of academic interrogation in Australia, the public lecture resource has received little academic attention in the

[27] Lord Reed, during his tenure as Deputy President, Lord Reed, 'The Supreme Court Ten Years On' (The Bentham Association Lecture 2019, University College London, 6 March 2019).

[28] This analysis only includes those Justices who have heard more than 50 cases during their tenure on the Court.

[29] Computational linguistics has been used elsewhere to identify the individual in joint judgments; whilst important, this work would not be suitable for this study as it does not adjust for the potential of compromise between the Justices to limit difference in collective decision making. See eg A Partovi, R Smyth, I Zukerman and J Valente, 'Addressing "Loss of Identity" in the Joint Judgment: Searching for "the Individual Judge" in the Joint Judgments of the Mason Court' (2017) 40(2) *University of New South Wales Law Journal* 670.

[30] See eg EG White, 'The Renaissance of Judicial Biography' (1995) 23 *Reviews in American History* 716; D Sugerman, 'From Legal Biography to Legal Life Writing: Broadening Conceptions of Legal History and Socio-legal Scholarship' (2015) 42(1) *Journal of Law and Society* 9; T Josev, 'Judicial biography in Australia: current obstacles and opportunities' (2015) 40(2) *University of New South Wales Law Journal* 842; P Scott, 'Judicial Biography in the National Security Constitution: Lord Diplock and a "Rather Silly Little Secret Racket"' (2024) 87(3) *Modern Law Review* 604.

[31] Biographies of former Supreme Court Justices include Lady Hale, *Spider Woman – A life by the former President of the Supreme Court* (London, Bodley Head, 2021) and Lord Hope has published his diaries from the time he sat on the court bench: see *Lord Hopes Diaries 2009–2015* (Edinburgh, *Avizandum* Publishing, 2019).

UK.[32] Akin to judgments, judicial public lectures are constrained by the conventions of the judicial role, as Lord Burrows highlights;

> Another aspect of the contrast in freedom is that, if giving a public lecture or talking to students about the law, a Supreme Court judge cannot just say whatever he or she likes about a decided case. For example, it would be regarded as inappropriate to criticise, by going beyond what one has said in a judgment, the views of colleagues whose reasoning has differed from one's own in deciding a case ...There is also a convention that, at least in general, one should not seek to reply to academic criticism of one's judgment. In addition, one clearly cannot disclose what went on behind the scenes in deciding the case, eg who said what in post-hearing deliberations. So, as a Supreme Court judge, and even though in an extra-judicial capacity, I have lost some of the previous freedom I enjoyed, as an academic, in talking about and writing about the law.[33]

Lectures are sometimes the product of a collaboration with the judicial assistant; yet, even in these highly constrained circumstances, public lectures do offer glimpses into who the Justices are and the factors that shape their decision making.[34] Lectures also offer an opportunity to understand the 'Court'. The lectures offer an opportunity to identify the norms and values that are shared by the Court.[35] The significant shift away from the individual judge to the 'Court' centres the institutional identity rather than the individual. Collective working and collaborative working practices shape that shared identity. As such, analysis of the content of public lectures offers an opportunity to view the individual within the collective court, to identify similarity and differences, and consider how the overt expression of difference shapes the future of judicial diversity.

This chapter draws on a subset of lectures (n = 80) between July 2020 and January 2025, published on the UKSC website, delivered by the Justices of the Court in the first four years of Lord Reed's tenure as President. During this time, 15 Supreme Court Justices decided cases, and Lady Arden, Lady Black and Lord Kitchin retired. Unusually, for the highest court in a common law system, the UK Supreme Court Justices may be joined by members of the senior judiciary and during this time period, the Lady Chief Justice of Northern Ireland, Siobhan Keegan, heard four cases, and Lord Chief Justice of England and Wales, Lord Burnett, heard six cases. The UK Supreme Court is unusual in inviting non-permanent judges to decide cases, a position justified by Lord Reed in reference to the invitation to Northern Irish senior judges:

> We also invite senior judges from Northern Ireland to sit with us in both Supreme Court and Privy Council hearings. That was not possible in the House of Lords unless the relevant judge also happened to be a peer, which was rarely the case. There are great benefits in

[32] See eg LJ Moran, 'Forming sexualities as judicial virtues' (2011) 14(3) *Sexualities* 273; H Roberts, 'Swearing Mary: the significance of the lectures made at Mary Gaudron's swearing-in as justice of high court of Australia' (2012) 34(3) *Sydney Law Review* 493; L Lindsay and D Tomkins, 'Hail to the chief! the roles and leadership of Australian chief justices as evidenced in extra-curial activity 1964–2017' (2017) 40(2) *University of New South Wales Law Journal* 712.

[33] Lord Burrows, 'Judges and Academics, and the Endless Road to Unattainable Perfection' (The Lionel Cohen Lecture 2021, 6 December 2021).

[34] In this collection see Chapter 8: J Kinghan, 'Beside the Bench: Education, Outreach and the Role of Judicial Assistants in Extrajudicial Discourse'.

[35] B Galligan, *Politics of the High Court* (St Lucia Qld, University of Queensland Press, 1987); L Zines, *The High Court and the Constitution* (Sydney, Butterworths, 1992).

> extending these invitations, both because they can strengthen the relationship between the Supreme Court and the intermediate appellate courts, and because they provide judges on those courts with experience of working on the Court and the opportunity to contribute to its judgments.[36]

Indeed, the invitation may encourage an application to join the Court. Notably, Lord Neuberger heard several cases with the Court, before he joined as President. There is increasing transparency regarding the invitation to join the bench. This invitation is typically associated with senior judicial position, although unusually, Lord Justice McCloskey and Lord Justice Horner (Court of Appeal of Northern Ireland) have also been invited to decide cases.

III. THE EXTERNAL 'VOICES' OF THE UK SUPREME COURT: LIMITED OVERT DIVERSITY

Much has been written about the role of the President in the allocation of workload in the UKSC.[37] In brief, the President selects both the panel who hear the case and, in the first meeting after the oral hearings, the lead author. Lord Reed, during his tenure, appears to have adopted a policy of pairing Justices to deliver the lead judgment, thus reducing the opportunities to write alone. When there are very few opportunities to take the lead and write alone, it is important to reflect on those who 'speak' for the Court and those who are rarely 'chosen'. On average, a Justice will deliver the lead judgment (alone or with another) in 12 per cent of cases. Two Justices, Lord Stephens and Lady Rose, were more likely than the others to deliver a lead judgment in the period under analysis, writing the lead in almost one-fifth of all cases they heard. In contrast, Lord Kitchin, who retired during Lord Reed's presidency, was unlikely to deliver the lead judgment; indeed he only did so in six per cent of cases he heard. Despite the impetus not to deliver concurring or dissenting judgments, on average a Supreme Court Justice will deliver an individual judgment in six per cent of cases (median four per cent). Two Justices, Lord Richards and Lord Lloyd-Jones never delivered a concurring or dissenting judgment alone. In contrast, Lord Briggs, Lord Sales, Lord Leggatt and Lord Burrows delivered an individual judgment in over one-tenth of cases they heard. There is a stark contrast between those who choose to be the voice of the 'Court' – for example, Lord Lloyd-Jones – and those who present as an individual within the collective, for example Lord Briggs.

Whilst many of the dominant voices of the Court are reflected in extrajudicial lectures, these lectures are an opportunity to hear the voices of those who do not, or seldom, deliver an individual judgment. With the exception of Lord Stephens, Lord Richards and Lord Kitchin, who did not have any lectures published on the website, every Justice has delivered a minimum of four public lectures (see Table 1).[38]

[36] Lord Reed, 'Why does the UK Supreme Court Matter for Northern Ireland?' (Belfast, 13 November 2024).

[37] For a detailed discussion see *Final Judgment* (above n 5).

[38] As with any public resource, there may be omissions from the website. At least one of the lectures is repeated to a different audience.

Table 1 Individual Judgments and Lectures[39]

Justice	Cases (n = 219)	Lead Judgment	Dissent (alone)	Individual judgment (not the lead judgment)	Judicial lecture (n = 80)
Reed	109	15 (14%)	0	3 (3%)	12
Hodge	99	12 (12%)	1	5 (6%)	7
Lloyd-Jones**	99	13 (13%)	0	0	2
Briggs	87	12 (14%)	3	9 (12%)	5
Kitchin	64	4 (6%)	0	1 (2%)	0
Sales	105	12 (11%)	3	10 (11%)	19
Hamblen	80	12 (15%)	0	1 (1%)	4
Leggatt*	74	12 (16%)	1	10 (16%)	6
Burrows*	74	9 (12%)	1	8 (12%)	9
Stephens*	67	13 (19%)	1	4 (7%)	0
Lady Rose*	52	10 (19%)	1	1 (2%)	16
Richards*	26	3 (11%)	0	0	0
Lady Simler*	3	1	0	0	0

* Justices appointed during the tenure of Lord Reed as President.
** Initially appointed by Lord Neuberger and retired at 70 years. Reappointed during Lord Reed's tenure when the retirement age changed to 75 years.

The judicial public lecture is also one of the ways in which the court can engage with a wider audience. The lecture is a shared experience and the audience both influence and are potentially influenced by the judicial lecture. Indeed, it is an important way to encourage diversity and the choice of audience reflects the courts priorities.

Debates surrounding increasing judicial diversity, drawing on social identity theory, highlight the importance of representativeness and the impact of overt diverse role models on the bench. In short, the argument is that a diverse bench encourages diverse applicants to consider the role, and thus those selected for the role in future are chosen from a wider pool of applicants, which in turn ensures the best candidates sit on the Supreme Court bench.[40] Whilst the lack of overt diversity on the bench highlights the limits of the Supreme Court appointment processes, the first step to remedy the deficit should be encouraging a diverse pool of applicants. In this context, it is important to reflect not simply on those who speak for the Court and the limited demographic diversity on display, but the audiences that they choose to address (see Figure 1).

[39] The data cases, judgment, dissent is the first complete four years (July 2020 – July 2024). The speeches extend to January 2025.

[40] For recent debates surrounding judicial diversity, see *Debating Judicial Appointments in the Age of Diversity* (above n 1); B Opeskin, *Future Proofing the Judiciary: Preparing for Demographic Change* (London, Palgrave McMillan, 2021).

Figure 1 The Audience the Court Chooses.

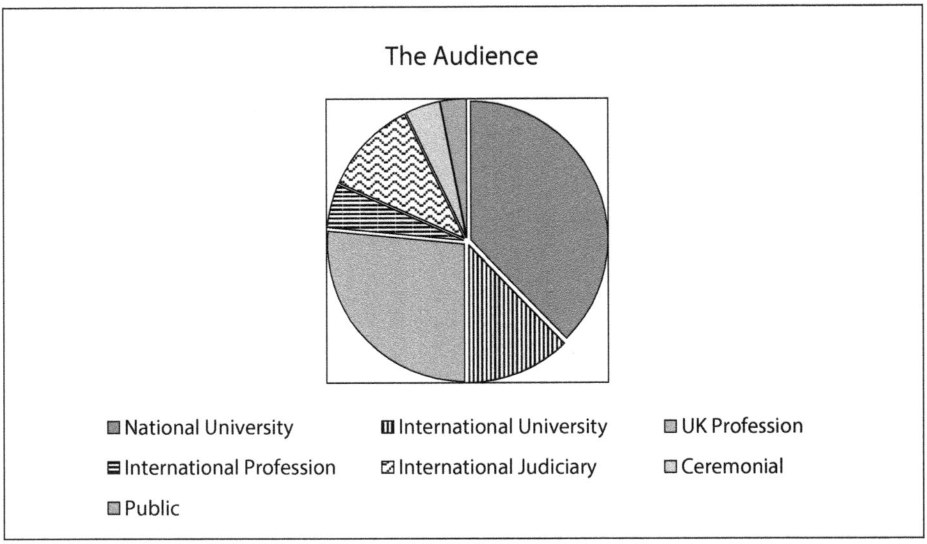

The data is presented as a percentage of the total lectures delivered (n = 80). It is not unexpected that a majority of the lectures are delivered to the profession, addressing associations and conferences. It is notable that many of the lectures are delivered at the Inns of Court, accounting for 41 per cent of the lectures delivered to the profession. This choice perpetuates the assumption that experience at the Bar is essential to the judicial role; something Lady Rose, a former private practice barrister, sought to rebut in a lecture highlighting the importance of the Judicial Appointments Commission, which notably does not regulate appointments to the Supreme Court:[41]

> The creation of the Judicial Appointments Commission in 2003 put the whole process of recruiting judges on a more transparent and fairer footing. It also opened up the judiciary for a much broader range of lawyers. It was a long overdue recognition that the previous idea that the qualities needed for joining the judiciary were to be found exclusively in the senior ranks of those in private practice was not true. Of course, many great barristers go on to be very good judges. But I think it is now clear that the skills involved, and the experience gained from being a good court advocate are neither necessary nor sufficient for being a good judge.[42]

Almost half of all the lectures were delivered in a national or international university setting – acknowledgment, perhaps, of the importance of the Supreme Court in shaping future generations of the profession. Whilst there is some attempt to address the breadth of the academic community, almost 60 per cent of lectures in this type of setting were delivered at Oxbridge. Indeed, in 2024, almost a quarter

[41] Members of the Judicial Appointments Commission do sit on selection panels for the Supreme Court, but the process is distinct. Indeed, it is a process that is significantly influenced by those who sit on the Supreme Court bench and hold significant judicial positions.

[42] Lady Rose, 'Speech to the Bar Council's Employed Bar Dinner and Awards' (Bar Council, London, 10 October 2024).

of *all* the lectures delivered by Supreme Court Justices were delivered in Oxbridge. There may be a range of reasons for the dominance of the Oxbridge audience, not least the educational allegiance of those on the Supreme Court bench, but the impact of the audience selection and those who the Court chooses to speak to should not be underestimated.[43] The dominant choice of audience mirrors the educational and professional constitution of the current Court and may in turn play a role in perpetuating the norms that exist and limit diversity. The shared educational experiences may result in shared cognitive skills that shape decision making, and cognitive structures such as values and beliefs. As such, the choice of audience may not only serve to embed a narrow conception of the educational experience required to be a judge, but it may also serve to limit the cognitive skills and structures. Indeed, the lectures provide some insight into how the educational experiences influence the judges.

IV. IDENTIFYING INDIVIDUAL DIFFERENCE: EXPERIENCES AND PRINCIPLES

The choice of audience may perpetuate the dominance of Oxbridge-educated members of the UKSC while the judicial lectures evidence the importance of education and the individuals who provide it on the judicial role. For example, Lord Sales, an alumnus of both Oxford and Cambridge, noted that

> I have always greatly valued the input that academia provides to our legal system, and so it is very pleasing to see so much activity and lively debate taking place in Oxford ... My own thinking on proprietary estoppel and much beyond has been shaped through conversations with Professor McFarlane and reading his work.[44]

Lord Hodge (Deputy President of the Court during sample time-frame), who was educated at Cambridge and read law at Edinburgh, highlighted the influence of his Edinburgh education, noting: 'I had the great privilege of studying jurisprudence under Professor Neil MacCormick'.[45]

The importance of academic outputs in informing the decision making of the Court emerges as a consistent theme in the data. It may be a reflection of the presence of Lord Burrows, who was the first Supreme Court Justice to be appointed from a full-time academic position at Oxford University. Indeed, it is unsurprising that he highlights the importance of academic writing: 'the writings of academics can help place a particular dispute into a larger context and can thereby assist the proper judicial development of principle'.[46] But it is a principle that is shared by other members of the Court. For example, Lord Hodge draws attention to the academic function in ordering the common law: 'The extensive case law which has developed in the last

[43] For further discussion of the judicial role in education, see C Mallory and H Tyrrell, 'The Extrajudicial Voice' (2024) 44(1) *Legal Studies* 1.

[44] Lord Sales, 'Proprietary Estoppel: Great Expectations and Detrimental Reliance' (Modern Studies in Property Law Conference, Oxford, 29 March 2022).

[45] Lord Hodge, 'The Scope of Judicial Law-Making in the Common Law Tradition' (*Max Planck Institute of Comparative and International Private Law*, Hamburg, 28 October 2019).

[46] 'Judges and Academics' (above n 33).

150 years together with academic writing which seeks to systematise the common law has assisted the judge's task in finding the relevant principles'.[47]

It is probably unsurprising that the Justices highlight their educational experiences, particularly at Oxford and Cambridge, as informative periods of their lives, and draw attention to the influence of the academe and specific individuals within it on their thinking. Educational experiences and professional training shape cognitive skills, value priorities and decision-making resources, and many of the Justices recognise the influence which their life experience has had on their decision making. For example, Lord Hamblen highlighted how his professional background at the Commercial Bar shaped his engagement with expert evidence, and Lord Briggs, how his 'career as a civil litigation lawyer' shaped his views of compliance with procedural rules.[48] Indeed, Lord Sales suggests that the area of practice influences how a judge considers the case to be decided: 'Even today, chancery lawyers and common lawyers have a tendency to think about issues in somewhat different ways'.[49]

Legal education and practice, as with any profession, embeds knowledge, skills and expertise, and Lord Hodge suggests that this also applies to jurisdiction, arguing that the jurisdiction in which the Justice was educated influences the process and structures of reasoning:

> As a lawyer trained in Scots law but not working principally in the field of English law, I detect subtle differences in the approach of lawyers from the two jurisdictions. I notice a marginally stronger tendency of lawyers from the mixed system of Scots law to go straight to a legal principle rather than build their legal submission by a historical presentation of the law, case by case. This may be because, in the early centuries of Scots law, it was the practice of lawyers to fill gaps in the law by referring to Roman law and the Corpus Juris Civilis of Justinian and the judges were able to rely on institutional writers to give structure to the argument.[50]

Each of these quotations highlight individual differences and how these differences shape decision making. Indeed, these individual differences underpin a diversity of knowledge, cognitive skills, structures, values and principles that are encompassed within deep-level diversity. Whilst the data suggests that the deep-level differences exist, these may be obscured in collective judgments and the associated narrative that is emerging about the collective 'Reed Court'.

A. Disrupting the Collective: Legal Principles

The judgments of the Court since the start of Lord Reed's tenure have underpinned a narrative that the collective 'Reed Court' adopts a more restrained, conservative

[47] 'The Scope of Judicial Law-Making in the Common Law Tradition' (above n 45).

[48] Lord Hamblen, 'The Commercial Court: Past, Present, and Future' (Annual Combar Lecture 2020, 13 October 2020); Lord Briggs, 'National Experience – Change of Civil Procedure Rules in the UK' (Cyprus Judicial Conference, 10 March 2021).

[49] Lord Sales, 'The Interface between Contract and Equity' (Lehane Memorial Lecture, Syndey, 28 August 2019).

[50] 'The Scope of Judicial Law-Making in the Common Law Tradition' (above n 45), published before the tenure of Lord Reed.

position than earlier iterations of the Court.[51] Graham asserts a more nuanced argument suggesting that the Reed Court has, in specific areas of public law, become more restrained, which is manifested as a deference to the separation of powers and a brightline boundary that prevents the Court stepping into the policy arena.[52] This position is reflected in the judicial lectures by Lord Hodge:

> [The judicial responsibility to keep law abreast with current social conditions and expectations] is discharged in the field of public law against the background of the United Kingdom's largely unwritten sovereignty third principle, the separation of powers. This principle calls for clear-eyed recognition of the limits of each branch of government, including the judiciary, and a shared respect for the roles of each branch.[53]

The debate surrounding the conservative Court centres on the judgments of the collective court. Implicit, both in the discourse on the 'Reed Court' and the structures of collective decision making and judgment writing of the Court, are judicial consensus and shared value priorities. This amplification of similarity obscures difference. The Court is a collection of individuals, and the lectures offer an opportunity to identify potential differences.

Graham's central argument is that the judgments of the Court reflect political constitutionalism at its most basic, a philosophical position that prioritises Parliamentary sovereignty. Indeed, the deference to Parliamentary sovereignty is a consistent theme in the lectures of Lord Hodge: 'I have no objection to the concept of the "purpose" of the legislation so long as it is [a] synonym for the objective assessment of parliamentary intention'.[54]

But the position is not as consistent as Graham's analysis of the Court would suggest. Indeed, Lady Rose offers a more nuanced reflection:

> It is that independence and impartiality which enables and indeed requires judges to take decisions which may be unpopular with the public, and also sometimes, with the Government or Parliament. This has been an important part of the judicial function for centuries – protecting the rights even of the most unpopular members of society against excessive action on the part of the State.[55]

The nuanced position of the individual is often lost in the analysis of the collective, and this is even more evident in the analysis of legal values. Graham noted a distinction between restraint and strict adherence to precedent and the exercise of discretion, drawing attention to the Court's preference for caution, prioritising certainty and

[51] C Gearty, 'In the shallow end' (*London Review of Books*, 27 January 2022); A Tomkins, 'Why did the Tories retreat from taking on the Supreme Court judges?' (*The Herald*, 11 August 2021); A Dean, 'The government wanted to rein in the Supreme Court. Now it may not need to' (*Prospect Magazine*, 16 October 2021).

[52] L Graham, 'Has the UK Supreme Court Become More Restrained in Public Law Cases?' (2024) 87 *Modern Law Review* 1073.

[53] 'The Scope of Judicial Law-Making in the Common Law Tradition' (above n 45).

[54] Lord Hodge, 'Statutory Interpretation: A Collaboration between Democratic Legislatures and the Courts' (Address to the Government Legal Service for Scotland, 10 November 2021).

[55] Lady Rose, 'Oxford Union Talk' (Oxford, 12 May 2022). A position that was espoused by earlier members of the UK Supreme Court. Lord Mance, 'Should the law be certain?' (Oxford Shrieval lecture, Oxford, 11 October 2011).

predictability over flexibility and justice. At the heart of this position are the values that shape the legal system, and the value priorities of the Court.

B. Disrupting the Collective: Values

A consistent theme in the lectures is the role of precedent and the opportunity for departure offered by the Practice Direction 1966, which sets out the principles guiding the exercise of the decision to depart from precedence.[56] The lectures identify the tension raised by the Practice Direction between the competing values of certainty and predictability associated with adherence to precedent in opposition to flexibility, responsiveness and change.[57] It is probably unsurprising that the dominant narrative in many lectures is the importance of certainty, especially in a commercial context.[58] Lord Hodge noted: 'A legal system which offers a high degree of certainty will tend to reduce the cost of transactions and so encourage commerce'.[59] Similarly, Lord Leggatt has reflected that '[i]t is desirable that they should, so far as possible, produce outcomes which are reasonably predictable: hence the importance of certainty in commercial law'.[60]

Indeed, the dominance on the bench of those with experience at the Commercial Bar may serve to amplify the values of this area of law.[61] As Mallory and Tyrrell note, when a Supreme Court Justice delivers a lecture, they are ambassadors not only for the Court but for the British legal system, and this is perhaps most evident in a commercial context.[62] This is evident in a keynote address delivered by Lord Reed at the London International Disputes Week, in which he stated:

> Those who can choose the law which will govern their contracts and the jurisdiction in which their disputes are resolved, and those who can choose the country where they will invest or carry on their business, need certainty that the contracts which they enter into will be interpreted and enforced in a predictable way.[63]

[56] See eg Lord Sales, 'Default Rules in the Common Law: Substantive Rules and Precedent' (Oxford, International Workshop on Default Rules in Private Law, 24 March 2023); Lord Leggatt, 'Precedent in English Law' (Keble College, Oxford, 26 April 2024); Lord Reed, 'Departing from Precedent: The Experience of the UK Supreme Court' (International Conference on Implementation of the Rule of Law, 20 January 2023); Lady Rose, '1966 and All That: Changing our Minds in a Post-Brexit World' (UK Association for European Law, Safra Theatre King's College London, 23 May 2022); the theme also appears in a number of other speeches, albeit not in the title: see eg Lord Reed, 'Time Present and Time Past: Legal Development and Legal Tradition in the Common Law' (Neill Law Lecture 2022, Oxford, 25 February 2022).

[57] See eg Lord Sales, 'Certainty and Flexibility in the Law' (Aston University, Birmingham, 30 January 2025).

[58] Please note the ambassadorial role of the Supreme Court Justice. See 'Extrajudicial Voice' (above n 43).

[59] Lord Hodge, 'Law and technological change' (British Irish Commercial Bar Association, Edinburgh, 4 April 2019).

[60] Lord Leggatt, 'What is the Point of Commercial Law?' (Brick Court Chambers, London, 2 November 2021)

[61] Other examples include 'Default Rules in the Common Law' (above n 56).

[62] 'Extrajudicial Voice' (above n 43).

[63] Lord Reed, 'Keynote Address London International Disputes Week' (London International Disputes Week, 11 May 2022).

But the dominance of certainty is not limited to the commercial context. It pervades other areas of law, including public law cases that involve the Human Rights Act 1998: '[i]t is reasonable to infer that Parliament did not intend such destructive effects on legal certainty and stability to be produced by the operation of the Human Rights Act',[64] and other areas of public law:

> The Supreme Court has not used the power in such cases; but the concern of the Practice Statement about certainty and predictability must be a relevant consideration in public law because the lack of predictability would be a major hinderance to good administration.[65]

It is notable that the more nuanced position of certainty tempered with flexibility in response to the needs of 'commercial practice or social values',[66] 'socially valuable purposes', and 'public expectations'[67] that was evident in a speech of Lord Hodge prior to the Presidency of Lord Reed is absent from the discussions of legal certainty by the Justices in the first four years of the Reed Court. Indeed, whilst word searches do not replace detailed content analysis, it is notable that 'certainty' appears in 28 lectures and is a dominant theme in seven. In stark contrast, flexibility only appears in 17 lectures and in the majority (n = 13) of these as a single reference, and where the term is used as a value of the common law, it is juxtaposed with certainty and strict adherence to legal rules. This is exemplified in a speech by Lord Sales on value pluralism and the power of the judge:

> The former end of the spectrum [bright line rules] best alleviates those rule of law concerns. However, it purchases clarity at the expense of flexibility and the lack of responsiveness to what may be significant shifts in the balance between the competing values which the rule of law seeks to accommodate.[68]

Flexibility was only positively affirmed by Lord Sales and Lord Briggs, and outside the commercial context, as Lord Sales states,

> [a]t the same time, alongside controlling abuse of power and abuse of rights, law has a function to provide a framework in which this new power can be deployed and used effectively for socially valuable purposes. In that sense, law should go with the flow and channel it, rather than merely resist it.[69]

But this flexibility is fettered when it conflicts with Parliament:

> [The case] also called for a decision which balanced competing fundamental institutional values in terms of whether the court should or should not strike the balance of moral values itself or accept the balance as struck by Parliament. Surely the justices were right that this was a context in which the public had a right to expect them to exercise their own judgment, as members of the highest court, regarding the legal outcome. It would have been

[64] Lord Sales, 'The developing jurisprudence of the Supreme Court on Convention rights' (Scottish Public Law Group Conference, 5 June 2023).

[65] Lord Hodge, 'The Scope of Judicial Law-making in Constitutional and Public Law' (Middle Temple, Treasurer's Lecture, London, 18 October 2021).

[66] 'The Scope of Judicial Law-making in the Common Law Tradition' (above n 45).

[67] ibid.

[68] 'Default rules in the Common Law' (above n 56).

[69] Lord Sales, 'Purpose in Law and Interpretation' (FA Mann Lecture, Lincoln's Inn, London, 19 November 2024).

> an abrogation of their duty if they had deferred, not to Parliament, but to the views of the court of first instance.[70]

Once again, analysis of the expression of some of the core values attributed to the common law system demonstrates evidence of individual difference, but these differences are masked by the dominance of specific norms, principles and values. It is the collective values which shape the external perception of the Court's priorities and the individuals who sit on the UKSC bench, and in doing so may limit the potential diversity of the Supreme Court bench.

V. CONCLUSION

It has long been recognised that in a common law system, the identity of the individual judge matters. This underpins the consensus advocating for judicial diversity. It is not simply about who the individual judge is; it is also about the characteristics which that judge displays. These characteristics are defined at two levels: the first is the 'surface' level, demographic characteristics, education and expertise; and the second, deep-level characteristics, values, knowledge and experiences. High-quality decision making requires diversity at both levels and overt evidence of diversity at a surface and deep level is essential to the recruitment of diverse candidates to the UKSC bench.

This chapter explores these facets of diversity through the lens of judicial lectures, a public resource which is rarely subject to academic scrutiny. The chapter analyses the lectures delivered by the Supreme Court bench during the first four years of Lord Reed's Presidency. This is an important time for the Supreme Court. Lord Reed, if he serves a full term, will be the longest serving President and will have participated in the appointment of the majority of the Supreme Court bench. Whilst there is overt recognition that judicial diversity on the Supreme Court bench is important, the Court remains dominated by white, male Oxbridge graduates, many of whom have experience at the Commercial Bar or on the Chancery Bench. Whilst there is some expectation that a court that is committed to diversity would seek to display its commitment by delivering lectures to less represented audiences, the audiences chosen by the Court during this period reflected the current image of a UKSC Justice, Oxbridge educated with experience at the Bar.

The collegiate practices of the Court have shifted the focus from the individual to the collective and increasingly the identity of the 'Reed Court' has started to dominate the academic and public discourse. The associated decrease in dissent underpins a conception of a collective court with shared principles, values and priorities: a narrative that centres on similarity rather than difference. The public lecture is one of the rare opportunities to hear the voice of the individual Justice, and albeit highly

[70] Lord Sales, was discussing the decision in *R (Nicklinson) v Secretary of State for Justice* [2014] UKSC 38, a case which centred on the right to life: Lord Sales, 'Proportionality Review in Appellate Courts: a Wrong Turning?' (ALBA Annual Lecture, London, Inner Temple, 1 November 2020), https://jcpc.uk/uploads/speech_181120_15214a472c.pdf.

constrained, it is an opportunity to present individual reflections, perspectives, and priorities. In doing so, the lecture either embeds or disrupts the perceptions of the Court and the Justices who populate it.

There is some evidence in the lectures of nuanced difference, but it is limited. Rather than displaying cognitive difference, even in the context of the public lecture there are dominant narratives, espousing shared values and principles. Judicial diversity and the high-quality decision making associated with it requires individuals who display difference, both overt and cognitive. In the UKSC it maybe that difference is expressed behind closed doors, but this is not sufficient. Difference needs to be on display if the Court is ever to achieve diversity.

11

Judicial Scholarship (in a Small-ish Democracy): Hallmark, Hobby, and/or Hazard?

DEAN R KNIGHT*

I. INTRODUCTION

RECEIVED CONSTITUTIONAL WISDOM used to be that judges should only speak through their judgments; in other words, the institutional product of the judiciary was, and should only be, rulings made when adjudicating cases.[1] However, this formalistic belief is, rightly, out of fashion nowadays. While adjudication, of course, continues to be the judiciary's preeminent function, judges also speak individually and collectively through various voices.[2] Linguistic metaphors such as dialogue (once fashionable but perhaps less so nowadays), discourse, voice and expression provide a helpful way to characterise the distinctive constitutional functions of different branches – their purpose, character, consequences and interaction.[3]

Academic publications by judges – judicial scholarship – are an especially enigmatic form of the extrajudicial voice. Scholarship penned by judges could be part of the *hallmark* of judicial office, adjunct to judicial stewardship of the common law and statutory interpretation and an essential tool in maintaining the legitimacy of the judiciary as an institution. Academic writing could be a judicial *hobby*, as judges dip their

*Thanks, subject to the usual caveat, to Alan Wendt and the editors of this collection for comments on a draft version of this chapter; thanks also to Jack Apperley and Zack Limbrick-Jones for research assistance.

[1] G Hammond, 'Judges and Free Speech in New Zealand' in HP Lee (ed), *Judiciaries in Comparative Perspective* (Cambridge, Cambridge University Press, 2011) 195; A Barak, *The Judge in a Democracy* (Princeton NJ, Princeton University Press, 2006); AW Bradley, 'Judges and the Media' [1986] *Public Law* 383; LB Dubeck, 'Understanding "Judicial Lockjaw"' (2007) 82 *New York University Law Review* 569.

[2] See eg, H Tyrrell and C Mallory, 'The Extrajudicial Voice' (2024) 44 *Legal Studies* 1; DR Knight and P Roycroft, 'A Supreme Voice: Non-adjudicative Expression by the Supreme Court' in M Littlewood and J McLean (eds), *The New Zealand Supreme Court: The Second Ten Years* (Auckland, LexisNexis, 2024) 95; R Cornes, 'A Constitutional Disaster in the Making?' [2013] *Public Law* 266.

[3] MSR Palmer and DR Knight, *The Constitution of New Zealand: A Contextual Analysis* (Oxford, Hart Publishing, 2022) 22.

toes into the world of academia. And, in either case, judicial scholarship could be a *hazard* – an unwelcome intervention into inter-branch constitutional dynamics or a risk to adjudicative impartiality.

In this chapter, I look at judicial scholarship as one of the non-adjudicative functions of our judiciary and lightly reflect on the virtue or otherwise of publication of academic articles by judges. Particular attention is paid, as an illustrative case study, to the practice and impact of judicial scholarship in Aotearoa New Zealand – a small democracy where judicial scholarship is especially common-place and judicial ruminations have profound effects on legal consciousness and public thought.[4]

II. SCHOLARSHIP AS NON-ADJUDICATIVE JUDICIAL VOICE

Judges are story-tellers. Adjudication of cases allows judges to tell the story of a dispute and its resolution in a set of reasons that supports their ultimate ruling. Yet, adjudicative authorship, especially in common law systems, is sometimes distinctive for its modesty and narrative parsimony. Judges are counselled to only speak to and determine the questions in issue in the case before them, and then, only those questions strictly necessary to dispose of the particular case; saying no more than necessary to dispose of the case is not unusual as a form of judicial posture in common law adjudication. Thus, publishing scholarship is a parallel and inviting way for judges to be story-tellers; this extrajudicial voice is closely allied to the function of delivering speeches – speeches which often have a second life as scholarship published in journals, edited collections or textbooks. Scholarship generally allows a more generous voice and more expansive story-telling than adjudicative authorship. At the same time, judicial scholarship is not free from limiting expectations, although the limits on public comment by judges – of which judicial scholarship is but one form – appear to have loosened in recent decades. I first explain the expectations about judges speaking extrajudicially, whether through oral remarks or published scholarship, including changes in emphasis in those expectations. I then turn to the practice, sketching the different types of scholarship.

A. Evolving Expectations

For judges in the United Kingdom, the so-called Kilmuir Rules framed expectations for extrajudicial comment and activity for much of the mid- to late-twentieth century and sought to keep the British judiciary 'insulated from the controversies of the day'.[5]

[4] For discussion of judicial scholarship in some other jurisdictions, see eg P McCormick, 'Judges, Journals and Exegesis: Judicial Leadership and Academic Scholarship' (1996) 45 *University of New Brunswick Law Journal* 139 (Canada); R Hunter and E Rackley, 'Judicial leadership on the UK Supreme Court' (2018) 28 *Legal Studies* 191 (as a form of 'community leadership', United Kingdom); S Bartie and J Gava, 'Some Problems with Extrajudicial Writing' (2012) 34 *Sydney Law Review* 637 (Australia); Dubeck, 'Understanding "Judicial Lockjaw"' (above n 1) 583ff especially (United States).

[5] Sir David Fyfe (Lord Kilmuir), Letter to Sir Ian Jacob (12 December 1955); reproduced in AW Bradley, 'Judges and the Media – the Kilmuir Rules' [1986] *Public Law* 383.

The rationale for restricting extrajudicial speech by judges was explained by Lord Chancellor, Lord Kilmuir in a letter to the Director-General of the BBC:

> So long as a Judge keeps silent [their] reputation for wisdom and impartiality remains unassailable: but every utterance which [they make] in public, except in the course of the actual performance of [their] judicial duties, must necessarily bring [them] within the focus of criticism.[6]

The mischief that led to the counselling of expressive restraint was a request from the BBC to interview a number of senior judges for a programme about famous judges from the past.[7] After consulting heads of different judicial divisions, Lord Kilmuir signalled that 'as a general rule it is undesirable for members of the Judiciary to broadcast on the wireless or to appear on television'.[8] However, the letter was taken as expressing a conventional rule against judicial participation in matters of public debate, thus, in principle, also constraining extrajudicial writing by judges. This expectation was, inevitably, conditioned by exceptions too. Judicial lectures and speeches were countenanced but only, as Lord Neuberger put it, 'on interesting but safe subjects such as the rule in *Foss v Harbottle*, or the principle in *Rylands v Fletcher*'.[9] More generally, 'steer[ing] clear of controversies' was the core expectation – an expectation Lord Neuberger noted also extended to 'any books or articles written by sitting judges'.[10]

Eventually, the conventional rule was abandoned in the mid-1980s at the instigation of Lord Mackay as Lord Chancellor; he took the view that the Kilmuir Rules were inconsistent with the separation of powers and explained that judges 'should have the judgment to decide such matters for themselves'.[11] Despite the formality of the expressive restraint being loosened and recasting of the judgement in to a matter for judges themselves, caution was still counselled:

> Judges should obviously be very cautious about publicly discussing the controversies of the day when speaking extra-judicially. Cautious not only in the choice of subject, but also in the manner in which their contributions to public debate are phrased.[12]

Neuberger explained the considerations in terms of judicial independence: 'A speech on a subject which may become the subject of judicial determination, and in which the judge's views on the subject are expressed in a particularly uncompromising or trenchant way', he said, could be seen as affecting a judge's ability to decide any particular case – thus 'compromising … judicial independence'.[13] Mutual respect between judges and politicians is also important, because judges 'can scarcely complain about Ministers criticising [them] for the way [they are] doing [their] job if [they criticise]

[6] ibid 385.

[7] Lord Neuberger, 'Where Angels Fear to Tread' (Presidential Address at the Holdsworth Club, London, 2 March 2012) 2. See also Lady Hale, 'Being a Judge in the Modern World' (2015) 48 *Israel Law Review* 387.

[8] Fyfe in Bradley (above n 5) 385.

[9] Neuberger (above n 7) 4.

[10] ibid.

[11] Lord Mackay, *The Administration of Justice* (London, Stevens & Co, 1993) 25.

[12] Neuberger (above n 7) 10.

[13] ibid 6.

Ministers for the way they are doing their jobs' and, 'if they slang each other off in public', both branches of government and democracy will be undermined.[14]

In New Zealand, expectations have ebbed-and-flowed somewhat. It is difficult to assess whether judges in New Zealand have been more or less vocal than their British counterparts; however, it is probably fair at least to say that judges have regularly pushed the boundaries of the controversial. Sanders, for example, recounts historical examples where judges have spoken 'off the bench' of matters on public controversy.[15] Especially notable are a celebrated judicial protest in colonial times and a number of incidents in recent decades where senior judges have courted controversy with public remarks and published scholarship.

The 'protest of bench and bar', as it came to be known, took place at the turn of the twentieth century.[16] Judges and lawyers, led by Chief Justice Stout, officially protested a ruling of the Privy Council overturning a decision of the New Zealand Court of Appeal, where the Judicial Committee criticised the motives of the local judges and their perceived lack of independence from the executive.[17] This unusual occasion provides a clue as to the attitude of colonial judges towards non-adjudicative speech on matters of controversy and stands as a major historical backdrop for modern extrajudicial speech.

The protest itself took place following an adjourned sitting of the Court of Appeal. Lengthy statements were read defending the local appeal court against, as Stout put it, a 'direct attack … upon its probity', 'baseless' imputations that it 'had lost its dignity and independence' and 'unfounded aspersions'.[18] These included a very strongly worded statement from one of the judges who sat on the New Zealand appeal, Williams J, read aloud by Stout on his behalf:

> [W]here the decision of the inferior Court has been not only reversed but has been reversed with contumely – where the inferior Court has been taunted with want of independence and subservience to the Executive Government – it is right that the members of the Court who pronounced the decision in question should come forward and defend the honour of the Court they represent.[19]

His lengthy rebuttal concluded with the acknowledgement that 'if we have spoken strongly, it is because we feel deeply'.[20]

The protest remarks were published verbatim in local newspapers and subsequently published in an appendix to the *New Zealand Privy Council Cases* law reports.[21] Public support was forthcoming from local executive government too, with the Premier,

[14] ibid 10.

[15] K Sanders, 'Away from the familiar – judges in public debate and as commissioners' in J Burrows and J Finn (eds), *Challenge and Change: Judging in Aotearoa New Zealand* (Auckland, LexisNexis, 2022) 223.

[16] Sanders (above n 15) 223. For further discussion of the incident, see J Tate, 'The Privy Council and Native Title: a Requiem for Wi Parata' (2004) 12 *Waikato Law Review* 99; R Cooke, 'The Nineteenth Century Chief Justices' in R Cooke (ed), *Portrait of a Profession* (Dunedin, AH & AW Reed, 1969) 36, 46.

[17] '*Wallis and others v Solicitor-General,* Protest of Bench and Bar, April 25, 1903', [1840–1932] NZPCC Appendix, 730; protesting *Wallis v Solicitor-General for New Zealand* [1903] UKPC 1, (1903) NZPCC 23.

[18] ibid 730 and 744.

[19] ibid 746.

[20] ibid 756.

[21] Sanders (above n 15) 224, fn 32. See also n 17 above.

Richard Seddon, describing the statements as a 'masterly and exhaustive refutation of their lordships' aspersions'.[22] Subsequently, Stout continued to rebuke the Privy Council in articles published in law journals: in the *Commonwealth Law Review*, he argued for the abolition of the Privy Council on the grounds that the Judicial Committee represented 'a denial of justice to many litigants on account of delay, cost, and the ignorance of the external Judges of what our laws have been, and are, and of want of acquaintance with our environment';[23] in the *Law Quarterly Review*, he noted that '[t]here is an impression amongst some New Zealand colonists that the Judicial Committee of the Privy Council must be a legislative body [because] recent deliverances of their lordships are regarded as indicating that … they do not consider themselves bound by those rules or canons by which our courts are guided'.[24]

After the colonial era, it is fair to say that the expectations relating to extrajudicial comment have ebbed-and-flowed. The adoption of the Kilmuir Rules in the United Kingdom, while not directly applicable, appears to have generated some halo effect for Antipodean judges. 'While New Zealand never formally adopted the Kilmuir rules', Hammond said, 'in practice, in the mid-1950s and for perhaps twenty years thereafter, the New Zealand judiciary acted very much in conformance with those rules'.[25] The latter part of the twentieth century and into the first part of the twenty-first century is notable for greater willingness on the part of judges to speak publicly, including through judicial scholarship, sometimes generating 'terse exchanges' between senior judges and the executive (as discussed further below).[26]

Nowadays, New Zealand's *Guidelines for Judicial Conduct* – based on the *Bangalore Principles of Judicial Conduct* – provide sage advice for judges considering speaking extrajudicially (relevant extracts reproduced in Appendix 1).[27] The guidelines are principle-based and illustrative: they are 'not intended to be a code of conduct' but 'designed to assist judges to make their own choices, informed by a checklist of general principles and illustrations drawn from experience'.[28]

Specific guidance is given on 'activities outside the courtroom', with a series of 'illustrations of issues relating to judicial independence'.[29] In general terms, the guidelines emphasise avoiding political controversy or judges otherwise compromising their judicial impartiality. The Chief Justice and Heads of Bench have a key role in responding to matters of public controversy if a response is needed. The virtue in public debate by judges, providing 'information relating to the administration of justice and the functions of the judiciary', is acknowledged as tempered by

[22] 'New Zealand and the Privy Council', *New Zealand Herald* (Auckland, 6 June 1903) 5 (Supplement), quoted in Sanders (above n 15) 225.

[23] R Stout, 'Appellate tribunals for the colonies' (1904–1905) 2 *Commonwealth Law Review* 3, 13.

[24] R Stout, 'Is the Privy Council a legislative body?' (1905) 21 *Law Quarterly Review* 9, 9.

[25] Hammond (above n 1) 196.

[26] ibid.

[27] *Guidelines for Judicial Conduct* (Courts of New Zealand, 2019) https://www.courtsofnz.govt.nz/assets/4-About-the-judiciary/judicialconduct/Guidelines-for-Judicial-Conduct-2019.pdf. Hammond mentions that these 'internal constraints' were previously set out in the Judges' Bench Book, issued by the Chief Justice: Hammond (above n 1) 196.

[28] ibid, Preface [3].

[29] ibid, Part G.

the need for 'care'.[30] Factors to bear in mind when deciding whether to contribute to public debate are listed. Publication in legal journals and remarks at seminars are described as 'not objectionable' with the caveat that judges should take 'care to avoid expressing firm views about matters which may come before the court for determination'.[31] The guidance does 'not resolve the tension between public engagement and … judicial "coinage"', Sanders argues, but 'is frank about the need for good judgement and continued attention to convention, community expectation and context'.[32]

Consistently with the spirit of the guidelines, Dame Sian Elias – one of the most prolific (and sometimes controversial) extrajudicial speakers – has suggested the practice in New Zealand charts a 'middle path' between 'judicial lock-jaw' and 'locked horns'.[33] On the one hand, judges may need to speak publicly about matters 'of legitimate concern' to the judiciary, such as diminishing funding for the courts, where judges have particular expertise, or to ensure that judges are not 'remote and mysterious' such that their authority is in doubt. On the other hand, caution is needed to avoid 'the risk to the appearance of impartiality in judging'.[34] Great freedom was also afforded to Chief Justices and other judicial leaders because, as Dame Sian Elias put it, they 'could be relied on to be uncontroversial and dull'.[35] Former Court of Appeal judge, Sir Grant Hammond, too, expressed similar sentiments.[36] Notably, he recognised that there was understood to be an exception for 'what might be termed "legal argument"'; that is, no objection would be taken to a judge taking issue, in a periodical or text, 'with something that commentators have said as to the validity, or strength of an argument which had been adopted by a judge even in a case'.[37] There was, he thought, public benefit in such contributions to 'an ongoing argument about what the law is on a particular point'.[38]

B. Diverse Typology and Styles

The stories of law and justice told by judges have taken many different forms: textbooks, technical digests, chapters in edited collections, journal articles and the like. The style of the stories told by judges in judicial scholarship also varies widely, from the descriptive to normative, from dull to the provocative, from the anodyne to the controversial, from the inert to the influential, and so forth. In the light of the expectations regulating the nature of the extrajudicial voice explained earlier, we might be especially interested how judges successfully – or unsuccessfully – position their

[30] ibid [50].
[31] ibid [52].
[32] Sanders (above n 15) 231.
[33] S Elias, 'Between "Lock-Jaw" and Locked Horns' (Address to the 14th Conference of Chief Justices of Asia and the Pacific, Seoul, 2011) 1.
[34] ibid 1.
[35] ibid.
[36] Hammond (above n 1).
[37] ibid 216.
[38] ibid.

scholarship on those continuums, especially navigating the need for impartiality and caution against controversy.

Authoring or editing textbooks and other legal digests is relatively common fodder for judges. By its general nature, this type of scholarship tends to lean towards the descriptive, dull and anodyne; however, explication of law can, of course, be highly influential.[39] Examples from the United Kingdom include Lord Collins continuing editorship of one of the reference texts on conflict of laws, *Dicey, Morris & Collins on the Conflict of Laws*, after his appointment to the bench,[40] along with Lady Hale's textbook on mental health law while serving on the Supreme Court, *Mental Health Law*.[41] So, too, in New Zealand. Justice Robertson was consulting editor for the leading looseleaf digest on criminal law, *Adams on Criminal Law*, for many years, with a large group of updating editors; Justice Downs now serves as first-listed consulting editor.[42] The leading civil procedure digest carries the name of Justice McGechan, *McGechan on Procedure*, and he was lead author and editor for decades.[43] Justice Blanchard was the co-author of a book on private receivers and also consulting editor for the *Civil Remedies in New Zealand* textbook.[44] Justice Palmer coauthors (with me) the New Zealand volume in the 'Constitutional Systems of the World' series: *The New Zealand Constitution: A Contextual Analysis*.[45] The encyclopaedic digest *Laws of New Zealand* lists extensive judicial involvement: the late Lord Cooke was an active founding editor-in-chief, followed by the late Justice McGrath and, today, Justice Kós; numerous other judges serve as consulting editors and on the advisory board.[46]

Judge-authored chapters in edited collections and journal articles, often consisting of published remarks given earlier in public addresses and conferences, are commonplace but there is greater diversity in the judicial voice in these types of publications. There are too many instances to catalogue here other than mentioning a few to give some flavour.

Some are predominantly *explanatory*, where a judicial author describes recent legal developments – often developments the judicial author was privy to. Lord Sales' recent article on the UK Supreme Court's treatment of European Convention rights is a good example.[47] Justice Glazebrook's article on two Supreme Court cases implicating cultural values, *Ellis* and *Deng*, is a recent instance from New Zealand.[48]

[39] J Varuhas, 'Mapping doctrinal methods' in Daly and Tomlinson (eds), *Researching Public Law in Common Law Systems* (Cheltenham, Edward Elgar Publishing, 2023) 70.

[40] L Collins (ed), *Dicey, Morris & Collins on the Conflict of Laws*, 11th–14th edns (London, Sweet & Maxwell, 1987–2016). The textbook was retitled in 2006 to include Collins and his editorship continued after his retirement.

[41] B Hale, *Mental Health Law*, 5th–6th edns (London, Sweet & Maxwell, 2010–2017).

[42] *Adams on Criminal Law* (Wellington, Brooker & Friend/Thomson Reuters, looseleaf, 1964–).

[43] *McGechan on Procedure* (Wellington, Thomson Brookers, looseleaf, 1995–).

[44] P Blanchard and M Gedye, *Private Receivers of Companies in New Zealand*, 1st edn (Auckland, LexisNexis, 2008); P Blanchard and A Barker (eds), *Civil Remedies in New Zealand*, 1st edn (Wellington, Thomson Brookers, 2003).

[45] Palmer and Knight (above n 3).

[46] *Laws of New Zealand* (Butterworths, 1992–).

[47] P Sales, 'The Developing Jurisprudence of the Supreme Court on Convention rights' [2024] *Public Law* 444.

[48] S Glazebrook, 'Tikanga and Culture in the Supreme Court: *Ellis* and *Deng*' (2023) 4 *Amicus Curiae* 287; *Deng v Zheng* [2022] NZSC 76; *Ellis v R* [2022] NZSC 114.

While legal description is never fully neutral, judicial scholarship of this type tends to avoid significant normative narrative. Sometimes more life is injected into the explanation, where a judicial author is *reflective* about developments, contextualising, conceptualising or, perhaps, lightly critiquing the shifts in the law; increasing normative content sometimes nudges a judicial author towards more controversy. Lady Hale's exploration of deference in recent cases is one example from the United Kingdom;[49] Chief Justice Winkelmann's chapter on narratives in the development of public law is a good example from New Zealand.[50] Occasionally, judges take a *predictive* turn, extrapolating from today and outlining legal issues that might fall for adjudication in the future, usually while refraining from giving too much away. Here, judges need to acutely avoid any loss of impartiality by expressing prior views too definitely. Bartie and Gava worry that extrajudicial writing on live legal issues often 'speaks of predispositions that are neither tentative nor academic [and] constitute a very real threat to a fair trial' – a complication I return to briefly later.[51] Lady Hale's remarks to students in Kuala Lumpur on the issues coming before the Court in the first Brexit case might be one example that fell very close to the line.[52] Sometimes a contribution is more *conceptual*, grappling with theoretical principles that underpin the legal order, such as Bingham's work on the rule of law.[53]

Sometimes judges avoid the currency of developments of today and look to the past: *historical* inquiry exploring old legal developments and figures. Lord Reed's portrait of Lord Reid, explored in the context of the famous quartet of cases that shaped English and Welsh administrative law fits this brief.[54] Justice Kós authored a blockbuster article diving deep into one of New Zealand's most significant constitutional cases from the mid-1970s, in 'Constitutional collision: Fitzgerald v Muldoon v Wild'.[55]

Relatively common are chapters and articles which are *self-referential*, where judicial authors narrate aspects of the judicial function and reflect on the practice of adjudicating cases. Lord Burrows' article, reproducing his 2021 Lionel Cohen lecture on the use of academic scholarship by judges, is an emblematic recent article.[56] New Zealand judges, especially Supreme Court judges in the early days of

[49] B Hale, 'Principle and Pragmatism in Public Law' (2020) 24 *Judicial Review* 315.

[50] H Winkelmann, 'The power of narrative – shaping Aotearoa New Zealand's Public Law' in E Carolan, J Varuhas and S Fulham-McQuillan (eds), *The Making and Re-Making of Public Law* (Oxford, Hart Publishing, 2025) 29.

[51] Bertie and Gava (above n 4) 658.

[52] B Hale, 'The Supreme Court: Guardian of the Constitution?' (Sultan Azlan Shah Lecture, Kuala Lumpur, 9 November 2016); see also 'Lady Hale will "Absolutely Not" Recuse Herself from Article 50 Appeal', *Solicitors Journal* (16 November 2016); G Gee, 'A Tale of Two Constitutional Duties: Liz Truss, Lady Hale, and Miller', *Judicial Power Project* (28 November 2016) https://judicialpowerproject.org.uk/graham-gee-a-tale-of-two-constitutional-duties-liz-truss-lady-hale-and-miller; BC Jones, 'Dissonant Constitutionalism and Lady Hale' (2018) 29 *King's Law Journal* 177.

[53] T Bingham, 'The Rule of Law' (2007) 66 *Cambridge Law Journal* 67.

[54] R Reed, 'Lord Reid: the Judge as Law Maker?' in TT Arvind et al (eds), *Executive Decision-Making and the Courts* (Oxford, Hart Publishing, 2021) 27.

[55] S Kós, 'Constitutional Collision: Fitzgerald v Muldoon v Wild' (2014) 13 *Otago Law Review* 243.

[56] A Burrows, 'Judges and Academics, and the Endless Road to Unattainable Perfection' (2022) 55(1) *Israel Law Review* 50.

establishment (2004–), commonly explained the operation of the courts, including adding insights from behind the scenes.[57] Allied to this type of scholarship are chapters or articles that reflect on the environment and settings within which law operates, especially changes which might unsettle the nature and practice of law. Lord Sales' writing on artificial intelligence and the law is a notable example of this style of scholarship.[58]

III. SITUATING JUDICIAL SCHOLARSHIP

Against the background of an industry of judicial scholarship, both in the United Kingdom and New Zealand, I turn to the question of whether extrajudicial scholarship is a hallmark, hobby and/or hazard – ultimately concluding that we see all three in practice. In doing so, I pay particular attention to instances in New Zealand that are emblematic of each, and explain these in greater detail.

A. Hallmark

There is a great deal of scholarship that we might regard as a hallmark of office; in other words, many stories told by judges arise from a sense of duty, especially the legal and institutional stewardship expected of judges. As curators and custodians of law, judges are increasingly expected to explain legal goings-on in order to provide transparency and legitimacy within the legal order. In addition, as members of the judiciary as an institution, judges – especially senior judges – are expected to explain their role, their work and their relationships with other institutions. It is no surprise that this talking-about-the-job is common for presiding members of courts or heads of bench; there are increasing expectations that judges will demystify the business of adjudication and promote a degree of openness in order to fortify the institutional legitimacy of the courts.

Examples from New Zealand are plentiful. Take, for example, Dame Sian Elias' article, 'Judgery and the rule of law', where she sought to give some insights into life as a judge; her reference to judgery was partly meant 'as a joke, and not even an original joke', partly to emphasise that that 'judging is hard work' and partly to 'disclaim the mantle of the hero judge'.[59] Another example is Matthew Palmer's article, 'Impressions of life and law on the High Court bench', where he reflected on his work, having kept a diary of his impressions since his appointment; 'greater public understanding and discussion of the judicial role', he said, 'ought to enhance support for the rule of law which is and ought to be a constitutional norm in New Zealand'.[60]

[57] See text at n 61.
[58] P Sales, 'Algorithms, Artificial Intelligence and the Law' (2020) 25 *Judicial Review* 46.
[59] S Elias, 'Judgery and the Rule of Law' (2015) 14 *Otago Law Review* 49, 51.
[60] M Palmer, 'Impressions of Life and Law on the High Court Bench' (2018) 49 *Victoria University of Wellington Law Review* 297, 313.

This form of 'judicial statecraft' is especially common in formative periods of a court's establishment and operation, as alluded to earlier.[61] Both Chief Justices to preside over the Supreme Court in New Zealand since its establishment in 2004 have published accounts of its establishment, role and associated issues. For example, Dame Sian nodded to appellate practice in several articles published on the eve of the Court's establishment, as well as regularly touching on it in later addresses and articles.[62] Dame Helen Winkelmann has since added her reflections, including discussing whether the Court might appropriately be described as a 'constitutional court'.[63] Roycroft and I have argued elsewhere that the application of the Court's non-adjudicative voice tracks its institutional creation story – 'from modest and largely functional beginnings to rising institutional stature' – in a deliberate effort to 'mark out its role and mana within our constitutional ecosystem'.[64]

Explication of legal developments is also a common topic of judicial scholarship, especially in order to demystify, situate and perhaps justify different turns taking in law. One of New Zealand's leading exponents of doctrinal elaboration was Lord Cooke, especially in the field of administrative law. As judge and later President of the Court of Appeal, he frequently published articles explaining developments in judicial review doctrine – often critiquing arcane precedent on the bases for judicial intervention or troublesome procedural rules.[65] Much of his extrajudicial analysis aligned with his adjudicative activities, as he is remembered for catalysing the reshaping and simplification of judicial review principles;[66] his extrajudicial comment was also based on a foundation of academic study, notably his PhD thesis at Cambridge entitled 'Jurisdiction'.[67]

[61] Knight and Roycroft (above n 2) 29. See eg, P Blanchard, 'The Early Experience of the New Zealand Supreme Court' in C Geiringer and DR Knight, *Seeing the World Whole: Essays in Honour of Sir Kenneth Keith* (Wellington, Victoria University Press, 2008) 321; P Blanchard, 'The Supreme Court: a Judge's View' in A Stockley and M Littlewood (eds), *The New Zealand Supreme Court: The First Ten Years* (Auckland, LexisNexis, 2015) 57; S Glazebrook, 'Intermediate and Final Courts of Appeal: Chalk and Cheese?' (2017) 26 *Journal of Judicial Administration* 98; see also fn 62. Examples from the United Kingdom include N Phillips, 'The Challenges of the Supreme Court' (2010) 15(4) *Judicial Review* 285; B Kerr 'The Impact of the Supreme Court on the Law of Northern Ireland ' in D Clarry (ed), *The UK Supreme Court Yearbook 2018–19* (London, Appellate Press, 2021) 86; this topic was often addressed in unpublished speeches including, eg D Hope, 'The Creation of the Supreme Court' (Barnard's Inn Reading, London, 24 June 2010); B Hale, 'Judgment Writing in the Supreme Court' (Supreme Court, *First Anniversary Seminar*, London, 30 September 2010).

[62] S Elias, '"The Next Revisit": Judicial Independence Seven Years on' (2004) 10 *Canterbury Law Review* 217; S Elias, 'Impartiality in Judging and the Passions of Mankind' (2005) 17 *Singapore Academy of Law Journal* 1; S Elias, 'Transition, Stability and the New Zealand Legal System' (2004) 10 *Otago Law Review* 475; S Elias, 'Something Old, Something New: Constitutional Stirrings and the Supreme Court' (2004) 2 *New Zealand Journal of Public and International Law* 121.

[63] H Winkelmann, 'The Supreme Court: a View from the Top' in M Littlewood and J McLean (eds), *The New Zealand Supreme Court: The Second Ten Years* (Auckland, LexisNexis, 2024) 503.

[64] Knight and Roycroft (above n 2) 29.

[65] See eg, R Cooke, 'Administrative law: the Vanishing Sphinx' [1975] *New Zealand Law Journal* 529; R Cooke, 'The struggle for simplicity in administrative law' in M Taggart (ed), *Judicial Review of Administrative Action in the 1980s* (Oxford, Oxford University Press, 1986) 1; R Cooke, 'Fairness' (1989) 19 *Victoria University of Wellington Law Review* 421.

[66] DR Knight, 'Simple, fair and discretionary administrative law' (2006) 39 *Victoria University of Wellington Law Review* 99.

[67] RB Cooke, 'Jurisdiction: An Essay in Constitutional, Administrative and Procedural Law' (PhD thesis, University of Cambridge, 1954).

Symbolic of his influence was his treatment of grounds of review in a chapter entitled 'The Struggle for Simplicity in Administrative Law', originally delivered at a conference held at the University of Auckland and a title later to be coopted as the title of a festschrift published in his honour.[68] His articulation of the expectations of decision-making in simplified tripartite form – that decision-makers 'must act in accordance with the law, fairly and reasonably' – was quickly canonised and remains the starting point for judicial review cases today.[69] A mirror reflection of Lord Diplock's famous tripartite statement in the *Council of Civil Service Unions* case, Sir Robin reminded his audience that his initial expression of these principles came five years before Lord Diplock's reformation.[70] In addition, the *Wednesbury* standard for unreasonableness was a frequent target in his extrajudicial scholarship, as his analysis sometimes became more forcefully normative. In his adjudicative work, he condemned *Wednesbury* as an 'unfortunately retrogressive decision in English administrative law'; in his extrajudicial scholarship, his disdain for *Wednesbury*'s 'distracting circumlocutions' was made plain: in his view, 'reasonable means reasonable', reasonableness was coterminous with the 'limits of reasons' and what is 'outside those limits is unreasonable [and] what is inside them is reasonable'.[71] His extrajudicial comment continued after his judicial tenure in New Zealand, while he continued to serve on the Appellate Committee of the House of Lords; notably, this period included the publication of his Hamlyn lectures, 'Turning Points of the Common Law', along with many other chapters and journal articles.[72]

This tradition of judicial engagement with the common law, along with other legal and interpretative developments, continues today. For example, Dame Susan Glazebrook has published analyses of the impact of international law on the shape of domestic law;[73] Dame Sian Elias's Hamlyn lectures on fairness in criminal justice is another example.[74] Constitutional histories, especially tracing key legal developments in New Zealand's maturation as a liberal democracy and allied developments in the discipline of public law, have been a common topic for New Zealand's most recent Chief Justices. Dame Sian has written about early colonial history, as well the nation's

[68] Cooke, 'Struggle for Simplicity' (above n 65); P Rishworth (ed), *The Struggle for Simplicity in the Law: Essays for Lord Cooke of Thorndon* (Wellington, Butterworths, 1997) 189.

[69] Cooke, 'Struggle for Simplicity' (above n 65) 5. For its continuing doctrinal legacy, see *NZ Fishing Industry Association v Minister of Agriculture & Fisheries* [1988] 1 NZLR 544, 552; *BNZ Investments Ltd v Commissioner of Inland Revenue* (2007) 23 NZTC 21,078 [15], [2007] NZCA 356; [2008] 1 NZLR 598; *Osbourne v Chief Executive of the Ministry of Social Development* [2010] 1 NZLR 559, [54] and Crown Law, *Judge Over your Shoulder*, 3rd edn (New Zealand, Crown Law Office, 2019) https://www.crownlaw.govt.nz/publications/judge-over-your-shoulder.

[70] Cooke, 'Struggle for Simplicity' (above n 65) 6, referring to R Cooke, 'Third Thoughts on Administrative Law' [1979] *NZ Recent Law Review* 218, 225, where he said it 'might not be an altogether absurd oversimplification to say that the day may come when the whole of administrative law can be summed up in the proposition that *the administrator must act fairly and reasonably*'. *Council of Civil Service Unions v Minister for the Civil Service* [1985] AC 374.

[71] Cooke, 'Struggle for Simplicity' (above n 65) 14; *Associated Provincial Picture Houses v Wednesbury Corporation* [1948] 1 KB 223.

[72] R Cooke, *Turning Points of the Common Law* (London, Sweet & Maxwell, 1997).

[73] S Glazebrook, 'Cross-Pollination or Contamination: Global Influences on New Zealand Law' (2015) 21 *Canterbury Law Review* 60.

[74] S Elias, *Fairness in Criminal Justice: Golden Threads and Pragmatic Patches* (Cambridge, Cambridge University Press, 2018).

moves to assert its independence;[75] Dame Helen Winkelmann has similarly traced the developments in nationhood and the ways in which the system of public law has been shaped by 'historical and social forces, operating as they do within a system without a constitutional charter'.[76] Other judges also frequently address indigenous dimensions of New Zealand's legal order, whether developments relating to *te Tiriti o Waitangi* / the Treaty of Waitangi or *tikanga Māori* as the first law of Aotearoa.[77] One of the most herculean such efforts – and extrajudicial analysis that has come to be much treasured – is Justice Joseph Williams' article in the *Waikato Law Review*, 'Lex Aotearoa: an heroic attempt to map the Māori dimension in modern New Zealand law'.[78] His explanation of the founding of Aotearoa New Zealand as a collision between two systems of law – Kupe's law (*tikanga Māori*) and Cook's law (English law) – and the recent emergence of comingled third law, *Lex Aotearoa*, has played a totemic role in recent framing of state law's relationship with indigenous law, including its mediation through *te Tiriti* / the Treaty.[79]

It seems fair to say that the ubiquity of judicial analysis of legal developments in New Zealand might be attributable in part to a combination of the smallness of the legal system and bigness of some judicial personalities. Justice Hammond in *Lab Tests* explained that our smallness translated to 'an irregular supply of cases' meaning it was 'difficult for senior judges to work at the problem systematically'.[80] Team this with a small academy, with the work of interpreting legal developments – explicating, synthesising and critiquing – falling to legal academics numbering fewer than 200. I wonder if these smallness factors incite judges to more frequently take an active role in explaining and situating legal developments? Add to the mix, too, the role Sir Robin Cooke played modelling active extrajudicial narration – an active role that has continued to be modelled by Chief Justices and other judges since. This modelling might also help us understand how the practice of extrajudicial commentary has become an entrenched habit.

B. Hobby

Judicial story-telling through scholarship is, for some, a hobby. Some judges publish legal scholarship exploring stories not directly related to their day-to-day adjudicative

[75] S Elias, 'Reclaiming New Zealand Legal Tradition' (2021) 27 *Auckland University Law Review* 16.

[76] Winkelmann (above n 50).

[77] See eg, Glazebrook (above n 48); C Whata, "Biculturalism in the Law' (2018) 26 *Waikato Law Review* 33; M O'Regan, 'The challenge of the Treaty for lawyers and judges: 25 years on' (2020) 28 *Waikato Law Review* 111.

[78] J Williams, 'Lex Aotearoa: An Heroic Attempt to Map the Māori Dimension in Modern New Zealand Law' (2013) 21 *Waikato Law Review* 1.

[79] See eg, M Mutu and M Jackson, *He Whakaaro Here Whakaumu Mō Aotearoa* (Matike Mai Aotearoa, Independent Iwi Working Group on Constitutional Transformation, 2016); Law Commission, *He Poutama* (NZLC Study Paper 24, 2023); and generally, DR Knight and M Pirini, '*Ellis*, tikanga Māori and the Common Law: Relations between the First, Second and Third Laws of Aotearoa New Zealand' [2023] *Public Law* 557.

[80] *Lab Tests Auckland Ltd v Auckland District Health Board* [2008] NZCA 385; [2009] 1 NZLR 776, [396].

duties or institutional responsibilities. For example, Lord Sumption is well known for this extrajudicial writing on historical topics, including his series on the hundred years war which continued while sitting at a judge on the UK Supreme Court (although the author's 'hobby' has its origins in a brief period as an academic historian before turning to law).[81] Justice Kós' historical enquiry into one of New Zealand's most famous constitutional cases, as mentioned earlier, is probably a good example of hobby scholarship.[82] *Plundering Beauty*, a book written by Judge Tompkins, on crimes involving artistic masterpieces, is another example.[83] A further example might be Justice Goddard's book drawing on his pre-judicial career exploring law-making and law reform: *Making Laws that Work*.[84] Characterisation of these types of works as a hobby might be more a question of degree, given the subjects loosely relate to law, albeit further away from law encountered in judges' day-to-day activities.

C. Hazard

Sometimes judicial story-telling approaches – and, occasionally, crosses – the controversy guideline, regardless of the particular form the extrajudicial remarks take. A couple of instances involving Chief Justice Elias demonstrate the delicate nature of extrajudicial scholarship and the potential friction that might be generated in a small-ish democracy. Again, Hammond J's reflections in *Lab Tests* on 'place' are apposite: tensions arising between the judiciary and executive from a single exercise of the judicial function in a 'smaller and more visible "Small Democracy"' are probably more problematic 'where a pebble in a pond has the effect of a boulder'.[85]

The first instance is a set of remarks made by Dame Sian about the sovereignty of Parliament, at the University of Melbourne in 2003 on the eve of the establishment of the Supreme Court; those remarks – 'Sovereignty in the 21st century: another spin on the merry-go-round' – were subsequently published in the *Public Law Review*.[86] Dame Sian tackled the 'fixation with parliamentary sovereignty and the relative democratic merits of parliament and the courts', which she considered 'impoverishing our constitutional thinking'.[87] She traced the origins of parliamentary sovereignty in New Zealand following the signing of *te Tiriti o Waitangi* / the Treaty of Waitangi and British settlement. Puzzled by the assumed application of parliamentary sovereignty, she explained the contested nature of the treatment of sovereignty in *te Tiriti* / the Treaty in the compact between the Crown and *rangatira* of *iwi* and *hapū* (tribal chiefs) that opened the door to assertion of British rule: the English version of the

[81] J Sumption, *The Hundred Years War IV: Cursed Kings* (Philadelphia PA, University of Pennsylvania Press, 2015).

[82] S Kós (above n 55), examining *Fitzgerald v Muldoon* [1976] 2 NZLR 615.

[83] A Thompkins, *Plundering Beauty: A History of Art Crime During War* (London, Lund Humphries, 2018).

[84] D Goddard, *Making Laws that Work: How Laws Fail and How We Can Do Better* (Oxford, Hart Publishing, 2022).

[85] *Lab Tests* (above n 80) [397].

[86] S Elias, 'Sovereignty in the 21st Century: Another Spin on the Merry-go-round' (2003) 14 *Public Law Review* 148.

[87] ibid 149.

Treaty spoke of Māori ceding 'sovereignty' to Queen Victoria and retaining 'undisturbed possession' of their lands and other properties; however, the *te Reo* version of *te Tiriti* spoke of the Crown assuming '*kawanatanga*' – a more limited concept akin to governorship – while Māori retained '*tino rangatiratanga*' – a stronger concept akin to unqualified chieftainship – over their lands and treasures. Hence, she recognised, there was an argument that 'the sovereignty obtained by the British Crown was a sovereignty qualified by the Treaty', despite no such qualification being recognised in domestic law.[88] Similarly, she pondered on whether legislative power might be qualified by human rights too, especially whether the courts might develop a declaratory remedy to alert Parliament to incompatibility of legislation with the Bill of Rights Act or, perhaps, the development of substantive limitations based on human rights.[89] She went on to argue – and 'release some energy' as she put it – that parliamentary sovereignty was 'an inadequate theory of our constitutions' and 'untrammelled freedom of parliament does not exist'.[90] Her remarks and article had commenced by enlisting Mitchell's metaphor of parliamentary sovereignty as a 'merry-go-round' and, in her final line, she concluded that we 'should get off the merry-go-round'.[91]

Perhaps unsurprisingly, Dame Sian's remarks raised a few eyebrows, including amongst those in executive government. Most notable was pushback from the then Attorney-General and Deputy Prime Minister, Michael Cullen, in a speech in Parliament and remarks elsewhere.[92] Narrating the evolution of Parliament in New Zealand, he went on to say he regarded it as 'settled doctrine' that 'sovereignty is exercised by Parliament as the supreme maker of law'.[93] He expressed concern about 'the increasing tendency to challenge the exercise of this sovereignty', noting that 'it comes not just from some radical Māori' but 'also comes from the heart of New Zealand's judiciary' – naming the Chief Justice and her comments.[94] He warned against 'a creeping process of eroding the sovereignty of Parliament to make laws' in circumstances where qualification of the law-making power is 'not discussed openly, not voted for by the people of New Zealand, and not assented to by Parliament', and cautioned the judiciary from entering such 'dangerous territory'.[95] Cullen went on to counsel his parliamentary colleagues to rise up against this threat: 'Parliament may need to be more assertive in defence of its own sovereignty, not just for its own sake but also for the sake of good order and government'.[96]

The rebuke from the Attorney-General continued in two published journal articles. In the first, 'Parliamentary sovereignty and the courts', Cullen expressed concern about senior judges 'taking sides' in these debates, especially because 'it is difficult

[88] ibid 153.

[89] ibid 159 and 162.

[90] ibid 163.

[91] ibid 148 and 163, drawing on J Mitchell, 'Sovereignty of Parliament – Yet Again' (1963) 79 *Law Quarterly Review* 196.

[92] M Cullen, 'Address to Her Excellency the Governor-General' (2004) 617 *New Zealand Parliamentary Debates* 13, 191 (in an address marking the 150th anniversary of the first sitting of the House of Representatives).

[93] ibid 13, 192.

[94] ibid.

[95] ibid.

[96] ibid.

to prevent ordinary educated New Zealanders from drawing inferences which are, though perhaps incorrect, unsettling'.[97] In the second, 'Parliament: supremacy over fundamental norms?', he worried that the credibility of both the courts and Parliament could be threatened if there was any 'perception that the courts are working to develop a common law jurisprudence which imposes new limits on the power of the Parliament and the legitimacy of the laws it enacts'.[98] The Attorney-General's conclusion, at this point, was more conciliary:

> I do not wish to place too much stress on this issue. I think New Zealanders have every reason to be confident in their Parliament and their judiciary. They are both robust institutions, pursuing their mandates with skill and determination. Some testing of the boundaries is necessary from time to time, and possibly healthy … However, I am confident that that reconciliation can leave both Parliament and the judiciary as stronger institutions, better able to serve the people.[99]

But this constitutional brouhaha did not go unnoticed; this discordant dialogue between the branches of government falling for mention in popular media, with speculation about an emerging constitutional battle.[100] In a profile around this time, one newspaper described Dame Sian as 'a lightning rod for trouble'.[101]

The second instance arose from remarks given by Dame Sian at the Wellington Women's Association's Shirley Smith address – 'Blameless Babes' – and published in *Victoria University of Wellington Law Review*.[102] Honouring the trailblazing woman lawyer who was celebrated in the named lecture – New Zealand's first female law lecturer and a barrister known for her work for vulnerable folk especially in the criminal and family law fields – the remarks and article anchored on a letter to the editor of the *Dominion*, penned by Shirley Smith herself:

> To provide only a prison at the bottom of the cliff is not a solution. Criminals will just go on falling into it, at great cost to the community. We have to find out why blameless babes become criminals. Writing as a lawyer who has read many probation reports I have no doubt that their life experience has been the cause. Society creates criminals, society must look at the conditions that create them.[103]

Riffing off these sentiments, Dame Sian then analysed the state of the criminal justice system and reformative challenges, informed, as she put it, by 'someone who has been involved in criminal justice in one way or another for forty years'.[104] A rising prison population ('second only to the United States in the proportion of prisoners to the total population') and failing efforts at effective rehabilitation were discussed,

[97] M Cullen, 'Parliamentary Sovereignty and the Courts' [2004] *New Zealand Law Journal* 243, 243.
[98] M Cullen, 'Parliament: Supremacy over Fundamental Norms?' (2005) 3 *New Zealand Journal of Public and International Law* 1, 5.
[99] ibid.
[100] R Berry, 'Cullen's Attack Draws Criticism', *New Zealand Herald* (Auckland, 2 June 2004); A Young, 'Cullen to judges: Speak up, don't make changes', *New Zealand Herald* (Auckland, 26 May 2005); 'Elias – Top Judge and Judicial Activist', *New Zealand Herald* (Auckland, 29 March 2005).
[101] 'Elias – Top Judge and Judicial Activist' ibid.
[102] S Elias, 'Blameless babes' (2009) 40 *Victoria University of Wellington Law Review* 581.
[103] S Smith, 'Kneejerk reaction', *The Dominion* (17 November 1999), referred to in Elias, 'Blameless babes', 582.
[104] Elias (above n 102) 582.

along with the way in which 'high public anxiety' tended to dominate public debate about penal policy to the exclusion of evidence-based strategies.[105] She suggested a number of strategies that might need to be explored, including 'community education; intervention strategies for those at risk; better support for probation; increased attention to mental health and substance abuse; and a frank policy of being prepared to reduce the prison population by management'.[106]

The final strategy was most controversial, something acknowledged by Dame Sian; at the same time she acknowledged that she did not know whether it was 'practical or politically acceptable'.[107] However, she closed by enlisting Shirley Smith's memory and remarks penned in other letters to the editor: 'the threat of imprisonment does not deter, and imprisonment does not reform' and '[a]s a society we create our criminals; we, as a whole, are responsible'.[108] The final Smith quote called in aid was blunt:

> To reduce crime it is necessary to identify what makes criminals and deal with the causes… This is the only long-term, effective way to help victims, to reduce their numbers. Punishment does not work.[109]

Dame Sian anticipated her analysis and turns-of-phrase would be provocative; a prescient line in her introduction identified the risk: 'I've also taken "blameless babes" as my working title, although I suppose I will have to alter it because it is bound to be misrepresented along the lines of "Chief Justice says murderers are 'blameless babes'"'.[110] However, she was unrepentant about exploring Smith's 'critical question', that is: 'What turns "blameless babes" (as all criminals once were) into the stuff of nightmares?'[111]

She was right. The reaction to the remarks was strong and swift, especially as significant reform of sentencing policy – and more punitive reform – was proposed by the then government. The Minister of Justice, Simon Power, recorded that the remarks did not represent government policy and that the job of the courts was 'to apply the law set by Parliament'.[112] The Prime Minister, John Key, said the Chief Justice had strayed 'over the line', into 'the justice minister's area'.[113] Calls were made for Dame Sian's resignation, including by the most high-profile victims' rights lobby group.[114] When later reflecting on the incident, Hammond spoke of the Attorney-General 'react[ing] sharply' and Dame Sian 'com[ing] under political fire'.[115] The incident provided much fodder for newspaper editorials and cartoons.[116]

[105] ibid 588.
[106] ibid 589.
[107] ibid 593
[108] ibid 595.
[109] ibid 595.
[110] ibid 582.
[111] ibid 582.
[112] R Tiffin, 'Irate Power tells Chief Justice to Butt out of Policy' *The New Zealand Herald* (Auckland, 17 July 2009); see also discussion in Hammond (above n 1) 202.
[113] 'Chief Justice crossed line on prisons – Key', *New Zealand Herald* (Auckland, 20 July 2009).
[114] 'Call for Chief Justice to Resign', *Stuff* (23 July 2009).
[115] Hammond (above n 1) fn 23.
[116] ibid 203.

Sparks continue to fly from extrajudicial scholarship today, as the controversy boundary is navigated – sometimes successfully, sometime not. For example, a business lobby group has taken aim at the Supreme Court, alleging 'activism', 'overreach' and improper 'judicial law-making' (albeit, in my view, many of the allegations are unfounded and the attack is a beat up).[117] For present purposes, it is interesting to note that one of their targets is an article by Justice Glazebrook on the rule of law; objection is taken to her suggestion that the rule of law might incorporate a need to provide redress to indigenous Māori for the deleterious effects of colonisation.[118]

One of the other potential hazards from judicial scholarship – loss of impartiality necessitating recusal – has not been particularly common or controversial in New Zealand but has arisen elsewhere.[119] The effect on impartiality from extrajudicial writing was famously one of the scenarios considered by the Court of Appeal of England and Wales in *Locabail (UK) Ltd v Bayfield Properties Ltd* in a set of consolidated appeals implicating different aspects of the principles of bias and predetermination.[120] In one of these appeals, *Timmins v Gormley*, the Court was called on to rule on whether a judicial officer's published writings on personal injury law disqualified him from hearing a claim in that same field; the Court found that there was a danger that the judge's 'pronounced pro-claimant anti-insurer views' generated an appearance of bias or loss of impartiality.[121] The standard for bias is similar in New Zealand, and is readily able to filter instances where extrajudicial writing crosses the line.[122] Curiously, though, New Zealand lacks headline instances where the impartiality standard has been contentiously implicated by judicial scholarship.

IV. CONCLUSION

Hallmark, hobby or hazard? Judicial scholarship in Aotearoa New Zealand – as well as in its common law parent jurisdiction, the United Kingdom – spans all of these three categories. Some of the scholarship arises from an expectation nowadays that extrajudicial elaboration of law, beyond explanatory reasoning in the course of adjudicating individual cases, is a function of judges as curators of the common law and an important aspect of fortifying the courts' institutional role and legitimacy. Chief Justices and heads of bench are especially prolific writers, given their leadership role; otherwise, the incidence of scholarship is spread unevenly amongst the judiciary. A small bundle of judicial scholarship might be regarded as more of a hobby, where judges share stories

[117] R Partridge, 'Who Makes the Law? Reining in the Supreme Court' (New Zealand Initiative, 2024). See also J Hodder, 'One Advocate's Opinions – The "Least Dangerous Branch"? Predictability and Unease' [2024] *New Zealand Law Review* 423.

[118] S Glazebrook, 'The Rule of Law: Guiding Principle or Catchphrase?' (2021) 29 *Waikato Law Review* 2.

[119] See especially Bertie and Gava (above n 4).

[120] *Locabail (UK) Ltd v Bayfield Properties Ltd* [2000] QB 451 (EWCA).

[121] ibid [89].

[122] *Saxmere Co Ltd v Wool Board Disestablishment Co Ltd* [2009] NZSC 72, [2010] 1 NZLR 35. On judicial recusal, see G Hammond, *Judicial Recusal: Principles, Process and Problems* (Oxford, Hart Publishing, 2009) 17.

animated by curiosity rather than institutional expectation. In either case, judicial scholarship is not without hazards. While the cautionary shadow generated by the Kilmuir Rules has formally lifted, expectations about avoiding controversy and maintaining judicial independence continue – probably with mixed success.

The incidence and effect of judicial scholarship in Aotearoa New Zealand perhaps reflect its status as a 'small-ish' democracy.[123] On the one hand, with around 5 million people, it is bigger in size that the widely-accepted definition of a 'small state'.[124] On the other hand, it lacks the multitude of people – and people in the business of law and government – seen in cognate democratic states. There are only around 60 senior court judges, fewer than 200 district court and other judges, just over 17,000 practising lawyers, and around 200 legal academics across six law schools.[125] And the unicameral Parliament only hosts 120 or so Members of Parliament. One consequence of this is that the nation has mature and sophisticated democratic structures and institutions, but operates with a smaller civic community in closer relationship with the general population itself.

These dynamics, I think, condition expectations about judges speaking extra-judicially about law and sometimes heighten the controversy stakes. First, there is probably more pressure upon judges, especially senior judges, to generate legal scholarship. Stewardship of the law and scholarly debate on its contours fall to fewer people and, thus, probably contribute to the heavy practice of judicial contribution to civic discourse. Secondly, the judicial voice is naturally amplified, as it takes place within this small legal and civic community. Thus, any controversy potentially carries an especially strong sting and is prone to produce inter-institutional ripples. These settings mean the tipping point for judicial scholarship – from hallmark or hobby, to hazard – is especially delicate. In the end, as Saunders puts it, the appropriateness of this form of judicial voice – and any move 'away from the familiar' – will be judged according to whether it is 'perceived to be well judged'.[126]

[123] DR Knight, 'Of Wise Decisions, Government Accountability and a Small-ish Democracy' (inaugural lecture, Victoria University of Wellington, 15 August 2024).

[124] World Bank, 'The World Bank in Small States' www.worldbank.org (small states are defined as having a population of up to 1.5 million or having a population greater than 1.5 million but sharing similar challenges); M Maass, 'The Elusive Definition of the Small State' (2009) 46 *International Politics* 65.

[125] H Winkelmann, 'Annual Report' (Office of the Chief Justice, 2023); New Zealand Law Society, 'Annual Report 2023/24'.

[126] Sanders (above n 15) 242.

Appendix 1

Guidelines for Judicial Conduct (2019)

G. ACTIVITIES OUTSIDE THE COURTROOM

Illustrations of issues relating to judicial independence

...

(e) Participation in public debate/media/judicial writing

50. If a matter of public controversy calls for a response from the judiciary or a particular court, it should come from the Chief Justice or Head of Bench or with his or her approval. In other cases it may be beneficial to public debate for judges to provide information relating to the administration of justice and the functions of the judiciary. Such participation is desirable but requires care. In particular a judge should avoid political controversy. It is important to avoid using judicial office to promote personal views and to avoid the appearance of capture by particular organisations or causes. Judges should avoid expressing opinions on matters which may arise in litigation and which may lead to concern about the impartiality of the judge.

51. Considerable care should be exercised to avoid using the authority and status of the judicial office for purposes for which they were not conferred. Points to bear in mind when considering whether it is appropriate to contribute to public debate on any matter include the following:

a. The place at which, or the occasion on which, a judge speaks may cause the public to associate the judge with a particular organisation, group or cause;

b. There is a risk that the judge may express views, or be led in the course of discussion to express views, that will give rise to issues of bias or prejudgment in cases that later come before the judge even in areas apparently unconnected with the original debate. A distinction might be drawn between opinions and comments on matters of law or legal principle, and the expression of opinions or attitudes about issues or persons or causes that might come before the judge;

c. Expressions of views on private occasions must also be considered carefully as they may lead to the perception of bias;

d. Other judges may hold conflicting views, and may wish to respond accordingly, possibly giving rise to a public conflict between judges which may bring the judiciary into disrepute or could diminish the authority of a court;

e. A judge, subject to the restraints that come with judicial office, has the same rights as other citizens to participate in public debate;

f. A judge who joins in community debate cannot expect the respect that the judge would receive in court and cannot expect to join and to leave the debate on the judge's terms.

52. Publication in legal journals or presentations at legal seminars is not objectionable but requires care to avoid expressing firm views about matters which may come before the court for determination.

(f) Taking part in conferences

53. Judges may deliver papers without a fee at legal conferences. Reasonable reimbursement of travel and accommodation expenses directly associated with the conference is acceptable.

54. Participation in, or the giving of papers without a fee at, non-legal conferences, is not objectionable. It is advisable to avoid speaking or writing on controversial or politically sensitive topics. A judge who is asked to speak at a non-legal conference should make sure that there is no risk of the judge appearing to be associated with the organisers or others who share the platform with the judge, if such association is likely to be controversial. Reasonable reimbursement of travel and accommodation expenses directly associated with the conference is acceptable.

(g) Comments on judicial decisions

55. Judgments must stand without further clarification or explanation. Where a decision is subject to inaccurate comment, any appropriate response should be from the Chief Justice or Head of Bench. Generally, the most effective response is to get the full text of the judgment into the public arena promptly. In major or high-profile cases, a short explanatory media release may be appropriate to accompany a judgment along the lines sometimes adopted by the Supreme Court.

(h) Judges explaining the legal system

56. Judges are often asked to speak to community groups and organisations to improve community understanding of the administration of justice. The precautions identified in [51] should be noted.

(i) Writing for newspapers or periodicals; appearing on television or radio

57. There is no objection to articles in news outlets (online or paper) or non-legal periodicals and other contributions intended to inform the public about the law and about the administration of justice generally. Before agreeing to write such an article, the judge should consult with the Head of Bench.

58. Occasionally a judge may be invited to contribute to public discussion on matters of public interest. Such contribution might be written comment, by radio, television or via the internet. There is no objection in principle to this, but the precautions identified in [52] should be considered and the Head of Bench should be consulted. Contribution via the media requires particular care. A court media officer should ensure that the host understands and will observe the limits on judicial participation and should be consulted about the making of necessary arrangements.

12

Methods of Extra-Judicial Participation in Parliament

ALEXANDER HORNE*

I. INTRODUCTION

Should the judiciary have any sort of extra-judicial participation in or contact with Parliament, and, if so, what should be the limits of their interactions with legislators? This chapter will explore the major changes to extra-judicial communication between the judges and Parliament that occurred in the twenty-first century – many of which were prompted by the passage of the Constitutional Reform Act 2005.

Extra-judicial interaction with Parliament can be justified for a number of reasons. It should be open to the senior judiciary to express concerns about Government policy which might have a significant impact on the administration of justice or the operation of the courts. This may be done via public responses to consultations, appearances before select committees,[1] or formal representations to Parliament under the Constitutional Reform Act itself. Judges may also wish to intervene when Government legislation would have an important impact on the constitution, or on human rights (although such interventions are likely to be rather more provocative).

It may also be necessary to hold the judiciary to account, provided that this can be done without impinging on judicial independence. Andrew Le Sueur has previously identified a number of ways that judicial accountability can occur. In the context of their interactions with Parliament, two seem particularly relevant: the publication of annual reports (which can be scrutinised) and the scrutiny of judicial appointments.[2]

*The author would like to thank the editors and Dr Ben Yong for comments on an earlier draft of this chapter. Any errors or infelicities remain his own.

[1] Mallory and Tyrrell have noted that 'for some judicial office holders, speaking is not merely a right but an expectation. In England and Wales, there is a practice that senior judges will attend when invited to Parliamentary Select Committees'. C Mallory and H Tyrrell, 'The Extrajudicial Voice' (2024) 44(1) *Legal Studies* 1, 4.

[2] A Le Sueur, 'Developing mechanisms for judicial accountability in the UK' in D Morgan (ed), *Constitutional Innovation – The Creation of a Supreme Court for the United Kingdom; domestic, comparative and international reflections* (A special issue of *Legal Studies*, Butterworths, 2004) 80. In the UK, scrutiny of appointments currently only takes place in respect of the appointment *process* as administered by the Judicial Appointments Commission, rather than the appointment of individual judges, however senior.

As Anthony Bradley put it:

> As an agency of state power, the judiciary as a body are, or ought to be, accountable for the general manner in which the court system serves the public at large. But methods of ensuring this form of accountability must not be such as to prejudice judicial independence.[3]

The chapter will argue that while extra-judicial contact between the judiciary and legislature can be perfectly appropriate, some of the formal structures in the UK remain less than transparent and could potentially benefit from some further clarification. The chapter will be informed not only by previous academic literature on the subject, but also by the author's experience working as a lawyer in Parliament for almost two decades.

II. SEPARATION OF POWERS AND THE CONSTITUTIONAL REFORM ACT 2005

The rather botched reforms proposed by the Blair Government in 2003, which were eventually enshrined in a slightly different form in the Constitutional Reform Act 2005, had a seismic role in changing the role of judges in Parliament. They were predicated, in part, on implementing the principle of the separation of powers. While the primary impact was seen in the reforms to the role of Lord Chancellor, the reforms also saw the Law Lords move across Parliament Square and metamorphose into Supreme Court Justices. If the principle of separation of powers were to be applied strictly, it would have been inconceivable for a person to combine the role of a member of the legislature and a member of the judiciary. As long ago as 1867, Walter Bagehot commented on the situation, stating that:

> It is a function which no theorist would assign to a second chamber in a new Constitution, and which is a matter of accident in ours. Gradually, indeed, the unfitness of the second chamber for judicial functions has made itself felt.[4]

In spite of these concerns, the separation of powers was never applied strictly under the UK constitution. The role of the Lord Chancellor was perhaps the apogee of this state of affairs. Prior to the reforms he (for it had always been a he) was nominally the highest-ranking minister in Government and sat in the Cabinet; was the head of the judiciary (and was entitled to sit as a judge on the Appellate Committee);[5] and acted as Presiding Officer in the House of Lords. As late as 2001, the office was described by

[3] A Bradley, 'The New Constitutional Relationship Between the Judiciary, Government and Parliament', Appendix 4 of the House of Lords Select Committee on the Constitution, 'Relations Between the Executive, the Judiciary and Parliament' (HL Paper 151, 2006–07) [18].

[4] W Bagehot, *The English Constitution* (London, Chapman & Hall, 1867; Reprinted by Oxford University Press, 2009) ch 3.

[5] Lord Irvine of Lairg, the final holder of the traditional office (1997–2003) sat in cases until at least 1999, after which a determination by the European Court of Human Rights in the case of *McGonnell v United Kingdom* (about the bailiff of Jersey) cast some doubt on the wisdom of this situation continuing. C Dyer, 'Verdict goes against lord chancellor', *The Guardian* (London, 20 February 2001) www.theguardian.com/politics/2001/feb/20/uk.labour3.

Michael Wills (then Parliamentary Secretary for the Lord Chancellor's Department in the House of Commons) as being

> unusual in the way that it combines different roles, but … also unusually useful because through it the judiciary have a representative in the Cabinet and the Cabinet has a representative in the judiciary. As such, we believe that the Lord Chancellor is well placed mutually to represent the views of each branch of our constitution to the other.[6]

Lord Irvine argued that the position was a 'natural conduit for communications between the judiciary and the executive, so that each fully understands the legitimate objectives of the other'.[7] Lest one think that this was an eccentric position, Robert Stevens recalled that at the time of the Royal Commission on the House of Lords (1999–2000) the Judges' Council had insisted that the Lord Chancellor's position should remain intact and said, in evidence, that the judges had

> no doubt that this dual role has historically proved invaluable in maintaining the independence of the judiciary in England and Wales and we have considerable anxiety that any other arrangement would result, in time, in the encroachment of executive government into the proper sphere of judicial independence essential in a democratic society.[8]

The significant reforms made to the office of Lord Chancellor, and the fact that the holder of the office ceased to be the head of the judiciary and is no longer considered to be the judges' voice in Cabinet, was bound to lead to material changes in the way in which judges communicated with Parliament extra-judicially, notably by placing new representative responsibilities on the Chief Justice of England and Wales and the President on the Supreme Court.

As for the position of the judges themselves, under the previous arrangements, to become a Law Lord, a judge usually had to be granted a peerage under the Appellate Jurisdiction Act 1876. Pursuant to the Appellate Jurisdiction Act 1887 such a peerage was a lifetime appointment, even though a Law Lord was required to retire from their judicial duties on reaching the mandatory retirement age.[9]

This was not the only crossover between the world of law and politics. J.Ll.J. Edwards recorded in his book, *The Law Officers of the Crown*, that the Attorney General historically had the right to be appointed a senior judge as a 'reward' for his official and political services. He highlighted, in particular, that in the 60 years between the passage of the Judicature Act 1873 and 1932, with one exception, 'every English Chief Justice has been an ex-Attorney General'.[10]

Even as late as the mid-1960s, Edwards noted that the elevation of Sir Reginald Manningham-Buller direct from the Attorney-Generalship to the Woolsack and of Sir Jocelyn Simon, a former Solicitor-General, to become President of the Probate and Admiralty Division of the High Court had revived 'speculation on the question of

[6] HC Deb, 4 December 2001, col 155.

[7] R Stevens, 'Reform in haste and repent at leisure: Iolanthe, the Lord High Executioner and *Brave New World*' (2004) 24 *Legal Studies* 1.

[8] R Stevens, *The English Judges* (Oxford, Hart Publishing, 2002) 129.

[9] G Cowie and D Torrance, 'The UK Supreme Court' (House of Commons Library, Research Paper No 09536, 1 October 2024) 55.

[10] J.Ll.J Edwards, *The Law Officers of the Crown* (London, Sweet and Maxwell, 1964) 310.

what claims, if any, the holders for the time being of the offices of Attorney-General and Solicitor-General may have to the reversion of the highest judicial offices in the state'.[11] The fact that these habits have been so quickly forgotten by most lawyers and lawmakers shows that we now have a very different mindset toward the relationship between law and politics.

Perhaps it would just be wise to admit, as Gavin Drewry has observed, that while we may traditionally seek to delineate the main areas of constitutional territory through the language of separation of powers, our executive government has 'rendered this vocabulary seriously out of date', having regard to the fact that members of the political executive are always members of one of the two Houses of Parliament. Nonetheless, the principle does have resonance in respect of the relations between the judiciary, Parliament and the executive. As Drewry argues: the 'distinctive role of the judiciary and its claims in democratic polities to constitutional independence … remains as robust and relevant as ever'.[12]

III. THE NEW ARRANGEMENTS

Richard Cornes recalls that, prior to the passage of the Constitutional Reform Act 2005, the Appellate Committee was an institution which did not advertise its activities. It 'had no annual reports, and no articulated strategic objectives, relevant to communications or otherwise. It had no separate institutional identity; it was a "court" yes, but a court which sat as a committee of Parliament'.[13] The changes made by the 2005 Act were significant in this regard and there is now no clearly defined institutional connection between the judges and Parliament.

All holders of 'high judicial office'[14] are precluded from sitting or voting in the House of Lords for as long as they hold a disqualifying office, under section 137(3) of the Constitutional Reform Act 2005. Yet the new arrangements were sufficiently pragmatic that they saw a continuing role for some judges in Parliament, albeit at the end of their judicial career. Thus, retired judges are not barred from sitting in the Lords and speaking on the floor of the House, or from participating in select committees. The House of Commons Library notes that when the UK Supreme Court was created in 2009, all of its inaugural 11 members were already peers (10 of them because they had been Law Lords, and one, Lord Clarke of Stone-cum-Ebony, because he had been given a life peerage a few months earlier).[15] This created a disparity: 'legacy' justices would be able to participate in the work of the House of Lords when they retired, whilst post-2009 appointees would not, unless they were already, or were otherwise made, a peer.

[11] ibid 311.

[12] G Drewry, 'Parliamentary Accountability for Justice' in A Horne, G Drewry, D Oliver, *Parliament and the Law* (Oxford, Hart Publishing, 2013) 340.

[13] R Cornes, 'A constitutional disaster in the making? The communications challenge facing the United Kingdom's Supreme Court' [2013] *Public Law* 266.

[14] Some MPs still hold part-time appointments, such as Recorder.

[15] 'The UK Supreme Court' (above n 9) 55.

During the scrutiny of reforms which became the Constitutional Reform Act 2005, the then House of Commons Constitutional Affairs Committee considered this question. It noted evidence from some Law Lords, such as Lord Hope, that the institutional link with Parliament was important, and evidence from stakeholders that judges could make an important contribution, particularly to the work of select committees.[16]

The Committee's report argued that 'from the point of view of preserving the reality and appearance of judicial independence, there are dangers in introducing a system which involves exercising patronage in favour of specific individual judges'. Accordingly, it recommended that all judges in the Supreme Court should be made peers on retirement, subject to the question of further reform of the House of Lords. If that were not feasible, it argued that none of them should be made peers.[17]

In response to that report the Government agreed with the Committee's recommendations that all Supreme Court Justices should be appointed to the House of Lords upon retirement.[18] However, the Constitutional Reform Act 2005 contained no provisions to guarantee that this would happen, and none has since been instituted. The commitment therefore depended on the emergence of a convention that Governments would nominate outgoing justices for peerages. The Commons Library indicates that this has not happened: 'no justices retired while Labour remained in office, and the envisaged arrangement did not materialise under subsequent Governments'.[19]

Some judges have been awarded peerages, including the current Supreme Court President, Lord Reed, the Lord Chief Justices (Lord Judge,[20] Lord Thomas, Lord Burnett and Baroness Carr) and the former Master of the Rolls, Lord Etherton. However, the failure to award John Dyson, a former Master of the Rolls and Supreme Court Justice, a peerage (a disappointment he made public in his autobiography)[21] highlighted the fact that the Government had failed to establish a sensible precedent for appointments.

Post-2005, there are now few examples of people moving in the other direction – from Parliament to the courts – to become senior judges. The only example I am aware of in recent years is Professor Sir Ross Cranston, who was briefly Solicitor General under the Blair administration. He returned to academia in 2005 and was made a

[16] Constitutional Affairs Committee, 'Judicial Appointments and a Supreme Court (court of final appeal)', First Report of Session 2003–4, HC 48–I [70]–[80] https://publications.parliament.uk/pa/cm200304/cmselect/cmconst/48/48.pdf. See further, on the work of retired judges in this context, Chapter 7: H Tyrrell, 'Extrajudicial Communication: What Changes in Retirement?'.

[17] First Report of Session 2003–4, ibid [80].

[18] 'Judicial appointments and a Supreme Court (court of final appeal)': The Government's response to the report of the Constitutional Affairs Committee, Cm 6150, [22].

[19] 'The UK Supreme Court' (above n 9) 55.

[20] Lord Judge was awarded a peerage in 2008 and in 2019 became Convenor of the cross-bench peers. Lord Hope also held this office between 2015 and 2019, following his retirement from the Bench. The role of Convenor is elected and is designed to allow the cross-bench peers to keep themselves up to date with the business of the House. While the cross-benchers are 'unwhipped', the Convenor can be invited to discussions with the 'usual channels'.

[21] M Cross, 'Back to tradition as master of the rolls appointed to Lords', *Law Society Gazette* (23 December 2020). Lord Dyson, *A Judge's Journey* (Oxford, Hart Publishing, 2019) 226.

High Court judge in 2007,[22] rising to become the lead judge in the Administrative Court. One may ask whether this trend against politicians becoming judges is good for law or politics. There must be at least a risk that it will lead to a lack of understanding between judges and politicians.[23]

IV. IS INCREASED TRANSPARENCY A RESULT OF THE MOVE FROM PARLIAMENT, AND DOES THIS MATTER?

The new arrangements have provided new opportunities for discussions about the administration of justice, both in respect of the Supreme Court and the justice system more generally. Drewry records that prior to the reforms, the prevailing orthodoxy was that the judges were 'exempt from even the most routine and non-partisan forms of parliamentary scrutiny', in part on the basis that Lord Chancellors tended to regard themselves as 'links or "buffers" between the judiciary and government/Parliament and fiercely resisted any hint of parliamentary intrusion into judicial territory'.[24]

Lord Reed has argued that one of the intentions of Parliament, when it created the Supreme Court to take over the functions previously performed by the Appellate Committee 'was that the workings of the highest court in the land should be much more visible and transparent than they previously were'.[25] In an evidence session before the House of Lords Constitution Committee, Lord Reed accepted that the constitutional reforms of 2005 had an impact on the way judges and Parliament interact. He contended that this was a constructive change and that it has had a knock-on, positive effect on the working practices of the Supreme Court:

> [It] is a good thing, of course, but the challenge it brings is that people have become aware of the work that the top court does, to an extent, when they were never aware of it previously. Some people have the impression that the court is activist and has taken on a new constitutional role. This is a consequence of the visibility of our work … Our judicial working methods have changed, and that is also partly because we are no longer in the House of Lords … We have user groups, which did not previously exist. I invite judges from lower courts to sit with us, which previously was not possible unless the judge happened to be a Peer; in modern times, it is only the Lord or Lady Chief Justice who is a Peer.[26]

[22] M Berlins, 'MP, academic – and now high court judge', *The Guardian* (London, 8 October 2007) www.theguardian.com/commentisfree/2007/oct/08/uk.law.

[23] Joshua Rozenberg reported in November 2024 that judges (including part-time fee paid judges) had been issued with unpublished guidance indicating that they should not express views on social media on government policy, or political and controversial social issues. Given that almost all politicians engage with some form of social media (and would be expected to comment on issues of the day), this guidance would make it very difficult for them to hold positions as fee paid judges or magistrates, despite the fact that they are nominally able to be politically active. See: J Rozenberg, 'What not to say on X', *Substack Blog* (15 November 2024) rozenberg.substack.com/p/what-not-to-say-on-x.

[24] G Drewry, 'Parliamentary Accountability for Justice' in A Horne, G Drewry and D Oliver, *Parliament and the Law* (Oxford, Hart Publishing, 2013) 341.

[25] House of Lords Constitution Committee, Oral evidence 1 May 2024, 2.

[26] ibid.

However, he also noted that the new arrangements distanced judiciary from Parliament:

> The only disadvantage that I have been conscious of … is the lack of daily contact with parliamentarians that we had previously, which had value. In retrospect, one of the weaknesses of the court during its first 10 years was a failure to build or maintain relationships with Parliament. Judges tend to be nervous about engaging with politicians. They were forced to when they were Members of this House, sitting as a committee within it, but once they moved across the road the default position was not to be involved in the world of politics. We saw some of the consequences of that in the fallout from the Brexit judgments. When I became president, I was very clear that I wanted to rebuild a relationship with Parliament … I am quite clear in my mind that the advantages of having our own institution … outweigh the disadvantages of being divorced from Parliament. However, I recognise that there is this consequent disadvantage. I have tried to address it by building up contacts between the court and Parliament in a way that did not happen during the first 10 years.[27]

This distance – combined with the reform of the office of Lord Chancellor (and the reduction in status of the role) and, at least between 2016 and 2024, a Government whose commitment to the rule of law was increasingly called into doubt – has undoubtedly impacted on the way in which the judges and executive interact, which may in turn have affected the nature of extra-judicial communication between the judges and Parliament.[28]

As an example, in a report published in 2023, the House of Lords Constitution Committee noted that while the Constitutional Reform Act 2005 required the Lord Chancellor to protect the judiciary,[29] there were some concerns about how this functioned in practice, particularly following the judgment of the High Court in the first *Miller* (Brexit) case. The *Daily Mail* published a front-page headline describing the judges involved as 'Enemies of the People'. When asked about her slowness to act, the then Lord Chancellor, Liz Truss MP, indicated to the Committee that senior judges were able to speak publicly about what they did and that 'it is dangerous for a government Minister to say this is an acceptable headline and this is not'.[30] Such a move must place more pressure on those judges in a leadership role, such as the Lady Chief Justice and President of the Supreme Court, since it has arguably opened up a gap in the defence of the judiciary.

While many contributors to the inquiry by the Constitution Committee argued that judicial independence had increased post-2005, the incident demonstrated that the judges are now more exposed and sometimes have to make their own case, both to Parliament and the press.

[27] ibid.

[28] See, for example, the way in which the Government's commitment to the rule of law was called into question during the passage of the United Kingdom Internal Market Act 2020, the Safety of Rwanda (Asylum and Immigration) Act 2024 and the Northern Ireland Protocol Bill 2022.

[29] See Constitutional Reform Act 2005, s 3.

[30] House of Lords Constitution Committee, 'The roles of the Lord Chancellor and the Law Officers' (18 January 2023, HL Paper 118).

V. FORMAL AND INFORMAL ENGAGEMENT WITH PARLIAMENT

How should judges engage with Parliament in this modern era, where some parliamentarians seem distinctly suspicious of judicial activism and where some Conservatives and most Reform MPs seem concerned about the way the courts make use of both judicial review procedures and the Human Rights Act 1998? It is important that the judiciary, as a whole, is able to be clear about effective ways to engage with the legislature on both formal and informal bases.

In an interview with Joshua Rozenberg, given to mark the 15th anniversary of the Supreme Court, Lord Reed explicitly acknowledged that the judgment in *Miller (No 2)* had raised concerns amongst some parliamentarians. He noted that he had taken action: as well as regular (annual) formal appearances before the House of Lords Constitution Committee,[31] he had begun to engage in informal outreach to Parliament to explain the work of the Supreme Court.[32] This had included regular meetings with the Speaker and Lord Speaker, engagement with the House of Commons Justice Committee and meetings with parliamentarians in Parliament. He stated that he saw the 2024 General Election as an opportunity to engage with new MPs and indicated that both a video and a booklet on the rule of law had been circulated to new MPs.[33]

Other, more esoteric, methods of informal engagement can also occur. In October 2024, Lord Reed attended a panel event in Parliament to mark the production of a House of Commons Library Paper on the Supreme Court.[34]

Similar activities have been undertaken by the Chief Justice of England and Wales. *The Politics of Judicial Independence in the UK's Changing Constitution* records how, from 2011, the appointment of a new Clerk in the House of Commons (Sir Robert Rogers) led to Parliament having more contact with the judiciary. This began with meetings in 2012 between the Lord Chief Justice and Master of the Rolls and the Speakers of both Houses to discuss breaches of injunctions in Parliament. However, the authors record that since then, regular meetings have occurred to discuss issues such as the *sub judice* rule and parliamentary privilege.[35]

The current Lady Chief Justice, Baroness Carr of Walton-on-the-Hill, has continued the practice of making regular appearances at the House of Commons Justice Select Committee. At an evidence session in January 2024, in addition to routine questions about her priorities and challenges, she was also asked some more politically charged questions about the Horizon Post Office case and the previous Conservative Government's proposed Rwanda scheme.[36] On the second of these,

[31] The most recent session occurred in May 2024 and was attended by Lord Reed and the Deputy President, Lord Hodge. See: committees.parliament.uk/oralevidence/14736/pdf/.

[32] See eg 'Lord Reed, How we will decide what constitutes a woman', *The Times* (4 October 2024) www.thetimes.com/uk/law/article/lord-reed-how-we-will-decide-what-constitutes-a-woman-mt7nn79hc.

[33] J Rozenberg, 'Putting MPs in their place', *Substack Blog* (8 October 2024) https://rozenberg.substack.com/p/putting-mps-in-their-place.

[34] 'The UK Supreme Court' (above n 9).

[35] G Gee, R Hazell, K Malleson and P O'Brien, *The Politics of Judicial Independence in the UK's Changing Constitution* (Cambridge, Cambridge University Press, 2015) 135.

[36] Courts and Tribunals Judiciary, 'Lady Chief Justice appears at the House of Commons Justice Committee' (17 January 2024), https://www.judiciary.uk/lady-chief-justice-appears-at-the-house-of-commons-justice-committee/.

she was particularly robust. When asked if the Government could fast-track appeals against deportation by drafting in 150 judges and freeing courtrooms, she replied:

> I'm afraid that this headline draws matters of judicial responsibility into the political arena. Parliament has legislated, we the judiciary have acted in preparation for that legislation but, to be absolutely clear, matters of deployment of judges, the allocation of work for judges, and the use of courtrooms is exclusively a matter for the judiciary, and more specifically a matter for myself and the Senior President of the Tribunals and it's really important, Chair, that people understand that clear division.[37]

This response was later briefed as a press release on the judiciary.uk website, demonstrating that such appearances can be used to send fairly direct messages to the Government of the day.

A. Representations to Parliament

Section 5 of the Constitutional Reform Act 2005 permits the Lord Chief Justice of any part of the United Kingdom to 'lay before Parliament written representations on matters that appear to him to be matters of importance relating to the judiciary, or otherwise to the administration of justice, in that part of the United Kingdom'. The same provision now allows the President of the Supreme Court to lay before Parliament written representations on matters that appear to the President to be matters of importance relating to the Supreme Court or to the jurisdiction it exercises. Initially, this was perceived to be a 'nuclear option', which these senior judges would only use if something had gone very wrong.[38] It was described this way by Lords Woolf, Phillips and Judge.[39] Yet, the judges now seem to have rowed back from this description and, as Graham Gee has noted, following discussions with the Clerks of both Houses, the judges have now invoked the provision for 'the more humdrum matter of laying before Parliament periodic reports on the management of the judiciary'.[40]

The back and forth between the judiciary and the parliamentary authorities over the use of this provision (and the lack of clarity about when it might be appropriate to use it) simply highlights the fact that, for all the discussion in advance of the passage of the 2005 Act, it has not been possible to replicate the situation where the serving Chief Justice could just raise important matters relating to the administration of justice on the floor of the House of Lords.

In February 2025, rather than utilising the provision in the Constitutional Reform Act, the Lady Chief Justice, Baroness Carr, used an annual news conference to raise concerns about exchanges that were made at Prime Minister's Questions about an

[37] ibid.

[38] For example, Gee, Hazell, Malleson and O'Brien argued that the power was intended to be used 'to alert Parliament to a threat to the administration of justice, such as a funding crisis'. See *The Politics of Judicial Independence* (above n 35) 134.

[39] G Gee, 'The Lord Chief Justice and Section 5 of the Constitutional Reform Act' (*UK Constitutional Law Association Blog*, 14 April 2014) www.ukconstitutionallaw.org/2014/04/14/graham-gee-the-lord-chief-justice-and-section-5-of-the-constitutional-reform-act/.

[40] ibid.

immigration case. She said that she was 'deeply troubled' by remarks made by the Prime Minister, Sir Keir Starmer and the Leader of the Opposition, Kemi Badenoch and called their comments 'unacceptable'. She suggested that these remarks conflicted with the duty of politicians to uphold the rule of law and respect the independence of judges, and argued that where parties disagree with judicial findings they should do so through the appellate process.[41]

The incident highlighted the fact that senior judges might not need to use formal mechanisms to bring their concerns to the attention of Parliament (and the broader public). Such an approach is interesting – but also potentially unwise. The media can be a treacherous friend and the incident was not as clear cut as it might have seemed: the Prime Minister did not directly criticise the judge who made the decision, but merely indicated that he thought it was the 'wrong decision' and indicated that the Government intended to change the law, rather than appeal.[42] It was a far cry from the sort of 'Enemies of the People' headline seen in the press during Brexit and, arguably, it seemed unnecessarily touchy in response to a fairly unremarkable comment.

Within days, the media was reporting that Jonathan Sumption had called Baroness Carr's intervention a 'mistake', arguing that that 'to say in perfectly moderate language that a judge was wrong is a perfectly legitimate thing to do'.[43] The spat between the Lady Chief Justice and parliamentarians highlighted the fact that tensions between judges and politicians can be hard to square, whatever the forum.

B. Select Committees

In terms of formal contact with Parliament, perhaps the most obvious and frequent example is the way in which judges interact with Parliament's select committees.[44] This can happen in two distinct ways. First, retired judges in the Lords often sit on select committees. As peers, retired judges can sit on committees in the Lords and on Joint Committees which are often used to conduct pre-legislative and legislative scrutiny.

During my 20 years in Parliament, I had the privilege to work with three senior judges: Lord Woolf on the Joint Committee on Human Rights; Lord Phillips on the Joint Committee on the draft Voting Eligibility (Prisoners) Bill, and Lord Thomas on the House of Lords European Union Committee and its Financial Affairs Sub-Committee. In my experience they added wisdom and gravitas to proceedings, particularly when dealing with contentious matters. On occasion, they would also raise issues which might not otherwise have been contemplated by lay members of a committee.

[41] D Casciani, 'Judge "deeply troubled" by PMQs exchange on Gazans settling in UK' (*BBC News*, 18 February 2025).

[42] Hansard 12 February 2025, vol 762 col 249.

[43] F Luck, 'Former Supreme Court Judge says Baroness Carr's intervention over PMQs immigration case comments was "mistake"' (*LBC*, 20 February 2025).

[44] See eg R Hazel and P O'Brien, 'Meaningful dialogue: judicial engagement with parliamentary committees at Westminster' [2016] *Public Law* 54.

Retired judges sit in a personal capacity and are not formal representatives of the judiciary (having ceased acting in a judicial capacity).[45] Any political involvement is likely to be low key: posing questions at evidence sessions, giving their thoughts on an issue to officials and other members of the committee in private sessions, or suggesting revisions to draft reports. Nonetheless, having *former* senior judges sitting on a select committee essentially allows the judiciary an informal voice in Parliament – particularly when policy and law are being developed. This is likely to be far less controversial than if a *serving* senior judge raised concerns about such issues in the public sphere, despite the fact that retired judges often tend to be more robust in their views and may be perceived by both parliamentarians and the public to be representing the voice of the judiciary in these interactions.

Serving judges and former judges can appear and give evidence to select committees. Such appearances are not uncommon and, unlike extra-judicial speeches and many of the other examples of extra-judicial communication considered in this volume, such appearances may not always be entirely discretionary: judges may be requested to attend select committee hearings.

In 2012, the Judicial Executive Board (JEB) published guidance for judges who were invited to appear before a committee. The tone of this guidance suggested a degree of concern about judges being drawn into the political discourse.[46] Notably, it suggested that such appearances should be regarded as 'exceptional' and stated that requests by Parliament should be sent to the Private Office of the Lord Chief Justice.[47]

The JEB guidance also set out that judges should not comment on the merits of individual cases or (subject to two provisos) on 'the merits, meaning or likely effect of provisions in any Bill or other prospective legislation and the merits of government policy'. It highlighted the fact that this convention is acknowledged in the *Cabinet Manual*, which states:

> [P]rinciples of judicial independence mean that the judiciary should not be asked to comment on the merits of proposed government policy, and individual judicial office-holders should not be asked to comment on matters that may then require the judge to disqualify him or herself in subsequent litigation.[48]

However, despite the clear reluctance of the senior judiciary to be dragged into the political sphere, the two provisos mentioned above have proved quite significant and are worth setting out in full:

> There are two qualifications to the convention against comment on Bill provisions or government policy. They both apply where the Bill or policy directly affects the operation of the courts or aspects of the administration of justice within the judge's particular area of judicial responsibility or expertise. The first is that, in these circumstances, the judge may comment on the practical operation or technical aspects of the Bill or policy. This

[45] In this volume, Chapter 7: H Tyrrell, 'Extrajudicial Communication: What Changes in Retirement?'.

[46] Judicial Executive Board, *Guidance to Judges on Appearances before Select Committees*. October 2012.

[47] Previously, some judges had been contacted directly by committees – particularly heads of division and judges acting in a representative capacity – for example the heads of the Council of Circuit Judges and the Association of District Judges.

[48] *Guidance to Judges* (above n 46).

> exception reflects the judiciary's interest in the effective administration of justice and the judiciary's jointly held responsibility for the operation of the courts. The second is that, in these circumstances, a judge may properly comment on the merit of a Bill or policy which affects the independence of the judiciary.[49]

In some respects, this has allowed the judiciary to have their cake and eat it – the administration of justice and the operation of the courts encompasses quite a wide sphere and contentious Government policies can often have knock-on effects which judges may feel emboldened to discuss (when they wish).

Rather oddly, the guidance is said to have application to retired judges, on the grounds that 'even in retirement a former judge may still be regarded by the general public as a representative of the judiciary and any activity that might tarnish the reputation of the judiciary should be avoided'.[50] Certainly, in respect of the most senior retired judges, I would suggest that any call to reticence is often ignored – although I am hard pressed to think of many examples where it could be a said that a judicial appearance before a committee has caused such a risk.[51]

The JEB guidance has no formal status in Parliament, although it is highly unlikely that a parliamentary committee would ever seek to formally summon a judge who had declined to give evidence.[52] Judges appearing before committees can reasonably expect some more mischievous or partisan MPs to pose political questions which go well beyond their self-denying ordinance.[53]

Patrick O'Brien has argued that the practice of judges giving evidence to parliamentary committees has been widely accepted as 'a positive and productive form of engagement' and it creates opportunities for dialogue and for judicial accountability. He suggested that: 'the reality is that the vast majority of judicial evidence sessions are uncontroversial'.[54] I agree.

[49] ibid 4.

[50] ibid 5.

[51] A good example of the type of evidence that retired judges can give is the wide-ranging evidence session that the Constitution Committee held with Lord Sumption and Baroness Hale on the Constitutional Implications of COVID-19. See Select Committee on the Constitution, 'Constitutional Implications of Covid-19' Corrected Oral Evidence (2 December 2020) committees.parliament.uk/oralevidence/1359/pdf/.

[52] Whether a committee could effectively summon a recalcitrant judge is a matter for conjecture. Select committees have few practical powers over people who are not parliamentarians. In theory, the two Houses of Parliament have the power to remove senior judges for misconduct, but it would be inconceivable that such a power would be used in practice in such circumstances. The only recent example I am aware of where a serving judge has been publicly criticised for non-attendance is in relation to a public inquiry. In 2015 the Northern Ireland Affairs Committee criticised Lady Justice Hallett for declining to attend a session to discuss a public inquiry she was then running.

[53] Mallory and Tyrrell cite a notable example in their article 'The Extrajudicial Voice' (above n 1) 13. In 2022, Lord Reed and Lord Hodge were faced with a series of pointed questions at the House of Lords Constitution Committee. When asked to comment on whether judges were, in one case, seeking to become the ultimate authority on constitutional matters, Lord Reed was forced to remind the panel '[w]e do not go looking for cases; they come to us'. Elsewhere in the same proceedings, they were pushed to further explain the reasoning in the *Miller; Cherry* case which concerned the prorogation of Parliament. It took Lord Reed to remind the Committee and its Chair that members of the Supreme Court are 'not accountable for [their] judgments to any institution'.

[54] P O'Brien, 'Judges and select committees: A developing accountability culture', *The Constitution Unit Blog* (22 September 2015) www.constitution-unit.com/2015/09/22/judges-and-select-committees-a-developing-accountability-culture/.

In *The Politics of Judicial Independence in the UK's Changing Constitution*[55] the authors argue that one consequence of the growth of judicial appearances before select committees is that judges are 'now called to account in a more collective sense'. It is suggested that whereas the judicial peers did not offer accountability for the courts system when they spoke in Parliament, 'more focused select committee inquiries allow greater scope for institutional accountability, with the agenda set principally by parliamentarians rather than the judiciary'.[56] In my experience, the attendance by judges before select committees that I advised was far from exceptional and added a great deal of value to inquiries, provided that members respected the restrictions under which the judges operated.

C. Contributions in the Chamber

Perhaps the most high-profile extra-judicial interactions with Parliament arise when former judges make direct interventions on the floor of the House of Lords. This happens more frequently that one might think.[57] It might be thought counterintuitive that retired judges are advised to be cautious in terms of select committee appearances, but are allowed to make (sometimes significant) speeches on the floor of the House of Lords and table amendments to Government legislation. Perhaps there is less concern because the office holders who get to make such contributions are inevitably very senior. Although that also means that such contributions are all the more high profile.

In truth, when scrutinising Government legislation, I have usually found judicial contributions to be extremely valuable.[58] Many will focus on problems that legislation might cause in respect of the administration of justice, or on constitutional or human rights issues that might arise. This may sound as though interventions are simply technical in nature. In fact, judges have felt free to make more far-reaching contributions on 'small p' political matters.

One clear example came during a debate on the Delegated Powers and Regulatory Reform Committee's pithily titled report, *Democracy Denied: The urgent need to rebalance power between Parliament and the Executive*. The former Lord Chief Justice, Lord Judge, rose and observed that during the Covid-19 pandemic, there had been 'government by proclamation'; that the parliamentary process did not exercise proper control over secondary legislation more generally; and that the executive enacts a vast swathe of legislation via statutory instruments because 'it's very friendly

[55] *The Politics of Judicial Independence* (above n 35) 101.

[56] ibid.

[57] To take but one example, in the two years before his death, Lord Brown of Eaton-under-Heywood made interventions in respect of (inter alia) the Illegal Migration Bill, the Public Order Bill, the Northern Ireland Protocol Bill and the Economic Crime and Corporate Transparency Bill, as well as on the issue of Imprisonment for Public Protection (IPP) Prisoners, UK Asylum and Refugee policy, and the Parole Board (Amendment) Rules 2022.

[58] As an example, as a legal adviser to Parliament's Joint Committee on Human Rights, I once asked Lord Brown of Eaton-under-Heyward to pursue an amendment in respect of the Committee's concerns about the sentencing provisions contained in the Cultural Property (Armed Conflicts) Bill. He made a forceful and informed speech: see HL Deb 6 September 2016, vol 774, col 948.

to do it that way, and because the controls that are supposed to be available are not being deployed'. He contended that while government by proclamation ended after the Stuarts, 'we have proclamations in disguise'.[59] Many of these assertions are indisputable – but they might be considered rather challenging when delivered by a former senior judge.

Retired judges do not always steer clear of more publicly contentious issues either. During the passage of the Safety of Rwanda (Asylum and Immigration) Bill, Baroness Butler-Sloss intervened on issues relating to modern slavery,[60] whilst Lord Etherton raised issues about the treatment of LGBT people.[61] In advance of the debate on the Terminally Ill Adults (End of Life) Bill, Baroness Hale of Richmond observed in the press that it is 'not a very Christian thing' to allow someone to continue suffering if they want help to end their lives and that it was 'terribly cruel' to deny someone an assisted death.[62]

None of the abovementioned contributions were in any way constitutionally inappropriate, in my view. They all related to questions on the operation of the law, in theory or in practice, where the former judge in question had a real interest. Nonetheless, each contribution will also have brought the views of the judge in question into the public domain, giving them a higher profile than might otherwise be the case.[63]

D. Which Judges Should Sit in Parliament Post-retirement?

The fact that there is no formal legal rule or convention as to which judges should sit in Parliament upon retirement is unfortunate. As the Constitutional Affairs Committee warned in 2004, there is a risk, however slight, that if it is perceived that the Government of the day is exercising patronage in favour of some judges ahead of others, this will damage judicial independence.

Clearly, at present, there is a clear desire, both in Government and Parliament, to bear down on the size of the House of Lords, and at the time of writing there were moves afoot to remove the remaining 92 hereditary peers. Further reforms are promised, which might result in a move to a second chamber elected on the basis of proportional representation, or one which reflects the nations and regions of the UK. It is hard to envisage, in either such circumstance, that retired judges would stand for election.

[59] HL Deb 12 January 2023, vol 826, col 1577.

[60] Tabling an amendment upon which the Government was defeated in the Lords.

[61] See, eg HL Deb 4 March 2024, vol 836, col 1422.

[62] T Hennessey, 'Denying assisted dying "not very Christian", former Supreme Court president says', *The Independent* (19 October 2024). Notably, Baroness Hale had been one of two Supreme Court Justices who had concluded that a declaration of incompatibility should be made in respect of the law in this area, on the basis that it allowed of no exceptions (*R (on the application of Nicklinson) v Ministry of Justice* [2014] UKSC 38, [301]).

[63] On extra-judicial speeches more generally, see Chapter 10: R Cahill-O'Callaghan, 'The Individual Voice in a Collective Court: Insights from Judicial Lectures'.

Being a cynic, and assuming that little will change in the medium term, in an ideal world, there would be clear legal rules about which judges should sit in the Lords. If a smaller House is required, it would be sufficient to award peerages to four judges: the President and Deputy President of the Supreme Court and the Lord Chief Justice of England and Wales and Master of the Rolls.[64] This would allow for a regular influx of new appointees, while keeping the numbers down, and frankly compares rather favourably to the preposterous representation of Church of England Bishops (26 bishops currently sit in the Lords).

VI. CONCLUSION

After the 2005 Constitutional Reform Act, the way judges engage with Parliament feels like it has grown up somewhat organically and in a rather haphazard way, which depends as much on personalities as new legal rules and conventions. The sensible approach of some senior judges and officials to the way in which the judiciary and Parliament interact means that matters of mutual interest can be discussed in informal ways, while there are a number of formal channels which allow the judiciary and Parliament to work in a constitutionally appropriate fashion.

As things stand, current judges may give evidence and engage in outreach to Parliament. Lord Reed has been an effective proponent of this in recent years. The Chief Justice frequently appears before the Justice Select Committee to discuss matters of mutual interest. Some former judges may choose sit on relevant select committees, or engage in debates on legislation. Two former judges have acted as Convenors of the Cross-Bench Peers. All of these contributions have been of value. But they depend very much on both the character and commitment of office holders, rather than any well-defined expectation or recognised convention.

As with so much of the UK constitution, how the extra-judicial relationship between the judiciary and Parliament develops in practice over the longer term is likely to depend as much on habit and practice than on formal rules. It is particularly unfortunate that there has been no attempt to formalise the practices relating to which judges are allowed to sit in the House of Lords following their retirement. The current set up risks claims that judges who have angered the executive may be excluded, and this surely damages the perception of judicial independence.

As is so often the case, these flaws in the system do not appear to preclude things functioning (broadly) effectively – although it is hard to tell whether the considerable disfunction in our criminal justice system is impacted by the fact that the judges have a less forceful voice in Government following the removal of the Law Lords from the legislature and the reform of the role of Lord Chancellor.

[64] Although arguably, if there was a desire to increase representation of the nations, we could also see the elevation of the Lady Chief Justice of Northern Ireland and Lord President of the Court of Session.

No urgent changes are required to the current arrangements. However, if we do see further efforts to reform the House of Lords in the future, MPs would be well advised to consider whether they wish to codify the rules as to how (if at all) former judges are allowed to sit in the legislature and whether any alternative means of communication should be put in place in the (still unlikely) event that we move towards an elected second chamber.

At present, much good work is done – transparently – through contributions in the Chamber and via select committees. Other good work is done through backchannel dialogue with officials and parliamentarians. If this were to end, it is possible that any increased distance between the judicial and legislative branches of Government could lead to increasing misunderstandings (and even mistrust), which could be profoundly damaging.

13

Whistleblowing in the Judiciary: Extrajudicial Communication

GAR YEIN NG*

I. INTRODUCTION

WHISTLEBLOWING IS RECOGNISED as attempting to 're-establish, whenever possible, confidence in the proper function of public institutions and private firms'.[1] Judiciaries are not immune from corruption and misconduct. In the United States of America, for example, two judges were convicted for 'conspiring with private prisons to hand young offenders maximum sentences in return for kickbacks amounting to millions of dollars'.[2] As a result, nearly 4000 sentences were expunged from records of juveniles wrongly convicted. Criticism was also levelled at the Judicial Conduct Board of Pennsylvania for failing to 'pursue to an anonymous complaint filed against [one of the judges] in 2006',[3] implying that someone had attempted to blow the whistle on at least one of the two judges found guilty of corruption.

A 2020 review in Australia looked at sexual harassment in courts by judges (and barristers), highlighting the lack of procedures and protections.[4] It was identified

*I would like to thank the following for their feedback and moral support in the writing of this chapter: Professor Dave Lewis (University of Middlesex) for invaluable comments on whistleblowing; David Sachar (National Center for State Courts) for his time and resources; Dr Dimitrios Kafteranis (University of Coventry) for his helpful feedback; and the editors of this volume for their generous feedback and boundless patience. I am also grateful to Dr Jessica Walsh (University of Buckingham) for being a sounding board. All work remains my own.

[1] K Manohar and D Santoro, 'A Justification of Whistleblowing' (2017) 43 *Philosophy & Social Criticism* 669, 670.

[2] C Gray, 'Top Judicial Ethics Stories of 2010: Pennsylvania "Cash for Kids" Scandal' (2011) 32(4) *Judicial Conduct Reporter* 7, https://ncsc.contentdm.oclc.org/digital/collection/judicial/id/702/rec/1.

[3] ibid 7.

[4] H Szoke AO, 'Review of Sexual Harassment in Victorian Courts: Preventing and Addressing Sexual Harassment in Victorian Courts and VCAT. Report and Recommendations' (March 2021) 26 https://courts.vic.gov.au/about-csv/sexual-harassment-main/sh-review-report; see also *Courts and Tribunals Judiciary Guide to Judicial Conduct* (July 2023), www.judiciary.uk/guidance-and-resources/guide-to-judicial-conduct-revised-july-2023.

'that sexual harassment and the silence surrounding these behaviours is perpetuated by the power inequalities in the court setting and a legal profession requiring patronage and a network to progress',[5] and that 'there are significant barriers preventing victim-survivors and witnesses from reporting sexual harassment that occurs in the courts'.[6] This report therefore identified the institutional context as a contributing factor to the ongoing problem of silence, and barriers to whistleblowing – either by ordinary staff workers or judges themselves.[7] Whilst it does not explicitly state where public confidence might be impacted (beyond the integrity of the judiciary),[8] the consequence of this could be that victims would refuse to bring any case forward. This shows that these courts themselves have created an access-to-justice barrier for victims – especially internally.[9]

Judicial whistleblowing aligns with the justifications for any form of extrajudicial communication: promoting transparency and accountability yet preserving freedom of speech. While other forms of extrajudicial communication may pursue a variety of aims, whistleblowing focuses entirely on exposition – reporting wrongdoing. Judicial whistleblowing therefore sits uncomfortably within frameworks, such as the England and Wales *Guide to Judicial Conduct*, which encourages extrajudicial work only insofar as it avoids harming the reputation of the judiciary. Damage to the reputation of the judiciary is arguably an almost inevitable consequence of whistleblowing.

The propriety of judicial whistleblowing thus rests on the extent to which this risk to reputation is outweighed by the contribution to transparency and the operation of the rule of law (for example, the prevention of miscarriages of justice). Two case studies of whistleblowing in the English judiciary provide a lens through which to assess this balance, considering the scope for whistleblowing and the protections for the judges involved. That analysis falls in favour of qualified whistleblowing. Judicial independence is the bedrock of the rule of law. However, while the perception of judicial independence is very important, protecting it at the cost of miscarriage of justice is arguably too high a price to pay. Although rare, no judiciary is totally immune from corruption.[10] As such, as a form of extrajudicial communication, judicial whistleblowing also reveals much about how judicial leaders and institutional contexts regulate judges and their speech to preserve perceptions of public confidence in the justice system at the cost of transparency.

I will first develop a theory of judicial whistleblowing. This will draw on two disciplines: whistleblowing literature found in political theory, and an international legal framework on the protecting of judicial whistleblowing (anti-corruption and freedom of expression). The chapter will then look at how the institutional context (institutions and rules) can shape judicial whistleblowing. This will take

[5] Szoke AO (above n 4) 8.

[6] ibid 8 and 48–49.

[7] ibid 36–47.

[8] ibid 75.

[9] There is no evidence in the report itself that this has impacted criminal cases brought to court of those accused of committing crimes of sexual harassment.

[10] S Masters, 'US Judge Receives 28-Year Jail Term for His Role in Kids-for-Cash Kickbacks', *The Independent* (London, 30 April 2013).

us to the two English cases and how they stand up to the qualified whistleblowing standards advanced by the international framework, while being shaped by their institutional context. Finally, I offer a brief conclusion, suggesting that there is a strong case for qualified judicial whistleblowing. Whilst judicial independence is a crucial part of the rule of law, both international law and the English *Guide to Judicial Conduct* state that the rule of law (including accountability) takes priority over judicial independence, especially where judges' behaviour does not warrant protection.[11]

An important caveat should be mentioned at this point. A Whistleblowing Policy internal to the English judiciary exists but I have been unable to access it. Three attempts were made to access this internal document: via a Freedom of Information Request;[12] by letter to the Judiciary of 5 October 2024 and an email to website enquiries on 9 January 2024.[13] This is an important limitation, precluding a comprehensive understanding of the institutional factors (such as management structures and the *Guide to Judicial Conduct*) to which this policy contributes.

II. A THEORY OF JUDICIAL WHISTLEBLOWING

The definition of whistleblowing found in political science literature centres around the activity of disclosure and the context in which information is disclosed:[14]

> Whistleblowing is the act of disclosing information from a public or private organization with the purpose of revealing cases of professional misconduct, or the violation of democratic procedures, that are of immediate or even potential danger to the public interest.[15]

Whistleblowing is an important tool to expose and attempt to take action to correct 'corruption, frauds, or general abuses of power',[16] where normal accountability mechanisms for wrongdoing are thought to be ineffective.[17]

The other side of this discussion is that whistleblowing is a 'violation of a promissory and role obligation'.[18] There is an assumption that a whistleblower will normally be a worker within an organisation, with a relationship of some loyalty to the organisation as well as other contractual obligations. In addition to contractual obligations,

[11] Szoke AO (above n 4) 26; see also *Guide to Judicial Conduct* (2023) (above n 4).

[12] Freedom of Information Request www.whatdotheyknow.com/request/whistleblowing_policy_for_the_ju#outgoing-1518400 requested 7 September 2023. The judiciary does not fall within the scope of Freedom of Information requests.

[13] Copies on files with the author.

[14] There are different definitions used for management/research purposes eg the International Organization for Standardization's *Whistleblowing management systems guidelines* (ISO 37002:2021) contain global recommendations for practice: www.iso.org/standard/65035.html.

[15] Manohar and Santoro (above n 1) 669; E Ceva and M Bocchiola, 'Theories of Whistleblowing' (2020) 15 *Philosophy Compass* 1, 2; M Martić, 'Protection of the Rule of Law through Whistleblowing' [2021] *Regional Law Review* 65, 67.

[16] Ceva and Bocchiola (above n 15) 2.

[17] Manohar and Santoro (above n 1) 671.

[18] ibid; ER Boot, 'The Feasibility of a Public Interest Defense for Whistleblowing' (2020) 39 *Law and Philosophy* 1, 2.

a judge in England and Wales has sworn a judicial oath.[19] Some organisations now also have non-disclosure agreements with their employees,[20] and employment law is engaged in the context of judicial whistleblowing. For example, in the *Gilham* case (discussed further below), a judicial whistleblower challenging the Ministry of Justice argued that she was a worker with rights to protection under the Employment Rights Act 1996.[21]

Whistleblowing disclosures attract two strands of justification. The first is that the judiciary should allow (and protect) whistleblowing where the public interest is served by a specific disclosure.[22] The other comes from a more general public interest debate around transparency, the need for informed public debate, democratic accountability and freedom of information.[23] The justifications for wider disclosures may be qualified where there exist internal procedures for whistleblowing which operate to preserve contractual obligations and allow time for the organisation to correct the situation. External disclosures may be justified if there are no internal procedures, or when such internal procedures are ineffective against corruption.[24] Disclosures in such circumstances may be especially important

> [w]hen sufficient evidence points to the complicity of top officials or limitation of the procedures to address wrongs [since] whistleblowing can be used to redress such limitations in order to uphold public interest and accountability.[25]

The framework for disclosure of private information, in public or private, can be classified into three areas (mirrored in the legal framework set out by the European Court of Human Rights (ECtHR) to protect judicial whistleblowing).[26] In the first place, (i) any information disclosed must be sufficiently detailed for the recipient to act upon it, (ii) it must not be false, and (iii) there must be sufficient evidence to support the disclosure.[27] Secondly, the whistleblower's motive must be to prevent or correct harm through the disclosure.[28] Finally, there must be a public interest in that disclosure being made.[29] In the literature cited so far, there is no clear agreement on how public interest is defined, and this is not the place to go into the larger debate set out above.

Legal frameworks emphasise a connection between the rule of law and whistleblowing, especially related to anti-corruption efforts, freedom of expression, and civil dissent in democracies.[30]

[19] *Guide to Judicial Conduct* (2023) (above n 4) 9; Courts and Tribunals Judiciary, 'Oaths' www.judiciary.uk/about-the-judiciary/our-justice-system/oaths.

[20] Martić (above n 15) 72.

[21] *Gilham v Ministry of Justice* [2019] UKSC 44; [2019] 1 WLR 5905.

[22] Martić (above n 15) 72.

[23] Boot (above n 18) 1.

[24] Manohar and Santoro (above n 1) 671; see also in Martić (above n 15) 73, which discusses 'dieselgate' as an example of a company failing to comply with regulations, involving Volkswagen's emissions scandal.

[25] Manohar and Santoro (above n 1) 671.

[26] *Kudeshkina v Russia* (Application no 29492/05) (ECtHR, Judgment of 14 September 2009).

[27] Manohar and Santoro (above n 1) 674; Martić (above n 15) 73; Ceva and Bocchiola (above n 15) 4.

[28] Ceva and Bocchiola (above n 15) 2; Manohar and Santoro (above n 1) 673; Boot (above n 18) 24.

[29] Manohar and Santoro (above n 1) 671.

[30] European Parliament, 'Resolution of 24 October 2017 on legitimate measures to protect whistle-blowers acting in the public interest when disclosing the confidential information of companies and public bodies' (2016/2224(INI)).

A. International Legal Framework and International Comparators: Anti-corruption

Several international and regional documents highlight the need for whistleblower protection in general. The American Bar Association (ABA) has done extensive development work globally, and its Codes and other documents are used in a global context.[31] The *ABA Model Code of Judicial Conduct*, Rule 2,15(A) provides that 'A judge having knowledge[32] that another judge has committed a violation of this Code that raises a substantial question regarding the judge's honesty, trustworthiness, or fitness as a judge in other respects shall inform the appropriate authority'.[33] Further '[a] judge who receives information indicating a substantial likelihood that another judge has committed a violation of this Code shall take appropriate action'.[34] If read in light of Rule 2.15(A), this would mean informing the appropriate authority. However, this only works if there are appropriate procedures and institutions in place for judges to disclose information they have about judicial misconduct.

The other parts of the international framework can be used to flesh out the ABA Model Code in terms of criteria such as 'knowledge', 'appropriate authority' and 'appropriate action'. It should be noted that the ABA places a (moral rather than legal) duty on judges to report misconduct that they have knowledge of. There is nothing in this international framework about how they should deal with the prospect of retaliation where judges decide or wish to disclose such information to the authorities. The remaining discussion in this section can provide some of the flesh to this judicial duty.

Firstly, the United Nations Convention Against Corruption (UNCAC) protects 'reporting persons'.[35] This is limited in scope to corruption only, although corruption as a concept is extremely broad. In line with the definition given in the introduction to this section of the chapter, Article 33 of UNCAC requires that the whistleblower is 'any person who reports in good faith and on reasonable grounds to the competent authorities'.[36] Similarly, the Organisation for Economic Co-operation and Development (OECD) provides a framework for protecting whistleblowers in the context of corruption, through its Recommendation on Improving Ethical Conduct

[31] ABA Center for Global Programs, https://www.americanbar.org/advocacy/global-programs/. An example of this is the Judicial Independence Monitor: www.americanbar.org/advocacy/global-programs/what-we-do/resources/2022/judicial-independence-monitor-toolkit/. This is used globally to support local initiatives in monitoring judicial independence and providing policy advice to improve local situations.

[32] American Bar Association, *ABA Model Code of Judicial Conduct* (2011): Preamble, 'Terminology' p 4: '"Knowingly," "knowledge," "known," and "knows" mean actual knowledge of the fact in question. A person's knowledge may be inferred from circumstances. See Rules 2.11, 2.13, 2.15, 2.16, 3.6, and 4.1'.

[33] American Bar Association, *ABA Model Code of Judicial Conduct*, Canon 2, Rule 2.15, 'Responding to Judicial and Lawyer Misconduct' www.americanbar.org/groups/professional_responsibility/publications/model_code_of_judicial_conduct/model_code_of_judicial_conduct_canon_2/rule2_15respondingtojudicialandlawyermisconduct/. '"Appropriate authority" means the authority having responsibility for initiation of disciplinary process in connection with the violation to be reported': Preamble, 'Terminology' p 3.

[34] ibid Rule 2.15(C).

[35] United Nations Convention against Corruption (adopted 31 October 2003, entered into force 14 December 2005) 2349 UNTS 41, Art 33.

[36] ibid.

in the Public Service (April 1998).[37] This document attempts to set out the political and legal environment to protect integrity and combat corruption in both private and public sectors, with the public sector especially responsible for paving the way.[38] This means that judiciary should have an environment conducive to whistleblowing, with respect to combatting corruption.

Secondly, the need for whistleblower protection against retaliation can be found in Article 5 of the Termination of Employment Convention 1982 (No 158), whereby

> 'The following ... shall not constitute valid reasons for termination:
>
> (c) the filing of a complaint or the participation in proceedings against an employer involving alleged violation of laws or regulations or recourse to competent administrative authorities.[39]

The International Labour Organization (ILO) discusses the protection of whistle-blowers from retaliatory measures through '[the] protection of whistle-blowers in the public service sector' and the working paper 'Law and practice on protecting whistle-blowers in the public and financial services sectors'.[40] These discussions take a broad approach to anti-corruption to protect any employee or former employee where they have reported 'illegal, immoral, or unethical practices under the control of their employers'.[41] These discussions further recognise the important place that whistleblowers have in alerting the public to issues of corruption.[42]

Finally, two Council of Europe Conventions would apply to the judiciary: the Civil Law Convention on Corruption (1999)[43] and the Criminal Law Convention on Corruption (1999).[44] The Council of Europe Civil Law Convention on Corruption requires states to offer whistleblowing protections. The Criminal Law Convention on Corruption is different and covers witness protection and collaborators of justice (informants). These have led to a Recommendation by the Council of Europe,[45] which includes a definition of whistleblowing and the protections that should be available to whistleblowers: 'The national framework should foster an environment that encourages reporting or disclosure in an open manner. Individuals should feel safe to freely raise public interest concerns'.[46] This means there should be internal processes preserving

[37] Organisation for Economic Co-operation and Development, *Recommendation of the Council on Improving Ethical Conduct in the Public Service, Including Principles for Managing Ethics in the Public Service* (adopted 23 April 1998, C/M(98)9/PROV).

[38] ibid.

[39] Termination of Employment Convention, 1982 (No 158) Art 5. This Convention was adopted by the General Conference of the International Labour Organization.

[40] I Chalouat, C Carrión-Crespo and M Licata, *Law and Practice on Protecting Whistle-Blowers in the Public and Financial Services Sectors* (Geneva, International Labour Office, Working Paper No 328, 2019).

[41] International Labour Office, *The Protection of Whistle-Blowers in the Public Service Sector: Technical Meeting on the Protection of Whistle-Blowers in the Public Service Sector* (Geneva, ILO 26–30 September 2022).

[42] Chalouat, Carrión-Crespo and Licata (above n 40) 2.

[43] Council of Europe, 'Civil Law Convention on Corruption' (adopted 4 November 1999) European Treaty Series No 174.

[44] Council of Europe, 'Criminal Law Convention on Corruption' (adopted 27 January 1999) European Treaty Series No 173.

[45] Council of Europe, *Recommendation CM/Rec(2014)7 of the Committee of Ministers to Member States on the Protection of Whistleblowers*, adopted 30 April 2014, with explanatory memorandum.

[46] ibid [12].

confidentiality, while acting upon the information and protecting informants against retaliation.[47] All whistleblowers (including judges) should have protections in place when they fulfil the criteria for legitimate whistleblowing.

In this framework, there is the foundational idea that judicial whistleblowers should be protected where they make disclosures in the public interest, on reasonable grounds, where an organisation has committed some sort of wrongdoing. What is not particularly clear is what reasonable grounds, public interest, information or wrongdoing means in each case and especially for judges. The *ABA Model Code of Judicial Conduct*, for example, describes disclosures made about violation of the Code by other judges as being required where that violation 'raises a substantial question regarding the judge's honesty, trustworthiness, or fitness as a judge in other respects'.[48] This type of explanation is absent in the international framework.

It is important to note that only one of the anti-corruption regulations examined here has considered specifically the role of the judge as whistleblower and, given their role in the courtroom and in the rule of law, this is arguably an important gap.

B. International Legal Framework: Freedom of Expression and Judicial Whistleblowing

There is a policy relationship between the freedom of expression and anti-corruption, with the understanding that the information imparted is important to combat corruption.[49] Article 10 of the European Convention on Human Rights (ECHR) protects freedom of expression, but with the express qualification that the right may be interfered with 'for maintaining the authority and impartiality of the judiciary'.[50] As with any other qualification to ECHR rights, '[no] restrictions shall be placed on the exercise of these rights other than such as are prescribed by law and are necessary in a democratic society'.[51]

The ECtHR has set out a proportionality test to balance out protection of freedom of speech for judges who have disclosed information about their organisations whether that freedom of expression can be interfered with 'for maintaining the authority and impartiality of the judiciary'.[52] The Court has set out six criteria:

> the public interest involved, the factual basis of the statements, their actual wording and possible interpretations, the applicant's motive for the statements, whether he or she had any alternative channels for disclosure, the damage suffered by the State authority, if any, and the severity of the sanction applied to the applicant.[53]

[47] ibid [12]–[26].

[48] *ABA Model Code of Judicial Conduct* (above n 33), Rule 2.15(A).

[49] D Kafteranis 'The International Legal Framework on Whistle-Blowers: What More Should Be Done?' (2020) 19 *Seattle Journal for Social Justice* 729.

[50] European Convention on Human Rights, Art 10(2).

[51] ibid Art 11(2).

[52] ibid Art 10(2).

[53] *Goryaynova v Ukraine* (Application no 41752/09) (ECtHR, Judgment of 8 January 2021), [51]; see also *Guja v Moldova* (Application no 14277/04) (ECtHR, Judgment of 12 February 2008), [73].

In the case of *Kudeshkina v Russia*,[54] when a Russian judge gave an interview in which she publicly criticised the Russian judiciary on the conduct of officials in a case of corruption, she highlighted that 'instances of pressure on judges were commonplace and that this problem had to be treated seriously if the judicial system was to maintain its independence and enjoy public confidence'.[55] Whether such extrajudicial communication fell within the scope of protection under Article 10 ECHR had to be examined in light of 'the duty of loyalty and discretion owed by… the judiciary [which] requires that the dissemination of even accurate information is carried out with moderation and propriety'.[56] As the ECtHR later explained in *Bilgen v Turkey*,[57] a judge's

> employment relationship with the State must … be understood in the light of the specific guarantees essential for judicial independence. Thus when referring to the special trust and loyalty that they must observe, it is loyalty to the rule of law and democracy and not to holders of State power.[58]

The protection of judicial independence is a recognised matter of public interest, especially in the context of corruption, and any restriction on judicial communication requires the application of the proportionality test, that looks at 'the factual basis of the statements, their actual wording and possible interpretations'.[59] In the *Kudeshkina* case, the ECtHR stated that:

> even if the applicant allowed herself a certain degree of exaggeration and generalisation, characteristic of the pre-election agitation, her statements were not entirely devoid of any factual grounds … and therefore were not to be regarded as a gratuitous personal attack but as a fair comment on a matter of great public importance.[60]

The Court found that, having raised an important issue that should be open to debate in a democratic society, the judge in *Kudeshkina* should not be prevented from speaking out.[61]

This is a rather permissive perspective on whether a judicial whistleblower has a factual basis for their disclosure. It has been argued that 'information regarding the context of the disclosure and its effects is always imperfect' and that 'unintended consequences may follow'.[62] This should not, however, stop judges from airing concerns, formally or informally. But the factual basis of the disclosure will be closely connected to the intentions of the disclosing party. The statements in *Kudeshkina* were considered to constitute 'fair comment' rather than a 'gratuitous personal attack' on the judiciary.

[54] *Kudeshkina v Russia* (above n 26).
[55] ibid [94].
[56] *Kudeshkina v Russia* (above n 26) [93].
[57] *Bilgen v Turkey* (Application no 1571/07) (ECtHR, Judgment of 9 June 2021).
[58] ibid [79].
[59] *Goryaynova v Ukraine* (above n 53) [51].
[60] *Kudeshkina v Russia* (above n 26) [95]; see also *Di Giovanni v Italy* (Application no 51160/06) (ECtHR, Judgment of 18 July 2013).
[61] *Kudeshkina v Russia* (above n 26) [94]–[95].
[62] Manohar and Santoro (above n 1) 673.

Had the Court found that the judge had been 'motivated by a personal grievance', the outcome would have been different.[63]

Following *Kudeshkina*, the ECtHR in *Morice* held that '[q]uestions concerning the functioning of the justice system, an institution that is essential for any democratic society, fall within the public interest'.[64] The *Morice* case was about limiting expression concerning the judiciary, and the limitation can be applied to extrajudicial communication, such as judicial whistleblowing. Freedom of expression can be interfered with even where there is a public interest in the disclosure, having regard to the 'special role of the judiciary in society',[65] especially if that disclosure impacts on the public confidence.[66] This confidence must be preserved in regard to the judiciary's functions in relation to dispute resolution and the findings of guilt or innocence in criminal cases.[67] The ECtHR goes on to state that 'save in the case of gravely damaging attacks that are essentially unfounded … they may as such be subject to personal criticism within the permissible limits, and not only in a theoretical and general manner'.[68] As such, 'maintaining the authority of the judiciary' is not an absolute qualification and would be allowable save for 'gravely damaging attacks that are essentially unfounded'.[69] Moreover, the ECtHR in *Kudeshkina* found that dismissal as a penalty 'did not correspond to the gravity of the offence [and] could undoubtedly discourage other judges in the future from making statements critical of public institutions or policies, for fear of loss of judicial office'.[70]

The ECtHR has therefore recognised the connection between free speech and public interest. While extrajudicial expression is subject to the Article 10(2) qualification protecting the reputation of the judiciary, interference is less likely to be justified where the expression is intended to protect the rule of law, in the public interest.

III. THE JUDICIAL INSTITUTIONAL CONTEXT IN ENGLAND AND WALES

There are two dimensions to the institutional context that are relevant to judicial whistleblowing. The first is the institutional governance of the judiciary, ie whether it is a system of self-governance, governance by the Ministry of Justice, or a mixed system. The model of governance will dictate communication behaviours and practices. The second is the *Guide to Judicial Conduct*,[71] which provides help to judges in deciding whether or not to disclose information.

[63] *Kudeshkina v Russia* (above n 26) [95].
[64] *Morice v France* (Application no 29369/10) (ECtHR, Judgment of 23 April 2015) [128].
[65] ibid; *Kudeshkina v Russia* (above n 26) [86].
[66] ibid; *Kudeshkina v Russia* (above n 26).
[67] *Morice v France* (above n 64) [129]–[130].
[68] ibid [131].
[69] ibid [130]–[131]. See also A Seibert-Fohr, 'Judges and Their Freedom of Expression' (2019) 45 *Revista Forumul Judecătorilor* (*Judiciary Forum Review*) 45, 54.
[70] *Kudeshkina v Russia* (above n 26) [98]; see also Seibert-Fohr (above n 69) 50–51.
[71] *Guide to Judicial Conduct* (above n 4).

A. Institutional Governance

The English judiciary can arguably be considered to be one that works to guarantee human rights and dignity,[72] which works to strengthen the rule of law,[73] instigates constitutional developments, and guards against extremism.[74] The judge under this model has an overriding 'duty to apply the law, the duty to develop the law and the duty to protect the law'.[75] While extrajudicial communication should not compromise the integrity of the judiciary,[76] protecting that integrity also provides the foundation for the 'public interest' argument in favour of disclosure.

This model results from a revised institutional architecture. The Constitutional Reform Act 2005 (CRA 2005) introduced the UK Supreme Court,[77] Judicial Appointments Commission,[78] and the Judicial Conduct Investigations Office (JCIO).[79] This brought judicial independence under the protection of a number of different organisations within the judiciary. Whereas before, there was a view of the judge in an ivory tower, removed from society, there has been a shift towards a metaphorical fortress – also termed the 'corporate' model.[80] New ways had to be found to garner support for collective positions, to handle internal dissent and to determine what decisions about the organisation and working patterns of the judiciary could be taken, by whom, and at what level in a larger, more complex and increasingly self-governed body.[81]

Whilst this has had the benefit of creating a community for judges to share best practices and discuss professional issues, it has added layers of management with consequences for the regulation of judicial conduct and communication. In England and Wales, at the top of this judicial corporation is the Lady Chief Justice.[82] As the professional head of the judiciary, the Lady Chief Justice is currently responsible for 'internal arrangements, including appointing judges to fulfil senior administrative roles, providing guidance and support to individual judges, and maintaining standards of conduct at all levels of the judiciary'.[83] This means that she helps to decide on cases of judicial discipline and conduct, along with the Lord Chancellor, as well as managing internal and external communications.

[72] K Dzehtsiarou, S Falcetta, D Giannoudopoulos and P Johnson (eds), *Human Rights in Action: Assessing the Positive Impact of the Human Rights Act 1998 in the UK* (Submission to the Independent Human Rights Act Review, March 2021) https://dx.doi.org/10.2139/ssrn.3797048, 23.

[73] ibid 27.

[74] ibid 36.

[75] P Kaczmarek and P Skuczyński, 'Three Models of Judicial Free Speech and Technological Challenges' (2022) 14(4) *Krytyka Prawa* 118, 127.

[76] *Guide to Judicial Conduct* (above n 4) 9.

[77] Constitutional Reform Act 2005 (CRA 2005), pt 3.

[78] ibid pt 4, ch 1.

[79] The JCIO was established in 2006 under powers conferred by the Act.

[80] G Gee, R Hazell, K Malleson and P O'Brien, 'Judicial Leadership and the Internal Governance of the Judiciary' in G Gee, R Hazell, K Malleson and P O'Brien (eds), *The Politics of Judicial Independence in the UK's Changing Constitution* (Cambridge, Cambridge University Press, 2015) 126, 126–27.

[81] ibid 129.

[82] ibid 130. Currently Baroness Carr of Walton-on-the-Hill.

[83] ibid.

Whilst the Lady Chief Justice is also responsible for managing and appointing the Senior Management Team, Senior Presiding Judge, Senior President of Tribunals and Heads of Division,[84] she has ultimate responsibility 'for the maintenance of appropriate arrangements for the deployment of the judiciary of England and Wales and the allocation of work within courts'.[85] She is responsible for managing external relations with the legislator and Lord Chancellor,[86] and for communicating any concerns about legislation or regulations that might impact the role and integrity of the judiciary.[87] This means that the judiciary present one position on matters pertaining to them that is represented through the Lady Chief Justice. Whistleblowing by other members of the judiciary might undermine that position.

There are other structures to filter information upwards towards the Lady Chief Justice. The Judges' Council is made up of approximately 28 members, with representatives from the Judicial Executive Board and from other levels of the judiciary.[88] It represents the views of the judges, and acts as a bridge between senior and junior judges.[89] The Judicial Office provides, in principle at least, a structured support system for judges and their work by offering 'training, communications, media support, human resources and judicial welfare and policy advice'.[90] Finally, the Judicial Communications Office manages media communications. Whilst there is a more relaxed approach to extrajudicial communication of judges with the media than when the Kilmuir Rules operated,[91] there is still some uncertainty as to whether judges have that right to approach the media or not: 'Judges are not required to check with the JCO before making a statement to the press or giving an interview, but it is increasingly common for judges to do so, particularly if the area is sensitive or newsworthy'.[92] Informally, the practice has evolved to 'secure advance approval from the Judicial Communications Office or senior judges for the wording of an extra-judicial statement on a controversial issue'.[93] Extrajudicial communications are therefore subject to fairly strong regulation by the Judicial Communications Office.

B. Guide to Judicial Conduct

The *Guide to Judicial Conduct* (Guide) is not a code but rather a guide to aid judges on their conduct. It is for each judge to decide, within the scope of their contractual obligations and oath, 'whether or not a particular activity or course of conduct is appropriate'.[94] When deciding whether to disclose information they feel is in the

[84] ibid 131–32.
[85] CRA (above n 77) s 7(2)(c).
[86] ibid ss 5 and 7(2)(a).
[87] H Siddique, 'Sue Carr Hits Back and Tells Sunak: The Judiciary Won't Be Cowed', *The Guardian* (London, 16 January 2024).
[88] Gee et al (above n 80) 141–42.
[89] ibid 142–43.
[90] ibid 144. See https://www.judiciary.uk/about-the-judiciary/training-support/judicial-office/.
[91] A Dennett, *Public Law Directions*, 3rd edn (Oxford, Oxford University Press, 2024) 308.
[92] Gee et al (above n 80) 146.
[93] ibid 147.
[94] *Guide to Judicial Conduct* (above n 4) 5.

public interest, judges would be expected to bear in mind the three main principles: judicial independence, impartiality and integrity.[95] Judicial office holders should also ensure their conduct 'maintains and enhances the confidence of the public … in their personal impartiality and that of the judiciary'.[96] Maintaining the 'authority of the court' requires, for example, that 'the risk of different judicial office holders expressing conflicting views in debate' should be 'borne in mind'.[97] Talking to the media is, 'for good reason' discouraged.[98] While the Guide does not directly state what the 'good reason' is, it is stated that judges are expected to follow the conventions to 'promote the dignity of the judicial office'.[99]

The Guide *does* allow extrajudicial communication where it adds to 'public understanding and to public confidence in the judiciary',[100] although it cautions against commenting on matters on which 'the judiciary intend to issue a formal, institutional comment, but have not yet done so'.[101] This is so that the judiciary can appear to speak with one voice, rather than have conflicting voices come out of the judiciary. Whistleblowing could be seen to damage the reputation of the judiciary and present conflicting voices on certain issues where it is claimed that there is one stance.[102]

Whistleblowing only appears once in the Guide, and that is under Annex A:

> If you see or experience bullying, harassment or discrimination or other behaviour that falls short of these expectations, you may raise it informally with the individual concerned if you feel comfortable or alternatively with your leadership judge, magistrate or another leadership judge. If you want to use a more formal route you may use the Judicial Grievance or whistleblowing procedures or report it to the Judicial Conduct Investigations Office.[103]

The discussion on *Kudeshkina*[104] above shows that internal pressures can be significant.[105] This Guide appears to strongly regulate internal discussions and concerns on possible issues of public interest. This offers strong protection to judicial independence, impartiality, integrity and dignity of the office, but perhaps at the cost of accountability.

IV. WHISTLEBLOWING IN THE JUDICIARY: ENGLAND

There have been two known reported cases of whistleblowing in England. The most recent case was in 2020, where Judge Keith Raynor blew the whistle during the COVID-19 pandemic over custody waiting times.[106] He claimed that there was a lack

[95] ibid 8.
[96] ibid 9.
[97] ibid 17.
[98] ibid 16.
[99] ibid. 'Dignity' is a word that appears six more times in the Guide and its Annex.
[100] ibid 17.
[101] ibid.
[102] ibid 17–18.
[103] ibid 26.
[104] *Kudeshkina v Russia* (above n 26).
[105] A Zamir, 'An Independent Judiciary: The Israeli Experience with a Mixed Jurisdiction System' [2021] *Regional Law Review* 13, 21.
[106] C Coleman, 'Judge Makes Formal Complaint Over Covid Custody Waits', *BBC News* (11 September 2020).

of sufficient resources to run trials in time, and that he was put under inappropriate pressure by another judge to extend remand cases. His decision to refuse to extend a remand case was later overruled by the High Court. The High Court clarified that overruling Judge Raynor on extension times was based on restarting jury trials safely during a pandemic, rather than a personal attack on Judge Raynor.[107] Judge Raynor was given a 'Formal Advice for Misconduct' by the JCIO,[108] which is issued 'when the Lord Chancellor and the Lady Chief Justice are satisfied that conduct, while not serious, was sufficiently improper to amount to misconduct, thereby warranting a formal response, recorded in writing, and kept on record'.[109]

Yet this disclosure can be argued to sit within the scope of 'public interest'. That a judge decides against extending remand, and felt pressured to change his decision, is valuable information to society, as it tells us that he did not feel that he was independent in making these decisions. This impacts on the liberty and lives of those who come before the courts and who have the right to an independent and impartial tribunal.[110]

In England, the relevant law for whistleblower protection is under sections 43A and 43B of the Employment Rights Act 1996 (ERA), which cover the concepts of qualifying and protected disclosures in Part IVA. Section 43A offers a definition of 'protected disclosure': 'In this Act a "protected disclosure" means a qualifying disclosure (as defined by section 43B) which is made by a worker in accordance with any of sections 43C to 43H'. Under section 43B, disclosures qualifying for protection means 'any disclosure of information which, in the reasonable belief of the worker making the disclosure, is made in the public interest', and should show that some type of damage has occurred or is likely to occur, such as a miscarriage of justice.[111]

That judges are supposed to be protected if they are whistleblowers was confirmed in the case of *Gilham v Ministry of Justice*.[112] Judge Gilham, a district judge, had complained about 'the lack of appropriate and secure court room accommodation, the severely increased workload placed upon district judges, and administrative failures' at the court where she worked. She raised these grievances internally with 'local leadership judges and senior managers in Her Majesty's Courts and Tribunal Service and eventually … a formal grievance',[113] and argued that her grievances fell under protected disclosures under ERA.

The district judge was subsequently signed off sick due to stress and returned to work in 2019. However, as a result of the uncertainty around whistleblower protections of judges, Judge Gilham was unable to bring her claim for whistleblower

[107] S Tobin, 'Judge Rebuked Over "Improper Pressure" Claim', *Law Society Gazette* (25 February 2022).
[108] Judicial Conduct Investigations Office, 'Statement JCIO 39/22' (24 February 2022).
[109] Judicial Conduct Investigations Office, *Judicial Discipline: Misconduct and Recommending Sanctions* (June 2024) 13 https://www.complaints.judicialconduct.gov.uk/rulesandregulations/MisconductandRecommendingSanctions.
[110] European Convention on Human Rights, Art 6.
[111] Section 43B(c) Employment Rights Act 1996.
[112] *Gilham v Ministry of Justice* (above n 21) [44].
[113] ibid [5].

protection against the judiciary in the employment tribunal. When the case came before the Supreme Court, the main issues were:

> whether a district judge qualifies as a 'worker' or a 'person in Crown employment' for the purpose of the protection given to whistle-blowers under Part IVA of the Employment Rights Act 1996 ('the 1996 Act'). If a district judge does not on the face of it qualify for whistle-blower protection, the further question is whether this is discrimination against her in the enjoyment of her right to freedom of expression under the European Convention on Human Rights. And if it is, what is the remedy?[114]

The Court determined that judges were not 'workers' under limb (b) of section 230(3) ERA but discussed the argument around whether judges are employees within the definition of 'crown employment',[115] which centred on the definition of 'employment under or for the purposes of a government department or any officer or body exercising on behalf of the Crown functions conferred by a statutory provision' in section 191(3).[116] The Supreme Court reasoned that judges work for the 'administration of justice in the courts of England and Wales in accordance with their oaths of office'.[117] Furthermore, judges fall under the Lord Chief Justice's statutory responsibility under section 7 of the CRA 2005, and as such have an employment relationship.[118]

The Supreme Court also determined that the detriments that the appellant suffered were an interference with the enjoyment of her right to freedom of expression under Article 10 ECHR. Furthermore, that the respondent had failed to extend Part IVA protections to judicial office holders constituted a violation of the appellant's rights under Article 14 ECHR (requiring that all of the rights and freedoms set out in the Convention (and by incorporation, the Human Rights Act) must be protected and applied without discrimination).[119] The remedy was to read and give effect to limb (b) as including

> an individual who works or worked by virtue of appointment to an office whereby the office-holder undertakes to do or perform personally any work or services otherwise than for persons who are clients or customers of a profession or business carried on by the office-holder,[120]

via its interpretative obligation under section 3(1) of the Human Rights Act 1998.

The Court concluded that:

> When considering whether the disclosures had been made in the public interest, it would of course be relevant to consider whether there were other more appropriate ways of trying to resolve the situation. This would include the judicial grievance procedures policies … however, the appellant did invoke the grievance procedure and the investigating judge, Tomlinson LJ, commented that it was not a suitable means of dealing with the sort of systemic failures which were being alleged.[121]

[114] ibid [1].
[115] ibid [23].
[116] ibid.
[117] ibid [24].
[118] ibid; also set out under County Courts Act 1984, s 6(5), discussed at [18]–[21].
[119] *Gilham v Ministry of Justice* (above n 21) [30], [36].
[120] ibid [43].
[121] ibid.

Therefore, this is a case that supports external judicial disclosures where the internal processes are not suitable or sufficient.

Looking at these two cases, one can see that the outcomes have been impacted by the institutional context of the English judiciary. One can see that the Guide and the institutional governance structures in place are there to protect independence and the appearance thereof. What is arguably lacking is the flexibility to deal with inadequate procedures, channels of communication, and judicial accountability in a meaningful and transparent way.

Freedom of expression is not absolute, and there is a qualification in Article 10(2) ECHR to maintain the authority of the judiciary. There is a proportionality test to be applied where judges are involved. It is therefore suggested that the judiciary takes a proportionality approach to whistleblowing in future. This indicates a lack of clear avenues for the judiciary to deal transparently with the issues raised by these judges.

V. CONCLUSION

As a form of extrajudicial communication, judicial whistleblowing reveals much about how judicial leaders and institutional contexts regulate judges and their speech to preserve perceptions of public confidence and the cost of this in terms of transparency.

Disclosures can come at great personal risk to the whistleblower.[122] For Judge Gilham above, blowing the whistle came at the expense of her health and a lengthy court battle.[123] For Judge Raynor, it was a formal write-up for misconduct. One consequence for the organisation was the development of a Whistleblowing policy which, at the time of writing, remains unavailable to the public. By keeping everything internal (including the whistleblowing policy), the judiciary insulates itself from public interest debates around its operations but also compromises transparency and accountability. The consequences of this could include miscarriages of justice, and a lack of trust by judges in the institutions that they work for. This could impact institutional issues such as retention and hiring of judges.

Whilst this author recognises the connection between the rule of law and judicial independence, the discussion here goes beyond the independence of the individual judge, to the integrity of the judiciary as an institution. The ECHR allows for restriction of the freedom of expression where it will impact negatively on the reputation of the judiciary, but not where it is a disproportionate measure. There is a strong case for qualified whistleblowing from within the England and Wales judiciary, internal and external, to highlight concerns judges might have, that have not been fully reflected upon by the institution. The rare instances where it has taken place in England and Wales, and in other common law countries, demonstrate that whistleblowing protection and procedures are necessary to combat corruption and deal with otherwise legitimate complaints to ensure the integrity of the judicial office. The reputation of the judiciary is for the judges to protect, but not at the expense of integrity and accountability, as set out by the international framework above.

[122] Manohar and Santoro (above n 1) 670.
[123] *Gilham v Ministry of Justice* (above n 21) [7].

14

Learning from Lord Hope's Diaries

LEWIS GRAHAM

I. INTRODUCTION

In late 2019, Avizandum Publishing released the last of five volumes of *Lord Hope's Diaries*, a series reproducing, apparently largely unedited, the personal diaries of Lord Hope of Craighead. The series covers the period 1978 to 2015, beginning with his time as Senior Counsel and ending with his tenure as Deputy President of the UK Supreme Court.[1]

Judges have released memoirs,[2] essay collections[3] and reflections on their time on the bench,[4] but in modern times we have seen nothing like the direct and at times intensely personal invitation to peek behind the curial veil like that provided by *Lord Hope's Diaries*. The diary is a special, and tantalising, format and one which is very important for assessing judicial individuality. A diary's audience is primarily the author (although it is clear that, through publication, Lord Hope is not *exclusively* writing for himself) and entries may well offer a more revealing and frank account of judicial motivations and behaviour than other similar formats. It is a unique kind of extrajudicial communication – one which could only be published after a judge's retirement.

I suggest that *Lord Hope's Diaries* are particularly helpful in shattering the stubborn and pervasive myth of absolute judicial impartiality. The caricature of

[1] Lord Hope, *Senior Counsel 1978–1986: Lord Hope's Diaries Volume I* (Edinburgh, Avizandum Publishing, 2018); Lord Hope, *Dean of Faculty 1986–1989: Lord Hope's Diaries Volume II* (Edinburgh, Avizandum Publishing, 2018); Lord Hope, *Lord President 1989–1996: Lord Hope's Diaries Volume III* (Edinburgh, Avizandum Publishing, 2018); Lord Hope, *House of Lords 1996–2009: Lord Hope's Diaries Volume IV* (Edinburgh, Avizandum Publishing, 2019); Lord Hope, *UK Supreme Court… and Afterwards 2009–2015: Lord Hope's Diaries Volume V* (Edinburgh, Avizandum Publishing, 2019).

[2] S Brown, *Playing Off the Roof & Other Stories: a Patchwork of Memories* (London, Marble Hill, 2021); S Brown, *Second Helpings & Last Scrapings* (London, Marble Hill, 2023). See also Chapter 15: J Lee, 'Judging Memoirs: Life-writing as Extra-Judicial Communication'.

[3] S Sedley, *Ashes and Sparks: Essays on Law and Justice* (Cambridge, Cambridge University Press, 2011); S Sedley, *Lions Under the Throne: Essays on the History of English Law* (Cambridge, Cambridge University Press, 2015); S Sedley, *Law and the Whirligig of Time* (Oxford, Hart Publishing, 2018).

[4] B Hale, *Spider Woman: A Life* (London, Bodley Head, 2021); J Dyson, *A Judge's Journey* (Oxford, Hart Publishing, 2019). On extrajudicial communication in retirement generally, see Chapter 7 in this volume, H Tyrrell, 'Extrajudicial Communication: What Changes in Retirement?'.

the modern judge is as simple as it is silly: judges apply objective, wholly detached reasoning, pertaining to some special kind of legal logic, rather than engaging with their own personal ideals, values or preferences. They look at the law, synthesise the correct answer from it, and apply it, in some completely disconnected way, to the case before them. If this is how the judicial function operates, the composition of the judiciary, and the personal values and preferences of the individual judges, would be totally irrelevant to the outcome of cases. We would agree with Patrick Atiyah that it would be 'largely immaterial' which judge from an available roster were to sit on a particular case, so long as each is doing their job correctly.[5]

This kind of neutrality, I suggest, is plainly impossible for any human being. And our judges are, like it or not, human beings. Therefore, to cast judges as simple decision-making machines, impervious to all influence, robs them of their humanity. It is a thin and crude representation of reality, and a largely false one. And nowhere is this clearer than in the pages of *Lord Hope's Diaries*. Put aside Holmes and Llewellyn: these diaries provide one of the strongest arguments in favour of judicial realism when it comes to the UK's highest appellate court.

There are at least three (interrelated) aspects to the myth of absolute judicial impartiality, or three ways of *expressing* the idea of absolute judicial impartiality, which are challenged and ultimately undercut by passages in *Lord Hope's Diaries*: firstly, that judges decide cases exclusively on the law before them; secondly, that the identity of the sitting judge does not matter; and thirdly, that judging has nothing to do with the humanity of the judges. Each will be taken in turn, with passages from *Lord Hope's Diaries* extracted to show how each is ultimately fallacious.

II. DO JUDGES EXCLUSIVELY DECIDE CASES ACCORDING TO THE LAW?

Unsurprisingly, my position from the outset will be that judges *do* decide cases for reasons other than the law. Lord Hope thinks so, too, at least some of the time. He notes that some judges had a 'curiously inflexible'[6] attitude towards the cases in front of them, and he chastised his colleagues at various points for deciding cases for reasons *other* than that was what the law required of them. This included for reasons of party sympathy (on one occasion it was suggested that Lord Hutton sided with a claimant in one case 'for reasons of sympathy… which did not appear to me entirely compatible with the strict [legal] rule')[7] and fear of upsetting the Government of the day (the majority in the case of *Bank Mellat*[8] adopted the position they did, in Hope's opinion, 'to avoid being criticised by the Government').[9]

[5] P Atiyah 'Judicial-Legislative Relations in Britain' in RA Katzmann (ed), *Judges and Legislators: Towards Institutional Comity* (Washington DC, Brookings Institution Press, 1988) 137.

[6] Lord Hope, House of Lords (above n 1) 63. The curiously inflexible attitude in question was ascribed to Lord Hutton, although it was conceded that he had 'a good brain'.

[7] ibid 118.

[8] *Bank Mellat v HM Treasury (No 2)* [2013] UKSC 39; [2014] 1 AC 700.

[9] Lord Hope, *Supreme Court* (above n 1) 180.

Sometimes, Lord Hope could predict, or at least found unsurprising, a number of judicial votes based on the fact that the judges seemingly had their minds made up from the outset. This included Lords Hoffmann, Steyn and Millett's positions in the *Pinochet* litigation;[10] Lords Nicholls, Bingham and Steyn in death penalty cases;[11] Lord Kerr in devolution cases;[12] Lord Judge in a miscarriage of justice case;[13] and Lady Hale in cases involving children.[14]

Two judges were singled out as particular offenders. First, Lord Steyn seemingly suffered from 'a serious bout of tunnel vision' when it came to cases involving human rights and civil liberties,[15] and it was apparent to Lord Hope that he had his mind made up from the start in a number of cases.[16] Steyn was described as being 'determined and quite dogged in holding on to his ideas, yet surprisingly uninterested in things that lie outside his vision of how things are'[17] and Hope worried that he 'impose[d] on the public the consequences of [his] own view of morality'.[18] Lord Bingham, who, as other passages show, Lord Hope clearly reveres, was another apparent offender. He approached a number of cases with his mind apparently very clearly made up,[19] which attracted Hope's scorn in one entry in particular concerning death penalty cases. Bingham was described as being 'incapable of deciding [cases] on the law'; he 'subscribes on paper' to the principle that judges should 'put aside personal inclinations and prejudices' when they judge, but he 'cannot grasp' it in practice.[20]

Judges such as Steyn and Bingham, in Hope's view, acted improperly by closing their mind to the issues before them. By contrast, he preferred judges, himself included, who 'believe in the constitution and the democratic process'.[21] The charge, of course, is that judges such as Steyn and Bingham did not subscribe to those ideals in practice.

These words are harsh. They could only really be published after a judge's retirement. But they might also reveal how many people might intrinsically feel about a judge approaching a case with their mind already made up, or with an ideal outcome in mind. Yet Hope's diary entries show that this is seemingly commonplace. Few judges escape Lord Hope's ire – even the judges who are not seen as entirely predictable are occasionally chastised for falling into a pattern or towing a particular line.

But could this be otherwise? Judges are human and have personal preferences and ideals. As Michael Kirby, former Justice of the High Court of Australia, put it,

[10] ibid 68, 74, 77.

[11] ibid 204–5, 212, 234.

[12] Lord Hope, *Supreme Court* (above n 1) 118.

[13] ibid 219.

[14] Lord Hope, *House of Lords* (above n 1) 347.

[15] ibid 127.

[16] Including *Arthur JS Hall v Simons* [2002] 1 AC 615; *Re A (No 2)* [2001] UKHL 25; [2002] 1 AC 45; *R v HM Advocate* [2002] UKPC D3; [2004] 1 AC 462 and see Lord Hope, *House of Lords* (above n 1) 110, 127, 164.

[17] Lord Hope, *House of Lords* (above n 1) 127.

[18] ibid 262.

[19] Including *A v Secretary of State for the Home Department* [2004] UKHL 56; [2005] 2 AC 68 and *R (Jackson) v Attorney General* [2005] UKHL 56; [2006] 1 AC 262. See Lord Hope, *House of Lords* (above n 1) 228 and 251.

[20] Lord Hope, *House of Lords* (above n 1) 214.

[21] ibid 234.

'if judges say that they have no sin of personal inclinations … they deceive themselves'.[22] And whether we like it or not, personal preferences and values play a part in judicial decision-making. Terence Etherton has stated that it is 'impossible to exclude' all personal preferences from case consideration.[23] He is right: it would be impossible for judges, or indeed any of us, to totally expunge these influences from our thinking when entering the courtroom.

And yet, this is what Hope seems to demand of his colleagues. He is *critical* when they do otherwise. He suggests that judges such as Lord Bingham and Lord Steyn are *wrong* to have carried their convictions with them; judges should be neutral and respect the constitution, much like, it is heavily implied, Lord Hope himself does. In contrast to some of his colleagues, Lord Hope does not, apparently, hold preferences or other values which would affect his decision-making. Indeed, Hope clearly thinks that leaving one's preferences at the courtroom door is not just *possible* but *required* of judges. What, then, would Lord Hope think of the academics and political scientists who have scrutinised his own records and analysed the preferences underlying his voting record?[24] What if Lord Hope is more human than he cares to admit?

A. Politics

Often, when we think of judicial preferences, we think immediately of *political* and *ideological* preferences, not least because of the popularity of scholarship, hailing mainly but not exclusively from the USA, which casts judicial behaviour in such a light.[25] Does Lord Hope see things in the same way? There are indeed some passages in his *Diaries* which touch on judicial politics, and they are worth investigating in their own right. Lord Hope casts some of his colleagues as liberals, and others as conservatives.

Among the list of progressive, liberal judges is Lord Bingham, who would get 'carried away by a crusade for human rights'[26] and let his deeply held convictions', and his consistently liberal attitude 'take complete control of him'[27] on occasion; at one point Hope cast him as being akin to a Liberal politician popular in the early twentieth century.[28] Another member is Lady Hale, whom Hope describes as holding

[22] M Kirby, 'A Darwinian Reflection on Judicial Values' in J Lee (ed), *From House of Lords to Supreme Court: Judges, Jurists and the Process of Judging* (Oxford, Hart publishing, 2011) 18. See also J Bell, *Policy Arguments in Judicial Decisions* (Oxford, Oxford University Press, 1983) 247: 'a judge does not come to a case neutral'. In this book, see Chapter 2: Allan C Hutchinson, 'Speaking Out: The More, the Better'.

[23] T Etherton, 'Liberty, the archetype and diversity: a philosophy of judging' [2010] *Public Law* 727, 743.

[24] See nn 48–50 below.

[25] See eg J Segal and H Spaeth, *The Supreme Court and the Attitudinal Model Revisited* (Cambridge University Press, 2002); L Epstein and J Knight, *The Choices Judges Make* (Washington DC, CQ Press, 1998); J Segal and H Spaeth, *The Supreme Court and the Attitudinal Model* (Cambridge, Cambridge University Press, 1993); J Segal and A Cover, 'Ideological Values and the Votes of U.S. Supreme Court Justices' (1989) 83(2) *American Political Science Review* 557; C Herman Pritchett, *Civil Liberties and the Vinson Court* (Chicago, University of Chicago Press, 1954).

[26] Lord Hope, *House of Lords* (above n 1) 214.

[27] ibid 262.

[28] ibid 251.

'much more radical' views than her colleagues[29] and being 'relentless' with her feminist 'agenda',[30] meaning she was 'confrontational' when she 'sense[d] an inefficiency or a gender issue' in a judgment.[31] She was, more generally, a 'forward-thinking'[32] judge 'with a strong agenda of her own'.[33] Finally, Lord Steyn was pegged as another strongly liberal judge; he was described, presumably not without some tongue in cheek, as a 'campaigner for the rights of man'[34] and was said to often go on a 'campaign against the police' during sittings.[35]

On the conservative side, we find Lord Rodger: at one point, Hope remarked that he risked being seen as 'far from … independent' and that his judicial behaviour in the Scottish courts gave credence to the apparently 'widely-held belief that he was put in my place as Lord President as a supporter of the [Conservative] Government'.[36] When he moved to the Supreme Court, he would espouse 'ideas rooted in the past Conservative government of which he was a member'.[37] Other conservatives included Lord Lloyd of Berwick, who consistently sided with the Conservative Government,[38] and Lord Carswell, a 'steady, conservative Ulsterman'.[39]

Interestingly, Hope's intuitive guesses as to the political persuasions of his colleagues appear to line up fairly well with the positions ascribed to judges in the academic literature.[40] What about Lord Hope himself? Does his diary reveal anything about his own politics? Unsurprisingly, there is little introspection as to whether he emerges as a liberal or a conservative thinker, although his derision regarding what he sees as more extreme partisanship on the part of some of his colleagues would suggest that he sees himself as neither. What we do find are a number of fascinating comments on party-politics.

He shows no consistent allegiance to any particular political party, but accepted that it was 'time for a change' when the New Labour Government took over in Westminster in 1997.[41] He admitted that he was 'much out of sympathy with the Tory government' at the time due to what he considered their draconian and unworkable positions on criminal punishment.[42] A few years later, he was described as a

[29] Lord Hope, *Supreme Court* (above n 1) 86.

[30] ibid 190.

[31] ibid 176. See further J Rozenberg, 'An insider's account of the Brenda Agenda' (*Law Gazette*, 3 February 2020) www.lawgazette.co.uk/commentary-and-opinion/an-insiders-account-of-the-brenda-agenda/5102903.article.

[32] Lord Hope, *House of Lords* (above n 1) 232.

[33] ibid 310.

[34] ibid 251.

[35] ibid 168.

[36] ibid 13.

[37] Lord Hope, *Supreme Court* (above n 1) 28.

[38] Lord Hope, *House of Lords* (above n 1) 59.

[39] ibid 232.

[40] See eg L Graham, *Judicial Individuality on the UK Supreme Court* (Oxford, Hart Publishing, 2025); C Hanretty, *A Court of Specialists* (Oxford, Oxford University Press, 2020); R Cahill-O'Callaghan, *Values in the Supreme Court: Decisions, Division and Diversity* (Oxford, Hart Publishing, 2020); TT Arvind and L Stirton, 'Legal ideology, legal doctrine and the UK's top judges' [2016] *Public Law* 418.

[41] Lord Hope, *House of Lords* (above n 1) 25 (notwithstanding his view that Tony and Cherie Blair 'lack gravitas': 26).

[42] ibid 26. He later agreed with the view that there was 'something of the night' about Michael Howard: 201.

'liberal' by the *Independent*, a label he was 'pleased' to have received.[43] By the time the House of Lords had become the Supreme Court, his tolerance of the Labour Party had slipped somewhat, primarily due to what Hope perceived as their 'disgraceful bias against landlords'.[44] He had become deeply suspicious of the Scottish National Party[45] but did not share his colleague Lord Rodger's hostility towards devolution.[46] His main political preoccupation seems to relate to the prospects of being made to pay more taxes, an all too human worry.[47]

Incidentally, academic assessments of Lord Hope's judicial output tend to cast him as a politically moderate judge without an extreme ideology.[48] Cahill-O'Callaghan argues that the values underpinning Hope's judicial output reflect, above all, an institutional attitude.[49] Elsewhere I have suggested that he is somewhat more likely than his contemporaries to side with a socio-economic underdog, but that he remains a fairly institutional figure, voting in favour of a smaller role for the court in general.[50] As such, whilst it would be wrong to say that Lord Hope has *no* political view, and that this has *no* impact on his judging, it might be fair to say that his *moderate* viewpoints and beliefs mean that personal political preferences have less of an *obvious* impact on judging, compared to some of his colleagues.

B. Beyond Politics

Decision-making is affected by the humanity of the judges in lots of indirect ways, too. We do not need to charge the judges with doing politics to accept that their decision-making is affected by a whole host of factors outside of the law.

Judicial decision-making is affected by practical considerations; Hope details how some discussions were delayed by judges' engagements abroad[51] or, at one point, a judge simply going on a cruise.[52] As Alan Paterson has masterfully detailed,[53] judges have different ways of influencing colleagues. Some, like Lord Carnwath, are keen on trying to convince others to come to his view, whereas others, like Lord Bingham, are content to let others be. Lord Hope details phoning up his colleagues to try and encourage them to come to his view, but he records only doing so occasionally.[54] Sometimes personal loyalty played a factor: in one case, Hope opined that some of

[43] ibid 34.
[44] Lord Hope, *Supreme Court* (above n 1) 180.
[45] ibid 309–10.
[46] ibid 28.
[47] ibid 129, 309.
[48] See eg Hanretty (above n 40) and Arvind and Stirton (above n 40).
[49] Cahill-O'Callaghan (above n 40), 129–134, 156, 170.
[50] Graham (above n 40) ch 9.
[51] Lord Hope, *House of Lords* (above n 1) 75, 290; *Supreme Court* (above n 1) 26, 170, 177.
[52] ibid 141.
[53] A Paterson, *Final Judgment: The Last Law Lords and the Supreme Court* (Oxford, Hart Publishing, 2013) and see also Lord Hope, *Supreme Court* (above n 1) 176.
[54] Lord Hope, *House of Lords* (above n 1) 165.

the judges would support Lord Phillips' view over his own view because they were 'close' to him personally.[55]

Sometimes the jurisdictional specialisms of judges played a part: in one case involving Scots law, Lord Bingham found himself disagreeing with the two Scottish judges on the panel. Rather than dissent, he chose to swallow his doubts and vote with the Scottish minority. Without Bingham's vote, the case would have gone the other way.[56] Similarly, Hope himself suggested that he would normally be very slow to disagree with a court below if the decision under appeal had been decided by an enlarged panel of judges.[57]

In each case, these considerations demonstrate that judges do not always decide cases *purely* on the law – other factors play a part, whether this is justifiable or not. Taken together, these factors show that a whole host of factors, including personal, practical and political ones, affect judicial decision-making. Nobody who reads *Lord Hope's Diaries* and takes their contents at face value could seriously believe that judges decide cases exclusively on the law.

III. DOES IT MATTER WHO SITS?

If judges have personal preferences, and these preferences affect their decision-making to the extent that Lord Hope can predict, or *claim* to predict, how judges will decide cases, what does this mean for the politics of panel selection – ie which judge gets to sit on each case?

In the Supreme Court, like the House of Lords before it, the full roster of judges almost never sits together on a single case; rather, they sit in panels, typically of five, but sometimes seven or more, judges at a time. If individual UKSC judges have different predilections from one another which affect the way they decide cases, answering the question 'who sits?' matters. There may be circumstances where some judges sitting on the Court might lean more heavily in one direction or another, and their presence or absence on a given case may well influence the outcome, especially as UKSC decisions are decided by majority vote. Indeed, Dickson has argued that 'the outcome of an appeal … can sometimes depend on which judges are sitting';[58] and Blom-Cooper and Drewry have claimed that 'a decision in a particular case might depend on the permutation of [judges] selected to sit'.[59] Indeed, Arvind and Stirton have wondered whether 'the entire direction of the development of the common law in certain areas could … be determined by the circumstances of the selection of a panel of the Supreme Court'.[60]

[55] Lord Hope, *Supreme Court* (above n 1) 4.

[56] Lord Hope, *House of Lords* (above n 1) 203, regarding *Burnett v Grainger* [2004] UKHL 8; 2004 SC (HL) 9.

[57] Lord Hope, *Supreme Court* (above n 1) 41.

[58] B Dickson, 'Close Calls in the House of Lords' in J Lee (ed) (above n 22) 302.

[59] L Blom-Cooper and G Drewry, *Final Appeal: A Study of the House of Lords in its Judicial Capacity* (Oxford, Oxford University Press, 1972), 402 and see also, at 262, fn 3: 'it is hard to believe that [*McEldowney v Forde*] would have gone the same way if Lord Reid presided rather than Lord Hudson'.

[60] Arvind and Stirton (above n 40) 430–31.

Currently, the factors governing how judges are allocated to panels remain fairly opaque.[61] The job primarily falls to the Court Registrar, subject to some tinkering from judges, most usually the President and Deputy President.[62] The judges determining permission to appeal in a given case also sometimes contribute to this decision.[63] Factors likely to be taken into account include a judge's availability, interest, expertise and workload.[64] An attempt is also made to ensure that judges from Scotland and Northern Ireland sit on cases involving their respective jurisdictions.[65]

This practice seems unobjectionable at first, and its inherent flexibility means that changes can be made at short notice if considered necessary. This allowed the Court to bring about last-minute changes necessitated by, for example, judges taking up other engagements and inquiries,[66] announcing their retirement,[67] and sudden ill-health.[68] Particular interruptions noted by Lord Hope include Lord Browne-Wilkinson suffering 'some kind of breakdown'[69] and Lord Kerr suffering from a 'badly poisoned foot'[70] as well as, of course, Lord Rodger's sudden illness, leading to his death in 2011.[71] In each case, the incapacitated judge due to sit on a case could simply be swapped out for another available member, limiting delay and disruption.

However, the informality of the procedure comes with a downside: panel selection may be subject to judicial influence. The idea that judges might 'stack' a panel in their favour, pulling in judges sympathetic to their own cause, is an almost heretical suggestion. However, Lord Hope does provide some evidence that panel-stacking – or something close to it – did occur on the UK's highest court at multiple points throughout the years. Lord Hope himself admitted that he once considered removing Lord Kerr from a potential future panel because of his apparent tendency to dissent in cases relating to devolution and human rights.[72] Whilst he ultimately decided that this was not a 'proper course … to take', the fact that such an opportunity was both open to him and, at one point, seriously considered, is of concern.

Unfortunately, this was not an isolated incident. Hope also alleges that Lord Judge once petitioned then-President Lord Phillips, to ensure that he, Judge, sat on a panel in an important case relating to compensation for miscarriages of justice.[73] It is not

[61] Pre-UKSC, Lord Dyson confessed that it was a 'mystery' how panels were allocated: (above n 4) 130.

[62] Paterson (above n 53), 72; Lord Reed, 'Collective Judging in the UK Supreme Court' in B Häcker and W Ernst (eds), *Collective Judging in Comparative Perspective* (Cambridge, Intersentia, 2020) 26.

[63] PTA panels 'give directions as to … the composition of the court' (Lord Reed, ibid 25, fn 11) and 'advise on the number of members of the Court who should sit' (Lord Reed, ibid 26).

[64] However, Lord Reed has stated that the Court registrar tries to specifically include on each panel at least one member of the Court who is not an expert in the field, in order to bring a fresh perspective to each case: ibid 27.

[65] See Lord Reed, 'The Supreme Court and Scotland: The First Ten Years' (UK Supreme Court Ten-Year Anniversary Lecture Series, London, 19 November 2019).

[66] Lord Hope, *House of Lords* (above n 1) 50–51, 119, 193.

[67] ibid 108. When Lord Browne-Wilkinson neared retirement, he expressed an interest in appearing in fewer cases to ensure he had little outstanding work at the end of his tenure.

[68] Lord Hope, *House of Lords* (above n 1) 118, 135–36, 168; Lord Hope, *Supreme Court* (above n 1) 77, 78.

[69] Lord Hope, *House of Lords* (above n 1) 84.

[70] Lord Hope, *Supreme Court* (above n 1) 37.

[71] ibid 78–97.

[72] ibid 118.

[73] *R (Adams) v Secretary of State for Justice* [2011] UKSC 18; [2012] 1 AC 48.

clear whether this was done after the draft panel was drawn up, or whether Judge was included in the original draft panel. According to Hope, Judge made the plea, not (only) because of his criminal law expertise, but because he was ideologically committed to a position on the law which he feared his fellow judges might depart from.[74] In the end, the case was decided 5–4, with Lord Judge's position winning a bare majority. Thus, without Judge's petitioning (and Lord Phillips' agreement), the decision may very well have been a different one.

The most worrying example, however, comes from an entry[75] which suggested that this kind of petitioning had occurred with respect to Privy Council cases concerning the use of the death penalty in Commonwealth jurisdictions. It seems that Lord Hoffmann, who had consistently upheld the constitutionality of the penalty in previous cases, had pushed for the inclusion of Edward Zacca (the former Chief Justice of Jamaica) on the panel hearing the case in place of Lady Hale. According to Lord Hope, his reasons for doing so were clear: Zacca, who had previously defended the practice and was considered likely to uphold the capital punishment regime, would be more likely to agree with Lord Hoffmann than the more predictably liberal Lady Hale. In the end, Hoffmann's plea was effective. Hale was replaced by Zacca, and the Board decided that the death penalty was constitutional in both Barbados and Trinidad and Tobago.[76] Each decision was decided by a bare majority of 5–4, with Zacca voting alongside Hoffmann in the majority. There is a very strong case that the change in the panel composition directly affected the outcome in these cases. Whilst it should be stressed that Hope's account of Hoffmann's behaviour is neither official nor verified, if it is at all accurate, it paints a fairly damning picture of how the flexibility and informality of the panel selection procedure can be subject to serious abuse. In the situation as Hope describes it, Lord Hoffmann could certainly be accused of engaging in a kind of judicial 'gerrymandering', a practice all the more remarkable when considering that these Privy Council cases are some of the very few which can be said to involve a literal matter of life or death. Remarkably enough, Lord Hope was not at all critical of Hoffmann's actions in his account of the affair. He himself voted with Hoffmann and Zacca in both cases.

The prospect of stacking panels therefore seems to be less theoretical than we might hope. Whilst it is not suggested that the practice is widespread, even these isolated examples suggest that *it matters very much who sits on a case*. We know this, and it seems the judges know it too: why else would they petition for a judge to be included, or excluded, in the above examples?

IV. IS JUDGING AN INHERENTLY HUMAN ACTIVITY?

It should come as no surprise, given the above, that there is something inherently *human* about the process of judging. Irritation and frustration over one's colleagues;

[74] ibid 219.

[75] Lord Hope, *House of Lords* (above n 1) 213.

[76] *Boyce v The Queen* [2004] UKPC 32; [2005] 1 AC 400; *Matthew v State of Trinidad and Tobago* [2004] UKPC 33; [2005] 1 AC 433.

ailments and injuries getting in the way of work; all of this is *all too human*. This, too, is reflected in the fact that many of the pages of *Lord Hope's Diaries* are filled not with grand theories about the nature of law, or with detailed analysis of the thorny issues he and his colleagues are considering, but instead with details of his laborious travel arrangements between London and Edinburgh,[77] and his notes on bird-watching – Lord Hope is a seasoned twitcher.[78] Sometimes a case is the most important thing on a judge's mind. Often it is not.

He chose not to remove the entries detailing petty complaints and irritants, from sharing a flight with a hen party 'screeching and larking about'[79] to having to listen to Clive Anderson on the radio.[80] He is overwhelmed by the installation of a fax machine and a 'new laser printer' at his home, and marvels at the fact that he could transport documents on a floppy disc.[81] He sends notes about judgments at 2:30 in the morning after a sudden flash of inspiration.[82] He doesn't take many notes during cases 'partly to avoid carrying too much stuff home with me at weekends'.[83] He notes that Lord Rodger switched flight providers because they decided to provide sandwiches for lunch instead of 'salad and pudding'[84] All of these are unmistakably human thoughts and worries.[85]

His humanity also shows when he learns of Lord Rodger's illness. The passages on cases, birds and travel come to an end, to be replaced by humane and sombre entries chronicling the sad period leading to his friend and colleague's death from brain cancer.[86] Here, the humanity of Lord Hope shines through.

This humanity, unfortunately, also shows when Hope makes some comments which, in retrospect, appear regressive or otherwise regrettable. He notes that a case before him featured a majority of advocates who were women, but soon complains that they spoke in 'light and high-pitched voices which I could barely hear';[87] he primarily finds it 'irritating' when an IRA attack disrupted his flight;[88] he sees student protests as having 'been taken over by anarchists bent on violence'[89] and becomes frustrated with what he sees as *lawfare*: 'Could we have won the war against Nazi Germany if our leaders had been playing safe for fear of claims under the Human Rights Act?'.[90] Whether jotted down in a moment of frustration or revealing more

[77] Lord Hope, *House of Lords* (above n 1) 12, 16–17, 19, 25, 26, 43, 55–56, 59, 117, 170–71, 173, 177, 182, 195, 206, 226 249, 257, 277–78, 305–6, 326–27, 341 and 365; *Supreme Court* (above n 1) 3–37, 54, 64, 67, 115, 118, 134–35, 141, 152, 175 and 181.

[78] Lord Hope, *House of Lords* (above n 1) 53, 82, 83, 102, 105, 120, 122, 158, 231, 232, 260, 293, 303, 350 and 357; Lord Hope, *Supreme Court* (above n 1) 22, 32, 43, 142, 144 and 173. Note also Lord Hope's amusement at being compared to an owl himself: *Supreme Court* (above n 1) 33.

[79] Lord Hope, *Supreme Court* (above n 1) 279.

[80] ibid 313.

[81] Lord Hope, *House of Lords* (above n 1) 20–21, 29, 50.

[82] ibid 49.

[83] ibid 143.

[84] ibid 327.

[85] An AI program wouldn't have a problem with note-taking capacity. And it is doubtful that Dworkin's Judge Hercules would care so much about aeroplane food.

[86] Lord Hope, *Supreme Court* (above n 1) 78–84, 91, 94–97.

[87] ibid 60.

[88] Lord Hope, *House of Lords* (above n 1) 26.

[89] Lord Hope, *Supreme Court* (above n 1) 66.

[90] Lord Hope, *House of Lords* (above n 1) 336.

deeply-held views or beliefs, these comments also show how human our judges are. They behave selfishly; they act imprudently; they hold prejudices. Judging is unmistakable an inherently *human* enterprise.

V. CONCLUSIONS

Judges are clearly well aware that, like all of us, they cannot hope to be totally and absolutely impartial in the cases they decide. But there remains an expectation that they must nonetheless appear to be so: as Lord Neuberger has noted, to be authoritative, 'justice has always to be detached, almost Olympian'[91] in nature. Lord Phillips argued that citizens must *see* judges as impervious to 'influences, pressures or inducements' to have any confidence in them.[92] There is a benefit, as Mulcahy notes, of playing up to the *Grundnorm* of absolute impartiality.[93] Judges must may lip service to this idea of absolute neutrality even if they do not believe in it themselves.[94] Such performances represent 'an institutional agreement that combines judicial exceptionalism with fostered ignorance'.[95] Even if there is 'widespread recognition of the truth' judges must continue, so to speak, to *talk the talk.*[96]

This is why the decision to publish *Lord Hope's Diaries* is so fascinating. Lord Hope does not *talk the talk*, at least on every occasion. Whilst he insists that judging should not depend on who sits, *he complains about how predictable his colleagues' votes are*. Whilst he is proud of the fact that he doesn't let his convictions get in the way of his judging, *he chastises others who do not show such restraint*. He insists that judges must leave their values and preferences at the courtroom door *whilst filling a diary with suggestions that personal values and preferences affected the cases he decided*. However helpful, the myth of absolute judicial impartiality is a false one. Judges differ from one another: '[i]ndividuality remains the essential characteristic of the English judicial function'.[97] The myth of absolute neutrality, does not reflect reality. Nobody can read Lord Hope's Diaries and seriously be in any doubt about this.

[91] Lord Neuberger and Paul Riddell, *The Power of Judges* (London, Haus Curiosities, 2018), 22

[92] Lord Phillips, 'Judicial Independence' (Commonwealth Law Conference, Nairobi, 12 September 2007) 2.

[93] L Mulcahy, 'The Possibilities and Desirability of Mediator Neutrality: Towards an Ethic of Partiality' (2001) 10(4) *Social & Legal Studies* 506.

[94] T Maroney, 'The Persistent Cultural Script of Judicial Dispassion' (2011) 99 *California Law Review* 629; K Mack and S Roach Anleu, 'Performing Impartiality: Judicial Demeanor and Legitimacy' (2010) 35(1) *Law and Social Inquiry* 137; R Hunter, S Roach Anleu and K Mack, 'Judging in lower courts: conventional, procedural, therapeutic and feminist approaches' (2016) 12(3) *International Journal of Law in Context* 337, 340–42.

[95] G Edmond and K Martire, 'Just Cognition: Scientific Research on Bias and Some Implications for Legal Procedure and Decision-Making' (2019) 82(4) *Modern Law Review* 633, 654.

[96] D Klein, 'Law in Judicial Decision-Making' in L Epstein and S Lindquist (eds), *Oxford Handbook of US Judicial Behaviour* (Oxford, Oxford University Press, 2017), 237. It is interesting, therefore, to see that Lord Hope spends so many passages in his *Diaries* discussing how his judgments, speeches and engagements were received in the press: Lord Hope, *House of Lords* (above n 1) 29–30, 45, 47, 79, 80, 85, 123, 230, 366; Lord Hope, *Supreme Court* (above n 1) 34, 47, 61, 75, 91–93, 120–21, 126.

[97] Blom-Cooper and Drewry (above n 59), 79.

15

Judging Memoirs: Life Writing as Extra-Judicial Communication

JAMES LEE*

I. INTRODUCTION

WHAT CAN WE learn from studying judicial autobiography?[1] I argue here that much can be learnt from this important contemporary example of extra-judicial communication. I develop my argument through the first sustained examination of four judicial memoirs[2] from members of the cohort of Justices from the early years of the United Kingdom Supreme Court (UKSC): Lady Hale, the late Lord Brown, Lord Dyson and Lord Hope. As the various chapters in this collection serve to illustrate, there is an increasing academic interest in the activities of judges beyond the bench[3] and, as Sir Ross Cranston has noted, there

*As well as when speaking at the workshop giving rise to this collection, I benefited from presenting on this theme at the Society of Legal Scholars Conference at King's College London, and a Colloquium at All Souls, Oxford, and I appreciated the valuable comments from participants at each of those events. The research for this chapter was supported by the generosity of a Visiting Fellowship at All Souls College, Oxford, the Beaufort Visiting Fellowship at Lady Margaret Hall, Oxford, and the 2022–23 Lee Kong Chian Visiting Professor, Yong Pung How School of Law, Singapore Management University, all of which I warmly acknowledge. I am also grateful to Edward Craven, Timothy Endicott, Wolfgang Ernst, Simon Lee, Michael Rudko, Eloise Scotford, Natasha Simonsen, and especially the Editors, Hélène Tyrrell and Conall Mallory. All views, and any errors, are my own.

[1] For a study of United States Supreme Court autobiographies, see L Krugman Ray, 'Lives of the Justices: Supreme Court Autobiographies' (2004) 37 *Connecticut Law Review* 233.

[2] I use 'memoir' as a compendious term, without claiming more generally that autobiography, memoirs and diaries are indistinguishable – see eg E Seidensticker, 'Autobiography' (1999) 22 *Biography* 46.

[3] See eg G Appleby and A Lynch (eds), *The Judge, the Judiciary and the Court Individual, Collegial and Institutional Judicial Dynamics in Australia* (Cambridge, Cambridge University Press, 2021); H Roberts, 'Women Judges, "Maiden Speeches", and the High Court of Australia' in B Baines, D Barak-Erez and T Kahana (eds), *Feminist Constitutionalism: Global Perspectives* (Cambridge, Cambridge University Press, 2012); K McLoughlin, *Law, Women Judges and the Gender Order: Lessons from the High Court of Australia* (Abingdon, Routledge, 2022), chs 3 and 7; H Tyrrell and C Mallory, 'The Extrajudicial Voice' (2024) 44 *Legal Studies* 1.

'is something of a renaissance in judicial memoirs'.[4] In taking judicial memoirs as my primary focus, I draw upon recent valuable scholarship on the nature and importance of legal biography as a discipline for understanding legal developments, but apply it to *auto*biographical work: for 'some judges have elected to be their own biographers'.[5]

Here, I examine four Justices (the 'Memoir Justices') but six books ('the Memoirs') written by them: Lady Hale's *Spider Woman: A Life*;[6] Lord Dyson's *A Judge's Journey*;[7] Lord Brown's *Playing off the Roof & Other Stories: A patchwork of memories*,[8] and *Second Helpings*;[9] and then two editions of Lord Hope's *Diaries, House of Lords 1996–2009*,[10] and *UK Supreme Court 2009–2015 ... and Afterwards 2009–2015*.[11] This assortment of books is an unusual, possibly unique, coincidence of publication within a narrow timeframe of life writing by Justices who served together, with their tenures overlapping. We therefore have different accounts of the final years of the House of Lords and the early years of the Supreme Court. The narrators of one version also appear as characters in those of the others. But, although the books were all published within two years, there is also some engagement *between* the writings – particularly in respect of Lord Hope's diaries. This study is therefore a miniature exercise in collective biography of a small elite group – known as prosopography.[12]

This is not a review essay, and there is such richness to the material that I cannot claim to do full justice to the Justices' books, careers or lives within the limits of this chapter. Rather, my modest aim here is to explore the judicial memoir as a distinct form of extra-judicial communication. There is certainly intrigue in the Memoirs: Lord Brown notes that biographies can include gossip,[13] while Regan described Lord Hope's House of Lords diary as like the tabloid '*Heat* magazine'.[14]

[4] R Cranston, 'Review of Lord Hope's Diaries: House of Lords 1976–2015' (2021) 137 *Law Quarterly Review* 170, 170. Less charitably, as Dominic Regan puts it in 'The insider' (2021) 171 (7948) *New Law Journal* 7, 'Former members of the judiciary have suddenly decided that the world needs their memoirs'. See also, on the writing of judicial biography more generally in the United States, GE White, 'The Renaissance of Judicial Biography' (1995) 23 *Review of American History* 716.

[5] S Burnside, 'Australian Judicial Biography' (2011) 57 *Australian Journal of Politics and History* 221, 240.

[6] Lady Hale, *Spider Woman* (London, Bodley Head/Penguin, 2021) ('Hale, *Spider Woman*').

[7] Lord Dyson, *A Judge's Journey* (Oxford, Hart Publishing, 2019) ('Dyson, *Journey*').

[8] S Brown, *Playing off the Roof & Other Stories* (London, Marble Hill Publishers, 2020) ('Brown, *Roof*').

[9] S Brown, *Second Helpings* (London, Marble Hill Publishers, 2021) ('Brown, *Second Helpings*'). Lord Brown published an expanded edition of *Second Helpings* shortly before his death in 2023 with several additional chapters included under the heading *Last Scrapings* (London, Marble Hill Publishers, 2023). I therefore use the shorthand 'Brown, *Last Scrapings*' when referring to the chapters added to the expanded edition.

[10] Lord Hope, *House of Lords 1996-2009: Lord Hope's Diaries Volume IV* (Edinburgh, Avizandum, 2018) ('Hope, *Lords*').

[11] Lord Hope, *UK Supreme Court. and Afterwards 2009–2015: Lord Hope's Diaries Volume V* (Edinburgh, Avizandum, 2019) ('Hope, *UKSC*').

[12] RFV Heuston, 'Judicial prosopography' (1986) 102 *Law Quarterly Review* 90. Stone sees prosopography as 'a means to bind together constitutional and institutional history on the one hand and personal biography on the other': L Stone, 'Prosopography' (1971) 100 *Daedalus* 46, 73.

[13] Brown, *Last Scrapings* (above n 9) 206–7. Prest notes the common concern that 'biography is an increasingly popular because irretrievably lightweight medium, with a fatal preference for sensational and ultimately trivial narrative over complex or reflective analysis': W Prest, 'History and Biography, Legal and Otherwise' (2011) 32 *Adelaide Law Review* 185, 186.

[14] D Regan, 'Book review: House of Lords 1996–2009: Lord Hope's Diaries' (2019) 169 (7845) *New Law Journal* 22. For further on this text, in particular, see Chapter 14: L Graham, 'Learning from Lord Hope's Diaries'.

In interrogating the Memoirs here, I highlight certain features and controversies in the discourse. I focus on three thematic insights from the Memoirs: judicial personalities, confidentiality on deliberations and confidentiality on appointments. There are controversial aspects, with revelations around decision-making in certain cases, and disclosure of information relating to previous appointment processes of Justices to the Court. Before concluding, therefore, I connect my argument to debates around ethical regulation for former Justices in final courts of appeal.[15]

As Burnside has noted, the importance of judicial life writing 'lies in the jural, political and discursive power possessed by judges in common law jurisdictions'.[16] This study thus explores how one method of extra-judicial communication enables us to develop our understanding of the Supreme Court as a complex institution. In addition, it is also one step towards a biography of the Court itself.[17]

II. LIMITS OF LIFE WRITING

As well as a fertile period of judicial memoirs, it is also a fertile period for both legal life writing and writing about legal life writing.[18] Some of the limitations of using autobiographical work or memoirs as sources (for example myopia, self-service, self-interest, imperfect recollection) are reduced by building the composite picture. We can consider contemporaneous sources from judges – including other modes of extra-judicial communication – in the form of judgments, extra-curial[19] speeches and academic interviews.[20] We may also add academic scholarship profiling the period in question. Victoria Barnes has termed this process 'triangulation'.[21] The challenge of triangulation is easier given that the period here is recent history, but with Memoirs as sources it is all the more important to rely on multiple other

[15] G Appleby and A Blackham, 'The Shadow of the Court: The Growing Imperative to reform Ethical Regulation of Former Judges' (2018) 67 *International and Comparative Law Quarterly* 505.

[16] S Burnside, 'Griffith, Isaacs and Australian Judicial Biography – An Evolutionary Development' (2009) 18 *Griffith Law Review* 151, 152.

[17] See also V Barnes, C MacMillan and S Vogenauer, 'On Legal Biography' (2020) 41 *Journal of Legal History* 115, 120: noting that, in the United Kingdom, 'the link between legal biographies and institutions is made with a view to particular courts or judicial offices'. See also J Thomson, 'Biographies and biographical writing' in T Blackshield, M Coper and G Williams (eds), *The Oxford Companion to the High Court of Australia* (Oxford, Oxford University Press, 2001).

[18] Barnes, MacMillan and Vogenauer (above n 17) 120; R Auchmuty and E Rackley, 'Feminist Legal Biography: A Model for All Legal Life Stories' (2020) 41 *Journal of Legal History* 186; See also the references in n 21 below.

[19] In this context, I prefer to use 'extra-curial' (meaning 'outside of the court') rather than 'extra-judicial', because it emphasises that what judges do outside of the courtroom is not always beyond or separate from their judicial work. Lord Dyson, for example, has published separately a collection of such writing – Lord Dyson, *Justice: Continuity and Change* (Oxford, Hart Publishing, 2018).

[20] Eg A Paterson, *Final Judgment: The Last Law Lords and the Supreme Court* (Oxford, Hart Publishing, 2013); E Mak, *Judicial Decision-Making in a Globalised World: A Comparative Analysis of the Changing Practices of Western Highest Courts* (Oxford, Hart Publishing, 2013).

[21] V Barnes, 'Interrogating the Self-told Narrative: Lord Lindley's Autobiography, his Life and his Legal Biography' (2020) 41 *Journal of Legal History* 143, 162; see also R Gwynedd Parry, 'Is Legal Biography Really Legal Scholarship?' (2010) 30 *Legal Studies* 208, 219 and D Sugarman, 'From Legal Biography to Legal Life Writing: Broadening Conceptions of Legal History and Socio-legal Scholarship' (2015) 42 *Journal of Law & Society* 7.

points of reference. In each case here, we are – unusually – able to use the other Justices' Memoirs as a means of triangulation and comparison, and avoid the risks of 'the distorting effect of the focus on one individual',[22] and 'becoming captive of the subject's personal myths'.[23] There are various approaches taken by the different Justices in writing about their lives, and judicial lives – different levels of personal candour can be seen, for example, and they focus on their own areas of interest. So, there are different limitations in using such self-reporting as sources: the accounts are necessarily subjective, and may be partial or biased. But their very publication offers us insights into the attitudes of the Justices involved. We must recall that 'all life writing is a constructed narrative'.[24]

An excellent recent article by Paul Scott has examined the relevance of Lord Diplock's wartime service for his subsequent record as a judge and chairing inquiries. Scott notes that

> if judges are less interesting to biographers than they once were, many seem to have chosen – either for that reason or, perhaps, for the far greater control it affords them, to say nothing of the demands of ego or the need to fill a longer retirement than was enjoyed by their predecessors – to produce more or less legally-focused memoirs whose value is in some cases more limited than is that of judicial biography from 'outside'.[25]

The topic of autobiography is thus a timely one not only because of the coincidence of the publication of the Memoirs under consideration here. Memoirs may also become a more common phenomenon. Girard has noted that 'the combination of greater longevity and mandatory judicial retirement … is only a sufficient and not a necessary condition for the production of such a literature'.[26] The retirement age for all of these judges was 75, given their date of initial appointment as judges (prior to March 1995). From 1995 onward, the retirement age was then reduced to 70 for a period of nearly 30 years, until it was raised again to 75 by the Public Service Pensions and Judicial Offices Act 2022. All of the Memoir Justices were 75 or over when they published their Memoirs – as noted below, Lords Hope and Brown, and Lady Hale all retired from the Court in the month of their 75th birthday; Lord Dyson retired as Master of the Rolls at 73, but his book came out three years later.[27]

Although all the Memoir Justices worked until near their mandatory retirement age, Supreme Court Justices may choose to retire early, as shown by recent retirements: Lord Hodge, for example, has at the time of submission of this chapter,

[22] Parry (above n 21) 219.

[23] J Woodford Howard Jr, 'Commentary' (1995) 70 *NYU Law Review* 533, 540.

[24] Sugarman (above n 21) 15.

[25] P Scott, 'Judicial Biography in the National Security Constitution: Lord Diplock and a "Rather Silly Little Secret Racket"' (2024) 87 *Modern Law Review* 604, 607.

[26] P Girard, 'Judging Lives: Judicial Biography from Hale to Holmes' (2003) 7 *Australian Journal of Legal History* 87, 101.

[27] I am grateful to the Editors for referring me to Lord Dyson's 2024 Birkenhead Lecture at Gray's Inn: 'Judicial after-life: should it be subject to any limits?' www.graysinn.org.uk/app/uploads/2024/08/20241112_GraysInn_Education_BirkenheaLecture2024_LordDyson.pdf. In that lecture, at paras 43 to 46, Lord Dyson argues that judges should be able to publish their memoirs and express their views within the law, but, with reference to Lord Hope's diaries, 'As for accounts of the deliberations of the Justices, it is surely obvious (and I always assumed) that these are confidential' (para 45).

announced his intention to retire as Deputy President in December 2025, when he would be 72½.[28] This point might be particularly relevant for judges who were appointed to the Supreme Court post-1995, believing that they could only serve until they were 70 rather than anticipating the extra five years which they now have in principle open to them.

III. CONFIDENCE: PERSONAS AND PERSONALITIES

Although in what follows I make thematic connections between the relevant books, it is helpful to begin with brief sketches of each judge's career[29] and a brief sketch of each judge's biography, especially for readers of this chapter who are unfamiliar with those sources. I also make some initial comments on the different personalities of the judges, for with 'legal biography we must … turn to the human, intuitive and individualistic forces in legal development'.[30]

Lady Hale qualified as a barrister, but her primary career was as an academic and as a Law Commissioner, with particular expertise in family law, prior to her appointment to the High Court in 1994. She became the second woman to be appointed to the Court of Appeal in 1999, and the first woman to be appointed Lord of Appeal in Ordinary in 2004. She succeeded Lord Hope as Deputy President of the Supreme Court in 2013, and Lord Neuberger as President in 2013. She retired in January 2020, a few weeks before her 75th birthday. Her approach in *Spider Woman* is one of autobiography,[31] but aimed at differing from a 'conventional lawyer's memoir'[32] by appealing to a wider audience.[33] She also draws on some of her extra-curial speeches, particularly in the later chapters.[34] Writing about Lady Hale, Harris and McKeever have referred to the 'pragmatism, humanity and social awareness that have characterised her decision-making'.[35]

Lord Hope of Craighead was a Scottish advocate and Dean of the Faculty of Advocates before being appointed directly to become Lord President of the Court of Session. He was awarded a peerage in 1995, and then appointed Lord of Appeal in Ordinary in 1996. He was Second Senior Law Lord by seniority in 2009, and then became Deputy President of the new Supreme Court in October 2009.[36] He retired

[28] Lady Black retired at 66 and Lord Kitchin at 68.

[29] 'Pen portraits' of Lady Hale, Lord Hope and Lord Brown as Lords of Appeal in Ordinary can be found in Appendix 4 of L Blom-Cooper, B Dickson and G Drewry (eds), *The Judicial House of Lords 1876–2009* (Oxford, Oxford University Press, 2009). Lord Dyson was appointed to the Supreme Court after the publication of the book.

[30] Parry (above n 21) 224.

[31] Hale, *Spider Woman* (above n 6) 3: 'This is the story of how that little girl from a little school in a little village in North Yorkshire became the most senior judge in the United Kingdom'.

[32] ibid, Acknowledgements, 249.

[33] ibid.

[34] Eg chapter 13 bears some relation to (and has a common title with) Lady Hale, 'What is the United Kingdom Supreme Court for?' (Mcfayden Lecture, Edinburgh, 28 March 2019) https://supremecourt.uk/uploads/speech_190328_b850f9ebdb.pdf.

[35] N Harris and G McKeever, 'The retirement of Lady Hale from the UK Supreme Court' (2020) 27 *Journal of Social Security Law* 1, 1.

[36] Constitutional Reform Act 2005, s 24(c).

from the UKSC on his 75th birthday in June 2013, and returned to sitting as a Cross-bencher in the House of Lords, later becoming the Convenor of such peers in 2015. Hope has published his diaries from distinct periods in his career. The diaries contain many (and it must be said somewhat repetitive)[37] accounts of Lord Hope's regular activities: for example, his role in graduation ceremonies at the University of Strathclyde each year and his travels from Scotland to London between sitting periods. Lord Hope notes in his preface:

> As the entries show, there were happy and amusing times which it was a privilege to share with them, and there were times of disagreement and tension too … This will, I hope, add colour to what was seen in public and can be detected from their published judgments. I have done my best to edit out those passages that should be kept private and to delete things that are best forgotten, of which in the event there were very few.[38]

We shall return later to whether Lord Hope's revelations simply add colour or rather betray confidences.[39]

Lord Brown of Eaton-under-Heywood, as a barrister, served as First Junior Treasury Counsel before becoming a judge of the Queen's Bench Division in 1984. He ascended to the Court of Appeal in 1992, acting as Vice-President of the Civil Division for two years, and was then appointed to be a Law Lord in 2004. He served on the Supreme Court for three years before reaching his retirement age in April 2012. His two and a half volumes of memoirs, while in broadly chronological order, feature selective reminiscences over his entire career, in the style of an engaging raconteur. His stories range from the courtroom to the lecture hall to the golf course. Lord Brown notes that in Professor Alan Paterson's seminal study of the House of Lords and Supreme Court, *Final Judgment*,[40] 'Flatteringly, [Paterson] describes me as having played the role of "social leader" in Tom Bingham's era, ascribing this not least to the strategic position of my room'.[41] Brown goes on to remark '[small] wonder that Alan Paterson is quite my favourite legal commentator'.[42]

Lord Dyson was appointed to the Queen's Bench Division in 1993, and the Court of Appeal in 2001, serving as Deputy Head of Civil Justice. He was the first Justice to be appointed after the inauguration of the Supreme Court, being sworn in in April 2010. Initially, he was referred to as Sir John Dyson SCJ, while all other members were already Lords or Ladies,[43] which made him feel 'uncomfortable … as if I was a

[37] See Sugarman (above n 21) 12: 'the details of the day-to-day practice of judges, lawyers, and jurists often seem trivial, repetitious, and boring even to those whose living depends upon them; to outsiders, the specifics are potentially interesting only when aggregated and used as guides to underlying structures or tendencies, "a task demanding the patience and skill to pick jewels out of mountains of junk"' (footnote omitted).

[38] Hope, *UKSC* (above n 11) Preface, vi.

[39] The legal commentator Joshua Rozenberg, reviewing Lord Hope's Diary, concluded that 'Legal historians will devour Hope's Diaries … But his former colleagues are bemused by what they regard as a five-volume misjudgement'. J Rozenberg, 'An insider's account of the "Brenda agenda"' *Law Society Gazette*, 3 February 2020.

[40] Paterson (n 20 above).

[41] Brown, *Roof* (above n 8) 189.

[42] Brown, *Roof* (above n 8) 190.

[43] Justices of the Supreme Court are not appointed as peers, and those who are otherwise members of the House of Lords (for instance, as former Lords of Appeal in Ordinary), are disqualified from sitting or voting in Parliament while they hold that judicial office.

second tier Justice'.[44] He was later[45] styled as Lord Dyson, a courtesy title by Royal Warrant, a practice adopted for all future Justices who did not hold a peerage.[46] He left the Supreme Court in October 2012, when he became Master of the Rolls (head of the Civil Division of the Court of Appeal). He retired at the age of 73. His book is a 'memoir',[47] with intensely personal reflections. Lord Neuberger wrote in warm terms on Lord Dyson's retirement, and noted that

> Alan Paterson, in his recent book about the Supreme Court records John's exceptional success in moving from the minority to the majority in a number of cases by writing such persuasive judgments that at least one colleague was converted to his view. I am no musician but that seems to show a remarkable ability to modulate – to shift from minor key to major key.[48]

These biographical details show that the Justices had overlapping judicial careers – they all served together on the Supreme Court for two years, between Lord Dyson's appointment in 2010 and Lord Brown's retirement in 2012; Lord Hope, Lady Hale and Lord Brown sat together for eight years on the House of Lords and Supreme Court. From Lord Hope's appointment to the Lords in 1996 to Lady Hale's retirement as President in 2020, the Memoirs cover a period of 24 years of history on our final court of appeal.

Because of the publication timelines, we find a dialogue between the memoirs. Lady Hale refers to Lord Dyson's memoir, noting that he had lived on the same Yorkshire road as the school where her aunt taught and which her sister attended.[49] She refers more often to Lord Hope's diaries:

> [I]t does appear from other entries in David Hope's diaries that he was uncomfortable with my advocacy of greater gender and other diversity in the judiciary, which he saw as Brenda's agenda, and indeed my interest in issues concerning women and children generally.[50]

And elsewhere, she notes, wryly, 'Unlike Lord Hope, I am not a great diary keeper, but I did keep a diary of my first week in the House of Lords'.[51] Responding to criticism of the revelations in Lord Hope's diaries, mentioned below, Lord Brown considered it 'excessively harsh to suggest that these entries involve the betrayal of confidential exchanges',[52] although he concedes that 'such references as the diaries make to me are unfailingly generous'.[53]

[44] Dyson, *Journey* (above n 7) 129.

[45] Lord Dyson says it took an 'unconscionably long time': Dyson, *Journey* (above n 7) 129.

[46] As Lady Hale notes (*Spider Woman* (above n 6) 210), the courtesy extends to the spouses of courtesy Lords but not of courtesy Ladies.

[47] Dyson, *Journey* (above n 7) Acknowledgements.

[48] Lord Neuberger, 'Framing a new procedural culture' (2015) 34 *Civil Justice Quarterly* 237, 237.

[49] Hale, *Spider Woman* (above n 6) 23.

[50] ibid 177.

[51] ibid 179.

[52] Brown, *Second Helpings* (above n 9) 140. Lord Brown does not directly refer to Lord Hope's disclosures on appointments; Lord Brown himself refers to a High Court judge having withdrawn an application for promotion to the Court of Appeal: Brown, *Last Scrapings* (above n 9) 195. See also – though not within a memoir, Lord Dyson's views in his Birkenhead Lecture (above n 27).

[53] Brown, *Second Helpings* (above n 9) 140.

A fascinating feature of all the Memoirs are the passages where the Justices reveal their own personal experiences with mental health, insecurity and self-doubt. In his final chapters, Lord Brown discusses how for most of his adult life he 'suffered from a most excruciatingly embarrassing physical ailment, profuse sweatiness', which he said was brought on by 'a feeling of mental pressure, perhaps allied to a sudden failure of self-confidence'.[54] That 'recurrent phenomenon cast a dismal pall over many years of my professional life'.[55] Lady Hale talks of imposter syndrome throughout her book, using it as a theme to frame important moments in her career. For example, when she was to apply to become President of the Supreme Court, she states that at the point 'I really did think that I could do the job',[56] yet 'there were still some qualms, imposter syndrome never quite defeated'.[57] Lord Dyson speaks movingly of his experience with depression for two years after suffering from post-viral fatigue: the 'experience gave [him] a real insight into this terrible mental illness'.[58] Lord Hope expresses doubts about his own abilities compared to certain of his colleagues: Lord Sumption was 'so incredibly well informed and so bright, I wondered whether I could keep up with him and remain interesting'.[59] Lord Hope also worried about giving an extra-curial lecture, observing that, while not all the Law Lords took up such invitations: '[those] who do (Bingham, Steyn, Hoffmann and Rodger) set very high standards. So it is hard for me to live up to what is expected of me'.[60]

These perspectives offer insights into the states of mind of our leading judges, and can humanise them in the eyes of the public. On the other hand, the personality clashes we can identify from the Memoirs can shed light: as Burnside has written in the Australian context, 'explorations of friendships and personality clashes amongst judges are also illuminating. The individuals sitting on [a final court of appeal] at any one time form a kind of corporate entity'.[61]

The Memoirs offer contemporary accounts of contemporaneous experiences on our highest court. I am conscious of the risk identified by Posner that 'a focus on the handful of exciting judges is apt to create a distorted impression of [the judicial] process'.[62] But this group is self-selecting, in that the Memoir Justices are those who have, so far, chosen (or been encouraged) to publish their Memoirs. By taking the four Justices as my subjects, I am not making any claims that, compared to other Justices on the Court, they are 'exciting', or 'great',[63] or

[54] Brown, *Last Scrapings* (above n 9) 183.

[55] ibid 184.

[56] Hale, *Spider Woman* (above n 6) 233–34.

[57] Hale, *Spider Woman* (above n 6) 234.

[58] Dyson, *Journey* (above n 7) chapter 9 and Epilogue.

[59] Hope, *UKSC* (above n 11) 138–39.

[60] Hope, *UKSC* (above n 11) 169. See also Lord Hope's lament of one case 'whether anyone will bother to refer to my speech, coming third after Lord Bingham and Lord Steyn, remains to be seen': Hope, *UKSC* (above n 11) 118.

[61] S Burnside, 'Australian Judicial Biography' (2011) 57 *Australian Journal of Politics and History* 221, 229.

[62] RA Posner, 'Judicial Biography' (1995) 70 *NYU Law Review* 502, 516.

[63] Barnes, MacMillan and Vogenauer (above n 17) 115; L Przybyszewski, 'The Dilemma of Judicial Biography or Who Cares Who Is the Great Appellate Judge?' (1996) 21 *Law & Social Inquiry* 135, 137; 170.

particularly distinguished;[64] only that they are distinctive because they are memoir authors. The study of memoirs does, though, invite us to assess the legacy of these judges: their writings give them a voice in that assessment, but also now form part of their legacy.

IV. CONFIDENCES: VIEWS OF VIEWS IN COURT

Primarily, this study focuses on *post*-judicial communication, since they are published after retirement. However, the Memoirs also speak to the communication between judges at the time of key decisions and moments. They are therefore a source of insight into the quotidian workings of the Court. The spectre of confidentiality looms large here. How far it is appropriate to disclose the discussions amongst Justices, and disagreements which may not previously have appeared on the public record?

Relatively few cases receive common substantive coverage across The Memoirs. The *Lumba*[65] case is one on which several of the Memoir Justices remark. The case required the UKSC to consider the position of foreign national criminals who had, upon completion of their sentence, been detained pending deportation pursuant to an unlawful secret policy. The case raised a number of issues, but for present purposes, it suffices to record that the Supreme Court determined by a majority that the men's detention was unlawful; that the men could sue; but that they were limited to nominal damages because, as violent offenders, they would have been detained anyway if the published policy (which allowed for discretionary detention) had been applied.

Lord Dyson, who wrote the leading judgment for the majority, cites *Lumba* as 'an extreme example of the problems created by multiple judgments'.[66] Lord Brown vehemently disagreed with the majority approach. His Lordship more generally grew frustrated by what he saw as the 'excessive soft-heartedness (I almost wrote woolly-mindedness) of a number of my colleagues, particularly in any case supposedly raising human rights concerns'.[67] Lord Hope, who was in the majority in *Lumba*, elsewhere mentions the disagreements he had with the late Lord Rodger, who concurred with Lord Brown.[68]

More broadly, Lord Hope's diary format sees him detail the discussions and machinations on various cases throughout his time in the Lords and the Supreme

[64] 'Distinction, among judges, is almost always a product of the assumptions, expectations, and appraisal of the legal profession': W Lucy, 'Judges, Distinguished' in P Cane and J Conaghan (eds), *The New Oxford Companion to Law* (Oxford, Oxford University Press, 2008) 649; Sugarman (above n 21) 13 fn38 'biographies, obituaries, and eulogies are a rich source for investigating lawyers' professional identity, the myths lawyers generate in defence of existing professional structures, and the culture and mindset of the legal community'. Prest (above n 13) 199.

[65] *R (Lumba) v Secretary of State for the Home Department* [2011] UKSC 12.

[66] Dyson, *Journey* (above n 7) 131.

[67] Brown, *Roof* (above n 8) xx.

[68] Lord Hope, 'Lord Rodger's Notebooks' in A Burrows, D Johnston QC and R Zimmermann (eds), *Judge and Jurist: Essays in Memory of Lord Rodger of Earlsferry* (Oxford, Oxford University Press, 2013) 80. See also Lord Brown's 'Dissenting Judgments' in the same collection.

Court. Lord Brown observes that the diaries 'provide unusually candid character descriptions and accounts of how certain judicial decisions were arrived at'.[69] Lord Hope admits to being insecure and sensitive to criticism from other Justices in deliberations, including expressing frustration when he was the sole dissentient in an enlarged panel.[70] Only a few pages later, Lord Hope in turn criticises Lady Hale for being the sole dissentient in a different case regarding the enforceability of pre-nuptial agreements.[71] He was similarly frustrated with Lord Kerr's approach to devolution cases.[72]

Lady Hale's approach to judicial deliberations is different: she talks generally about the approach to judgment writing and debate, but without disclosing confidential details.[73] She refers to her own judgments that caused some controversy amongst her fellow Justices. But her account of, for example, the two Brexit cases in the final chapter[74] explains how the President (Lord Neuberger in 2016, Lady Hale herself in 2019) led the 11 Justices in each case through the discussion and judgment writing process. She does not reveal disagreements beyond those that appear in judgments themselves.

The question over whether discussions between Justices about judging should be confidential is a vexed one.[75] Such revelations, of course, are a valuable resource for judicial scholars. Prest has noted that this can be a contribution from judicial life writing:

> Judicial findings can also present a 'black box' problem, due to the frequent difficulty of identifying the distinctive character of an individual judge's personal contribution to a court's decision with which he or she is recorded merely as concurring or dissenting.[76]

And yet there is a sense of unease about the potential betrayal of confidences and its implications for trust between serving judges. Furthermore litigants, and their lawyers, may be discomfited or disgruntled by hearing how close they came to winning (or losing).[77] I consider below how we may address such concerns.

[69] Brown, *Second Helpings* (above n 9) 140.

[70] Referring to *Her Majesty's Treasury v Ahmed* [2010] UKSC 5, Hope, *UKSC* (above n 11) 13, 26–7, 28–9. Meanwhile in a later case he notes that he, with Lords Reed and Kerr, dissented 'on grounds of principle', and that Lord Neuberger writing for the majority 'recognis[ed] the force of the objections of the minority': Hope, *UKSC* (above n 11) 180 and fn 188 (speaking of *Bank Mellat v HM Treasury (No 2)* [2013] UKSC 38.

[71] Hope, *UKSC* (above n 11) 35–36: 'Brenda, perhaps out of a feeling that there were issues here that the rest of us did not fully understand' (referring to *Granatino v Radmacher* [2010] UKSC 42). At a different point in his diaries Lord Hope admits to wondering whether he had been 'guilty of double standards' when presiding over an appeal: Hope, *UKSC*, 176.

[72] Hope, *UKSC* (above n 11) 116 and 118: 'I fear that the chances of steering [Lord Kerr] off this line are rather remote' (At 118).

[73] Eg, Hale, *Spider Woman* (above n 6) 211.

[74] Hale, *Spider Woman* (above n 6) chapter 13, 'What is the Supreme Court For?', especially 232ff; the two cases are *R (on the application of Miller) v Secretary of State for Exiting the European Union* [2017] UKSC 5 and *R (on the application of Miller) v The Prime Minister* [2019] UKSC 41.

[75] Cranston supports their publication on the ground of public interest: Cranston (above n 4) 173.

[76] Prest (above n 13) 195.

[77] cf H Cecil, *The English Judge*, 22nd Hamlyn Lectures (London, Stevens & Sons, 1970), 64 'Most losing parties will go away from the court slightly happy if they merely lose the case without also being called unmitigated liars'.

V. CONFIDENTIALITY: APPOINTMENTS

Another theme in the Memoirs relates to judicial appointments, at early stages, then to the Lords and the UKSC, and to the leadership positions which several of the Justices held. The Justices write interestingly about their own experiences on initial appointment and then later through the judicial hierarchy, and also their views of the processes more generally, since their careers spanned the periods before and after the changes introduced by the Constitutional Reform Act 2005 (CRA 2005).

Lord Brown writes of his appointment to the High Court bench that he was summoned by the Lord Chancellor and given 'less of an invitation than an instruction',[78] and admits to feeling some trepidation, even reluctance, about joining the Lords.[79] When offered an appointment to the bench by Lord Mackay of Clashfern, Lord Dyson asked for some time to reflect, only then to be chased by Sir Tasker Watkins V-C, for an answer.[80] Lady Hale found out about her own appointment as the first woman to be Lord of Appeal in Ordinary inadvertently from the pass officer at the entrance to the House of Lords![81]

For appointments that involved applications under the provisions of the 2005 Act, Lord Dyson speaks about applying (unsuccessfully) to be Master of the Rolls first in 2009, when Lord Neuberger and he were the only candidates.[82] Lady Hale writes about her applications to be President (twice) and Deputy President of the Court.[83] In both cases, it is the judge's own choice to reveal his original application.

Lord Hope discloses various details of the appointments processes, as well as his views of them. We may begin with a key passage:

> Somebody who knew a lot of the facts was prepared to talk to [*The Times*' Legal correspondent) … the general tenor of the article was right – that the appointments system was mishandled. It was never going to be easy or leak-proof. The old system, warts and all, was preferable in that respect to the ponderous one which we now have. It is such a pity that, in the interests of political correctness, we have had to abandon it. The result is a system which is open to the criticism that it can be manipulated by vested interests. That is most unfair on the very deserving characters who are selected.[84]

Here, Lord Hope casts doubt on the reform to appointments, taking it away from being in the gift of the Government of the day to become a politically independent process. He calls the system 'ponderous', and suggests it was introduced 'in the interests of political correctness', which is presumably a reference to the desire for greater representative diversity in the higher judiciary, although his Lordship does not elaborate on his claim.

[78] Brown, *Roof* (above n 8) 89.

[79] Brown, *Roof* (above n 8) 174–76. 'I had indeed long felt, and occasionally said, about the Lords: "I'd love to be asked but only if I can say no." On being asked, however, I felt I *could* not, and certainly I *did* not, say no'.

[80] Dyson, *Journey* (above n 7).

[81] Hale, *Spider Woman* (above n 6) 125.

[82] Dyson, *Journey* (above n 7) 127.

[83] Hale, *Spider Woman* (above n 6) 217, 233–34.

[84] Hope, *UKSC* (above n 11) 28.

Beyond his personal thoughts, Lord Hope's diaries contain other revelations about appointments, unlike the memoirs of his colleagues. There is discussion of Lord Sumption's prior applications to the Supreme Court[85] albeit this was widely known, since Lord Sumption confirmed it himself.[86] Lord Brown discusses this too,[87] as does Lord Dyson, who was appointed in the 2009–10 around when Lord Sumption had first applied.[88]

In addition, Lord Hope discloses that Lady Arden had more than one unsuccessful occasion for appointment to the final court of appeal (including to the House of Lords, when there was no application process).[89] In Lady Arden's case, there is the further dimension that she is, and was then, married to Lord Mance, who was serving in the Lords and on the Supreme Court at the same time.[90] Lord Hope also reveals that Lord Burrows was interviewed in 2012,[91] some eight years before his eventual appointment to the Court.

There is a question of wisdom here – candour about one's own experience going through an appointments process is to be expected; candour about the experience of others, including disclosure of unsuccessful applicants, is something else. It is one thing to disclose one's personal feelings as someone consulted by those involved with appointments (particularly in the House of Lords, when there was no formal application process, but the views of serving Law Lords were sought on possible candidates); it is another to disclose details of the application process when one was on the panel. In Lord Hope's case, that includes not only the identities of unsuccessful applicants and his views on the process, but also reporting the feedback of others. This may matter because it may disincentivise applicants from applying – not least those from under-represented groups. Transparency as to the process should not extend to individual members of a panel disclosing confidential information – it would be a different matter if it was a condition of the process that names would indeed be disclosed, as some have suggested as a viable reform.[92]

As noted above, Lord Brown considered it 'excessively harsh to suggest' that Lord Hope's diaries 'involve the betrayal of confidential exchanges'.[93] As far as the disclosures relate to appointments to the Supreme Court, however, there is more than an

[85] Hope, *UKSC* (above n 11) 25 and 28.

[86] F Gibb, 'Supreme ambition, jealousy and outrage', *The Times*, 4 February 2010, www.thetimes.co.uk/article/supreme-ambition-jealousy-and-outrage-rv8fzvbx536 (Lord Hope refers to this article in Hope, *UKSC* (above n 11) 28). See further 'Judges oppose appointment of Sumption, QC, to the Supreme Court', *UKSC Blog*, 15 October 2009, www.ukscblog.com/judges-oppose-appointment-of-sumption-qc-to-the-supreme-court/

[87] Brown, *Roof* (above n 8) 191–93. Lord Sumption provided Lord Brown with a jacket quote for *Second Helpings* (above n 9): 'I really enjoyed *Second Helpings*. Simon Brown has that elusive quality which the eighteenth century called "bottom": a combination of wisdom, experience, empathy and humour'.

[88] Dyson, *Journey* (above n 7) 127.

[89] Hope, *UKSC* (above n 11) 172.

[90] Lord Hope observes that 'happily' Lady Arden was later appointed (Hope, *UKSC* (above n 11) 172), to one of three vacancies created in 2018, including by the retirement of Lord Mance.

[91] Hope, *UKSC* (above n 11) 172.

[92] See for example the views of Dinah Rose QC (quoted from Twitter), referred to in 'Retired Supreme Court justice returns after age bar is raised', *The Times*, 30 August 2022 www.thetimes.co.uk/article/retired-supreme-court-justice-returns-after-age-bar-is-raised-8kfszwk2j.

[93] Brown, *Second Helpings* (above n 9) 140.

expectation to be honoured that Justices will be discreet. There is in fact a specific duty of confidentiality, imposed by section 139 of the CRA 2005:

> (1) A person who obtains confidential information, or to whom confidential information is provided, under or for the purposes of a relevant provision must not disclose it except with lawful authority.[94]
>
> (2) These are the relevant provisions—
>
> (a) sections 26 ['Selection of members of the Court'] and 27 ['Selection process'] and regulations under section 27A;
>
> ...
>
> (3) Information is confidential if it relates to an identified or identifiable individual (a 'subject').

Section 139(7) provides that the duty of confidentiality does not 'prevent the disclosure of information which is already, or has previously been, available to the public from other sources'.[95] But, as noted above, at least some of the information about applications and the Justices' views of applicants was not public before Lord Hope disclosed it. Not does it appear that Lord Hope secured the consent of the relevant individuals (which would be lawful authority under section 139(4)(a); none of the other reasons would seem to apply). Referring to Lord Hope's revelations of the views inside and outside the Court when she applied to be Deputy President, Lady Hale has described him, with understatement, as 'indiscreet',[96] which would suggest that her consent was not secured. Unusually, the statute provides that a breach of the duty of confidence under section 139 is privately actionable,[97] at the suit of the subject of the information.[98]

Lord Hope does not expressly refer to section 139 of the CRA 2005 in his diaries; his Lordship does get as far as section 137,[99] which provides for the Parliamentary disqualification of serving Judges of the Supreme Court, from sitting and voting in the Lords even if they otherwise hold a peerage. He does mention, in a passage noting that Lady Hale had been disappointed with one shortlist, 'of course she knows nothing of what we have been told about the candidates, and as this was given to us in confidence we cannot tell her'.[100]

When it comes to appointments, then, there is an existing, statutory, confidentiality requirement imposed on Justices, which is not limited to their time serving on the Court. But this example perhaps serves to show that the existence of the duty, even where it has been made privately actionable, is not a sufficient mechanism to prevent disclosures of confidential processes. And it may seem unlikely that serving Justices of the Court would seek to sue a retired Justice.

[94] Under the Act, 'relevant provisions' include those relating to Supreme Court selection commission processes (s 139(2)).

[95] It is not therefore a breach of the duty of confidentiality to discuss Lord Hope's published revelations in this chapter.

[96] Hale, *Spider Woman* (above n 6) 217.

[97] CRA 2005, s 139(8).

[98] CRA 2005, s 139(9).

[99] Hope, *Lords* (above n 10) 368.

[100] Hope, *UKSC* (above n 11) 69.

VI. PUBLIC CONFIDENCE? POST-RETIREMENT ACTIVITY

Having reviewed some of the controversies, I now make some suggestions for changes with respect to Memoirs. As Girard has perceptively observed, 'As public interest in, and media criticism of, judges has become more prevalent, autobiography provides judges an avenue for telling their side of the story, something they cannot do while still holding judicial office'.[101]

That public interest continues after judges have retired. Appleby and Blackham have drawn attention to the ethical challenges relating to former judges,[102] and the potential for those challenges to affect public confidence.[103] They have argued for an approach which recognises 'former judges' rights as private individuals, while still ensuring the maintenance and protection of the integrity of the judicial institution'.[104]

As noted earlier, Justices of the Supreme Court are by Royal Warrant granted the courtesy title of Lord or Lady, which they retain for life. They are not, however, given peerages by virtue of their office. Since 2009, no Supreme Court Justice has been appointed to the House of Lords after their retirement. Lord Reed of Allermuir was granted a peerage upon his appointment as President, his Lordship being the Court's first President not already to be a peer.[105] So the currently serving Justices may not expect to sit in the House of Lords after their judicial retirement. But by virtue of their courtesy title and their record of judicial service, Justices retain a certain status in the eyes of the media and the public.

The Supreme Court has a *Guide to Judicial Conduct* for serving Justices,[106] and a separate Guide for conduct for Retired Justices who are also members of the Supplementary Panel, who can serve until they reach 75 if they have otherwise retired from the Court before then.[107] All the Memoir Justices had retired altogether from the bench by the time they published their Memoirs: In June 2025, the Court published a Guide to Conduct for Retired Justices:[108] so far no retired Justice has published a memoir since that Guide was introduced.

[101] P Girard, 'Judging Lives: Judicial Biography from Hale to Holmes' (2003) 7 *Australian Journal of Legal History* 87, 101.

[102] G Appleby and A Blackham, 'The Shadow of the Court: The Growing Imperative to reform Ethical Regulation of Former Judges' (2018) 67 *International and Comparative Law Quarterly* 505.

[103] ibid 507.

[104] ibid 546. See also P O'Brien and B Yong, *Work in Judicial Retirement. A Policy Report* (The Judicial Afterlife Project, June 2023) https://sites.google.com/brookes.ac.uk/the-judicial-afterlife.

[105] Lord Phillips and Lady Hale were among the last Law Lords and the first members of the Supreme Court as provided for by s 24 of the CRA 2005. Lord Neuberger served in the House of Lords until 2009, but stepped down before the inauguration of the UKSC, in order to become Master of Rolls in October 2009, and then became President of the Supreme Court in 2012, retiring at 69 in 2017 (his Lordship turned 70 in January 2018).

[106] UK Supreme Court, *Guide to Judicial Conduct* (revised 2019) https://www.supremecourt.uk/uploads/uksc_guide_to_judicial_conduct_a456af62f8.pdf.

[107] UK Supreme Court, *Guide to Conduct for Members of the Supplementary Panel* (last updated August 2021) https://www.supremecourt.uk/uploads/UKSC_guide_to_conduct_supplementary_panel_cdcf133083.pdf.

[108] The Supreme Court of the United Kingdom and the Judicial Committee of the Privy Council, *Guide to Conduct for Retired Justices* (revised 2025) https://www.supremecourt.uk/uploads/Guidance_for_retired_justice_3858fbeb7b.pdf. For further consideration of retired judges in this collection see Chapter 7: H Tyrrell, 'Extrajudicial Communication: What Changes in Retirement?'.

The 2019 Guide places emphasis on the primary responsibility being upon each Justice individually to make decisions about the appropriateness of particular activities, with the opportunity if in doubt to seek the advice of the President or Deputy President.[109] The Guide recognises that Justices may carry out extra-curial activities such as lectures, attending conferences or teaching. The aim of such work, says the Guide, 'is to enhance professional and public understanding of the issues and of the role of the Court'.[110] But in promoting public understanding, Justices must show 'appropriate caution and restraint when explaining or commenting publicly upon their decisions in individual cases'.[111] We have seen above that this practice has not been consistently observed in the Memoirs.

In 2021, the Court published the *Guide to Conduct for Members of the Supplementary Panel*. This Guide notes that the Guide for serving Justices does not apply to them. The 2025 Guide for Retired Justices applies to all retired members of the Court, whether or not they are also subject to the Guide for Supplementary Panel members by serving in that capacity. Interestingly, both Guides contain an almost identical list of examples of relevant post-retirement[112] activity:

> Retired Justices of the Supreme Court have accepted appointment as arbitrators, conducted inquiries, sat as judges of foreign courts, given speeches to commercial or trade promotion organisations, published their memoirs, participated in the work of the House of Lords, and contributed to public debate, for example by taking part in discussion panels or giving media interviews[113]

The only difference in the list is that the Retired Justices' Guide goes on to specify that the media interviews have been 'on legal matters and the administration of justice'.[114]

We can note that the publication of memoirs is expressly mentioned as an example of post-retirement activity. We can then compare how the Guides deal with the activities of retired Justices who are Panel Members and those who are not. The Supplementary Guide continues:[115]

> None of these post-retirement activities necessarily runs counter to the UKSC Conduct Guide, but some of them are capable of presenting risks to public confidence in the independence and impartiality of Panel members, and in the Supreme Court generally.[116]

The 2021 Guide continues to note that such extra-judicial activities of Panel members 'are therefore relevant to the Court's reputation for the duration of their membership

[109] 2019 Guide (above n 106), para 1.4.
[110] ibid para 3.4.
[111] ibid para 2.5.
[112] In this instance I use 'post-retirement' to mean retiring from serving as a Justice of the Court, rather than potentially also from the Supplementary Panel.
[113] 2021 Guide (above n 107), para 4; 2025 Guide (above n 108) para 5.
[114] 2025 Guide (above n 108), para 5.
[115] 2021 Guide (above n 107), para 4.
[116] ibid.

of the Panel, whether or not they are ever invited to sit on a case'.[117] As a result, Panel members are asked to provide an undertaking as to conduct

> which will (i) hold Panel members to high standards, equivalent to those expected of serving Justices; (ii) protect the Court's reputation; and (iii) take account of the legitimate extra-judicial activities which many Panel members undertake.[118]

That undertaking provides that the judge:

> will so conduct myself, in court and out of it, as not to throw doubt on my character, integrity, or continuing fitness to serve on the Supplementary Panel, and will not engage in any activity which would compromise my independence or impartiality or the performance of my duties or functions in respect of cases on which I may be invited to sit.[119]

It is notable that the *undertaking* does not refer directly to the *Court*'s independence or institutional integrity, which is identified as vulnerable in the 2021 Guide.

The Retired Justices' Guide notes after the list of activities above[120] that

> None of these post-retirement activities necessarily runs counter to this guidance, but some of them are capable of presenting risks to public confidence in the independence and impartiality of Justices, and in the Court itself. Retired Justices are publicly identified as such and their post-retirement activities are therefore relevant to the Court's reputation.[121]

The wording here refers to Justices, plural, which points to the potential for any activity to have a bearing on the perception of other members of the Court, as well the individual retired Justice.

There is no undertaking required of retired Justices who are not members of the Supplementary Panel. Instead, the Retired Justices' Guide asks for discretion: 'Retired Justices should therefore exercise discretion as to whether their retirement activities might compromise the Court's independence or impartiality, actual or perceived'.[122] Particular areas are then identified, such as avoided party-political activities or public commentary on issues of party-political controversy.[123] The Guide states

> Caution should also be exercised about the public expression of opinions about high-profile issues of public policy or about matters that have come before the Court. In cases of doubt, advice should be sought from the President of the Court.[124]

It may be thought that the Memoirs involve examples of public expression of opinion about matters that have come before the Court. We have thus seen that there are provisions in the Guides which may engage some of the controversies raised by memoirs, and indeed the Supplementary Guide and Retired Justices' Guide *expressly* refer to memoirs. But despite that express mention, the measures required do not address specific ways in which memoirs can be challenging in this context. There is only one

[117] ibid para 5.
[118] ibid para 10.
[119] ibid para 12.
[120] Text to n 113 above.
[121] 2025 Guide (above n 108), para 6.
[122] ibid.
[123] 2025 Guide (above n 108), para 7.
[124] ibid.

mention of confidentiality in any of the three Guides, which is the 2019 Guide for serving Justices. It provides that 'Confidential information acquired by a Justice in his or her judicial capacity will not be used or disclosed by the Justice for any purpose not related to his or her judicial duties'.[125] The Guide could usefully clarify the definition of confidential information. It might be understood to refer to information relating to trade secrets or financial information of the parties, for example. But expectations of confidence might also extend to the deliberations of Justices. And there could be express reference to the statutory duty of confidence with respect to appointments. The *Guide to Conduct for Members of the Supplementary Panel* and the *Guide to Conduct for Retired Justices* do not refer to confidentiality at all.

I would therefore argue that there is a case for articulating the expectations on retired Justices when it comes to their memoirs. The current Guides to Conduct are not sufficient. There will be a range of views over what the approach should be,[126] but it should be considered amongst the Justices and addressed. Collective discussion would be a better approach than resting so much on individual judgement, and on discretion being the better part of valour. Indeed, Lord Dyson has called for an obligation of confidentiality with respect to judicial deliberations to be added to the *Guide to Judicial Conduct*.[127] Finally, there should be express reference to the continuing statutory duty of confidence with respect to appointments processes included in all three Guides.[128]

VII. CONCLUSIONS

My argument here has been that there is value in engaging with the memoir as a form of extra-judicial communication. At a time of scholarly interest in life writing more widely, the distinctive category of judicial autobiography merits attention. The coincidence of four Justices' memoirs appearing in close temporal proximity gives us fresh perspectives on the early life of the United Kingdom Supreme Court. My aim has been to highlight ways in which such memoirs can be both a valuable source for judicial scholars and a discrete genre worthy of examination. As Justice Felix Frankfurter of the US Supreme Court once wrote,

> A member of the Supreme Court is at once a soloist and part of an orchestra. While dissenting opinions seem like solo performances, even that is not always true and, in any event, the private rehearsals, as it were, behind the impenetrable draperies of judicial secrecy may tell much more about the soloist and the rest of the orchestra than the public performance even remotely reveals.[129]

[125] 2019 Guide (above n 106), para 5.4.

[126] As shown by the wide range of views on post-retirement activities more generally found by O'Brien and Yong in their interviews: *Work in Judicial Retirement* (above n 104).

[127] Dyson, Birkenhead Lecture (above n 27) para 45.

[128] It might be thought to be rare that judges would publish any form of memoirs while they are still serving, but the 2019 Guide should still address the point.

[129] Letter from Frankfurter to Professor Charles Fairman from 27 December 1948, published in C Fairman, 'The Writing of Judicial Biography – A Symposium' (1949) 24 *Indiana Law Journal* 363, 367.

The publication of judicial memoirs, and the study of them, can reveal much of what goes on backstage, by pulling back the curtain. They can offer insights that contextualise the public history of a court.

In addition, I have identified and addressed various issues – what the approach should be to confidentiality, for example, with respect to discussions amongst the Justices and with respect to appointments. We have seen that the Supreme Court has increased its self-governance in respect of extra-curial activities of serving Justices, those on its Supplementary Panel and those who have retired: memoirs are expressly mentioned as an example of an activity which is 'capable of presenting risks to public confidence in … the Supreme Court generally'. As it stands, the only clear obligation of confidentiality is the statutory duty with respect to confidential information obtained during a process relating to a selection commission. Lord Hope nonetheless disclosed extensive information in his diaries: the existing mechanisms for enforcing that duty, notably the prospect of a civil suit by a serving Justice of the Supreme Court against a retired Justice, may be thought to be a limited deterrent.

Judicial memoirs typically represent 'each author's deliberate effort to generalize from particular experiences and to convey a personal vision of a public life'.[130] The revelations in these memoirs are not merely about who said what when, and who changed their minds, but rather each Justice reveals their own thoughts. Speaking in the American context, J Woodford Howard, Jr has noted bluntly that 'judicial biographies are basically case studies in judic[i]al politics'.[131] Judicial (auto-)biographies may thus also be case studies in judicial politics, enduring after retirement. The authors of memoirs have many different purposes: two of the most common are to remember well, but also to be well-remembered.

[130] Krugman Ray (above n 1) 240.

[131] J Woodford Howard, Jr, 'Judicial Biography and the Behavioral Persuasion' (1971) 65 *American Political Science Review* 704, 707.

16

Ermine Trims and Marmite Toast: Judicial Portraits from Extrajudicial Aesthetics

ANURAG DEB

I. INTRODUCTION

ACROSS THE UK, the veil of judicial unknowability is gradually being lifted. Courts – so we are asked to believe – are staffed by people no different from anyone else, and in this vein, judges too are like anyone else, marked only by the seriousness of their work rather than the aloofness of their characters. Judges now more readily give interviews in national newspapers, appear in documentaries and podcasts and even star in bespoke outreach videos designed for recruitment, all while holding office – rare or unthinkable as these things once might have been. Greater prominence in the public eye brings greater public scrutiny, with senior judges pointedly asked questions around politically controversial decisions or issues, continued gender imbalance in the courts and their personal tastes. In contrast to the more traditional modes of extrajudicial appearance, such as lectures or infrequent parliamentary engagement, these more recent modes purport to make the judge much more publicly accessible – literally, on anyone's personal entertainment device. But who is this judge? And to what extent is this judge – who remains frequently robed and wigged both in and out of court – accessible?

This chapter critically explores the idea of the judge in the public eye through a series of illustrative examples of extrajudicial appearances, exploring their aesthetic framing and what this framing tells us about the judiciary today.

II. SETTING THE SCENE: THE JUDGE IN THE PUBLIC EYE

In an October 2024 article in *The Times*, Lord Reed, President of the UK Supreme Court, is credited with expanding the visibility of the Supreme Court, particularly among underrepresented cohorts within the judiciary: 'The idea is that they get to know the set-up, see what a friendly place it is, how nice my colleagues are. Hopefully, they will think about applying. It's important … that we're not regarded as some sort of ivory tower'.[1] The accompanying pictures, while not necessarily setting Lord Reed in an ivory tower, nevertheless place him in august surroundings. He is robed in the gold-trimmed, black silk damask of his office (and those of his colleagues), standing in one photo and sitting in another amid the 'art nouveau gothic'[2] décor of Middlesex Guildhall, which houses the Court. The article briefly explores Lord Reed's childhood and his entry into law, finishing with some anodyne details (questions include 'Whisky or beer?' and 'Country weekend or city break?') about his personal tastes. Nevertheless, the only pictorial accompaniment firmly situates the President in his own court, arguably echoing the truism 'The Court *is* its judges; its judges *are* the Court'.[3]

Similarly, interviews with and articles about Dame Siobhan Keegan, Lady Chief Justice of Northern Ireland, and Baroness Carr of Walton-on-the-Hill, Lady Chief Justice of England and Wales, the first women to lead their respective judiciaries (with Dame Siobhan additionally being the first woman to lead any of the UK's three jurisdictions), situate both presiding judges in their own courts. Dame Siobhan sits in her warmly lit and richly wood-panelled judicial chambers under the portraits of her male predecessors,[4] while Lady Carr gazes out from the Royal Courts of Justice in London, wearing the ermine-trimmed, scarlet robes and full-bottomed wig of her office.[5] Yet, much like the personal detail afterthoughts in Lord Reed's interview, Dame Siobhan speaks briefly (and in general terms) about the women who inspired her younger self, while among the scant personal details of Lady Carr's story are her birthplace (Surrey) and that of her father having been a one-time director of Arsenal Football Club.

The point I am making here, that judges appear extrajudicially in specific aesthetic surroundings, is far from novel. Aesthetics have played defining roles in leadership for a long time and, although frequently associated with political leaders,[6] judges are leaders in their own right. But the aesthetics of the extrajudicial appearance in the examples I have set out thus far foreground the judicial *office* and are therefore dissonant with the accompanying (albeit brief) attempts to personalise the judicial *subject*. Why, for example, is Lord Reed, being fond of both whisky and beer,[7] not pictured with a glass of either? This dissonance – and the aesthetic harmony which sometimes

[1] F Gibb, 'Lord Reed: How we will decide what constitutes a woman', *The Times* (London, 4 October 2024).

[2] N Pevsner, *London: The cities of London and Westminster* (London, Penguin, 1973) 513.

[3] L Graham, *Judicial Individuality in the Supreme Court* (Oxford, Hart Publishing, 2025) 1.

[4] S Clarke, 'Dame Siobhan Keegan on legacy, bringing the legal system into the digital age and wearing a wig' *ITV* (31 October 2022).

[5] D Casciani, 'Dame Sue Carr is first Lady Chief Justice, the top judge for England and Wales', *BBC* (2 October 2023).

[6] See eg VA Howard, 'The Aesthetic Face of Leadership' (1996) 30(4) *The Journal of Aesthetic Education* 21; D Pels, 'Aesthetic Representation and Political Style; Re-balancing Identity and Difference in Media Democracy' in J Corner and D Pels (eds), *Media and the Restyling of Politics* (Sage, 2003) 41; and R Ramirez, 'Aesthetics and Leadership: An Essay' (2021) 41(7) *Psychoanalytic Inquiry* 488.

[7] Gibb (above n 1).

contrasts with it – ultimately provides insights into the nature of the publicly accessible judge.

Before we turn to the detail – of the aesthetics, its dissonance and harmony – we must appreciate the role played by extrajudicial 'art' and its value as a social critique.

III. FRAMING THE PORTRAIT: ADORNO AND THE 'BEING-IN-ITSELF' OF ART

The study of aesthetics as a way of discerning the nature of beauty is a long-established field of philosophical enquiry. Within this field, the work of German philosopher Theodor Adorno focuses on the mediation between art and its viewer:

> The being-in-itself of art is not an imitation of something real but an anticipation of a being-in-itself yet to come, of an unknown that will determine itself through the subject. Works of art state that there is an in-itself, but they do not spell out what it is.[8]

In its autonomy from something real, art thus exists to signify its own aesthetic value, determined through those who view it. Moreover, art serves to 'affront prevailing needs by throwing new light on the familiar, thus meeting the objective need for a change in consciousness that might ultimately lead to a change of reality.'[9]

These themes – art containing its own aesthetic value discernible by its viewers and serving as a social critique simply by virtue of its own existence – enable a reflexively critical exploration of artistic representations of society. The viewer is an active – indeed enthusiastic – participant in the determination of aesthetic value which underlies the critique of the viewer's society, simultaneously generating and answering a 'call to action'.[10] What this call to action is and how it is answered are fundamental questions which serve to shine a light on (for example) institutions and offices of great social importance – in this case, the court and the judge.

Aesthetic critiques in legal scholarship are well established, especially in critical legal scholarship.[11] Specific examples include Illan rua Wall and Daniel Matthews' exploration of the aesthetic dimensions of the concept of sovereignty in constitutional thinking,[12] Marett Leiboff's exploration of law through theatre[13] and Nathan Moore's exploration of law's controlling social influence through icons.[14] I situate this chapter within these wider traditions of aesthetic legal critiques and ask what insights the aesthetics of extrajudicial appearances tell us about the judge and

[8] T Adorno, *Aesthetic Theory* (Christian Lenhardt trans, Gretel Adorno and Rolf Tiedemann (eds), London, Routledge and Keegan Paul, 1984) 114.

[9] ibid 345.

[10] ibid.

[11] For a detailed overview, see eg A Philippopoulos-Mihalopoulos, 'Law is Stage: from Aesthetics to Affective Aestheses' in E Christodoulidis, R Dukes and M Goldoni (eds), *Research Handbook on Critical Legal Theory* (Cheltenham, Edward Elgar Publishing, 2019) 201.

[12] I Wall and D Matthews, 'Sovereignty and the Persistence of the Aesthetic' (2024) 87(6) *Modern Law Review* 1393.

[13] M Leiboff, 'Threatricalizing Law' (2018) 30(2) *Law and Literature* 351.

[14] N Moore, 'Icons of Control: Deleuze, Signs, Law' (2007) 20(1) *International Journal for the Semiotics of Law* 33.

the court today. I devote the next two sections to two different kinds of extrajudicial aesthetics: the first with examples of the dissonance which I briefly explored earlier, where the aesthetic surroundings of the judicial subject are largely at odds with the subject itself; and the second with examples of aesthetic harmony with the judicial subject, where the subject is situated within their aesthetic surroundings, leading to an integrated whole of subject and surroundings.

Before moving on, I pause to make two caveats. First, I am not saying that the majority or even plurality of extrajudicial appearances is grounded in an aesthetic which is dissonant with attempts to personalise the judicial subject. I am not interested in the numerical prevalence of one or other kind of aesthetic framing; I am simply interested in what aesthetic dissonance says about judges and courts, especially when compared to aesthetic harmony. Art (broadly defined) does not provide social critique because its themes or aesthetic values permeate some critical numerical mass of artworks; it critiques simply by existing (as above).

Second, because the aesthetic value – the 'being-in-itself' – of art is determined through the subject, I am not interested in the intentions behind the aesthetic choices explored in this chapter. For example, interviews with judges may be subject to myriad factors and interests which condition and constrain the aesthetic choices in which these interviews are presented. Considerations of what is properly disclosable by the judge, how far the judge in question is comfortable being pushed in specific directions, the interview's target audience, and so on, are just some of the factors which may condition the aesthetic choices of the interview (most obviously, for example, whether the judge is comfortable being interviewed in their own home). But these factors, some of which are explored extensively and much more insightfully by the other contributors in this volume,[15] are not the focus of this chapter. Instead, I am interested in what insights can be gleaned solely from what is presented – in other words, the *finished product*. From a scholarly perspective, these insights are part of critical scholarship on the interaction between law and society. More practically, these critical reflections can enable those who create the kinds of aesthetics explored here to reflect on their impact and to modify such aesthetics accordingly.

IV. SEEING AND SAYING

The first example of aesthetic dissonance is the interview series *The Judges: Power, Politics and the People*, hosted by legal journalist Frances Gibb and The University of Law.[16] I draw some broad aesthetic themes from this series rather than exploring each (hour-or-so-long) episode of a 12-part series in detail. Most episodes follow the same format: Gibb interviews a former judge about their judicial career, with brief glimpses into their background and entry into the legal profession, discussions about

[15] See eg Chapter 9: Alan Paterson, 'Judicial Interviews'; Chapter 10: Rachel Cahill O'Callaghan, 'The Individual Voice in a Collective Court: Insights from Judicial Lectures'.

[16] The University of Law Podcast, *The Judges: Power, Politics and the People* www.youtube.com/playlist?list=PLIr_gf3NNn2jvMHVS4oFnGTigu8mroujy.

some interesting, memorable or influential cases which they have tried and more pointed discussions about the judge's concerns with the legal system, and frequently, the attitude of the government towards it. In these discussions, the judges provide rich, insightful and sometimes frank commentary, pushing back against publicly held (or reported) notions of who they are and how they work.

Much like its format, the series aesthetic is also largely the same across its 12-episode run. The background in most episodes is unmistakeably *official*: heavy tomes and collections of papers line shelves and the interior decor – with instances of traditional wood-panelling and intricately decorated fireplaces[17] – evokes institutional endurance and longevity (especially the episode filmed inside the 'vast and handsome' Victorian gothic Royal Courts of Justice on the Strand).[18] Other aesthetics – for example the interview of Baroness Elizabeth Butler-Sloss[19] in what appears to be a domestic[20] setting – nevertheless exude a strong sense of tradition. Gibb and Lady Butler-Sloss sit across from one another in large chesterfield chairs, framed by floral curtains, bathed in natural light which enters through a set of double doors leading out to a balcony behind them. In front of them are richly varnished wooden tables (one of which is intricately carved), each with delicately patterned porcelain teacups.[21] This strong sense of tradition continues in the interview of Lord Mackay of Clashfern,[22] who sits in what appears to be a dining room, complete with two ornately framed paintings rendered in a classical style, darkly lacquered and traditional wooden furniture with intricate glassware, a bookshelf and elaborately decorated sconces.

The dissonance of the series' aesthetic with the personalisation of the judges is, on one level, obvious: there is no connection between the two. Even where interviewees such as Lady Butler-Sloss, Lord Mackay of Clashfern, and Lord Phillips of Worth Matravers[23] sit in clearly domestic surroundings, there is no attempt – either within the interview or in the precis of each episode – to *situate* the judge in their surroundings. It is not so much that the judicial subject needs to account for or personalise each aesthetic element in their surroundings, but more that the surroundings – especially the domestic surroundings – should have some personal connection with the subject. The lack of personalisation is at odds with the content of many of the episodes – whether the personal reflections on the role of women in the senior judiciary by Lady Butler-Sloss and Lady Hale[24] or the frequent and frank (and at times terse) reflections on judicial relationships with ministers and the media. But the lack of personalisation

[17] A standout being the elaborately decorated gothic fireplace in the interview of former Lord Chief Justice of England and Wales Lord Burnett of Maldon (2017–23), *The Judges: Power, Politics and the People* (above n 16) Episode 9: Lord Burnett (14 March 2024).

[18] E Anthony, 'The Royal Courts of Justice' (1899) III(3) *Chicago Law Times* 269, 270. The episode in question is the interview of Lord Burnett, ibid.

[19] President of the Family Division of the High Court of England and Wales (1999–2005).

[20] At no point are we told whether this is in fact a domestic setting or whose home it is.

[21] *The Judges: Power, Politics and the People* (above n 16) Episode 7: Lady Butler-Sloss (8 February 2024).

[22] Lord Chancellor (1987–97). *The Judges: Power, Politics and the People* (above n 16) Episode 8 (29 February 2024).

[23] President of the UK Supreme Court (2009–12). *The Judges: Power, Politics and the People* (above n 16) Episode 5: Lord Phillips (10 January 2024).

[24] President of the UK Supreme Court (2017–20).

ultimately makes the broader aesthetic themes of each episode – tradition and professionalism – largely interchangeable with one another, which are in any event subservient to the discussions between Gibb and the judges. These discussions, although personalised, are personalised in the distinctly *professional* sphere; in other words, each interviewee reflects personally on their career – especially their judicial career – much more so than on their personal background, temperament, character and relationships.

What thus aesthetically emerges is a judicial archetype – with packed bookshelves, traditionally designed furniture and classical art acting as its symbols. This archetype sustains the legitimacy of the judicial role within the state: even at their most emotive, when discussing tensions between ministers and judges, the judges anchor their answers to the proper functioning of the constitution and of government itself. During his extensive and forthright commentary[25] on his fraught relationship with then Lord Chancellor, Elizabeth Truss, for example, Lord Thomas of Cwmgiedd speaks of the *official* tension: not between Truss and Thomas, but between the Lord Chancellor and the Lord Chief Justice. I return to this theme of the judicial archetype as a symbol sustaining judicial legitimacy further below.

The second example of aesthetic dissonance is Dame Siobhan in a brief appearance in the BBC podcast series *Lady Killers with Lucy Worsley*, hosted by historian Lucy Worsley. The format of this is very different from the interview series hosted by Gibb. Worsley discusses historical offences committed by women, taking her audience through the facts of the offences, the lives of the women who were convicted, situating these stories in their historical and sociopolitical (especially gendered) contexts, with guests contributing to specific aspects of Worsley's discussion. It is also primarily an aural experience,[26] with the only visual point often being the series' title cover.

The episode – 'Jane and Ann Boyd – Secret Baby'[27] – is set in nineteenth-century Holywood, presently a town outside Belfast, Northern Ireland, along the shores of the Belfast Lough. Worsley takes us through the grim story of an infanticide committed – it is strongly suggested – by the grandmother of the newborn baby, her hand greatly forced by the poverty, religiosity, lack of privacy and wider sexual politics of rural nineteenth-century Ireland. Like every other episode in the series, Worsley narrates the facts of the case and its wider social context, brought to life by actors playing some of the relevant people involved in the case (such as neighbours and police officers) and emotionally anchored by an anxious musical score.

Dame Siobhan provides the legal context of the case. After some brief remarks from Worsley about Dame Siobhan's rise through the legal profession to the senior judiciary and appointment as Northern Ireland's first female Chief Justice, as well as the changing gender balance within the legal profession and the judiciary in

[25] *The Judges: Power, Politics and the People* (above n 16) Episode 4: Lord Thomas (12 December 2023).

[26] Though some episodes feature a video recording (see eg Series 3 episode 21, available at https://www.youtube.com/watch?v=4u0CVvT-1j4&list=PL4Z-TOtZ0iIMnelGR9LMpn2dQnOvAZ1b9) the episode analysed in this chapter is an audio recording only.

[27] *Lady Killers with Lucy Worsley*, Series 3, episode 23: 'Jane and Ann Boyd – Secret Baby', BBC (8 January 2024).

Northern Ireland, she asks Dame Siobhan to provide insights on the legal modalities of the case: the ingredients of the offence, the evidence and credibility of the witnesses and the mind of the judge trying the case. These insights are peppered with Dame Siobhan's brief and general reflections on the sociopolitical context of the case.

Analytically, although the primarily aural experience of the podcast might appear to preclude an exploration of its aesthetics in the same way as the video recordings of Gibb's judicial interviews at the start of this section, the podcast can also have a powerfully visual impact without a commensurately prominent (or even explicit) visual component. Elements such as the involvement of actors and an emotionally resonant musical score – both prominent in Worsley's series – engage with a listener's 'cinematic imagination'. As film and media critic Dario Llinares observes, 'Podcasting is simply a secondary platform whereby sound properties are utilised to affirm the primary experience of cinema'.[28] Consequently, the aesthetic of Worsley's podcast is distinctly personal: bringing the stories of Victorian women convicted of serious offences to life through the immersive use of actors, sounds and music.

What is important for this chapter, however, is Dame Siobhan's engagement with this aesthetic. The Lady Chief Justice's reflections on the Boyd case are mainly general and impersonal: primarily through the lens of an impartial observer of the case as it unfolds, rather than the judge trying *that* case. Equally general and impersonal are Dame Siobhan's reflections on the sociopolitical context of the Boyd case. In response to Worsley revealing the rise in infanticide at the relevant time, for example, stressing the lack of options for unwanted pregnancies in nineteenth-century Ireland, Dame Siobhan observes, 'I think it [the rise in infanticides] correlates with how children were viewed and valued in society, linked to poverty and social conditions and social hierarchy'[29] without offering what those views, values, conditions and hierarchies might have been or how different (or similar) these might have been to her own experiences – whether personal or as a notable family lawyer, High Court judge and Lady Chief Justice. Whatever the motivations or intentions behind the impersonal quality of these reflections, what matters for my analysis is that these reflections are impersonal, contrasting with the deeply personal aesthetics of the episode and the podcast in general. The polarity of the aesthetic dissonance here is reversed from that in Gibb's interviews, where the personalised nature of the judges' answers contrasted with the impersonal, largely interchangeable aesthetics of each episode. The reversal reflects the role of the judge in each example: Gibb spotlit the judges themselves, whereas Worsley delves into the offences and the women who committed them.

I contrast the examples of aesthetic dissonance discussed in this section with examples of aesthetic harmony in the next section, taken from one (albeit notable) source.

[28] D Llinares, 'A Cinema for the Ears: Imagining the Audio-Cinematic through Podcasting' (2020) 24(3) *Film-Philosophy* 341, 342.

[29] 'Jane and Ann Boyd – Secret Baby' (above n 27), between 21:12 and 21:25.

V. S(AY)EEING

In 2011, the BBC broadcast a documentary about the then two-year-old UK Supreme Court. This documentary, entitled *The Highest Court in the Land: Justice Makers* featured four of the Court's first Justices: its then President, Lord Phillips, then Deputy President, Lord Hope, Lady Hale and Lord Kerr. The Justices mostly discuss the work of the Court and how they approach the kinds of controversial issues – such as the expenses scandal involving UK Members of Parliament[30] – which end up on appeal before them. Interspersed with these discussions are personal reflections on justice and the rule of law, as well as personal insights. In the latter context, two vignettes stand out: Lord Kerr and Lady Hale.

In the first vignette, Lord Kerr is in the kitchen of his London home preparing breakfast for his wife. He prepares eggs, toast with Marmite and tea – of which he is, by his own admission, fond of none. Nevertheless, he says, 'I say to [his wife] that I earn, in consequence, zillions of brownie points. But it's a bit like airmiles – you never get to spend them'.[31] The aesthetic is (in contrast with the general domestic aesthetics of the judges in Gibb's interviews in the previous section) modern, even sparse: the kitchen walls, cupboards and countertop are all cream coloured, with a small pop art print of four jars of Marmite hung on one of the walls. The space is lit by soft recessed lighting. On a shelf sit anthropomorphically decorated egg cups wearing colourful little egg cosies. A toaster, an electric kettle and two cafetieres can be seen on the countertop in the background as Lord Kerr assembles his wife's breakfast meticulously on a tray before bringing it to her.

The second vignette is also set in a kitchen, this time with Lady Hale and her husband sitting around a table with a bag of groceries. Lady Hale peels apples while her husband reads a newspaper. She says, 'my husband does most of the main course cooking, so I tend to do the starters and the puddings and he does the main course'.[32] The kitchen, in contrast to the sparse modernity of Lord Kerr, is much more varied and colourful in its décor, with wooden cupboards and a wooden cabinet, the table topped with a colourful cover of fruits and flowers and candles sitting in candleholders with intricately detailed fruit and foliage. Through a window in the upper left corner of the shot, a hedge can be seen, its top half gleaming in the sun.

The point here is not to draw insights about either Justice's cooking, their relationships with their spouses or even for either Justice to account for their interior design – it is simply about the fact that both vignettes *situate* their judges in their aesthetic surroundings. Lord Kerr and Lady Hale are not simply in their respective homes, they are talking about and carrying out domestic tasks which have nothing to do with their judicial roles. There is something deeply personal in each vignette, before even delving into their aesthetic details. This contrasts with the vignettes about the other two Justices in the 2011 documentary. Lord Phillips and Lord Hope, when pictured at home, are shown reading case papers intently while discussing the way

[30] *R v Chaytor* [2010] UKSC 52, [2011] 1 AC 684, which involved a number of MPs charged with false accounting relating to their expenses as MPs.

[31] *The Highest Court in the Land: Justice Makers*, BBC (27 January 2011), between 17:28 and 17:42.

[32] ibid between 20:25 and 20:42.

they both work. Additionally, in the only scene in the documentary in which Lord Hope takes the viewer around his living room, he shows and comments on two of his professional portraits – the first as Dean of the Faculty of Advocates in Scotland and the second as Lord Justice General of Scotland[33] – explaining, 'you wanted to see some pictures of my previous existence'.[34] It is telling that Lord Hope's existence prior to the Supreme Court – at least in this scene – is limited to the apex of both the Scottish legal profession and its judiciary. The foregrounding of the judicial role for both Lord Phillips and Lord Hope – whether they are pictured in the Supreme Court or at home – blurs any kind of aesthetic distinction between their workplaces and their homes. Aesthetically, this blurring makes the workplace and the home largely interchangeable in terms of broader aesthetic themes; in contrast with Lord Kerr and Lady Hale who have clearly separated existences in each sphere, Lord Phillips and Lord Hope appear as *Justices* both in court and at home.

VI. DISSONANCE AND THE PARADOX OF THE PUBLICLY ACCESSIBLE JUDGE

Aesthetic dissonance in the extrajudicial sphere has significant effects for the idea of the publicly accessible judge. Consider the aesthetics of Gibb's interviews. Although the interviews are largely unscored, shortened versions of the series' opening musical score play at moments of each episode which mark a change in the topic of discussion. This makes the music of the series interchangeable between judges, the topics Gibb covers with them and their reflections on these topics. The interchangeability of the music thus parallels the interchangeability of the visual themes in each episode (as covered above) and across the episodes more generally. Here, any aesthetic particularities – whether visual or musical – disappear in the face of the discursive content of each episode. Moreover, the musical score of the series has an unmistakably classical resonance, with a terse arrangement of strings which musically underscores the gravity and solemnity of the judicial role. What thus comes across – both visually (as above) and musically – in terms of aesthetics is a judicial archetype rooted in professionalism and tradition.

In Worsley's podcast, the musical score complements the discussions of violent offences committed by the women on whom she focuses, as well as the actors who bring these women and their circumstances to life for the listener. This complementarity is missing in the discussions with Dame Siobhan: her segments are unscored, and what she says is more general of the role of a judge in trying cases than the particular circumstances of the case of the Boyd infanticide. The judge in the Boyd case is not analysed in his own right or with reference to Dame Siobhan's particular experience as a judge, but de-contextualised in favour of a judicial archetype. This makes Dame Siobhan's reflections among the least personal part of the episode.

[33] The presiding judge of the High Court of Justiciary, Scotland's highest criminal court. The post is held concurrently with that of the Lord President of the Court of Session, and thus also at the apex of civil justice in Scotland.

[34] *The Highest Court in the Land* (above n 31), between 14:34 and 14:37.

The judicial archetype is writ large in the pictures accompanying the interview of Lord Reed and the article about Lady Carr: pictured in the ceremonial dress of their offices, the personal yields almost entirely to the professional. In Dame Siobhan's interview (explored at the start of this chapter) her predecessors in office gazing down from their portraits in which they are also ceremonially robed and wigged leave little if, any room, for any personal aesthetic accompaniment to the Lady Chief Justice.

The role of this archetype in sustaining judicial legitimacy recalls critical scholarship on legal semiotics, in particular, Nathan Moore's work on law as a sign of control. Moore looks to the works of philosophers Charles Sanders Peirce and Giles Deleuze to conceptualise the relationship between law and control as a sign, and more specifically as an icon. The conceptual reasoning is somewhat dense, and its detail is largely unnecessary for present purposes. Importantly, Moore tells us that law as a sign resolves to three kinds of sign: an icon, an index and a symbol. Law as a symbol of control, 'refer[s] to modulated conceptualisations, where what is capable of being thought is dependent upon what it is appropriate and efficient to think in any given situation'.[35] The judicial archetype's aesthetic symbols covered in this chapter (robes, wigs, books and papers, traditional furniture and classical art and music) serve to condition the thinking around the institution which they represent (the judiciary) by reference to how to think *appropriately* about that institution. The judiciary is largely traditional *and* legitimate, but it is legitimate *because* it is largely traditional. In this sustenance of legitimacy through tradition therefore, the idiosyncratic personal disappears almost entirely beneath the stable and homogenous professional. As former Israeli Supreme Court President Aharon Barak puts it:

> Inside and outside the court, judges must act in a manner that preserves public confidence in them. They must understand that judging is not merely a job but a way of life. It is a way of life that does not include the pursuit of material wealth or publicity; it is a way of life based on spiritual wealth; it is a way of life that includes an on objective and impartial search for truth.[36]

A distinct problem arises, however, in the interaction of this archetype with the claim at the start of this chapter – that it is important to view judges accessibly. Accessibility matters because it is a stated goal of the judiciary to be more representative of the society which it serves.[37] Accessibility is thus an important part of how the public views the judiciary and, by extension, its legitimacy.[38] So important is judicial accessibility, that an explicit part of the role of a UK Supreme Court Justice is outreach work,[39] and judges appearing in video recordings designed for recruitment

[35] Moore (above n 14) 52.

[36] A Barak, *The Judge in a Democracy* (Princeton NJ, Princeton University Press, 2006) 110.

[37] See eg, House of Lords Constitution Committee, transcript of Evidence Session 1 (1 May 2024), Lord Reed's answer to Question 7, p 12, See also the UKSC website, 'Diversity and Inclusion'. On this see in this volume, Chapter 6: Erika Rackley, 'Uncomfortable truths, clichés and real dilemmas: Extrajudicial discourse on judicial diversity'.

[38] See the Judicial Diversity and Inclusion Strategy 2020–2025 applicable in England and Wales, p 10.

[39] See eg UK Supreme Court, *UK Supreme Court Justice recruitment – 2023* (28 April 2023) www.youtube.com/watch?v=1JyKTZa4j-k, between 1:07 and 1:10.

are a growing genre of extrajudicial appearances, whether at the senior[40] or junior[41] curial level.

But although judges are more available to the wider public through appearances outside of the courts in which they work, availability does not necessarily mean *accessibility*. Instead, the inner workings of the court – as an archetypal institution – are being made somewhat more publicly available than they might have been in decades past.

Access is more complex. According to disabled dancer and choreographer Alice Sheppard, it is an aesthetic in itself as well as 'building a relationship with [the] audience. It is in invitation to relationship, not a checklist of things to be done'.[42] It is also 'a deeply personal experience, forged in the specific material, sociocultural and embodied contexts of individual users [of media]'.[43] Access is thus not simply about the tools by which different users experience media – it is also about the aesthetics of the media itself. Sheppard, for example, states: 'access and art are less about accessibility for audience and artist, but about access as art and aesthetic', offering an example of the use of a ramp (an access tool for wheelchair users) in her dance duet, where the ramp is transformed into a work of art, 'yielding to movement desire' and 'designed for beauty and for the potential of wheeled movement'.[44] A tool by which access can be enabled is thus made part of the aesthetics of a performance.

This is where the accessibility *of* extrajudicial aesthetics jars with the access *to* extrajudicial appearances. When the personal largely disappears in the face of the professional, it is difficult to forge a relationship between judges and the wider public. Greater public access to the previously explored aesthetic themes of institutional longevity, tradition and professionalism in extrajudicial appearances thus simply reinforces the *personal* inaccessibility of those themes. As critical legal scholar Costas Douzinas and art historian Lynda Nead observe:

> The self in art – as painter or viewer – is free, desiring, corporeal, it has gender and history. The subject of law – as judge or litigant – is constrained, censored, and ethereal. The legal person is a collection of rights and duties, a point of condensation of capacities and obligations of a general or universal nature; the judge is at the service of the law of reason, which has no history, no past or future, but is omnipresent.[45]

The corporeality of the self in art has a particular resonance in art depicting the law, because representations of the law – in the form of the judge – can be almost

[40] UK Supreme Court, *Lord Reed Justice recruitment October 2020* (30 October 2020) www.youtube.com/watch?v=dzVfRwSuJSE&t=1s.

[41] Northern Ireland Judicial Appointments Commission, *Isobel Brownlie introduces the role of District Judge* (9 October 2020) www.youtube.com/watch?v=8_0ne-SbFDY.

[42] A Sheppard, 'Staging Bodies, Performing Ramps: Cultural-Aesthetic Disability Technoscience' (2019) 5(1) *Catalyst: Feminism, Theory, Technoscience* 1, 2.

[43] E Ellcessor, 'Digital media accessibility: An evolving infrastructure of possibility' in K Ellis, G Goggin, B Haller and R Curtis (eds), *The Routledge Companion to Disability and Media* (London, Routledge, 2020) 249–50.

[44] Sheppard (above n 42) 8.

[45] C Douzinas and L Nead, 'Introduction' in Costas Douzinas and Lynda Nead (eds), *Law and the Image: The Authority of Art and the Aesthetics of Law* (Chicago IL, University of Chicago Press, 1999) 3.

entirely incorporeal. A prime example of this – Victorian painter Abraham Solomon's *Waiting for the Verdict* (1857) – features the scene of a family waiting outside a court for the verdict in a legal case of great importance to them. The impact of waiting on the family is rendered in careful detail: the anxious and tense expressions of the two women who face forward, with one's right hand clasping her left hand as its nails dig into her dress; the sense of complete dejection in the man who holds his head in his hand obscuring his eyes; and the tension in the frame of the woman who turns away from the viewer to peek through an open door to the court beyond it. By contrast, the legal personalities are far less distinct. The lawyers all disappear under the uniformity of their robes and wigs, and the person of the judge is barely noticeable – appearing at the top right corner of the painting in a whisper of scarlet and faint white lines suggestive of a wig, despite being the vanishing point of the painting. The importance of the law and its social impact in *Waiting for the Verdict* can hardly be overstated, and the almost complete incorporeality of the judge furthers this importance. The law – and the judge – transcend the self, its desires and its fears and thus exert such awesome influence over them.

In this vein, extrajudicial appearances in digital media – a tool enabling wider public access – are not aesthetically particularised or indeed personalised to enable greater accessibility to the judge. The line between the judge in the court and the judge outside the court thus blurs, returning us to Lewis Graham at the start of this chapter – 'The Court *is* its judges; its judges *are* the Court'. Aesthetically, the judge has certainly become more distinguishable since Solomon's celebrated painting, but the judge has not yet become fully corporeal. This paradox – the publicly accessed yet inaccessible judge – reveals deeper disquiets in how the court presents itself and how it is, in turn, presented.

VII. TRANSPARENCY AND TURBULENCE

On 19 December 2024, Mr Justice Williams in the Family Division of the England and Wales High Court handed down his judgment on the applications by a number of journalists and media groups to access and publish papers relating to historic proceedings involving Sara Sharif, who suffered brutally at the hands of her father and stepmother, before they murdered her in 2023. The judgment, to which certain of the media applicants reacted with 'fury'[46] and which they considered to be an 'unprecedented departure from open justice',[47] contained a number of general observations from Williams J on the media reporting of judgments and judges. Calling these observations highly critical would be an understatement. On the question of naming the

[46] R Camber, 'Fury as Sara Sharif judge says the Press can't be trusted to be fair as he controversially blocked the identification of professionals', *The Daily Mail* (20 December 2024) www.dailymail.co.uk/news/article-14215541/Fury-Sara-Sharif-judge-says-Press-trusted-fair-controversially-blocked-identification-professionals.html.

[47] J Rozenberg, 'Judge hits back', *A Lawyer Writes* (23 December 2024) rozenberg.substack.com/p/judge-hits-back.

individual professionals (such as social workers) and judges who were involved in the historic proceedings, Williams J sternly remarked:

> [I]ndividuals associated with the case will I have no doubt be subject to an exceptional level of attention. That attention will I have little doubt range from measured commentary through to rude and discriminatory slurs, moving onto vilification, abuse and threats. That I think is reasonably certain in the online world where a virtual lynch mob will readily be assembled in the current febrile atmosphere engendered online and fanned by the undermining of the rule of law and the judiciary worldwide notably in the USA but in this country also where a headline identifying senior judiciary as 'Enemies of the People' was seen as legitimate comment.[48]

And further:

> The likely level of online abuse will be high. However, the reality currently is that in addition to that there is real possibility of some individuals going further – much further. The BBC reported only last week on the case of a man who attacked a firm of solicitors identified in the Daily Mail as being involved in processing asylum applications. Hotel's [*sic*] housing asylum seekers were firebombed. That is not to make the press responsible for the actions of those who perpetrate such acts but putting names and faces in the public domain bring with it potential consequences from those who are unstable, aggrieved, fanatical. Attacks upon those in authority by those with grievances have led to death (Jo Cox) and serious assault (HHJ Perusko), arson on the home of an expert witness (although the perpetrator accidently fire-bombed the neighbour's home) and stalking (judges).[49]

Williams J buttressed these remarks with claims about the 'growing' levels of 'abusive and threatening' communications and behaviour, and data which showed a significant level of concern among judges about their personal safety.[50]

The judge's remarks are grounded in a number of events, ranging from the political climate in a different country to a notorious and scathingly criticised[51] headline published almost a decade ago – none of which relate to the Sharif case. However, what Williams J's remarks disclose is the turbulence which the judiciary sometimes faces in the public eye.

The 'Enemies of the people' headline to which the judge made particular reference is an example of this turbulence.[52] The article following the headline reported on the Divisional Court judgment in *R (Miller) v Brexit Secretary*,[53] which determined that the UK Government could not trigger the process to exit the European Union without statutory endorsement from Parliament, and the appeal against which was dismissed

[48] *Tickle and others v Surrey County Council and others* [2024] EWHC 3330 (Fam) [75].

[49] ibid [76].

[50] ibid [77].

[51] See, eg the evidence of Lord Thomas of Cwmgiedd before the House of Lords Constitution Committee in Select Committee on the Constitution, *Oral evidence session with the Lord Chief Justice* (22 March 2017), answer to Q4.

[52] J Slack, 'Enemies of the people: Fury over "out of touch" judges who have "declared war on democracy" by defying 17.4m Brexit voters and who could trigger constitutional crisis', *The Daily Mail* (London, 3 November 2016).

[53] *R (on the application of Miller) v Secretary of State for Exiting the European Union* [2016] EWHC 2768 (Admin).

by a majority of the UK Supreme Court.[54] The article is peppered with references to personal details of the members of the Divisional Court – such as the finances of then Lord Chief Justice, Lord Thomas of Cwmgiedd, the sexual orientation of then Master of the Rolls, Sir Terence Etherton (the late Lord Etherton), and the earnings of Lord Justice Sales (now Lord Sales) before his appointment to the bench – which were wholly irrelevant to the Court's judgment with which the article purported to concern itself. Certain captions which accompanied the professional photos of the judges – such as 'Blair's pal billed you £3m', accompanying the photo of Sales LJ, and 'Out of touch', accompanying a photo of the Lord Chief Justice – painted their subjects in a distinctly negative light.

The reference to a notorious headline and its article – made all the more notable by the backlash it faced[55] – might perhaps be considered a stretch if it was used to sustain judicial approaches to transparency in unconnected cases – as Williams J might appear to have done. Williams J's judgment was subsequently overturned on appeal, which was allowed, among other grounds, on the basis of the unfairness against the media which some of the judge's 'colourful language' demonstrated.[56] Nevertheless, the Court of Appeal made serious enquiries as to the safety of the judges whose identities might now be disclosed,[57] and allowed time for the Courts and Tribunals Service to 'put measures in place to protect them from any potential harm once their names are released'.[58] This indicates that, notwithstanding the overturning of Williams J's judgment, the risk which may arise from public accessibility remains a live concern of judges. This may suggest that vignettes of the kind featuring Lord Kerr and Lady Hale may become even rarer than they once were. Extrajudicial appearances, in other words, may become even less personalised. Such rarity would parallel recent trends which suggest increasing constraints on extrajudicial commentary.[59]

VIII. CONCLUSION

Looking beyond the content of extrajudicial appearances, this chapter focuses on their aesthetic framing and characteristics instead. In 2026, it is no longer unusual for a judge – even a Justice of the UK Supreme Court – to appear on a podcast or documentary available to be played in homes across the UK. But this embrace of modernity still largely feels traditional. The personalisation of the aesthetics of extrajudicial appearances is discounted in favour of a de-contextualised and strong sense of tradition and professionalism. Such de-contextualisation reveals sometimes loud echoes of judicial disquiet about the negative aspect of public exposure – and

[54] *R (on the application of Miller) v Secretary of State for Exiting the European Union* [2017] UKSC 5, [2018] AC 61.

[55] 'Brexit ruling: Lord Chancellor backs judiciary amid row', *BBC News* (5 November 2016).

[56] *Tickle and others v BBC and others* [2025] EWCA Civ 42, [75]–[79] per Vos MR.

[57] ibid [9].

[58] ibid [81].

[59] J Rozenberg, 'What not to say on X' (*A Lawyer Writes* 15 November 2024) rozenberg.substack.com/p/what-not-to-say-on-x.

its associated extremes – for the institution of the court and its judges. But much as a de-contextualised aesthetic might serve to reassure judges that public access does not lead to public intrusion; it also hinders judicial accessibility at a time when the courts have all committed to increasing their social representativeness as a way of enriching their understanding of the society which they serve. Representativeness is difficult to achieve when, in the eyes of the viewer, judicial corporeality disappears beneath the ubiquitous and ancient robes and wigs.

Greater availability to the public therefore presents a dilemma for the judge: to disappear beneath the institution of the court or to bring greater attention to one's individuality? While it is not for this chapter to set out how to resolve this dilemma, the insights offered here are relevant to it and may assist those who seek a resolution.

Index

www.ingramcontent.com/pod-product-compliance
Ingram Content Group UK Ltd.
Pitfield, Milton Keynes, MK11 3LW, UK
UKHW020243290926
15470UKWH00002B/716

9 781509 98183(